# interchange

## FIFTH EDITION

3

Teacher's Edition

## Jack C. Richards

with Jonathan Hull and Susan Proctor

CAMBRIDGE
UNIVERSITY PRESS

# CAMBRIDGE
## UNIVERSITY PRESS

University Printing House, Cambridge CB2 8BS, United Kingdom

One Liberty Plaza, 20th Floor, New York, NY 10006, USA

477 Williamstown Road, Port Melbourne, VIC 3207, Australia

314–321, 3rd Floor, Plot 3, Splendor Forum, Jasola District Centre, New Delhi – 110025, India

103 Penang Road, #05-06/07, Visioncrest Commercial, Singapore 238467

Cambridge University Press is part of the University of Cambridge.

It furthers the University's mission by disseminating knowledge in the pursuit of education, learning and research at the highest international levels of excellence.

www.cambridge.org
Information on this title: www.cambridge.org/9781316622803

© Cambridge University Press 1992, 2017

First published 1992
Second edition 1998
Third edition 2005
Fourth edition 2013

20  19  18  17  16  15  14  13  12  11  10  9  8  7  6  5

Printed in Great Britain by CPI Group (UK) Ltd, Croydon CR0 4YY

A catalogue record for this publication is available from the British Library

ISBN  978-1-316-62051-9  Student's Book 3 with Online Self-Study
ISBN  978-1-316-62053-3  Student's Book 3A with Online Self-Study
ISBN  978-1-316-62054-0  Student's Book 3B with Online Self-Study
ISBN  978-1-316-62055-7  Student's Book 3 with Online Self-Study and Online Workbook
ISBN  978-1-316-62056-4  Student's Book 3A with Online Self-Study and Online Workbook
ISBN  978-1-316-62058-8  Student's Book 3B with Online Self-Study and Online Workbook
ISBN  978-1-316-62276-6  Workbook 3
ISBN  978-1-316-62277-3  Workbook 3A
ISBN  978-1-316-62279-7  Workbook 3B
ISBN  978-1-316-62280-3  Teacher's Edition 3 with Complete Assessment Program
ISBN  978-1-316-62230-8  Class Audio CDs 3
ISBN  978-1-316-62405-0  Full Contact 3 with Online Self-Study
ISBN  978-1-316-62407-4  Full Contact 3A with Online Self-Study
ISBN  978-1-316-62409-8  Full Contact 3B with Online Self-Study
ISBN  978-1-108-40307-8  Presentation Plus 3

Additional resources for this publication at www.cambridge.org/interchange

# CONTENTS

# Plan of Book 3

| Titles/Topics | Speaking | Grammar |
|---|---|---|
| **UNIT 1** — PAGES 2–7 | | |
| **That's my kind of friend!** Personality types and qualities; relationships; likes and dislikes | Describing personalities; expressing likes and dislikes; agreeing and disagreeing; complaining | Relative pronouns as subjects and objects; *it* clauses + adverbial clauses with *when* |
| **UNIT 2** — PAGES 8–13 | | |
| **Working 9 to 5** Jobs; career benefits; job skills; summer jobs | Talking about possible careers; describing jobs; deciding between two jobs | Gerund phrases as subjects and objects; comparisons with adjectives, nouns, verbs, and past participles |
| PROGRESS CHECK — PAGES 14–15 | | |
| **UNIT 3** — PAGES 16–21 | | |
| **Lend a hand.** Favors; formal and informal requests; messages | Making direct and indirect requests; accepting and declining requests | Requests with modals, *if* clauses, and gerunds; indirect requests |
| **UNIT 4** — PAGES 22–27 | | |
| **What happened?** The media; news stories; exceptional events | Narrating a story; describing events and experiences in the past | Past continuous vs. simple past; past perfect |
| PROGRESS CHECK — PAGES 28–29 | | |
| **UNIT 5** — PAGES 30–35 | | |
| **Expanding your horizons** Cultural comparisons and culture shock; moving abroad; emotions; customs; tourism and travel abroad | Talking about moving abroad; expressing emotions; describing cultural expectations; giving advice | Noun phrases containing relative clauses; expectations: *the custom to*, *(not) supposed to, expected to, (not) acceptable to* |
| **UNIT 6** — PAGES 36–41 | | |
| **That needs fixing.** Consumer complaints; everyday problems; problems with electronics; repairs | Describing problems; making complaints; explaining something that needs to be done | Describing problems with past participles as adjectives and with nouns; describing problems with *need* + gerund, *need* + passive infinitive, and *keep* + gerund |
| PROGRESS CHECK — PAGES 42–43 | | |
| **UNIT 7** — PAGES 44–49 | | |
| **What can we do?** The environment; global challenges; current issues | Identifying and describing problems; coming up with solutions | Passive in the present continuous and present perfect; prepositions of cause; infinitive clauses and phrases |
| **UNIT 8** — PAGES 50–55 | | |
| **Never stop learning.** Education; learner choices; strategies for learning; life skills | Asking about preferences; discussing different skills to be learned; talking about learning methods; talking about life skills | *Would rather* and *would prefer; by* + gerund to describe how to do things |
| PROGRESS CHECK — PAGES 56–57 | | |

| Titles/Topics | Speaking | Grammar |
|---|---|---|
| **UNIT 9**  PAGES 58–63 | | |
| **Getting things done**  Everyday services; recommendations; self-improvement | Talking about things you need to have done; asking for and giving advice or suggestions | Get or have something done; making suggestions with modals + verbs, gerunds, negative questions, and infinitives |
| **UNIT 10**  PAGES 64–69 | | |
| **A matter of time**  Historic events and people; biography; the future | Talking about historic events; talking about things to be accomplished in the future | Referring to time in the past with adverbs and prepositions: *during, in, ago, from…to, for, since*; predicting the future with *will*, future continuous, and future perfect |
| PROGRESS CHECK  PAGES 70–71 | | |
| **UNIT 11**  PAGES 72–77 | | |
| **Rites of passage**  Milestones and turning points; behavior and personality; regrets | Describing milestones; describing turning points; describing regrets and hypothetical situations | Time clauses: *before, after, once, the moment, as soon as, until, by the time*; expressing regret with *should (not) have* + past participle; describing hypothetical situations with *if* clauses + past perfect and *would/could have* + past participle |
| **UNIT 12**  PAGES 78–83 | | |
| **Keys to success**  Qualities for success; successful businesses; advertising | Describing qualities for success; giving reasons for success; interviewing for a job; talking about ads and slogans | Describing purpose with infinitive clauses and infinitive clauses with *for*; giving reasons with *because, since, because of, for, due to*, and *the reason* |
| PROGRESS CHECK  PAGES 84–85 | | |
| **UNIT 13**  PAGES 86–91 | | |
| **What might have been**  Pet peeves; unexplained events; reactions; complicated situations and advice | Drawing conclusions; offering explanations; describing hypothetical events; giving advice for complicated situations | Past modals for degrees of certainty: *must (not) have, may (not) have, might (not) have, could (not) have*; past modals for judgments and suggestions: *should (not) have, could (not) have, would (not) have* |
| **UNIT 14**  PAGES 92–97 | | |
| **Creative careers**  Movies; media and entertainment professions; processes | Describing how something is done or made; describing careers in film, TV, publishing, gaming, and music | The passive to describe process with *is/are* + past participle and modal + *be* + past participle; defining and non-defining relative clauses |
| PROGRESS CHECK  PAGES 98–99 | | |
| **UNIT 15**  PAGES 100–105 | | |
| **A law must be passed!**  Recommendations; opinions; community issues; controversial topics | Giving opinions for and against controversial topics; offering a different opinion; agreeing and disagreeing | Giving recommendations and opinions with passive modals: *should be, ought to be, must be, has to be, has got to be*; tag questions for opinions |
| **UNIT 16**  PAGES 106–111 | | |
| **Reaching your goals**  Challenges; accomplishments; goals; inspirational sayings | Giving opinions about inspirational sayings; talking about the past and the future | Accomplishments with the simple past and present perfect; goals with the future perfect and *would like to have* + past participle |
| PROGRESS CHECK  PAGES 112–113 | | |
| GRAMMAR PLUS  PAGES 132–150 | | |

# Informed by teachers

Teachers from all over the world helped develop *Interchange Fifth Edition*. They looked at everything – from the color of the designs to the topics in the conversations – in order to make sure that this course will work in the classroom. We heard from 1,500 teachers in:

- Surveys
- Focus Groups
- In-Depth Reviews

We appreciate the help and input from everyone. In particular, we'd like to give the following people our special thanks:

Jader Franceschi, **Actúa Idiomas,** Bento Gonçalves, Rio Grande do Sul, Brazil

Juliana Dos Santos Voltan Costa, **Actus Idiomas,** São Paulo, Brazil

Ella Osorio, **Angelo State University,** San Angelo, TX, US

Mary Hunter, **Angelo State University,** San Angelo, TX, US

Mario César González, **Angloamericano de Monterrey, SC,** Monterrey, Mexico

Samantha Shipman, **Auburn High School,** Auburn, AL, US

Linda, **Bernick Language School,** Radford, VA, US

Dave Lowrance, **Bethesda University of California,** Yorba Linda, CA, US

Tajbakhsh Hosseini, **Bezmialem Vakif University,** Istanbul, Turkey

Dilek Gercek, **Bil English,** Izmir, Turkey

Erkan Kolat, **Biruni University, ELT,** Istanbul, Turkey

Nika Gutkowska, **Bluedata International,** New York, NY, US

Daniel Alcocer Gómez, **Cecati 92,** Guadalupe, Nuevo León, Mexico

Samantha Webb, **Central Middle School,** Milton-Freewater, OR, US

Verónica Salgado, **Centro Anglo Americano,** Cuernavaca, Mexico

Ana Rivadeneira Martínez and Georgia P. de Machuca, **Centro de Educación Continua – Universidad Politécnica del Ecuador,** Quito, Ecuador

Anderson Francisco Guimerães Maia, **Centro Cultural Brasil Estados Unidos,** Belém, Brazil

Rosana Mariano, **Centro Paula Souza,** São Paulo, Brazil

Carlos de la Paz Arroyo, Teresa Noemí Parra Alarcón, Gilberto Bastida Gaytan, Manuel Esquivel Román, and Rosa Cepeda Tapia, **Centro Universitario Angloamericano,** Cuernavaca, Morelos, Mexico

Antonio Almeida, **CETEC,** Morelos, Mexico

Cinthia Ferreira, **Cinthia Ferreira Languages Services,** Toronto, ON, Canada

Phil Thomas and Sérgio Sanchez, **CLS Canadian Language School,** São Paulo, Brazil

Celia Concannon, **Cochise College,** Nogales, AZ, US

Maria do Carmo Rocha and CAOP English team, **Colégio Arquidiocesano Ouro Preto – Unidade Cônego Paulo Dilascio,** Ouro Preto, Brazil

Kim Rodriguez, **College of Charleston North,** Charleston, SC, US

Jesús Leza Alvarado, **Coparmex English Institute,** Monterrey, Mexico

John Partain, **Cortazar,** Guanajuato, Mexico

Alexander Palencia Navas, **Cursos de Lenguas, Universidad del Atlántico,** Barranquilla, Colombia

Kenneth Johan Gerardo Steenhuisen Cera, Melfi Osvaldo Guzman Triana, and Carlos Alberto Algarín Jiminez, **Cursos de Lenguas Extranjeras Universidad del Atlantico,** Barranquilla, Colombia

Jane P Kerford, **East Los Angeles College,** Pasadena, CA, US

Daniela, **East Village,** Campinas, São Paulo, Brazil

Rosalva Camacho Orduño, **Easy English for Groups S.A. de C.V.,** Monterrey, Nuevo León, Mexico

Adonis Gimenez Fusetti, **Easy Way Idiomas,** Ibiúna, Brazil

Eileen Thompson, **Edison Community College,** Piqua, OH, US

Ahminne Handeri O.L Froede, **Englishouse escola de idiomas,** Teófilo Otoni, Brazil

Ana Luz Delgado-Izazola, **Escuela Nacional Preparatoria 5, UNAM,** Mexico City, Mexico

Nancy Alarcón Mendoza, **Facultad de Estudios Superiores Zaragoza, UNAM,** Mexico City, Mexico

Marcilio N. Barros, **Fast English USA,** Campinas, São Paulo, Brazil

Greta Douthat, **FCI Ashland,** Ashland, KY, US

Carlos Lizárraga González, **Grupo Educativo Anglo Americano, S.C.,** Mexico City, Mexico

Hugo Fernando Alcántar Valle, **Instituto Politécnico Nacional, Escuela Superior de Comercio y Administración-Unidad Santotomás, Celex Esca Santo Tomás,** Mexico City, Mexico

Sueli Nascimento, **Instituto Superior de Educação do Rio de Janeiro,** Rio de Janeiro, Brazil

Elsa F Monteverde, **International Academic Services,** Miami, FL, US

Laura Anand, **Irvine Adult School,** Irvine, CA, US

Prof. Marli T. Fernandes (principal) and Prof. Dr. Jefferson J. Fernandes (pedagogue), **Jefferson Idiomass,** São Paulo, Brazil

Herman Bartelen, **Kanda Gaigo Gakuin,** Tokyo, Japan

Cassia Silva, **Key Languages,** Key Biscayne, FL, US

Sister Mary Hope, **Kyoto Notre Dame Joshi Gakuin,** Kyoto, Japan

Nate Freedman, **LAL Language Centres,** Boston, MA, US

Richard Janzen, **Langley Secondary School,** Abbotsford, BC, Canada

Christina Abel Gabardo, **Language House,** Campo Largo, Brazil

Ivonne Castro, **Learn English International,** Cali, Colombia

Julio Cesar Maciel Rodrigues, **Liberty Centro de Línguas,** São Paulo, Brazil

Ann Gibson, **Maynard High School,** Maynard, MA, US

Martin Darling, **Meiji Gakuin Daigaku,** Tokyo, Japan

Dax Thomas, **Meiji Gakuin Daigaku,** Yokohama, Kanagawa, Japan

Derya Budak, **Mevlana University,** Konya, Turkey

B Sullivan, **Miami Valley Career Technical Center International Program,** Dayton, OH, US

Julio Velazquez, **Milo Language Center,** Weston, FL, US

Daiane Siqueira da Silva, Luiz Carlos Buontempo, Marlete Avelina de Oliveira Cunha, Marcos Paulo Segatti, Morgana Eveline de Oliveira, Nadia Lia Gino Alo, and Paul Hyde Budgen, **New Interchange-Escola de Idiomas,** São Paulo, Brazil

Patrícia França Furtado da Costa, Juiz de Fora, Brazil

Patricia Servín, Chris Pollard, **North West Regional College SK,** North Battleford, SK, Canada

Olga Amy, **Notre Dame High School,** Red Deer, Canada

Amy Garrett, **Ouachita Baptist University,** Arkadelphia, AR, US

Mervin Curry, **Palm Beach State College,** Boca Raton, FL, US

Julie Barros, **Quality English Studio,** Guarulhos, São Paulo, Brazil

Teodoro González Saldaña and Jesús Monserrrta Mata Franco, **Race Idiomas,** Mexico City, Mexico

Autumn Westphal and Noga La`or, **Rennert International,** New York, NY, US

Antonio Gallo and Javy Palau, **Rigby Idiomas,** Monterrey, Mexico

Tatiane Gabriela Sperb do Nascimento, **Right Way,** Igrejinha, Brazil

Mustafa Akgül, **Selahaddin Eyyubi Universitesi,** Diyarbakır, Turkey

James Drury M. Fonseca, **Senac Idiomas Fortaleza,** Fortaleza, Ceara, Brazil

Manoel Fialho S Neto, **Senac – PE,** Recife, Brazil

Jane Imber, **Small World,** Lawrence, KS, US

Tony Torres, **South Texas College,** McAllen, TX, US

Janet Rose, **Tennessee Foreign Language Institute,** College Grove, TN, US

Todd Enslen, **Tohoku University,** Sendai, Miyagi, Japan

Daniel Murray, **Torrance Adult School,** Torrance, CA, US

Juan Manuel Pulido Mendoza, **Universidad del Atlántico,** Barranquilla, Colombia

Juan Carlos Vargas Millán, **Universidad Libre Seccional Cali,** Cali (Valle del Cauca), Colombia

Carmen Cecilia Llanos Ospina, **Universidad Libre Seccional Cali,** Cali, Colombia

Jorge Noriega Zenteno, **Universidad Politécnica del Valle de México,** Estado de México, Mexico

Aimee Natasha Holguin S., **Universidad Politécnica del Valle de México UPVM,** Tultitlàn Estado de México, Mexico

Christian Selene Bernal Barraza, **UPVM Universidad Politécnica del Valle de México,** Ecatepec, Mexico

Lizeth Ramos Acosta, **Universidad Santiago de Cali,** Cali, Colombia

Silvana Dushku, **University of Illinois Champaign,** IL, US

Deirdre McMurtry, **University of Nebraska – Omaha,** Omaha, NE, US

Jason E Mower, **University of Utah,** Salt Lake City, UT, US

Paul Chugg, **Vanguard Taylor Language Institute,** Edmonton, Alberta, Canada

Henry Mulak, **Varsity Tutors,** Los Angeles, CA, US

Shirlei Strucker Calgaro and Hugo Guilherme Karrer, **VIP Centro de Idiomas,** Panambi, Rio Grande do Sul, Brazil

Eleanor Kelly, **Waseda Daigaku Extension Centre,** Tokyo, Japan

Sherry Ashworth, **Wichita State University,** Wichita, KS, US

Laine Bourdene, **William Carey University,** Hattiesburg, MS, US

Serap Aydın, Istanbul, Turkey

Liliana Covino, Guarulhos, Brazil

Yannuarys Jiménez, Barranquilla, Colombia

Juliana Morais Pazzini, Toronto, ON, Canada

Marlon Sanches, Montreal, Canada

Additional content contributed by Kenna Bourke, Inara Couto, Nic Harris, Greg Manin, Ashleigh Martinez, Laura McKenzie, Paul McIntyre, Clara Prado, Lynne Robertson, Mari Vargo, Theo Walker, and Maria Lucia Zaorob.

# The Fifth Edition of *Interchange*

*Interchange*, the world's favorite English course, has a long tradition of teaching students how to speak confidently. Millions of people all over the world attest to its effectiveness.

## What Makes *Interchange* Special?

**Jack C. Richards' communicative methodology**: Refined over years and in countless classrooms, the *Interchange* approach is rooted in solid pedagogy.

**Flexible units**: Instructors can change the order of the activities in each unit, keeping lessons fresh and students engaged. Additional photocopiable activities and a full video program give teachers even more freedom to make *Interchange* their own.

**Students speak right from the start**: The solid research and winning content give students the confidence to speak early and often.

## What's New in the Fifth Edition?

**50% new content**: Readings, listenings, conversations, and Snapshots have been updated throughout the books.

**Improved exercises for listenings and readings**: We listened to teachers' requests for greater variety in the activities that accompany the listenings and readings.

**New digital tools**: Self-study for every student available online. An online workbook with fun games.

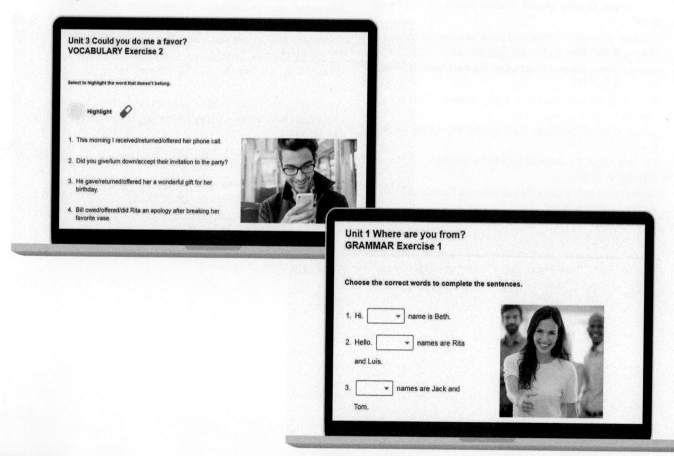

# Student's Book overview

Every unit in *Interchange Fifth Edition* contains two cycles, each of which has a specific topic, grammar point, and function. The units in Level 3 contain a variety of exercises, including a Snapshot, Conversation, Grammar focus, Pronunciation, Discussion (or Speaking/Role Play), Word power, Perspectives, Listening, Writing, Reading, and Interchange activity. The sequence of these exercises differs from unit to unit. Here is a sample unit from Level 3.

## Cycle 1 (Exercises 1–6)

**Topic:** past events
**Grammar:** past continuous vs. simple past
**Function:** describe ongoing actions and events in the past

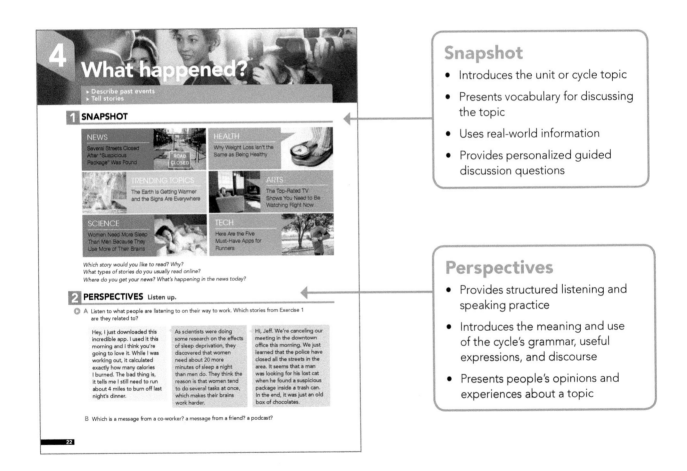

### Snapshot

- Introduces the unit or cycle topic
- Presents vocabulary for discussing the topic
- Uses real-world information
- Provides personalized guided discussion questions

### Perspectives

- Provides structured listening and speaking practice
- Introduces the meaning and use of the cycle's grammar, useful expressions, and discourse
- Presents people's opinions and experiences about a topic

## Grammar focus

- Includes audio recordings of the grammar
- Provides controlled grammar practice in realistic contexts, such as short conversations
- Provides freer, more personalized speaking practice

## Pronunciation

- Provides controlled practice in recognizing and producing sounds linked to the cycle grammar
- Promotes extended or personalized pronunciation practice

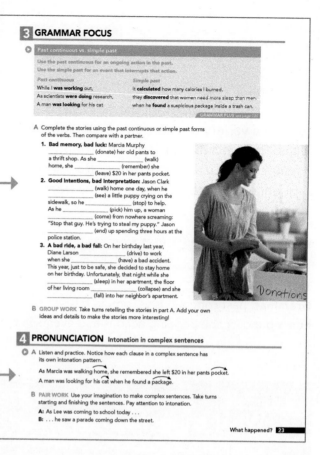

### 3 GRAMMAR FOCUS

**Past continuous vs. simple past**

Use the past continuous for an ongoing action in the past.
Use the simple past for an event that interrupts that action.

| Past continuous | Simple past |
|---|---|
| While I **was working** out, | it **calculated** how many calories I burned. |
| As scientists **were doing** research, | they **discovered** that women need more sleep than men. |
| A man **was looking** for his cat | when he **found** a suspicious package inside a trash can. |

GRAMMAR PLUS see page 138

**A** Complete the stories using the past continuous or simple past forms of the verbs. Then compare with a partner.

1. **Bad memory, bad luck:** Marcia Murphy _____ (donate) her old pants to a thrift shop. As she _____ (walk) home, she _____ (remember) she _____ (leave) $20 in her pants pocket.

2. **Good intentions, bad interpretation:** Jason Clark _____ (walk) home one day, when he _____ (see) a little puppy crying on the sidewalk, so he _____ (stop) to help. As he _____ (pick) him up, a woman _____ (come) from nowhere screaming: "Stop that guy. He's trying to steal my puppy." Jason _____ (end) up spending three hours at the police station.

3. **A bad ride, a bad fall:** On her birthday last year, Diane Larson _____ (drive) to work when she _____ (have) a bad accident. This year, just to be safe, she decided to stay home on her birthday. Unfortunately, that night while she _____ (sleep) in her apartment, the floor of her living room _____ (collapse) and she _____ (fall) into her neighbor's apartment.

**B** GROUP WORK Take turns retelling the stories in part A. Add your own ideas and details to make the stories more interesting!

### 4 PRONUNCIATION Intonation in complex sentences

**A** Listen and practice. Notice how each clause in a complex sentence has its own intonation pattern.

As Marcia was walking home, she remembered she left $20 in her pants pocket.
A man was looking for his cat when he found a package.

**B** PAIR WORK Use your imagination to make complex sentences. Take turns starting and finishing the sentences. Pay attention to intonation.

A: As Lee was coming to school today . . .
B: . . . he saw a parade coming down the street.

What happened? 23

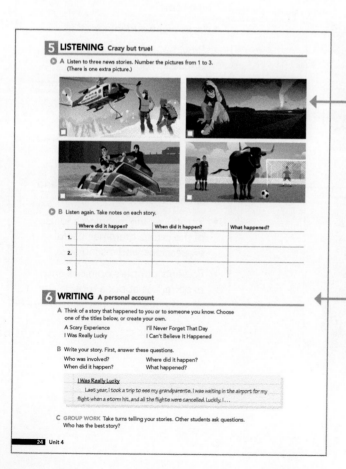

### 5 LISTENING Crazy but true!

**A** Listen to three news stories. Number the pictures from 1 to 3. (There is one extra picture.)

**B** Listen again. Take notes on each story.

| | Where did it happen? | When did it happen? | What happened? |
|---|---|---|---|
| 1. | | | |
| 2. | | | |
| 3. | | | |

### 6 WRITING A personal account

**A** Think of a story that happened to you or to someone you know. Choose one of the titles below, or create your own.

A Scary Experience      I'll Never Forget That Day
I Was Really Lucky      I Can't Believe It Happened

**B** Write your story. First, answer these questions.

Who was involved?      Where did it happen?
When did it happen?      What happened?

> **I Was Really Lucky**
> Last year, I took a trip to see my grandparents. I was waiting in the airport for my flight when a storm hit, and all the flights were cancelled. Luckily, I . . .

**C** GROUP WORK Take turns telling your stories. Other students ask questions. Who has the best story?

24 Unit 4

## Listening

- Provides pre-listening focus tasks or questions
- Develops a variety of listening skills, such as listening for main ideas and details
- Includes post-listening speaking tasks

## Writing

- Provides a model writing sample
- Develops skills in writing different texts, such as blogs and email messages
- Reinforces the vocabulary and grammar in the cycle or unit

# Cycle 2 (Exercises 7–12)

**Topic:** past events
**Grammar:** past perfect
**Function:** tell stories about past events

## Conversation

- Provides structured listening and speaking practice
- Introduces the meaning and use of Cycle 2 grammar, useful expressions, and discourse
- Uses pictures to set the scene and illustrate new vocabulary

## Grammar focus

- Presents examples from the previous conversation
- Provides controlled grammar practice in realistic contexts, such as short conversations

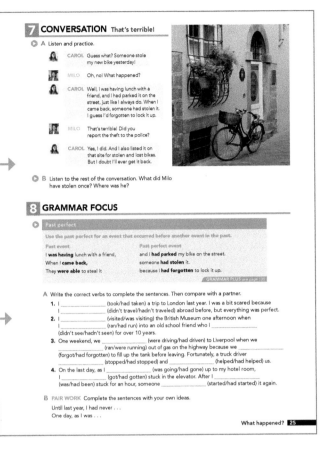

### 7 CONVERSATION That's terrible!

A Listen and practice.

CAROL  Guess what? Someone stole my new bike yesterday!

MILO  Oh, no! What happened?

CAROL  Well, I was having lunch with a friend, and I had parked it on the street, just like I always do. When I came back, someone had stolen it. I guess I'd forgotten to lock it up.

MILO  That's terrible! Did you report the theft to the police?

CAROL  Yes, I did. And I also listed it on that site for stolen and lost bikes. But I doubt I'll ever get it back.

B  Listen to the rest of the conversation. What did Milo have stolen once? Where was he?

### 8 GRAMMAR FOCUS

Past perfect

Use the past perfect for an event that occurred before another event in the past.

| Past event | Past perfect event |
|---|---|
| I was having lunch with a friend, | and I had parked my bike on the street. |
| When I came back, | someone had stolen it. |
| They were able to steal it | because I had forgotten to lock it up. |

GRAMMAR PLUS see page 135

A  Write the correct verbs to complete the sentences. Then compare with a partner.
1. I _____ (took/had taken) a trip to London last year. I was a bit scared because I _____ (didn't travel/hadn't traveled) abroad before, but everything was perfect.
2. I _____ (visited/was visiting) the British Museum one afternoon when I _____ (ran/had run) into an old school friend who I _____ (didn't see/hadn't seen) for over 10 years.
3. One weekend, we _____ (were driving/had driven) to Liverpool when we _____ (ran/were running) out of gas on the highway because we _____ (forgot/had forgotten) to fill up the tank before leaving. Fortunately, a truck driver _____ (stopped/had stopped) and _____ (helped/had helped) us.
4. On the last day, as I _____ (was going/had gone) up to my hotel room, I _____ (got/had gotten) stuck in the elevator. After I _____ (was/had been) stuck for an hour, someone _____ (started/had started) it again.

B  PAIR WORK  Complete the sentences with your own ideas.
Until last year, I had never . . .
One day, as I was . . .

What happened? 25

### 9 WORD POWER Exceptional events

A  Match the words in column A with the definitions in column B.

| A | B |
|---|---|
| 1. coincidence ____ | a. an unexpected event that brings good fortune |
| 2. dilemma ____ | b. a situation that involves a difficult choice |
| 3. disaster ____ | c. something puzzling or unexplained |
| 4. emergency ____ | d. an event that causes suffering or destruction |
| 5. lucky break ____ | e. a great success or achievement |
| 6. mishap ____ | f. an accident, mistake, or unlucky event |
| 7. mystery ____ | g. a sudden, dangerous situation that requires quick action |
| 8. triumph ____ | h. a situation when two similar things happen at the same time for no reason |

B  PAIR WORK  Choose one kind of event from part A. Write a situation for it.

A man bought an old house for $10,000. As he was cleaning the attic of his new home, he found an old painting by a famous painter. He had never collected art, but when he took it to a museum, he found out it was worth almost one million dollars. (lucky break)

C  GROUP WORK  Read your situation. Can others guess which kind of event it describes?

### 10 SPEAKING It's a story about . . .

GROUP WORK  Have you ever experienced the events in Exercise 9, part A? Tell your group about it. Answer any questions.
A: It's a story about a coincidence.
B: What happened?
A: My sister bought a new dress for her graduation party. She had saved for months to buy it. When she got to the party, another girl was wearing the exact same dress!
C: Wow! That's more than a coincidence. It's a disaster! And what did she do?

### 11 INTERCHANGE 4 Spin a yarn

Tell a story. Go to Interchange 4 on page 117.

26 Unit 4

## Word power

- Presents vocabulary related to the unit topic
- Provides practice with collocations and categorizing vocabulary
- Promotes freer, more personalized practice

## Speaking

- Provides communicative tasks that help develop oral fluency
- Includes pair work, group work, and class activities

## Reading

- Presents a variety of text types
- Introduces the text with a pre-reading task
- Develops a variety of reading skills, such as reading for main ideas, reading for details, and inferencing
- Promotes discussion that involves personalization and analysis

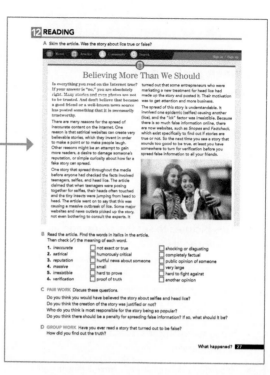

A Skim the article. Was the story about lice true or false?

### Believing More Than We Should

Is everything you read on the Internet true? If your answer is "no," you are absolutely right. Many stories and even photos are not to be trusted. And don't believe that because a good friend or a well-known news source has posted something that it is necessarily trustworthy.

There are many reasons for the spread of inaccurate content on the Internet. One reason is that satirical websites can create very believable stories, which they invent in order to make a point or to make people laugh. Other reasons might be an attempt to gain more readers, a desire to damage someone's reputation, or simple curiosity about how far a fake story can spread.

One story that spread throughout the media before anyone had checked the facts involved teenagers, selfies, and head lice. The article claimed that when teenagers were posing together for selfies, their heads often touched and the tiny insects were jumping from head to head. The article went on to say that this was causing a massive outbreak of lice. Some major websites and news outlets picked up the story, not even bothering to consult the experts. It

turned out that some entrepreneurs who were marketing a new treatment for head lice had made up the story and posted it. Their motivation was to get attention and more business.

The spread of this story is understandable. It involved one epidemic (selfies) causing another (lice), and the "ick" factor was irresistible. Because there is so much false information online, there are now websites, such as Snopes and Factcheck, which exist specifically to find out if stories are true or not. So the next time you see a story that sounds too good to be true, at least you have somewhere to turn for verification before you spread false information to all your friends.

B Read the article. Find the words in italics in the article. Then check (✓) the meaning of each word.

1. *inaccurate* ☐ not exact or true ☐ shocking or disgusting
2. *satirical* ☐ humorously critical ☐ completely factual
3. *reputation* ☐ hurtful news about someone ☐ public opinion of someone
4. *massive* ☐ small ☐ very large
5. *irresistible* ☐ hard to prove ☐ hard to fight against
6. *verification* ☐ proof of truth ☐ another opinion

C PAIR WORK Discuss these questions.

Do you think you would have believed the story about selfies and head lice?
Do you think the creation of the story was justified or not?
Who do you think is most responsible for the story being so popular?
Do you think there should be a penalty for spreading false information? If so, what should it be?

D GROUP WORK Have you ever read a story that turned out to be false?
How did you find out the truth?

What happened? 27

# In the back of the book

## Interchange activity

- Expands on the unit topic, vocabulary, and grammar
- Provides opportunities to consolidate new language in a creative or fun way
- Promotes fluency with communicative activities such as discussions, information gaps, and games

## Grammar plus

- Explores the unit grammar in greater depth
- Practices the grammar with controlled exercises
- Can be done in class or assigned as homework

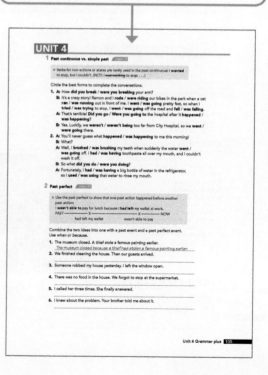

### INTERCHANGE 4 Spin a yarn

A GROUP WORK Place a pen on the CHARACTER spinner and spin it. Repeat for the other two spinners. Use the elements the pen points at to create a story. If the pen points at YOU DECIDE, you can use any element from that spinner, or you can invent a new one.

a young woman

CHARACTER

YOU DECIDE

on the street

SETTING

YOU DECIDE

mishap

lucky break

EVENT

YOU DECIDE

"One day a clumsy man was having dinner at a restaurant when . . ."

B CLASS ACTIVITY Share your group's stories with your classmates. Who created the most interesting story? the most unexpected? the most creative?

Interchange 4 117

### UNIT 4

**1 Past continuous vs. simple past**

▪ Verbs for non-actions or states are rarely used in the past continuous: I wanted to stop, but I couldn't. (NOT: I was wanting to stop . . .)

Circle the best forms to complete the conversations.

1. A: How did you break / were you breaking your arm?
   B: It's a crazy story! Ramon and I rode / were riding our bikes in the park when a cat ran / was running out in front of me. I went / was going pretty fast, so when I tried / was trying to stop, I went / was going off the road and fell / was falling.
   A: That's terrible! Did you go / Were you going to the hospital after it happened / was happening?
   B: Yes. Luckily we weren't / weren't being too far from City Hospital, so we went / were going there.

2. A: You'll never guess what happened / was happening to me this morning!
   B: What?
   A: Well, I brushed / was brushing my teeth when suddenly the water went / was going off. I had / was having toothpaste all over my mouth, and I couldn't wash it off.
   B: So what did you do / were you doing?
   A: Fortunately, I had / was having a big bottle of water in the refrigerator, so I used / was using that water to rinse my mouth.

**2 Past perfect**

▪ Use the past perfect to show that one past action happened before another past action:
I wasn't able to pay for lunch because I had left my wallet at work.
PAST ——— X ——————— X ——— NOW
          had left my wallet    wasn't able to pay

Combine the two ideas into one with a past event and a past perfect event. Use when or because.

1. The museum closed. A thief stole a famous painting earlier.
   *The museum closed because a thief had stolen a famous painting earlier.*

2. We finished cleaning the house. Then our guests arrived.

3. Someone robbed my house yesterday. I left the window open.

4. There was no food in the house. We forgot to stop at the supermarket.

5. I called her three times. She finally answered.

6. I knew about the problem. Your brother told me about it.

Unit 4 Grammar plus 135

# Online Self-study overview

*Interchange Fifth Edition* online Self-study provides students with hundreds of additional exercises to practice the language taught in the Student's Book on their own, in the classroom, or in the lab.

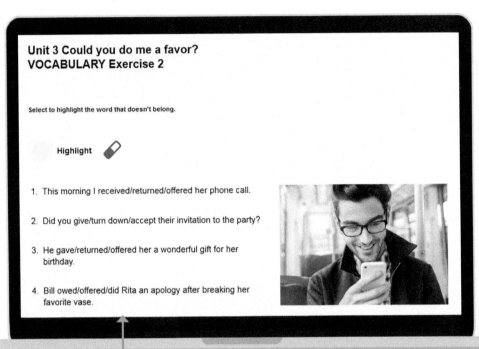

**Unit 3 Could you do me a favor?**
**VOCABULARY Exercise 2**

Select to highlight the word that doesn't belong.

Highlight

1. This morning I received/returned/offered her phone call.

2. Did you give/turn down/accept their invitation to the party?

3. He gave/returned/offered her a wonderful gift for her birthday.

4. Bill owed/offered/did Rita an apology after breaking her favorite vase.

## Interactive exercises

Hundreds of interactive exercises provide hours of additional:

- vocabulary practice
- grammar practice
- listening practice
- speaking practice
- reading practice

## The complete *Interchange* video program

The entire *Interchange* video program for this level is included online with exercises that allow the students to watch and check comprehension themselves.

2:56 / 3:43

# Online Workbook overview

The *Interchange Fifth Edition Online Workbook* provides additional activities to reinforce what is presented in the corresponding Student's Book. Each *Online Workbook* includes:

- A variety of interactive activities that correspond to each Student's Book lesson, allowing students to interact with workbook material in a fresh, lively way.

- Instant feedback for hundreds of activities, challenging students to focus on areas for improvement.

- Simple tools for teachers to monitor students' progress such as scores, attendance, and time spent online, providing instant information.

The *Interchange Fifth Edition Online Workbooks* can be purchased in two ways:

- as an institutional subscription,
- as part of a Student's Book with Online Workbook Pack.

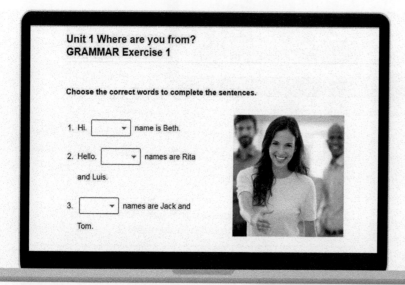

## Games

- Fun, interactive, self-scoring activities in the Online Workbooks offer a fresh change of pace.

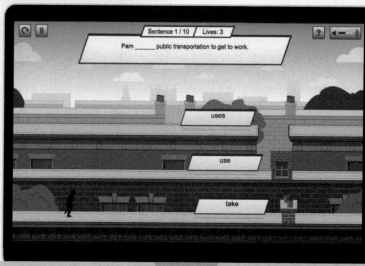

# Workbook overview

*Interchange Fifth Edition* provides students with additional opportunities to practice the language taught in the Student's Book outside of the classroom by using the Workbook that accompanies each level.

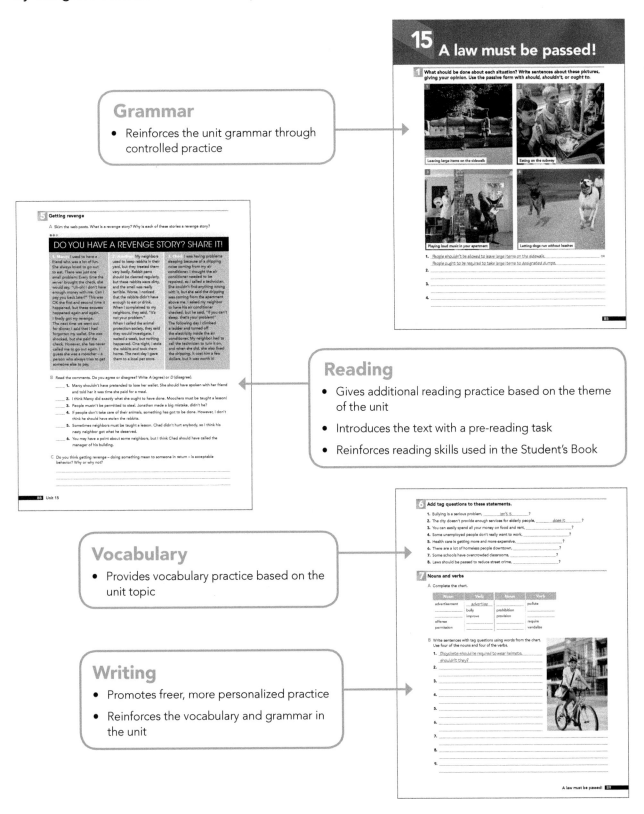

## Grammar
- Reinforces the unit grammar through controlled practice

## Reading
- Gives additional reading practice based on the theme of the unit
- Introduces the text with a pre-reading task
- Reinforces reading skills used in the Student's Book

## Vocabulary
- Provides vocabulary practice based on the unit topic

## Writing
- Promotes freer, more personalized practice
- Reinforces the vocabulary and grammar in the unit

# Teacher's Edition overview

The Teacher's Editions provide complete support for teachers who are using *Interchange Fifth Edition*. They contain Supplementary Resources Overview charts to help teachers plan their lessons (for more information see page xx), Language summaries, Workbook answer keys, Audio scripts, Fresh ideas, and Games. They also include detailed teaching notes for the units and Progress checks in the Student's Books.

## Teaching notes

- Learning objectives for each exercise
- Step-by-step lesson plans
- Audio scripts
- Answers and Vocabulary definitions
- Stimulating and fun Games to review or practice skills such as grammar and vocabulary
- Alternative ways to present and review exercises in the Fresh ideas
- Tips that promote teacher training and development
- Options for alternative presentations or expansions
- Suggestions for further practice in other *Interchange Fifth Edition* components and online
- Suggestions for regular assessment using quizzes and tests

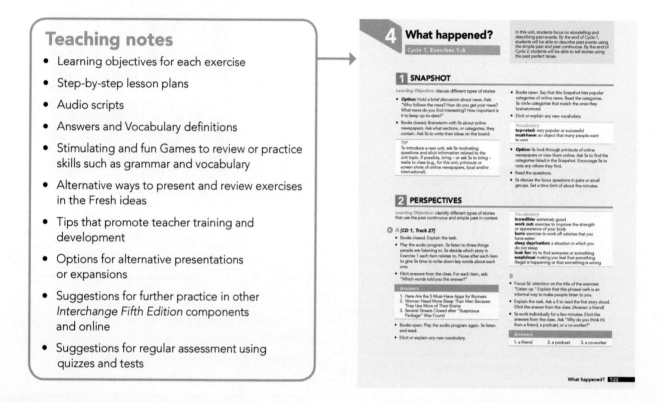

# Complete Assessment Program

The complete assessment program contains oral and written quizzes and tests. It includes PDF and Microsoft Word versions of all quizzes, mid-term and final tests, the placement test program, audio, audio scripts, and answer keys.

# Presentation Plus overview

*Interchange* Presentation Plus is a complete classroom presentation package, combining the contents of the Student's Book, the class audio, and the video program for each level of the series into a convenient one-stop presentation solution. It can be used with all types of interactive whiteboards or with just a projector and a computer to present *Interchange* core materials in the classroom in a lively and engaging way.

Presentation Plus simplifies several of the teaching tasks that take place in the classroom.

You can use Presentation Plus to display the answers for the exercises in an uncomplicated way, zoom in on a page to more efficiently focus students' attention on an activity or image, and even annotate pages for future lessons.

# cambridge.org/interchange

Go online for a variety of materials to assist with your teaching of the series. Here you will find practical articles, correlations, language summaries, overviews of supplementary materials, ideas for games and extra activities, as well as a number of downloadable worksheets for projects and extra practice of vocabulary, grammar, listening, writing, and speaking.

## Supplementary Resources Overviews

Indicate all the activities available in the various ancillary components that can be used after each exercise in the Student's Book units for extra practice, review, and assessment.

## Downloadable worksheets

- Offer extra speaking opportunities
- Provide guidance for projects and extra practice of grammar, vocabulary, listening, and writing

# Video Program overview

The *Interchange* Video Program is designed to complement the Student's Books. Each video provides further practice related to the topics, language, and vocabulary introduced in the corresponding unit of the Student's Book.

## PROGRAM COMPONENTS

### Video

The sixteen videos in each level's video program complement Units 1 through 16 of the corresponding Student's Book. There are a variety of genres: dramatized stories, documentaries, interviews, profiles, and travelogues.

### Video Resource Book

The Video Resource Book contains the following:

- engaging **photocopiable worksheets** for students
- detailed **teaching notes** for teachers
- **answer keys** for the student worksheets
- complete **video transcripts**

## TEACHING A TYPICAL VIDEO SEQUENCE

The **worksheets** and **teaching notes** for each video are organized into four sections: *Preview*, *Watch the video*, *Follow-up*, and *Language close-up*. The unit-by-unit teaching notes in the Video Resource Book give detailed suggestions for teaching each unit.

### Preview

The *Preview* activities build on each other to provide students with relevant background information and key vocabulary that will assist them in better understanding the video.

### Watch the video

The carefully sequenced *Watch the video* activities first help students focus on gist and then guide them in identifying important details and language. These tasks also prepare them for *Follow-up* speaking activities.

### Follow-up

The *Follow-up* speaking activities encourage students to extend and personalize information by voicing their opinions or carrying out communicative tasks.

### Language close-up

Students finish with the *Language close-up*, examining and practicing the particular language structures and functions presented in the video.

# Introduction to the CEFR

## Introduction to the Common European Framework of Reference (CEFR)

The overall aim of the Council of Europe's Common European Framework of Reference (CEFR) is to provide objective criteria for describing and assessing language proficiency in an internationally comparable manner. The Council of Europe's work on the definition of appropriate learning objectives for adult language learners dates back to the '70s. The influential Threshold series (J.A. van Ek and J.L.M. Trim, Cambridge University Press, 1991) provides a detailed description in functional, notional, grammatical, and sociocultural terms, of what a language user needs to be able to do in order to communicate effectively in the sort of situations commonly encountered in everyday life. Three levels of proficiency are identified, called Waystage, Threshold, and Vantage (roughly corresponding to Elementary, Intermediate, and Upper Intermediate).

The Threshold series was followed in 2001 by the publication of the Common European Framework of Reference, which describes six levels of communicative ability in terms of competences or "can do" statements: A1 (Breakthrough), A2 (Waystage), B1 (Threshold), B2 (Vantage), C1 (Effective Operational Proficiency), and C2 (Mastery). Based on the CEFR descriptors, the Council of Europe also developed the European Language Portfolio, a document that enables learners to assess their language ability and to keep an internationally recognized record of their language learning experience.

## *Interchange Fifth Edition* and the Common European Framework of Reference

The table below shows how *Interchange Fifth Edition* correlates with the Council of Europe's levels and with some major international examinations.

| | CEFR | Council of Europe | Cambridge ESOL | IELTS | TOEFL iBT | TOEIC |
|---|---|---|---|---|---|---|
| **Interchange** | | | | | | |
| Level Intro | A1 | Breakthrough | | | | 120+ |
| Level 1 | A2 | Waystage | | | | 225+ |
| Level 2 | | | | | | |
| | B1 | Threshold | KET (Key English Test) | 4.0–5.0 | 57–86 | 550+ |
| Level 3 | | | PET (Preliminary English Test) | | | |
| **Passages** | | | | | | |
| Level 1 | B2 | Vantage | FCE (First Certificate in English) | 5.5–6.5 | 87–109 | 785+ |
| Level 2 | C1 | Effective Operational Efficiency | CAE (Certificate in Advanced English) | 7.0–8.0 | 110–120 | 490+ (Listening) 445+ (Reading) |

Source: http://www.cambridgeesol.org/about/standards/cefr.html

# Essential teaching tips

## Classroom management

### Error correction

- During controlled practice accuracy activities, correct students' wrong use of the target language right away, either by correcting the error yourself or, whenever possible, having the student identify and/or correct the error. This way, the focus is on accuracy, and students can internalize the correct forms, meaning, and use of the language.
- During oral fluency activities, go around the room and take notes on errors you hear. Do not interrupt students. Instead, take notes of their errors in the use of target language and write these errors on the board. Encourage students to correct them first. Be sure to point out and praise students for language used correctly as well.

### Grouping students

It is good to have students work in a variety of settings: individually, in pairs, in groups, and as a class. This creates a more student-centered environment and increases student talking time.

- The easiest and quickest way to put students in pairs is to have two students sitting close to one another work together. This is good for when students need to have a quick discussion or check answers.
- To ensure students don't always work with the same partner and/or for longer activities, pair students by name, e.g., Maria work with Javier.
- One way to put students in groups is to give them a number from 1 to 4, and then have all number 1s work together, all number 2s work together, and so forth.

### Instructions

- Give short instructions and model the activity for the students.
- Check your instructions, but avoid asking, Do you understand? Instead ask concept questions such as, Are you going to speak or write when you do this activity?

### Monitoring

- Make sure you go around the room and check that the students are doing the activity and offer help as necessary.
- Monitor closely during controlled practice, but don't make yourself too accessible during fluency activities; otherwise, students may rely on you to answer questions rather than focus on communicating their ideas to their partner or group.

## Teaching lower-level students

- Teach the Classroom Language on page xxiii and put useful language up in the classroom, so the students get used to using English.
- Don't rush. Make sure all the students have had enough time to practice the material.
- Do a lot of repetition and drilling of the new target language.
- Encourage students to practice and review target language by doing activities in the Workbook and Self-study.
- Elicit answers from your students and involve them in the learning process. Even though they are beginners, they may have a passive knowledge of English. Find out what they already know by asking them questions.
- Use the optional activities within the Teaching Notes and the Supplementary Resources Overview charts at the beginning of each unit in this Teacher's Edition to add variety to your lessons.

### Teaching reading and listening

- Reading and Listening texts are meant to help the students become better readers / listeners, not to test them. Explain to your students why they need to read or listen to a text several times.
- Adapt the reading speed to the purpose of the reading. When the students read for gist, encourage them to read quickly. When students read for detail, give them more time.

# Classroom Language

# Unit 1 Supplementary Resources Overview

| | After the following SB exercises | You can use these materials in class | Your students can use these materials outside the classroom |
|---|---|---|---|
| **CYCLE 1** | **1 Snapshot** | | |
| | **2 Conversation** | | **SS** Unit 1 Speaking 1–2 |
| | **3 Grammar Focus** | | **SB** Unit 1 Grammar plus, Focus 1<br>**SS** Unit 1 Grammar 1<br>**GAME** Sentence Stacker (Relative pronouns as subject or object of a clause)<br>**GAME** Sentence Runner (Relative pronouns and personalities) |
| | **4 Word Power** | **TSS** Unit 1 Vocabulary Worksheet<br>**TSS** Unit 1 Extra Worksheet | **SS** Unit 1 Vocabulary 1–2<br>**GAME** Spell or Slime (Adjectives for personality traits) |
| | **5 Listening** | **TSS** Unit 1 Listening Worksheet | |
| | **6 Discussion** | | |
| | **7 Writing** | | **WB** Unit 1 exercises 1–5 |
| **CYCLE 2** | **8 Perspectives** | | |
| | **9 Pronunciation** | | |
| | **10 Grammar Focus** | **TSS** Unit 1 Grammar Worksheet<br>**TSS** Unit 1 Writing Worksheet | **SB** Unit 1 Grammar plus, Focus 2<br>**SS** Unit 1 Grammar 2<br>**GAME** Word Keys (Relative pronouns, personalities, and clauses) |
| | **11 Interchange 1** | | |
| | **12 Reading** | **TSS** Unit 1 Project Worksheet<br>**VID** Unit 1<br>**VRB** Unit 1 | **SS** Unit 1 Reading 1–2<br>**SS** Unit 1 Listening 1–3<br>**SS** Unit 1 Video 1–3<br>**WB** Unit 1 exercises 6–10 |

**Key**

| | | | | |
|---|---|---|---|---|
| **GAME:** Online Game | **SB:** Student's Book | **SS:** Online Self-study | **TSS:** Teacher Support Site |
| **VID:** Video DVD | **VRB:** Video Resource Book | **WB:** Online Workbook/Workbook | |

# My Plan for Unit 1

Use the space below to customize a plan that fits your needs.

| With the following SB exercises | I am using these materials in class | My students are using these materials outside the classroom |
|---|---|---|
| | | |
| | | |
| | | |
| | | |
| | | |
| | | |
| | | |
| | | |
| | | |
| | | |
| | | |
| | | |
| | | |

| With or instead of the following SB section | I am using these materials for assessment |
|---|---|
| | |
| | |
| | |

# 1 That's my kind of friend!

▸ Discuss personalities and qualities
▸ Discuss likes and dislikes

## 1 SNAPSHOT

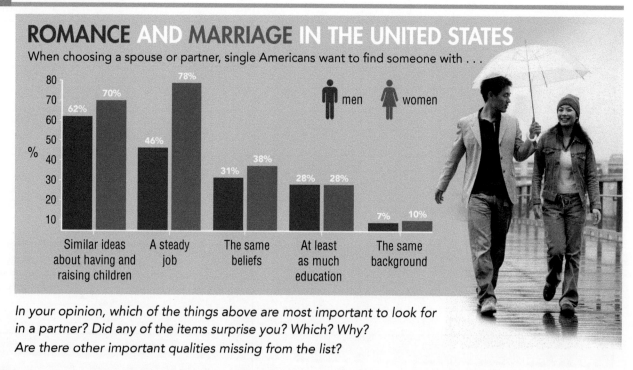

**ROMANCE AND MARRIAGE IN THE UNITED STATES**

When choosing a spouse or partner, single Americans want to find someone with . . .

men     women

| | Similar ideas about having and raising children | A steady job | The same beliefs | At least as much education | The same background |
|---|---|---|---|---|---|
| men | 62% | 46% | 31% | 28% | 7% |
| women | 70% | 78% | 38% | 28% | 10% |

*In your opinion, which of the things above are most important to look for in a partner? Did any of the items surprise you? Which? Why?*
*Are there other important qualities missing from the list?*

## 2 CONVERSATION  What *are* you looking for?

▸ **A** Listen and practice.

**Joe:** What are you doing?

**Roy:** I'm setting up my profile for this online dating site. I have to describe the kind of person I'm looking for.

**Joe:** I see. And what are you looking for?

**Roy:** Oh, I like people who aren't too serious and who have a good sense of humor. You know, someone I can have fun with.

**Joe:** OK. Uh, what else?

**Roy:** Well, I'd like someone I have something in common with – who I can talk to easily.

**Joe:** I think I know just the girl for you: my cousin Lisa. She's a lot of fun and she loves sports, just like you.

**Roy:** Well, why not? I'll give it a try.

**Joe:** OK, I'll invite her over for dinner, and you can tell me what you think.

▸ **B** Listen to Joe and Roy discuss Lisa after they had dinner together. What did Roy think of her?

# 1 That's my kind of friend!

## Cycle 1, Exercises 1–7

In this unit, students practice talking about personalities and qualities and likes and dislikes. By the end of Cycle 1, students will be able to discuss ideal friends and partners using relative pronouns *who* and *that*. By the end of Cycle 2, students will be able to discuss things they like and don't like using clauses with *it* and adverbial clauses with *when*.

- **Option:** Brainstorm questions Ss might ask to find out about classmates. Write Ss' ideas on the board:

  *Wh- questions*
  Where do you live?
  What do you do?
  Why are you studying English?

  *Yes/No questions*
  Do you speak any other languages?
  Are you married?
  Do you have any children?

- Ss work in pairs (preferably with someone they don't know). They take turns interviewing each other. Remind Ss to use the questions on the board and others of their own.

- After ten minutes, stop the activity. Pairs take turns introducing their partners to the class.

## 1 SNAPSHOT

**Learning Objective:** discuss relationships and ideal partners

- Books closed. Ask: "What do you think women look for most in a partner? What do men look for most in a partner?"

- Ss discuss these questions in pairs. Elicit ideas and write them on the board.

- Books open. Ss read the Snapshot individually. Answer vocabulary questions, or allow Ss to use their dictionaries.

- Ask Ss to look carefully at the information in the Snapshot. Ask: "What are some important differences between men and women?" Elicit ideas.

- Read the questions. Discuss the questions as a class, or ask Ss to discuss them in pairs or small groups.

- **Option:** Ask Ss to write a paragraph about some qualities they look for in a partner. Encourage them to give reasons for their choices.

## 2 CONVERSATION

**Learning Objective:** use relative pronouns *who* and *that* in a conversation about dating preferences

### ▶ A [CD 1, Track 1]

- As a warm-up, ask: "What do you think of online dating? Does it work?" Elicit ideas.

- Books closed. Write these focus questions on the board:

  1. What is Roy doing?
  2. Who does Joe suggest?
  3. How will Roy meet her?

- Play the audio program and elicit Ss' answers. (Answers: 1. Roy is setting up his online profile. 2. Joe suggests his cousin Lisa. 3. Joe will invite her for dinner.)

- Write on the board:

  Roy likes girls who . . .
  1. are serious
  2. have a good sense of humor
  3. are sensitive
  4. have something in common with him

- Ask Ss to listen to find out which sentences are true.

- Play the audio program again. Elicit answers. (Answers: 2 and 4)

- Books open. Play the audio program again. Ss listen and read silently.

- Ss practice the conversation in pairs.

  ! For a new way to teach this Conversation, try **Look Up and Speak!** – download it from the website.

### ▶ B [CD 1, Track 2]

- Read the focus question aloud.

- Play the audio program once or twice. Ss listen for the answer to the question. (Answers: Roy liked her a lot. / He thought she was smart, funny, and very pretty.)

### Audio script

See page T-168.

# 3 GRAMMAR FOCUS

**Learning Objective:** use relative pronouns *who* and *that* as subjects and as objects of clauses

▶ **[CD 1, Track 3]**
### Relative pronouns

- Focus Ss' attention on the Grammar Focus box. Explain that relative pronouns (*who* and *that*) do two jobs at the same time. They enable us to:
  1. join two ideas (e.g., *Roy likes girls*, and *they aren't too serious*).
  2. add information (e.g., *Roy likes girls. What kind of girls? Girls who aren't too serious.*).

### Relative pronouns as subjects and objects

- Point to *I like people who/that aren't too serious.* Tell Ss to underline the relative clause. (Answer: *who/that aren't too serious*) Ask: "What's the subject in the relative clause? Who or what 'aren't too serious'?" (Answer: *who/that, people*) Explain that the relative pronoun is the subject here. Repeat for the second sentence.

- Point to *I'd like someone (who/that) I can talk to easily.* Tell Ss to underline the relative clause. (Answer: *(who/that) I can talk to easily*) Ask: "What's the subject in this relative clause? Who can talk to someone easily?" (Answer: *I*) Explain that the relative pronoun is the object here. Repeat for the other sentence.

- Explain that a relative pronoun *who* or *that* is necessary when the relative pronoun is a subject. When the relative pronoun is an object, we can omit it.

- Focus Ss' attention on the Conversation on page 2. Ask Ss to find four examples of relative clauses.

- Play the audio program for the Grammar Focus box. Ss listen and repeat.

**A**

- Explain the task. Model the first item. Point out that more than one answer is possible.

- Ss complete the task individually. Then they compare answers in pairs. Go over answers with the class.

| Possible answers | | | |
|---|---|---|---|
| 1. c | 3. g | 5. d | 7. f |
| 2. e | 4. b | 6. a | |

**B**

- Ss complete the task individually. Then they compare answers in pairs. Go over answers with the class.

| Answers |
|---|
| *Who/that* is optional in sentences 2, 5, and 7. |

### C *Pair work*

- Model with your own information (e.g., *I don't like to work with people who are lazy.*).

- Ss complete the sentences individually. Encourage Ss to be creative and use their own ideas.

- Ss work in pairs. They take turns reading their sentences to each other. The goal is to find where they have similar opinions.

# 4 WORD POWER

**Learning Objective:** paraphrase definitions and use adjectives that describe personal characteristics

**A**

- Ss do the matching individually or in pairs. When finished, Ss can check a dictionary.

| Answers | | | | |
|---|---|---|---|---|
| 1. h, P | 3. a, N | 5. f, P | 7. d, P | 9. e, N |
| 2. c, N | 4. i, P | 6. b, N | 8. g, N | |

### B *Pair work*

- Tell Ss to cover the definitions. Read the example sentence. Ask a S to complete it.

- Explain the task. Ss work in pairs. They take turns talking about the adjectives.

### C *Pair work*

- Model the task by using some adjectives to describe a relative.

- Ss work individually to write down adjectives to describe their relatives. Go around the class and give help as needed.

- Then Ss work in pairs. Ss take turns sharing their descriptions.

- For more practice with vocabulary from Exercises 1–4, play **Prediction Bingo** – download it from the website. Read aloud the definitions, not the adjectives.

# 3 GRAMMAR FOCUS

> **Relative pronouns**

| As the subject of a clause | As the object of a clause |
|---|---|
| I like people **who/that** aren't too serious. | I want someone **(who/that)** I can have fun with. |
| I like people **who/that** have a good sense of humor. | I'd like someone **(who/that)** I can talk to easily. |

GRAMMAR PLUS see page 132

**A** Match the information in columns A and B. Then compare with a partner.

**A**
1. I don't like to work with people who/that __c__
2. I have some good, old friends who/that _____
3. I discuss my problems with people who/that _____
4. I don't want to have a roommate who/that _____
5. I'd like to have a boss who/that _____
6. I enjoy teachers who/that _____
7. I'm looking for a partner who/that _____

**B**
a. help me understand things easily.
b. is messy.
c. are too competitive.
d. I can respect as a leader.
e. I met in middle school.
f. I have a lot in common with.
g. can give me good advice.

**B** Put a line through *who/that* in part A if it's optional. Then compare with a partner.

**C** PAIR WORK Complete the sentences in column A with your own information.
Do you and your partner have similar opinions?

**A:** I don't like to work with people who are too competitive.
**B:** Neither do I. I like to work with people who are friendly and helpful.

# 4 WORD POWER Personality traits

**A** Match the words with the definitions. Then decide whether the words
are positive (**P**) or negative (**N**). Write **P** or **N** after each word.

__h__ 1. easygoing __P__
___ 2. egotistical _____
___ 3. inflexible _____
___ 4. modest _____
___ 5. outgoing _____
___ 6. stingy _____
___ 7. supportive _____
___ 8. temperamental _____
___ 9. unreliable _____

a. a person who doesn't change easily and is stubborn
b. someone who doesn't like giving or spending money
c. someone who has a very high opinion of him- or herself
d. someone who is helpful and encouraging
e. a person who doesn't do what he or she promised
f. a person who enjoys being with other people
g. a person who has unpredictable or irregular moods
h. a person who doesn't worry much or get angry easily
i. someone who doesn't brag about his or her accomplishments

**B** PAIR WORK Cover the definitions. Take turns talking about the adjectives
in your own words.

"An easygoing person is someone who . . ."

**C** PAIR WORK Think of at least two adjectives to describe your favorite
relative. Then tell a partner.

## 5 LISTENING What's new?

**A** Listen to conversations that describe three people. Are the descriptions positive (**P**) or negative (**N**)? Check (✓) the box.

| | | |
|---|---|---|
| **1.** Emma | ☐ P | ☐ N |
| **2.** Mrs. Leblanc | ☐ P | ☐ N |
| **3.** Pablo | ☐ P | ☐ N |

**B** Listen again. Write two adjectives that describe each person in the chart.

## 6 DISCUSSION The right qualities

**A** What is the ideal friend, parent, or partner like? Add your own type of person under **People**. Then write one quality each ideal person should have, and one each should *not* have.

| People | This person is . . . | This person is not . . . |
|---|---|---|
| The ideal friend | | |
| The ideal parent | | |
| The ideal partner | | |
| The ideal _____ | | |

**B** GROUP WORK Take turns describing your ideal people. Try to agree on the two most important qualities for each person.

**A:** I think the ideal friend is someone who is supportive and who is a good listener.

**B:** I agree. The ideal friend is someone who isn't critical . . .

**C:** Oh, I'm not sure I agree. . . .

## 7 WRITING A good friend

**A** Think about a good friend. Answer the questions. Then write a paragraph.

What is this person like?
How long have you known each other?
How did you meet?
How are you similar?
How are you different?
What makes your relationship special?

> My friend Nolan is easygoing and doesn't take life too seriously. He's someone who loves to have fun, and he makes sure everyone else has a good time, too. We met about six years ago . . .

**B** PAIR WORK Exchange paragraphs. How are your friends similar? How are they different?

# 5 LISTENING

**Learning Objective:** listen to descriptions of people for specific information, and make inferences about them

### A [CD 1, Track 4]

- Books closed. Divide the class into teams. Each team brainstorms positive and negative adjectives to describe personalities.
- Set a time limit of three minutes. Call on different Ss from each team to write the adjectives in two columns on the board.
- Books open. Set the scene. Ss will listen to descriptions of three people. After listening to each conversation, Ss decide if the general feeling is positive (P) or negative (N).
- Play the audio program. Ss listen and check (✓) the positive or negative box.

### Audio script

See page T-169.

- Go over answers with the class.

### Answers

1. Emma: N
2. Mrs. Leblanc: P
3. Pablo: P

### B [CD 1, Track 5]

- Play the audio program again. Pause after each conversation. Ss write two adjectives that describe each person.
- Elicit answers from the class. Ask Ss to explain why they chose those words (e.g., *Emma is unreliable because she didn't do what she said she would.*).

### Possible answers

1. Emma: unreliable; inflexible
2. Mrs. Leblanc: supportive; modest
3. Pablo: easygoing; sociable

# 6 DISCUSSION

**Learning Objectives:** describe personal qualities using relative pronouns; agree or disagree with descriptions

### A

- Focus Ss' attention on the picture. Ask: "What is happening? What kind of friend is that?"
- Explain the task. Read the discussion question, and go over the chart.
- Ss complete the chart.

### B Group work

- Explain the task. Have three Ss model the conversation.
- Ss work in small groups. Ss take turns describing their "ideal people" using information from their chart in part A. Go around the class and give help as needed.
- **Option:** Ss discuss other ideal people (e.g., the ideal boss/employee/teacher/student/brother/sister).

! For a new way to practice discussion, try the **Onion-Ring** technique – download it from the website.

# 7 WRITING

**Learning Objective:** write a paragraph describing a friend using relative pronouns

### A

- Explain the task. Go over the example paragraph.
- Read the questions. Ask Ss to find the answers to the first two questions in the paragraph.
- Ask Ss to identify the two relative clauses in the paragraph.
- Have Ss think about a good friend and write answers to the questions.
- Ss write the first draft of their paragraph. Write one paragraph focusing on three areas: (1) content, (2) organization, (3) grammar.
- **Option:** Ss write the paragraph for homework.

### B Pair work

- Ss work in pairs to complete the task.
- Call on pairs to explain how their friends are similar and different.
- Ss make final revisions. Then they turn in their work for checking.

### End of Cycle 1

See the Supplementary Resources chart at the beginning of this unit for additional teaching materials and student activities related to this Cycle.

# 8 PERSPECTIVES

**Learning Objective:** agree or disagree with statements using clauses with *it* and adverbial clauses with *when* in context

### A [CD 1, Track 6]

- Ss cover the text and look only at the picture. Ask Ss to discuss these questions in pairs:
  *What is the boy doing?*
  *Would this annoy you? Why?*

- While Ss are talking, write on the board:
  <u>Common complaints - topics</u>
  *someone takes the last cookie*
  *people who text "Call me."*
  *people who tell you to calm down*
  *an early morning phone call*
  *friends who answer their phone at dinner*
  *children who scream in restaurants*
  *friends who forget birthdays*
  *doctors who are late*

- Books closed. Set the scene. Ss will hear eight common complaints. They are written on the board but in the wrong order.

- Tell Ss to listen and number the complaints on the board in the order they hear them. Play the audio program. Then Ss open their books and check their answers. (Answers: someone takes the last cookie: 4;

people who text "Call me.": 8; people who tell you to calm down: 2; an early morning phone call: 6; friends who answer their phones at dinner: 7; children who scream in restaurants: 1; friends who forget birthdays: 5; doctors who are late: 3)

- Next, Ss complete the quiz individually.

### B

- Explain the task. Ss read the quiz again and count their score.

- **Option:** Ss find out who is similar to them by going around the class and asking people what their score was. Then tell Ss to choose the situation that bothers them the most.

- Call on Ss to read each complaint in turn. Ask Ss to raise their hand if they chose that complaint. Note how many people chose each complaint, and count the score. Which one bothers people the most?

- **Option:** Ss with the same complaint work in groups. They discuss these questions:
  *Why does that situation annoy you so much?*
  *When did it last happen? What did you do about it?*

- **Option:** Tell Ss to look at the sentences in the quiz. Elicit four ways of saying *I don't like it.* Write Ss' answers on the board. (Answers: *I hate it. / It bothers me. / I can't stand it. / It upsets me.*)

# 9 PRONUNCIATION

**Learning Objective:** sound more natural when using linked sounds

### A [CD 1, Track 7]

- Explain that English speakers often link words together. They often link a final consonant to the vowel sound that follows it (e.g., **It u**psets me. I can't stan**d i**t.).

- Point out that we link *sounds* together, not letters. Write some examples on the board:
  I ha**te it** = /ti/       I lo**ve it** = /vi/

- Give Ss time to read the two example sentences and to study the examples of consonant + vowel links in each sentence.

- Play the audio program. Ss practice the sentences.

### B [CD 1, Track 8]

- Explain the task. Ss read the sentences and decide which sounds are linked. They mark the linked sounds.

- Play the audio program. Ss listen and check their answers.

- Go over answers with the class. Write the sentences on the board. Call on Ss to mark the linked sounds.

#### Answers

1. I ha**te i**t whe**n a** cell phone goe**s o**ff at the movies.
2. I can't stan**d i**t when a perso**n i**s inflexible.
3. Doe**s i**t bother you whe**n a** frien**d i**s **u**nreliable?

### C Pair work

- Explain the task. Model the first sentence in the quiz.

- Ss work in pairs. They take turns saying the sentences. Go around the class and listen for linking.

- Play the audio program again, if needed.

## 8 PERSPECTIVES Are you difficult to please?

▶ **A** Listen to some common complaints. Check (✓) the ones you agree with.

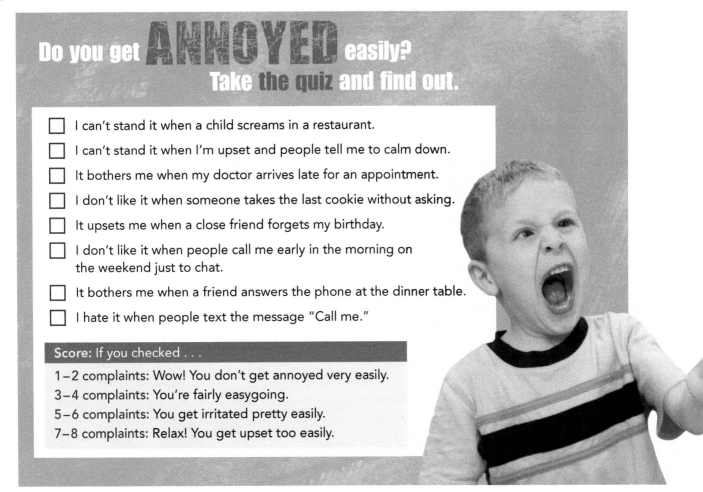

# Do you get ANNOYED easily?
## Take the quiz and find out.

☐ I can't stand it when a child screams in a restaurant.

☐ I can't stand it when I'm upset and people tell me to calm down.

☐ It bothers me when my doctor arrives late for an appointment.

☐ I don't like it when someone takes the last cookie without asking.

☐ It upsets me when a close friend forgets my birthday.

☐ I don't like it when people call me early in the morning on the weekend just to chat.

☐ It bothers me when a friend answers the phone at the dinner table.

☐ I hate it when people text the message "Call me."

**Score: If you checked . . .**

1–2 complaints: Wow! You don't get annoyed very easily.
3–4 complaints: You're fairly easygoing.
5–6 complaints: You get irritated pretty easily.
7–8 complaints: Relax! You get upset too easily.

**B** Calculate your score. Do you get annoyed easily?
Tell the class what bothers you the most.

## 9 PRONUNCIATION Linked sounds

▶ **A** Listen and practice. Final consonant sounds are often linked to the vowel sounds that follow them.

It upsets me when a friend is late for an appointment.
I love it when a friend is supportive and kind.

▶ **B** Mark the linked sounds in the sentences below.
Listen and check. Then practice saying the sentences.

**1.** I hate it when a cell phone goes off at the movies.

**2.** I can't stand it when a person is inflexible.

**3.** Does it bother you when a friend is unreliable?

**C** PAIR WORK Take turns saying the sentences in
Exercise 8. Pay attention to linked sounds.

# 10 GRAMMAR FOCUS

▶ *It* clauses + adverbial clauses with *when*

| I like **it** | **when** my roommate cleans the apartment. |
| I don't mind **it** | **when** a friend answers the phone at the dinner table. |
| I can't stand **it** | **when** I'm upset and people tell me to calm down. |
| **It** makes me happy | **when** people do nice things for no reason. |
| **It** bothers me | **when** my doctor arrives late for an appointment. |
| **It** upsets me | **when** a close friend forgets my birthday. |

GRAMMAR PLUS *see page 132*

**A** How do you feel about these situations? Complete the sentences with *it* clauses from the list. Then compare your sentences with a partner.

| I love it | I don't mind it | It annoys me | It really upsets me |
| I like it | It doesn't bother me | I don't like it | I can't stand it |
| It makes me happy | I hate it | | |

1. _____ when a friend gives me a present for no special reason.

2. _____ when someone criticizes a friend of mine.

3. _____ when friends start arguing in front of me.

4. _____ when people call me late at night.

5. _____ when salesclerks are temperamental.

6. _____ when people are direct and say what's on their mind.

7. _____ when someone corrects my grammar in front of others.

8. _____ when a friend is sensitive and supportive.

9. _____ when people throw trash on the ground.

10. _____ when a friend treats me to dinner.

**B GROUP WORK** Do you ever get annoyed by a certain type of person or situation? Write down five things that annoy you the most. Then compare in groups.

**A:** I can't stand it when someone takes food off my plate.

**B:** I feel the same way. Especially when the person didn't order his or her own food!

**C:** Yeah, but it bothers me more when . . .

# 11 INTERCHANGE 1 Personality quiz

Interview a classmate to find out about his or her personality.
Go to Interchange 1 on page 114.

# 10 GRAMMAR FOCUS

**Learning Objective:** use clauses with *it* and adverbial clauses with *when* to express opinions about situations

▶ *[CD 1, Track 9]*
### Clauses with *it* and *when*

- Focus Ss' attention on the quiz on page 5. Ask Ss to find examples of sentences that begin with *I*. Write the sentences on the board like this:

| 1 | 2 | 3 | 4 | 5 |
|---|---|---|---|---|
| I | can't stand | it | when | I'm upset... |
| I | don't like | it | when | someone... |
| I | hate | it | when | people text... |

- Ask Ss what is in each column to elicit the rule:
  <u>Clause with *it*</u>     <u>Adverbial clause with *when*</u>
  *subject + verb + it + when + subject + verb*

- Point out that we use *it when* in this structure.

### Sentences beginning with *it* and adverbial clause with *when*

- In the same quiz, ask Ss to find two examples of sentences that begin with the word *it*. Write the sentences on the board. Also add the phrase *it embarrasses me*.

| 1 | 2 | 3 | 4 | 5 |
|---|---|---|---|---|
| It | bothers | me | when | my doctor... |
| It | upsets | me | when | a close friend... |
| It | embarrasses | me | when | a friend... |

- Ask Ss what is in each column to elicit the rule:
  <u>Clause with *it*</u>     <u>Adverbial clause with *when*</u>
  *It + verb + object   +   when + subject + verb*

- Play the audio program.

- **Option:** For additional practice, write these cues on the board and ask Ss to complete them orally:

  I like it when...          It bothers me when...
  I don't like it when...    It really upsets me when...

### A

- Focus Ss' attention on the picture. Ask: "What is happening? How do you feel when someone takes food from your plate?" Elicit ideas from the class.

- Ss read the expressions and clauses silently.

- Explain any new vocabulary. Elicit which phrases are positive (e.g., *I love it.*), neutral (e.g., *I don't mind it.*), and negative (e.g., *It really upsets me.*).

- Explain the task. Model the first one by eliciting suggestions.

- Ss complete the task individually. Go around the class and give help as needed.

- **Option:** Tell Ss to use each expression only once.

- Ss work in pairs. They take turns reading their sentences aloud to compare responses. Remind Ss to focus on linking the words.

- Elicit Ss' responses. Accept any sentences that are logical and grammatically correct. Let Ss self-correct before you correct them.

> **TIP**
> To deal with common errors, write the word on a note card (e.g., the word *when* or *it*). Each time Ss make the error, show the card.

▦ For more practice with the expressions, play **Tic-Tac-Toe** – download it from the website.

### B Group work

- Explain the task. Have three Ss model the conversation.

- Ss work individually to write down five things that annoy them. Go around the class and give help as needed.

- Write some useful phrases on the board. Point out that these are ways to agree with someone:

  I feel the same way.        Absolutely!
  I know what you mean!       Me too./Me neither.
  You can say that again.

- Ss work in small groups and compare what annoys them.

- Encourage Ss to use some of the phrases on the board. Remind them to ask follow-up questions and to give their own opinions. Set a time limit of about ten minutes.

# 11 INTERCHANGE 1

See page T-114 for teaching notes.

## A

- Books closed. Read the pre-reading questions aloud, or write them on the board. Ask Ss to discuss the questions in pairs and write down some options for things that get their attention (pictures of people/ animals, funny videos, inspirational messages . . .)
- Write the title of the article on the board. Ss predict what kind of information they will read in the article.
- Books open. Ss read the article silently. Ss should read the article without stopping to ask questions or use a dictionary.
- Then tell Ss to go back through the text and circle words they can't guess from context. Ss work in pairs to figure out unfamiliar vocabulary.
- Elicit or explain any remaining new vocabulary.

### Vocabulary

**pursue:** try to find, do, or achieve something
**supportive:** giving help or encouragement
**play-date:** an arrangement for children to spend time together and play
**entrepreneur:** someone who starts his or her own business
**keep up with:** continue to be informed about something
**improve:** make better

! For a good way to find the meaning of unknown words, try **Vocabulary Mingle** – download it from the website.

## B

- Explain the task. Ss decide which sentence belongs to which website based on the article.
- Ss reread the article individually and answer the questions.
- **Option:** Ss compare answers in pairs. Ss show their partners where in the article they can find this information.
- Go over answers with the class.

### Answers

1. S   2. P   3. P   4. H   5. S   6. H

### TIP
Two or three smaller, purposeful readings can be more productive than one long, detailed reading.

## C

- Explain the task. Ask Ss to find the first word. (Answer: *sufficient*) Read the sentence aloud. Elicit context clues that help Ss figure out the meaning.
- Ss work individually or in pairs to find the phrases and choose the meanings.
- Go over answers with the class.

### Answers

1. sufficient       4. activists
2. forums           5. strategies
3. appreciate

- **Option:** Write the names of the websites on the board:

*Stache Passions*
*Purrsonals*
*Horyou*

- Ss work in pairs to find out why the sites have their names (Answers: Stache Passions: The name *Stache* is short for *mustache*; Purrsonals: A *purr* is a noise cats make when they are happy; Horyou: It means *What humanity can do for you and what we can do for humanity*).

## D *Pair work*

- Explain the task. Read the questions.
- Ss discuss the questions in pairs.
- Play **Just One Minute** – download it from the website. Ask Ss to talk about the article or other social media sites.

## End of Cycle 2

See the Supplementary Resources chart at the beginning of this unit for additional teaching materials and student activities related to this Cycle.

**A** Are you a frequent social media user? What kinds of things get your attention on social media?

| HOME | NEWS | ABOUT | CULTURE | | Q |

# SOCIAL NETWORKS THAT AREN'T FOR EVERYONE

Since social networking websites first appeared, many have come and some have gone. However, their purpose has generally been the same: keeping up with old friends, making new friends, and sharing pictures, videos, and bits of interesting news. In addition, some sites make it possible to pursue new relationships, either online or in the real world.

For some people who have very specific interests, generic sites like Facebook or Twitter are not sufficient. They want to be part of a supportive online community that shares their particular passions.

A good example is Stache Passions, a social site for people who wear, admire, or have an interest in moustaches. It features photos of men with all sizes and styles of moustaches, forums  for discussing the history, growing, and styling of the 'stache, and even a meet-up page to help you meet other moustache-lovers.

Purrsonals is a specialized site for those who love cats. Here you can meet and chat with cat-loving friends, set up feline play-dates with local people and their pets, and even find a home for a cat in need. And if your friends don't like it when you share endless cute cat videos on your regular social site, Purrsonals is where people are sure to appreciate them!

On a more serious note, Horyou is a website for people that want to do good in the world. On the site, you can connect with other social activists and entrepreneurs, plan meetings, share fund-raising strategies, and keep up with thousands of people who are working hard to make the world a better place. There are no funny videos here, but Horyou offers its own web-based video channel that features programs and documentaries about efforts to improve people's lives around the globe.

**B** Read the article. Which website is good for the people below? Write **S** (Stache Passions), **P** (Purrsonals), or **H** (Horyou).

This site would be good for someone who . . .

**1.** has a strong interest in personal appearance. _____

**2.** is hoping to adopt a new pet. _____

**3.** wants to watch a bit of light entertainment. _____

**4.** wants ideas for improving others' lives. _____

**5.** is interested in styles from the past. _____

**6.** wants to raise money for a charity. _____

**C** Find the words in the article that mean the following.

**1.** enough for a purpose _____

**2.** places where a discussion can take place _____

**3.** to like and be grateful for something _____

**4.** people who want to accomplish political or social change _____

**5.** plans of action _____

**D** **PAIR WORK** Do you belong to any specialized social networking sites? If yes, what is the focus? If not, what type of specialized site might you join?

# Unit 2 Supplementary Resources Overview

| | After the following SB exercises | You can use these materials in class | Your students can use these materials outside the classroom |
|---|---|---|---|
| **CYCLE 1** | 1 Snapshot | | |
| | 2 Perspectives | | |
| | 3 Grammar Focus | | **SB** Unit 2 Grammar plus, Focus 1<br>**SS** Unit 2 Grammar 1<br>**GAME** Speak or Swim (Gerund phrases) |
| | 4 Word Power | | **SS** Unit 2 Vocabulary 1–2 |
| | 5 Speaking | **TSS** Unit 2 Writing Worksheet | **GAME** Name the Picture (Career choices and professions) |
| | 6 Writing | | **GAME** Say the Word (Expressions for describing pros and cons)<br>**WB** Unit 2 exercises 1–4 |
| **CYCLE 2** | 7 Conversation | | **SS** Unit 2 Speaking 1–2 |
| | 8 Grammar Focus | **TSS** Unit 2 Vocabulary Worksheet<br>**TSS** Unit 2 Grammar Worksheet | **SB** Unit 2 Grammar plus, Focus 2<br>**SS** Unit 2 Grammar 2<br>**GAME** Sentence Stacker (Comparisons) |
| | 9 Pronunciation | **TSS** Unit 2 Listening Worksheet | |
| | 10 Listening | | |
| | 11 Discussion | **TSS** Unit 2 Extra Worksheet | |
| | 12 Interchange 2 | | |
| | 13 Reading | **TSS** Unit 2 Project Worksheet<br>**VID** Unit 2<br>**VRB** Unit 2 | **SS** Unit 2 Reading 1–2<br>**SS** Unit 2 Listening 1–3<br>**SS** Unit 2 Video 1–3<br>**WB** Unit 2 exercises 5–8 |

| With or instead of the following SB section | You can also use these materials for assessment |
|---|---|
| **Units 1–2 Progress Check** | **ASSESSMENT PROGRAM** Units 1–2 Oral Quiz<br>**ASSESSMENT PROGRAM** Units 1–2 Written Quiz |

**Key**   **GAME:** Online Game   **SB:** Student's Book   **SS:** Online Self-study   **TSS:** Teacher Support Site
**VID:** Video DVD   **VRB:** Video Resource Book   **WB:** Online Workbook/Workbook

# My Plan for Unit 2

Use the space below to customize a plan that fits your needs.

| With the following SB exercises | I am using these materials in class | My students are using these materials outside the classroom |
|---|---|---|
| | | |
| | | |
| | | |
| | | |
| | | |
| | | |
| | | |
| | | |
| | | |
| | | |
| | | |
| | | |
| | | |

| With or instead of the following SB section | I am using these materials for assessment |
|---|---|
| | |
| | |
| | |

# 2 Working 9 to 5

▸ Discuss opinions, advantages, and disadvantages of jobs
▸ Compare various jobs

## 1 SNAPSHOT

### What do you want from your career?

 **☐ Security**
If you want to have stability, choose a job that you can keep for your whole life. You could be a federal judge, a public school teacher, or a university professor.

 **☐ Adventure**
Perhaps you can't picture yourself doing the same thing, at the same place, for years and years. In that case, be something that will allow you to explore other places and other cultures, like an environmentalist or a tour guide.

 **☐ Money**
Do you want to have a high-paying job? You may want to look into being a financial analyst, a doctor, or a stockbroker.

*Rank the factors from 1 (most important) to 3 (least important). Compare with a partner.*
*Which factors did you consider when you chose your present job or your future career? Why?*

## 2 PERSPECTIVES Career choices

A Listen to students discuss career choices. Do you agree or disagree?
Check (✓) the speaker you agree with more.

 I'd like to work in the video game industry. Playing games all day would be lots of fun. ☐

 I disagree! Playing the same game every day for months would be boring. ☐

 Designing clothes is not a man's job. Women are much more fascinated by fashion. ☐

 Being a flight attendant sounds very exciting. Traveling all the time would be really interesting. ☐

 But flight attendants get tired of traveling. They spend most of their time in airports! ☐

That's not true! Many great fashion designers are men. Just look at Michael Kors!  ☐

B Compare your responses with your classmates. Give more reasons to support your opinions.

 I'd enjoy working with animals. I think working as a veterinarian could be rewarding. ☐

I'm not so sure. Animals can be very unpredictable. Getting a dog bite would be scary!  ☐

# 2 Working 9 to 5

## Cycle 1, Exercises 1–6

In this unit, Ss discuss the advantages and disadvantages of various jobs and careers. By the end of Cycle 1, students will be able to discuss their opinions of jobs using gerund phrases as subjects and as objects. By the end of Cycle 2, students will be able to discuss jobs using comparisons with adjectives, adverbs, nouns, and past participles.

## 1 SNAPSHOT

**Learning Objective:** discuss opinions of various jobs

- Books closed. Introduce the topic of careers and factors that influence your decision on choosing a job.
- Explain that some jobs or careers will be more stable whereas others will be more adventurous or better paying.
- With the class, brainstorm some other jobs and careers for each of the factors. Write Ss' ideas on the board. Ask Ss to guess which ones will be mentioned in the Snapshot.
- Books open. Give Ss a few minutes to read the Snapshot on their own. Allow Ss to use a dictionary after they finish reading, if they wish.
- Elicit or explain any new vocabulary.

### Vocabulary

**stability:** the quality of not being likely to change or move
**perhaps:** possibly
**picture:** imagine something in a particular way
**environmentalist:** someone who tries to protect the natural environment from being damaged
**stockbroker:** someone whose job is to buy and sell stocks and shares in companies for other people

- Read the questions aloud. Then Ss discuss the questions in pairs.
- **Option:** Ask Ss to discuss other factors that need to be considered when choosing a career (e.g., *responsibility*). Write Ss' ideas on the board.

For a new way to review jobs vocabulary, try **Vocabulary Steps** – download it from the website.

To practice jobs vocabulary, play **Hot Potato** – download it from the website. Ask Ss to brainstorm one job beginning with each letter of the alphabet.

## 2 PERSPECTIVES

**Learning Objective:** agree or disagree with statements about jobs using gerund phrases in context

### ▶ A [CD 1, Track 10]

- Books closed. Set the scene. Ss will hear people talking about four jobs. Two people give different opinions about each job.
- Play the audio program. Ss listen and write down the four jobs. (Answers: video game player, flight attendant, fashion designer, veterinarian)
- Books open. Tell Ss to read the Perspectives to check their answers.
- Elicit or explain any new vocabulary. Elicit that Michael Kors is one of the most successful male fashion designers in the world.
- Explain the task. Ss read and check which of the two speakers they agree with more.

### B

- Explain the task. Go over the language used by the speakers in part A to agree or disagree (e.g., *I disagree! I'm not so sure.*).
- Ss compare their answers in pairs. Encourage Ss to ask follow-up questions.
- Play the audio program again. Tell Ss to focus on the intonation used for disagreeing and presenting opinions.
- Ss practice the conversations in pairs. Tell Ss to try to imitate the original speakers' intonation.

## 3 GRAMMAR FOCUS

Learning Objective: use gerund phrases as subjects and objects in opinions about jobs

▶ *[CD 1, Track 11]*

- Elicit or explain that a gerund is formed by adding -*ing* to a verb (e.g., *playing, being*). This is the same form as the present continuous. However, a gerund is a noun, so it can be a subject or an object in a sentence.

> **TIP**
> To help Ss remember the structure, encourage them to try to work out rules themselves. Training Ss in this skill will help them deal with new structures in the future.

- Write on the board:

  Gerund phrases
  1. As the subject of a sentence:
  Being a flight attendant sounds exciting.
  2. As the object of the verb:
     He'd love being a flight attendant.
  3. As the object of a preposition:
     I'm interested in being a flight attendant.

- Play the audio program.

- Focus Ss' attention on the Perspectives on page 8. Tell Ss to underline the gerunds. Call on Ss to write the gerunds on the board. (Answers: *playing, being, traveling, designing, working, getting*)

  Note: *Clothing designer* is a noun phrase; *exciting* and *rewarding* are participial adjectives.

- **Option:** Ask Ss to use the gerunds on the board as subjects. Then ask Ss to use the gerunds as objects (e.g., *Designing clothes is a job for men and women. Michael Kors is great at designing clothes.*).

### A

- Explain the task. Use the example sentence to model the task. Have Ss read the gerund phrases in column A. Explain any new vocabulary.

- **Option:** Review or present other adverbs that Ss can use with the adjectives in column C (e.g., *pretty, kind of, really, very, extremely, so, quite, incredibly*).

- Ss work individually to write their opinions of each job. Go around the class and give help as needed.

- Go over answers with the class. Accept any answers that are logical and grammatically correct.

> **TIP**
> Let Ss correct problems themselves. Then explain those errors that Ss can't correct.

### B *Pair work*

- Explain the task. Model the task with several Ss using the example conversation in the book.

- Ss work in pairs to give reasons for their opinions about the jobs in part A. Go around the class and give help as needed. Make notes of errors with gerund phrases.

- When pairs finish, write some of the errors on the board. Elicit corrections from the class.

### C *Group work*

- Explain the task. Ss complete the sentences with gerund phrases as objects. Ask a S to read the example sentence.

- Ss work individually to complete the task. Go around the class and give help as needed.

- Then Ss work in small groups, taking turns reading their sentences. Encourage Ss to ask follow-up questions and to give more information.

- Ask each group to choose the three most interesting sentences. Different Ss read them aloud to the class.

- **Option:** Ss go around and exchange their information with classmates.

For more practice with gerund phrases, play **True or False?** – download it from the website.

# 3 GRAMMAR FOCUS

▶ **Gerund phrases**

| Gerund phrases as subjects | Gerund phrases as objects |
|---|---|
| **Playing games all day** would be lots of fun. | She'd be good at **testing games**. |
| **Being a flight attendant** sounds exciting. | He'd love **being a flight attendant**. |
| **Designing clothes** is not a man's job. | He wouldn't like **being a fashion designer**. |
| **Working as a veterinarian** could be rewarding. | She'd enjoy **working with animals**. |

GRAMMAR PLUS *see page 133*

**A** Look at the gerund phrases in column A. Write your opinion of each job by choosing information from columns B and C. Then add two more gerund phrases and write similar sentences.

| A | B | C |
|---|---|---|
| 1. working from home | seems | awful |
| 2. doing volunteer work | could be | stressful |
| 3. having your own business | would be | fantastic |
| 4. working on a movie set | must be | fascinating |
| 5. being a teacher | wouldn't be | pretty difficult |
| 6. making a living as a tour guide | doesn't sound | kind of boring |
| 7. taking care of sick people | | really rewarding |
| 8. retiring at age 40 | | very challenging |
| 9. _____ | | |
| 10. _____ | | |

> 1. Working from home could be very challenging.

**B** **PAIR WORK** Give reasons for your opinions about the jobs in part A.

**A:** In my opinion, working from home could be very challenging.
**B:** Really? Why is that?
**A:** Because you have to learn to manage your time. It's easy to get distracted.
**B:** I'm not sure that's true. For me, working from home would be . . .

**C** **GROUP WORK** Complete the sentences with gerund phrases. Then take turns reading your sentences. Share the three most interesting sentences with the class.

1. I'd get tired of . . .
2. I'd be interested in . . .
3. I'd be very excited about . . .
4. I'd enjoy . . .
5. I think I'd be good at . . .
6. I wouldn't be very good at . . .

"I'd get tired of doing the same thing every day."

# 4 WORD POWER Suffixes

**A** Add the suffixes *-er, -or, -ist,* or *-ian* to form the names of these jobs. Write the words in the chart and add one more example to each column.

| software develop _er_ | freelance journal_____ | marketing direct_____ | politic_____ |
| computer technic_____ | guidance counsel_____ | project manag_____ | psychiatr_____ |

| -er | -or | -ist | -ian |
|---|---|---|---|
| software developer | | | |
| | | | |
| | | | |

**B** PAIR WORK Can you give a definition for each job?

"A software developer is someone who creates apps for computers and other devices."

# 5 SPEAKING Career paths

GROUP WORK Talk about a career you would like to have. Use information from Exercises 1–4 or your own ideas. Other students ask follow-up questions.

**A:** I'd enjoy working as a guidance counselor.
**B:** Why is that?
**A:** Helping kids must be really rewarding.
**C:** Where would you work?
**A:** Well, I think I'd like to work at a high school. I enjoy working with teens.

# 6 WRITING What's more satisfying?

**A** GROUP WORK What would you choose: a job that you love that doesn't pay well, or a high-paying job that you don't like? Discuss and list the consequences of the two alternatives.

**B** Use the list to write a paragraph justifying your choice.

> Having a high-paying job that you don't like could be very frustrating. First of all, you'd have to do something you don't like every day. You would have a lot of money. However, it's not worth it if . . .

**useful expressions**

First of all, . . .
In addition, . . .
Furthermore, . . .
For example, . . .
However, . . .
On the other hand, . . .
In conclusion, . . .

**C** PAIR WORK Read your partner's paragraph. Do you agree or disagree? Why or why not?

# 4 WORD POWER

**Learning Objective:** describe jobs using suffixes *-er*, *-or*, *-ist*, and *-ian*

## A

- Explain the task. Ask a S to read the example.
- Ss complete the task individually or in pairs. First, Ss add suffixes to form names of jobs. Then Ss write the words in the chart. Remind Ss to add one more example to each column.
- To check answers, draw the chart on the board. Ask Ss to come up to complete it.

### Answers

| **-er** | **-ist** |
|---|---|
| software develop**er** | freelance journal**ist** |
| project manag**er** | psychiat**rist** |
| *baby sitter* | *dentist* |

| **-or** | **-ian** |
|---|---|
| guidance counsel**or** | computer techni**cian** |
| marketing direct**or** | politi**cian** |
| *actor* | *librarian* |

*(note: additional examples are italicized)*

- Pronounce the words. Explain that the *p* is silent in words beginning with *psy-*.
- **Option:** Ask Ss to name jobs where the verb and noun are the same (e.g., *coach, cook, guide, TV host*).
- **Option:** Ask Ss to talk about the jobs in the chart, using gerunds as subjects or objects.

## B  *Pair work*

- Ask a S to read the example definition.
- Ss work in pairs and take turns making definitions. Remind Ss to use *someone who* or *someone that*.

For a new way to talk about jobs and their suffixes, try **Mime** – download it from the website.

# 5 SPEAKING

**Learning Objective:** discuss possible careers using gerund phrases

## *Group work*

- Ask three Ss to model the conversation. Point out the follow-up questions.

- Ss work in small groups. Set a time limit of about ten minutes. Ss take turns talking about possible careers. Tell Ss to ask two follow-up questions each per discussion. Go around the class and give help as needed.

# 6 WRITING

**Learning Objective:** write a paragraph about the advantages and disadvantages of a job using gerund phrases

## A  *Group work*

- Ss work in small groups to discuss the question. Ss choose one of the jobs they talked about in Exercise 5 (or another job). Ss make a list of advantages and disadvantages of both alternatives.
- Go around the class and give help as needed.

## B

- Explain the task. Ask a S to read the model paragraph aloud.
- Ss work individually to write their paragraphs.
- Encourage Ss to write positive and negative consequences. Remind Ss to add a title.
- **Option:** Ss do this step for homework.

## C  *Pair work*

- Ss exchange and read each other's paragraphs about jobs. Partners say if they agree or disagree and explain why.

### End of Cycle 1

See the Supplementary Resources chart at the beginning of this unit for additional teaching materials and student activities related to this Cycle.

## 7 CONVERSATION

**Learning Objective:** use comparisons in a conversation about jobs

### ▶ A [CD 1, Track 12]

- Books closed. Set the scene. Tyler and Emma are talking about summer jobs. Explain that in the United States, young people often get a job during summer vacation to pay for their studies or to gain experience.
- Ask: "What job has Tyler found?" Tell Ss to listen for the answer.
- Books open. Play the first five lines of the audio program. Elicit the answer. (Answer: working at a beach resort)
- Explain that *leads* are possible jobs. Elicit that an intern is a person working to gain experience, usually for little or no pay.
- Books closed. Play the audio program.

- Ss compare Emma's two job leads in pairs. Ask Ss to discuss the advantages of each.
- Books open. Play the audio program again. Ss listen and read. Ask different Ss to read each line aloud.
- Ss practice the conversation in pairs.

### ▶ B [CD 1, Track 13]

- Read the focus question aloud. Ss listen for the answer to the question.
- Play the second part of the audio program. Encourage Ss to take notes.

#### Audio script

See page T-168.

#### Answer

Tyler is going to work with the entertainment staff. He'll have to organize and take part in daytime and evening activities, like games, shows, and parties.

## 8 GRAMMAR FOCUS

**Learning Objective:** use comparisons with adjectives, adverbs, nouns, and past participles

### ▶ [CD 1, Track 14]

- Play the audio program. Ask Ss to underline the adjectives, verbs, nouns, and past participles.
- Point out that all the comparisons are based on the same few structures. Write them on the board:

  more...than    better...than    as...as
  less...than    worse...than    not as...as

- Give a few examples with familiar occupations. Elicit other examples.

#### A

- Explain the task.
- Ss work individually to complete the sentences with the words in parentheses. Remind Ss that there are several correct answers for each item.
- Ss go over their answers in pairs. Then go over answers with the class.

#### Possible answers

1. In my opinion, being a firefighter is **more stressful than** being a sales associate. In addition, sales associates have **better hours than** firefighters.
2. In general, doctors need **more training than** nutritionists. However, they usually **earn more than** nutritionists.
3. Game testers don't need **as much experience as** software developers. As a result, they **earn less than** software developers.
4. A career in banking is often **more demanding than** a career in sales, but it is also **better paid**.

### B *Pair work*

- Ask a S to read the first sentence in Part A. Ask Ss to make another comparison between the two jobs. They do not need to use the words in parentheses (e.g., *Being a firefighter is more dangerous than being a sales clerk.*).
- Ss work in pairs. They think of one more comparison for each pair of jobs. They take turns making up sentences. They can change the comparative word, the sentence structure, or both. Go around the class and give help as needed.
- Go over answers with the class. Elicit Ss' responses around the class.

## 7 CONVERSATION  It doesn't pay as much.

▶ **A** Listen and practice.

**Tyler:** Guess what? . . . I've found a summer job!

**Emma:** That's great! Anything interesting?

**Tyler:** Yes, working at a beach resort.

**Emma:** Wow, that sounds fantastic!

**Tyler:** So, have *you* found anything?

**Emma:** Nothing yet, but I have a couple of leads. One is working as an intern for a news website – mostly answering emails and posts from readers. Or I can get a job as a camp counselor again.

**Tyler:** Being an intern sounds more challenging than working at a summer camp. You could earn college credits, and it's probably not as much work.

**Emma:** Yeah, but the internship doesn't pay as much as the summer camp job. Do they have another opening at the beach resort? That's the kind of job I'd really enjoy.

▶ **B** Listen to the rest of the conversation. What is Tyler going to do at the resort?

## 8 GRAMMAR FOCUS

▶ | **Comparisons** | |
|---|---|
| **with adjectives** | **with verbs** |
| . . . sounds **more/less** challenging **than** . . . | . . . earns **more/less than** . . . |
| . . . is hard**er than** . . . | . . . earns **as much as** . . . |
| . . . is **not as** hard **as** . . . | . . . does**n't** pay **as much as** . . . |
| **with nouns** | **with past participles** |
| . . . has **better/worse** hours **than** . . . | . . . is **better** paid **than** . . . |
| . . . has **more** education **than** . . . | . . . is **as** well paid **as** . . . |
| . . . is**n't as much** work **as** . . . | . . . is**n't as** well paid **as** . . . |

GRAMMAR PLUS *see page 133*

**A** Complete the sentences using the words in parentheses. Compare with a partner. (More than one answer is possible.)

**1.** In my opinion, being a firefighter is _____ (stressful) being a sales associate. In addition, sales associates have _____ (hours) firefighters.

**2.** In general, doctors need _____ (training) nutritionists. However, they usually _____ (earn) nutritionists.

**3.** Game testers don't need _____ (experience) software developers. As a result, they _____ (earn) software developers.

**4.** A career in banking is often _____ (demanding) a career in sales, but it is also _____ (paid).

**B** **PAIR WORK** Compare the jobs in part A. Which would you choose? Why?

## 9 PRONUNCIATION  Stress with compound nouns

▶ **A** Listen and practice. Notice that the first word in these compound nouns has more stress. Then add two more compound nouns to the chart.

| ● | ● | ● | ● |
|---|---|---|---|
| firefighter | game tester | guidance counselor | |
| hairstylist | flight attendant | project manager | |

**B GROUP WORK** Which job in each column would be more challenging? Why? Tell the group. Pay attention to stress.

## 10 LISTENING  It's not what I thought.

▶ **A** Listen to Caden talk to Janelle about his job as a video game tester. Which parts of the job does he like and dislike? Check (✓) Like or Dislike.

|  | | Like | Dislike |
|---|---|---|---|
| **1.** | The pay | ☐ | ☐ |
| **2.** | The hours | ☐ | ☐ |
| **3.** | Testing games | ☐ | ☐ |
| **4.** | Playing video games at home | ☐ | ☐ |
| **5.** | Thinking of new ideas for games | ☐ | ☐ |

▶ **B** Listen again. What does Caden decide to do?

**C PAIR WORK** What other advice would you give Caden?

## 11 DISCUSSION  Which job would you take?

**A** What is a job you would like to have? What is a job you wouldn't like to have? Write each one on a separate slip of paper.

kindergarten teacher

tour guide

**B GROUP WORK** Mix all the slips from your group. One student picks two slips and the group helps him or her decide between the two jobs.

**A:** You should take the job as a kindergarten teacher because you enjoy working with kids.

**B:** But being a tour guide sounds more exciting. I could travel more and earn more money.

**C:** But you'd work longer hours and . . .

## 12 INTERCHANGE 2  Networking

Would you be a good party planner? Go to Interchange 2 on page 115.

# 9 PRONUNCIATION

**Learning Objective:** sound more natural when using stress in compound nouns

## ▶ A [CD 1, Track 15]

- Books closed. Write the following jobs on the board. Ask: "What do these nouns have in common?"

  *firefighter    game tester    guidance counselor*

- Elicit that these are all compound nouns (two-word nouns). In compound nouns, the main stress falls on the first word.
- Play the audio program. Signal stressed words by tapping a pencil or clapping.
- Books open. Play the audio program again. Ss listen and repeat, tapping or clapping on each stressed word.

- Ss work individually to add two more compound nouns to the chart. Ss can look back through Unit 2 for ideas. (Possible answers: software developer, computer technician)
- Write Ss' answers on the board. Ss practice pronouncing the words.

## B Group work

- Dictate this sentence, or write it on the board:

  *Being a _____ would be more challenging because . . .*

- Ask Ss to complete the sentence. After each S has completed the sentence, have Ss discuss the answers in groups.
- Elicit a few answers. Remind Ss to use the correct stress and to ask follow-up questions.

# 10 LISTENING

**Learning Objective:** listen for details in job descriptions discussed using comparisons

## ▶ A [CD 1, Track 16]

- Ask Ss to identify the job in the picture. (Answer: a game tester)
- Play the audio program. Ss listen and check which aspects of the job Caden likes and dislikes.

### Audio script

See page T-169.

### Answers

1. Like
2. Like
3. Dislike
4. Like
5. Like

## ▶ B [CD 1, Track 17]

- Explain the task. Read the focus question.
- Play the audio program again. This time Ss take notes.

### Answer

Caden is going to keep working for a while and then go back to school to become a software developer.

## C Pair work

- Ss work in pairs and write down some advice to give Caden. Elicit answers from the class. Are the pieces of advice similar?

# 11 DISCUSSION

**Learning Objective:** compare various jobs using comparisons with adjectives, adverbs, nouns, and past participles

## A

- Explain the task. Ss choose a job they would like and a job they would not like from the unit and write them on two separate slips of paper.

## B Group work

- Three students model the conversation.
- Ss discuss in small groups. Go around the class and listen in. Take notes on problems.
- Set a time limit of eight to ten minutes. When time is up, call on groups to say which jobs they chose.
- Write some problems you heard on the board. Elicit Ss' suggestions on how to correct them.

# 12 INTERCHANGE 2

See page T-115 for teaching notes.

# 13 READING

**Learning Objectives:** scan a professional social networking site; read for specific information and make inferences

## A

- Books closed. To introduce the topic, ask: "Who has a job now? Where do you work? Is that a traditional workplace?"

- *Option:* If none of the students have jobs, give them some examples and discuss if those workplaces are traditional or not.

- Books open. Ask Ss to look at the pictures, skim the webpage, and discuss who has the most and the least traditional workplace. (Possible answers: Catherine's office is the most traditional workplace. Lauren's office is the least traditional workplace.)

- Ask a S to read the title of the webpage. Explain that three people have responded to a question about their workplace.

- Elicit or explain any new vocabulary. Ss read the webpage individually.

> **Vocabulary**
> **stimulating:** interesting and making you think
> **membership:** the state of belonging to a group or an organization
> **perk:** an advantage, such as money or a car, that you are given because of your job
> **tedious:** boring
> **greenhouse:** a building made of glass, used for growing plants that need warmth and protection
> **luxurious:** very comfortable and expensive
> **tiny:** very small
> **make up for:** reduce the bad effect of something, or make something bad become something good

## B

- Explain the task. Ask different Ss to read the sentences aloud. Say that the comments express opinions of people on the webpage, in different words.

- Ss work individually to match the comments to the names. Allow Ss to consult with others near them if they want help.

- *Option:* Explain that we can infer or guess people's opinions based on other opinions that they state directly.

- Go over answers with the class. Ask: "Who would probably say 'Working in different locations keeps me from getting bored'?" (Answer: Mark). Alternatively, ask an early finisher to write the answers on the board.

> **Answers**
> 1. Mark
> 2. Lauren
> 3. Catherine
> 4. Lauren
> 5. Mark
> 6. Catherine

> ! For a new way to practice scanning for specific information, try **Reading Race** – download it from the website.

## C

- Explain the task. Point out that Ss should find the words in the webpage and guess the meaning from context.

- Ss work individually to complete the sentences.

- Go over answers with the class.

> **Answers**
> 1. perk        3. cubicle        5. tedious
> 2. stimulating    4. luxurious

## D *Pair work*

- Read the discussion question.

- Ss discuss the question in pairs. Ask one S to write down notes.

- Ask pairs to share their opinions on the workplaces and some features. Write them on the board. Also ask the pairs to share other interesting ideas from their discussions.

## End of Cycle 2

See the Supplementary Resources chart at the beginning of this unit for additional teaching materials and student activities related to this Cycle, and for assessment tools.

**A** Skim the web posts. Which person works in the most traditional workplace? the least traditional?

## ── THE PERFECT WORKPLACE? ──

**What is your workplace like?** Tell us and see how other places compare!

My workplace is cooler than any office I've ever seen. Working here is really stimulating. I share a table with my co-workers, and the workplace is flooded with light. Getting free meals is great, and there are relaxing activities like billiards and board games. Plus we get a membership to a local gym! It isn't all play, of course – we work very hard – but the perks make it better than any other job I can imagine.
**Lauren L.,** *Palo Alto, California*

When I got my job as a project manager for a finance company in London, I imagined a modern building with views of the city and open workspaces. When I arrived for my first day, I was pretty surprised. I found a typical cubicle farm, with desks as far as the eye could see. It works for me, though. I can concentrate in my own space and then talk with colleagues in the meeting rooms. We do have a great gym on the ground floor, so that's a bonus!
**Catherine D.,** *London, UK*

I work in a research laboratory at a botanical garden. Working in a lab isn't as tedious as it sounds. That's because a lot of my work takes place in the greenhouses or outdoors. I love spending time among plants, and I enjoy working with other scientists who share my interests. True, the workplace isn't very luxurious. We have a tiny break room that some people complain about, and there isn't a place to work out or anything, but being outdoors so much makes up for the disadvantages.
**Mark T.,** *Bronx, New York*

**B** Read the web posts. Who would have written these sentences about their workplace? Write the names.

1. Working in different environments keeps me from getting bored. _____
2. It's a perfect environment for sharing new ideas with co-workers. _____
3. There's nothing unique about it, but it's fine for the kind of work we do. _____
4. Visitors might get the idea that we don't take our work seriously. _____
5. Some employees are dissatisfied with the workplace, but I don't mind it. _____
6. I love being able to exercise without leaving the building. _____

**C** Find the words below in the web posts. Then complete the sentences with the words.

| stimulating | perk | cubicle | tedious | luxurious |
|---|---|---|---|---|

1. One _____ of my job is that we get free tickets to cultural and sporting events.
2. Working with creative people is very _____ because we can share lots of great ideas!
3. The disadvantage of working in a _____ is that you can hear everything that's going on around you.
4. The marketing director's office is very _____, with beautiful furniture and valuable paintings.
5. Working with numbers all day seems _____ to some people, but I enjoy it.

**D** **PAIR WORK** Which of the workplaces would you like the best? What features of a workplace matter most to you?

## SELF-ASSESSMENT

How well can you do these things? Check (✔) the boxes.

| I can . . . | Very well | OK | A little |
|---|:---:|:---:|:---:|
| Describe personalities (Ex. 1) | ☐ | ☐ | ☐ |
| Ask about and express preferences (Ex. 1) | ☐ | ☐ | ☐ |
| Understand and express complaints (Ex. 2) | ☐ | ☐ | ☐ |
| Give opinions about jobs (Ex. 3) | ☐ | ☐ | ☐ |
| Describe and compare different jobs (Ex. 4) | ☐ | ☐ | ☐ |

## 1 SPEAKING Doing things together

**A** What two qualities would you like someone to have for these situations?

*A person to . . .*

**1.** be your business partner _____ _____

**2.** share an apartment with _____ _____

**3.** go on vacation with _____ _____

**4.** work on a class project with _____ _____

**B** CLASS ACTIVITY Find someone you could do each thing with.

**A:** What kind of person would you like to be your business partner?

**B:** I'd choose someone who has initiative and is hardworking.

**A:** Me, too! And I'd like someone who I can . . .

## 2 LISTENING I know what you mean!

**A** Listen to Suki and Andy discuss these topics. Complete the chart.

| | Andy's biggest complaint | Suki's biggest complaint |
|---|---|---|
| **1.** websites | | |
| **2.** children | | |
| **3.** taxi drivers | | |
| **4.** restaurant servers | | |

**B** PAIR WORK What is your biggest complaint about any of the topics in part A?

"I hate it when you can't find the products you want on a company's website."

# Progress check

## SELF-ASSESSMENT

**Learning Objectives:** reflect on one's learning; identify areas that need improvement

- Ask: "What did you learn in Units 1 and 2?" Elicit Ss' answers.
- Ss complete the Self-assessment. Encourage them to be honest, and point out that they will not get a bad grade if they check (✓) "a little."

- Ss move on to the Progress check exercises. You can have Ss complete them in class or for homework, using one of these techniques:
  1. Ask Ss to complete all the exercises.
  2. Ask Ss: "What do you need to practice?" Then assign exercises based on their answers.
  3. Ask Ss to choose and complete exercises based on their Self-assessment.

## 1 SPEAKING

**Learning Objective:** demonstrate one's ability to use relative clauses

**A**

- Explain the task. Model with an example of your own. Say: "Let's see. I'd like to have a business partner who is organized, so I'll write *organized* here. And I'd also like someone who is calm, so I'll write *calm.*"

- Ss complete the task individually. Remind them to write two qualities for each situation. Go around the class and give help as needed.

**B** *Class activity*

- Explain the task. Ask two Ss to model the conversation.
- Ss go around the class to agree on the qualities they want and to find someone they could do each thing with.

## 2 LISTENING

**Learning Objectives:** demonstrate one's ability to listen and respond to complaints; demonstrate one's ability to express likes and dislikes

▶ **A** *[CD 1, Track 18]*

- Explain the task. Ask a S to read the chart.
- Ask Ss to predict complaints they might hear.
- Tell Ss to listen for the complaints. Play the audio program once or twice. Ss complete the chart. Remind Ss to use their own words.
- Play the audio program again for Ss to check their answers.
- Go over answers with the class.

### Audio script

See page T-169.

### Answers

|  | Andy's biggest complaint | Suki's biggest complaint |
|---|---|---|
| **1. websites** | When a website makes you sign up to read an article | When the website sends you emails every day |
| **2. children** | When the kid behind you keeps kicking your seat | When people let their children cry in restaurants |
| **3. taxi drivers** | When taxi drivers are dishonest and take longer routes to charge more money | When taxi drivers say they don't know the area and you don't know if they're lying |
| **4. restaurant servers** | When servers don't write down your order and they get it wrong | When servers get annoyed if you order something cheap off the menu and they're impolite |

**B** *Pair work*

- Explain the task. Read the question. Ask a S to read the example.
- *Option:* Elicit verbs for expressing likes and dislikes (e.g., *can't stand, hate, love*). Write them on the board.
- *Option:* Play the audio (CD 1, Track 18) again. Have Ss listen for verbs to express likes and dislikes and write them down. Elicit examples and write them on the board.
- Ss discuss complaints in pairs. Remind them to use clauses with *it* and *when.*
- Ask Ss to share complaints with the class. Write each new complaint on the board. See which complaint was mentioned most often.

## 3 SURVEY

**Learning Objective:** demonstrate one's ability to express likes and dislikes using gerund phrases

### A Group work

- Explain the task. Ask four Ss to model the conversation.
- Go over the list of useful expressions with the class.
- Ss work in groups of four to ask and answer questions about jobs. Each S completes the chart.

### B Group work

- Explain the task. Read the questions.
- Ss work in the same group or a different one. Point out that Ss can talk about other aspects of the jobs.
- Ask one S from each group to share the most unusual, the best, and the worst jobs from the group.
- **Option:** Each S writes a short paragraph about the job he or she chose and the job one of the group members chose.

## 4 ROLE PLAY

**Learning Objective:** demonstrate one's ability to make comparisons to talk about jobs

- Explain the task.
- Divide the class into pairs, and assign A/B roles. Student As are the job helpers. Student Bs are the job seekers. Ask two Ss to model the conversation. Read the questions.
- Give Ss time to plan what they are going to say.

- Ss role-play in pairs. Encourage Ss to ask as many questions as possible, rather than choosing a job quickly.
- Ss change roles and repeat the role play.
- **Option:** Divide the class in half. Half of the Ss are job helpers, and the other half are job hunters. The job helpers sit at the front of the class and tell the class which two jobs each has. The job hunters then come up and talk to any of the job helpers. Set a time limit of five to ten minutes. When time is up, each S chooses a job.

## WHAT'S NEXT?

**Learning Objective:** become more involved in one's learning

- Focus Ss' attention on the Self-assessment again. Ask: "How well can you do these things now?"
- Ask Ss to underline one thing they need to review. Ask: "What did you underline? How can you review it?"
- If needed, plan additional activities or reviews based on Ss' answers.

## 3 SURVEY Job evaluation

**A** GROUP WORK What job would you like to have? Ask and answer questions in groups to complete the chart.

| | Name | Job | Good points | Bad points |
|---|---|---|---|---|
| 1. | | | | |
| 2. | | | | |
| 3. | | | | |
| 4. | | | | |

**A:** What job would you like to have?
**B:** I'd like to be a flight attendant.
**C:** What would be the good points?
**B:** Well, traveling around the world would be exciting.
**D:** Would there be any bad points?
**B:** Oh, sure. I'd dislike packing and unpacking all the time. . . .

**useful expressions**

I would(n't) be good at . . .
I would enjoy/dislike . . .
I would(n't) be interested in . . .
I would(n't) be excited about . . .

**B** GROUP WORK Who thought of the most unusual job? the best job? the worst job?

## 4 ROLE PLAY Choosing a job

*Student A:* Your partner, Student B, is looking for a job. Based on his or her opinions about jobs in Exercise 3, suggest two other jobs that Student B might enjoy.

*Student B:* You are looking for a job. Student A suggests two jobs for you. Discuss the questions below. Then choose one of the jobs.

Which one is more interesting? harder?
Which one has better hours? better pay?
Which job would you rather have?

**A:** I thought of two other jobs for you. You could be a hairstylist or a truck driver.
**B:** Hmm. Which job has better hours?
**A:** Well, a hairstylist has better hours, but it's not as . . .

Change roles and try the role play again.

## WHAT'S NEXT?

Look at your Self-assessment again. Do you need to review anything?

# Unit 3 Supplementary Resources Overview

| | After the following SB exercises | You can use these materials in class | Your students can use these materials outside the classroom |
|---|---|---|---|
| **CYCLE 1** | **1 Snapshot** | | |
| | **2 Conversation** | | **SS** Unit 3 Speaking 1–2 |
| | **3 Grammar Focus** | | **SB** Unit 3 Grammar plus, Focus 1<br>**SS** Unit 3 Grammar 1<br>**GAME** Sentence Runner (Requests with modals, *if* clauses, and gerunds) |
| | **4 Pronunciation** | | |
| | **5 Listening** | | |
| | **6 Writing** | **TSS** Unit 3 Writing Worksheet | |
| | **7 Interchange 3** | | **WB** Unit 3 exercises 1–4 |
| **CYCLE 2** | **8 Word Power** | **TSS** Unit 3 Vocabulary Worksheet | **SS** Unit 3 Vocabulary 1–2<br>**GAME** Say the Word (Collocations) |
| | **9 Perspectives** | | |
| | **10 Grammar Focus** | **TSS** Unit 3 Grammar Worksheet<br>**TSS** Unit 3 Listening Worksheet<br>**TSS** Unit 3 Extra Worksheet | **SB** Unit 3 Grammar plus, Focus 2<br>**SS** Unit 3 Grammar 2<br>**GAME** Sentence Stacker (Indirect requests)<br>**GAME** Word Keys (Indirect requests) |
| | **11 Speaking** | | |
| | **12 Reading** | **TSS** Unit 3 Project Worksheet<br>**VID** Unit 3<br>**VRB** Unit 3 | **SS** Unit 3 Reading 1–2<br>**SS** Unit 3 Listening 1–3<br>**SS** Unit 3 Video 1–3<br>**WB** Unit 3 exercises 5–9 |

**Key**

**GAME:** Online Game    **SB:** Student's Book    **SS:** Online Self-study    **TSS:** Teacher Support Site
**VID:** Video DVD    **VRB:** Video Resource Book    **WB:** Online Workbook/Workbook

# My Plan for Unit 3

Use the space below to customize a plan that fits your needs.

| With the following SB exercises | I am using these materials in class | My students are using these materials outside the classroom |
| --- | --- | --- |
|  |  |  |
|  |  |  |
|  |  |  |
|  |  |  |
|  |  |  |
|  |  |  |
|  |  |  |
|  |  |  |
|  |  |  |
|  |  |  |
|  |  |  |
|  |  |  |
|  |  |  |

| With or instead of the following SB section | I am using these materials for assessment |
| --- | --- |
|  |  |
|  |  |
|  |  |

# 3 Lend a hand.

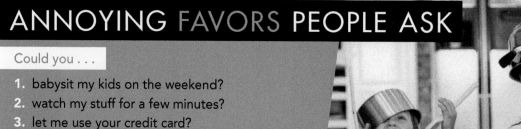

▶ Discuss favors, borrowing, and lending
▶ Leave messages with requests

## 1 SNAPSHOT

### ANNOYING FAVORS PEOPLE ASK

Could you . . .

1. babysit my kids on the weekend?
2. watch my stuff for a few minutes?
3. let me use your credit card?
4. drive me to the airport?
5. let me use your passcode to download a movie?
6. help me move to my new apartment?
7. come with me to my niece's school concert?
8. let me stay at your place for a couple of weeks?
9. donate to my favorite charity?
10. co-sign a bank loan for me?

*Imagine that a close friend asked you each of these favors. Which would you agree to do?*
*What are three other favors that you dislike being asked?*

## 2 CONVERSATION Thanks a million.

▶ **A** Listen and practice.

**Carlos:** Hey, Keiko. What's up?

**Keiko:** Hi, Carlos. I was wondering if you could help me. I'm moving to my new apartment this weekend, and my car is pretty small. Can I borrow your truck, please?

**Carlos:** Um, I need it on Saturday, but you can borrow it on Sunday.

**Keiko:** Thanks so much.

**Carlos:** Sure. So, have you packed already?

**Keiko:** Uh-huh. I mean, I'll have everything packed by Sunday. You know, I think some of my boxes are going to be kind of heavy. Would you mind helping me put them in your truck on Sunday?

**Carlos:** I guess not. I suppose you want my help taking them out of the truck, too?

**Keiko:** Oh, that'd be great. Thanks a million, Carlos!

▶ **B** Listen to two more calls Keiko makes. What else does she need help with? Do her friends agree to help?

# 3 Lend a hand.

**Cycle 1, Exercises 1–7**

In this unit, students discuss favors, borrowing and lending, and leaving messages and requests. By the end of Cycle 1, students will be able to discuss favors, borrowing, and lending using modals, *if* clauses, and gerunds. By the end of Cycle 2, students will be able to leave messages using indirect requests.

## 1 SNAPSHOT

**Learning Objective:** discuss favors

- **Option:** Books closed. Introduce a well-known proverb: "A friend in need is a friend indeed." Elicit the meaning. (Answer: A friend who helps you when you need it is a true friend.) Then ask: "Should you always say 'yes' to a friend? What would you do if your friend asked you a favor you didn't feel good about?"

- Explain that people were interviewed about favors they dislike being asked. Elicit that a *favor* is something you do to help someone else.

- With the class, brainstorm the favors the people might have mentioned (e.g., *Can you lend me some money?*). Write Ss' ideas on the board. Ask Ss to guess what the top three were.

- Books open. Tell Ss to read the Snapshot. Did Ss guess any of the favors people dislike being asked?

- Read the questions. Ss discuss the questions in pairs. Go around the class and give help as needed.

- Then each pair joins another pair to compare their answers.

- **Option:** Clarify the difference between *lend* and *borrow*. *To lend* is to give; *to borrow* is to take. If helpful, ask an artistic S to draw a picture on the board that shows the difference between the two verbs.

- **Option:** Clarify the expression *co-sign a bank loan*. Explain that it means to guarantee to a bank that you will pay a debt if the person who gets the loan does not.

## 2 CONVERSATION

**Learning Objective:** use modals, *if* clauses, and gerunds in a conversation about a favor

### ▶ A [CD 1, Track 19]

- Ask Ss to cover the text and look at the picture. Ask: "What are they doing? What are they talking about? What does Keiko want from Carlos? Will Carlos help? How do you know?" Elicit ideas.

- Tell Ss to listen to find out if their predictions are correct. Play the audio program.

- Write this incorrect summary on the board:

  *This weekend Keiko is going to move to her new house. Carlos is only free on Saturday. She already has everything packed.*

- Ask Ss to listen and correct three mistakes. Play the audio program again. Go over Ss' answers. (Answers: This weekend Keiko is going to move to her new <u>apartment</u>. Carlos is only free on <u>Sunday</u>. She will have everything packed by Sunday.)

- Ss read the conversation silently.

- Elicit or explain any new vocabulary.

#### Vocabulary
**What's up?:** How are you? *or* Is there a problem?
**I was wondering if . . . :** a polite way to ask someone for something
**pack:** put your things into bags or boxes
**Thanks a million.:** Thank you very much.

- Play the audio program again. Ss listen and read. Ask Ss to focus on how Carlos agrees to Keiko's request (e.g., *sure, I guess not.*).

- Ss practice the conversation in pairs.

- For a new way to practice this conversation, try **Moving Dialog** – download it from the website.

### ▶ B [CD 1, Track 20]

- Read the focus questions aloud.

- Play the second part of the audio program. Pause after each conversation. Ss take notes.

- Ss compare answers in pairs. Elicit Ss' responses around the class.

#### Audio script
See page T-169.

#### Answers
Keiko wants Hunter to take care of her goldfish.
Hunter agrees.
Keiko wants Claire to help her pack her things.
Claire doesn't agree.

# 3 GRAMMAR FOCUS

**Learning Objective:** use modals, *if* clauses, and gerunds to ask for favors

▶ *[CD 1, Track 21]*

### Requests with modals, if clauses, and gerunds

- Books closed. Ask a few favors around the class, using modals *can* and *could*. Write them on the board:

  *Can I borrow your pen, please?*
  *Could you lend me your cell phone?*

- Books open. Focus Ss' attention on the Conversation on page 16. Ask Ss to find two examples of requests with *could* or *would*. Ask a S to write them on the board:

  *I was wondering if you could . . . ?*
  *Would you mind helping me . . . ?*

- Explain that there are many ways to ask favors. They also vary in degrees of formality.

- Point out that we use *can* and *could* for informal requests. Elicit that the structures with *would* are more formal. We use them with people we don't know well or with friends if the request is very demanding.

- Play the audio program. Point out the continuum.

- Elicit or explain the structures used in requests.

  **1. Requests with *if* clauses and the present tense**
  *Is it OK if . . . ?* and *Do you mind if . . . ?* are followed by the present tense:
  *Is it OK if I borrow your phone?*
  *Do you mind if I use your credit card?*
  Note: *Is it OK if . . .* is answered with "yes" if the request is granted. "No" means the person denies the request. *Do you mind if . . .* is answered with "no" if the request is granted. "Yes" means the person denies the request.

  **2. Requests with *if* clauses and the past tense**
  *Would it be all right if . . . ?* and *Would you mind if . . . ?* are followed by the past tense:
  *Would it be all right if I used your credit card?*
  *Would you mind if I borrowed your truck?*
  Note: *Would you mind* is answered with "no" if the request is granted. "Yes" means the person denies the request.

  **3. Requests with gerunds (*-ing*)**
  *Would you mind* (without *if*) is followed by a gerund:
  *Would you mind letting me use your laptop?*
  Note: *Would you mind* + gerund is answered with "no" if the request is granted. "Yes" means the person denies the request.

  **4. Requests with *if* clauses and modals**
  *Wonder* + *if* is followed by a modal:
  *I wonder if I could borrow your car.*
  *I was wondering if you could help me move.*
  Note: *wonder* + *if* is a statement, not a question.
  Possible responses if the request is granted: "Sure, that's fine."/"Of course."/"No problem."
  Possible response if the request is denied: "Sorry" + explanation.

- For more practice with requests, play **Run For It!** - download it from the website. Assign a structure to each wall: Present tense, past tense, modals, and gerunds.

- Tell Ss to make their own requests and ask favors around the class.

## A

- Read the first conversation. Ss choose the correct answer as a class. Then ask a S to read the first conversation with you.

- Ss complete the task individually. Elicit Ss' responses to check answers. Then Ss practice the conversations in pairs.

### Answers

1. A: **Is it OK if** I use your cell phone?
2. A: Would you mind if I **stayed** at your place for the weekend?
3. A: I was wondering **if I could** borrow your car tomorrow.
4. A: Could you **lend** me $20?
5. A: Would you mind **helping** me pack my stuff this weekend?
6. A: **Can** you feed my cats while I'm on vacation, please?

## B

- Explain the task. Model the first example.
- Elicit more examples.
- Ss complete the task individually.

### Possible answers

1. Would you mind coming to my cousin's wedding with me?
2. Is it OK if I borrow your notes to study for the test?
3. Could you lend me your camera to take with me on my vacation?
4. I was wondering if you could drive me to the airport.
5. Could you help me paint my apartment?
6. Do you mind if I borrow your cell phone to call a friend in London?

- Ask different Ss to read their formal requests aloud. Model accepting some and declining others.
  S1: Would you mind if I borrowed some money for a soda?

  T: No. Not at all. Here you go./I'm really sorry. All I have is a dollar.

- Tell Ss to look at part A for more examples of ways to accept and decline.

- Ss work in pairs. They take turns making requests and responding. Go around the class and check for logical and grammatical responses.

▶ **Requests with modals, *if* clauses, and gerunds**

| Less formal | **Can I** borrow your truck, please? |
| | **Could** you lend me your truck, please? |
| | **Is it OK if** I use your credit card? |
| | **Do you mind if** I use your credit card? |
| | **Would it be all right if** I us**ed** your credit card? |
| | **Would you mind if** I borrow**ed** your truck? |
| | **Would you mind** help**ing** me on Sunday? |
| More formal | **I was wondering if** you **could** help me move. |

GRAMMAR PLUS *see page 134*

**A** Circle the correct answers. Then practice with a partner.

1. **A: Is it OK if / Would / Do you mind** I use your cell phone? Mine just died.
   **B:** No problem, but can you keep it short? I'm expecting an important phone call.

2. **A:** Would you mind if I **stay / staying / stayed** at your place for the weekend?
   **B:** Not at all. It'll be fun to have you stay with us.

3. **A:** I was wondering **I could / if I could / if I would** borrow your car tomorrow.
   **B:** Sure, that's fine. Just be careful. I've only had it for a couple of months.

4. **A:** Could you **lend / lending / lent** me $20?
   **B:** I'm sorry. I don't have any money to spare right now.

5. **A:** Would you mind **help / helped / helping** me pack my stuff this weekend?
   **B:** No, I don't mind. I'm not doing anything then.

6. **A: Would you mind / Can / Is it OK if** you feed my cats while I'm on vacation, please?
   **B:** Sorry, I don't get along with cats.

**B** Rewrite these sentences to make them more formal requests. Then practice making your requests with a partner. Accept or decline each request.

1. Come to my cousin's wedding with me.
2. Can I borrow your notes to study for the test?
3. Can you lend me your camera to take with me on my vacation?
4. Drive me to the airport.
5. Help me paint my apartment.
6. I'd like to borrow your cell phone to call a friend in London.

> 1. *Would you mind coming to my cousin's wedding with me?*

## 4 PRONUNCIATION Unreleased consonants

▶ **A** Listen and practice. Notice that when /t/, /d/, /k/, /g/, /p/, and /b/ are followed by other consonant sounds, they are unreleased.

Coul**d** Crai**g** ta**ke** care of my pe**t** skunk?
Can you as**k** Bo**b** to hel**p** me?

▶ **B** Circle the unreleased consonants in the conversations. Listen and check. Then practice the conversations with a partner.

1. **A:** I was wondering if I could borrow that book.
   **B:** Yes, but can you take it back to Doug tomorrow?
2. **A:** Would you mind giving Albert some help moving that big bed?
   **B:** Sorry, but my doctor said my back needs rest.

## 5 LISTENING I was wondering . . .

▶ **A** Listen to three telephone conversations. Write down what each caller requests. Does the other person agree to the request? Check (✓) Yes or No.

|   | Request | Yes | No |
|---|---------|-----|-----|
| **1.** Jesse | | ☐ | ☐ |
| **2.** Liz | | ☐ | ☐ |
| **3.** Min-jun | | ☐ | ☐ |

**B PAIR WORK** Use the chart to act out each conversation in your own words.

## 6 WRITING A message with requests

**A** Write a message to a classmate asking for several favors. Explain why you need help.

**B PAIR WORK** Exchange messages. Write a reply accepting or declining the requests.

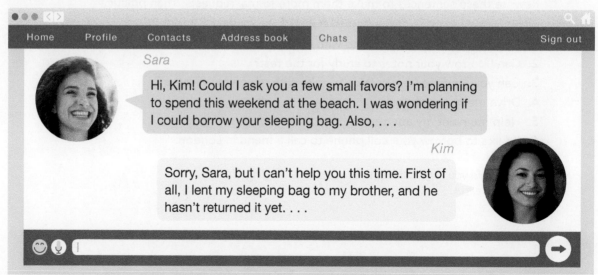

**Sara**
Hi, Kim! Could I ask you a few small favors? I'm planning to spend this weekend at the beach. I was wondering if I could borrow your sleeping bag. Also, . . .

**Kim**
Sorry, Sara, but I can't help you this time. First of all, I lent my sleeping bag to my brother, and he hasn't returned it yet. . . .

# 4 PRONUNCIATION

**Learning Objective:** sound more natural when using unreleased consonants

## ▶ A [CD 1, Track 22]

- Read the explanation. Tell Ss to compare /d/ in a fully released form (e.g., *did*) with /d/ in the phrase "could Craig" in an unreleased form.
- Play the first part of the audio program once or twice. Pause to allow Ss to repeat. Encourage Ss to say the unreleased consonants softly, blending them with the next word.
- Explain that it is easier to blend these consonants than it is to pronounce them separately.

## ▶ B [CD 1, Track 23]

- Explain the task. Ss work individually.
- Play the second part of the audio program. Ss listen and check their answers.

### Answers

1. A: I was wondering if I coul**d** borrow tha**t** book.
   B: Yes, bu**t** can you take i**t** bac**k** to Dou**g** tomorrow?
2. A: Would you min**d** giving Alber**t** some hel**p** moving tha**t** bi**g** bed?
   B: Sorry, bu**t** my doctor sai**d** my ba**ck** needs rest.

- Then Ss practice the conversations in pairs.

# 5 LISTENING

**Learning Objective:** listen for specific information in requests for favors using modals, *if* clauses, and gerunds

❗ To practice recognizing different types of requests, try **Stand Up, Sit Down** – download it from the website.

## ▶ A [CD 1, Track 24]

- Explain the task. Ss listen first for what each caller requests.
- Play the audio program. Pause briefly after each conversation for Ss to write down the requests.

### Audio script

See page T-170.

- Play the audio program again. Ss listen to find out whether the other person agrees to the request.
- Ss work in pairs to compare information. Elicit responses around the class to check answers.

### Answers

1. Jesse: He wants to borrow an electric mixer; no
2. Liz: She wants to borrow a book; yes
3. Min-jun: He wants Silvia to watch his cat while he's away; yes

## B *Pair work*

- Model the task by role-playing the phone conversations with Ss. Write phrases on the board to help Ss begin and end the conversations:

  Hello/Hi, . . . This is . . .
  What's up?
  Well, actually, would you mind . . . ?
  No problem.
  Thanks a million! See you in class tomorrow.
  Yeah, see you then. Bye!

- Remind Ss to use their own words. Tell Ss to role-play accepting and declining each request.
- Ss work in pairs. Go around the class and note any problem areas. Go over the problems with the class after the role play.
- *Option:* Tell Ss to sit back-to-back to do the role play to help mimic a phone call.

# 6 WRITING

**Learning Objective:** write an informal email asking for a favor using modals, *if* clauses, and gerunds

## A

- Explain the task. Ask a S to read the sample message.
- Ss work individually. They write a message to a classmate asking several favors. Remind Ss to include reasons for their requests. Set a time limit of about five minutes. Go around the class and give help as needed.

## B *Pair work*

- Explain the task. Ss exchange messages and write replies accepting or declining requests.
- Tell Ss to give reasons for declining requests.
- Set a time limit of five minutes. When time is up, Ss exchange again and read the replies.

See page T-116 for teaching notes.

See the Supplementary Resources chart at the beginning of this unit for additional teaching materials and student activities related to this Cycle.

## End of Cycle 1

## Cycle 2, Exercises 8–12

# 8 WORD POWER

**Learning Objective:** talk about making requests and responding using collocations with common words for making requests

**A**

- Focus Ss' attention on the example and explain why *make* is crossed out.
- Ss complete the task individually or in pairs. Challenge Ss to do it without checking a dictionary.
- Ss compare answers in pairs. Then elicit responses.

| Answers | | | |
|---------|---------|---------|---------|
| 1. make | 3. offer | 5. do | 7. do |
| 2. do | 4. do | 6. offer | |

**B** *Pair work*

- Read the questions. Ask Ss to underline the collocations. Elicit the answers (return a favor, turn down an invitation, declined a request).
- Elicit questions Ss can use to add to the list. Write them on the board:

  *When was the last time you . . . ?*
  *How often do you . . . ?*
  *How would you feel if . . . ?*
  *What would you say if . . . ?*

- Ss work in pairs. Ss choose two collocations from part A to write two more questions. Then they take turns asking and answering all five questions.

- Practice the collocations with **Vocabulary Tennis** – download it from the website (e.g., Team A – return; Team B – a compliment; Team B – a gift; Team A – refuse).

# 9 PERSPECTIVES

**Learning Objective:** complete messages using indirect requests in context

▶ **A** *[CD 1, Track 25]*

- Books closed. Set the scene. Six people left messages for Mary Martin at the school where she teaches.
- Write the topic of each message in random order on the board:

  tests     students' reports    phone
  homework   teachers' meeting   meet in the cafeteria

- Play the audio program. Pause after the first message. Ss listen and decide what the message was about. (Answer: her phone)
- Play the rest of the audio program. Pause after each message. Ss listen. Elicit what the message was about.
- Books open. Ss read the messages and work individually to complete them with *ask* or *tell*.
- Play the audio program again. Have Ss listen and check their answers.

| Answers | | | | | |
|---------|--------|--------|---------|--------|--------|
| 1. tell | 2. ask | 3. ask | 4. tell | 5. ask | 6. ask |

- Elicit or explain any new vocabulary.

**B**

- Explain the task. Ask a S to read the list of people. Explain that more than one answer is possible.
- Ss work individually to decide *who* left each message.
- Ss go over their answers in pairs. Answer any questions Ss may have.

| Possible answers |
|------------------|
| 1. another teacher |
| 2. the school coordinator |
| 3. a student |
| 4. the school coordinator |
| 5. a teacher |
| 6. a student |

## 7 INTERCHANGE 3 Beg and borrow

Find out how generous you are. Go to Interchange 3 on page 116.

## 8 WORD POWER Verb-noun collocations

A Which verb is not usually paired with each noun?
Put a line through the verb. Then compare with a partner.

1. return / do / ask for / ~~make~~        a favor
2. owe / offer / do / accept              an apology
3. receive / accept / turn down / offer   an invitation
4. do / receive / give / accept           a gift
5. do / return / make / receive           a phone call
6. accept / make / decline / offer        a request
7. receive / return / do / give           a compliment

B **PAIR WORK** Add two questions to the list using the
collocations in part A. Then take turns asking and
answering the questions.

1. What are nice ways to return a favor? How do you usually return favors?
2. Have you ever invented an excuse to turn down an invitation? What excuse did you give?
3. When was the last time you declined a request? What was the request?
4. _____
5. _____

## 9 PERSPECTIVES Can you tell her . . . ?

A Listen to the requests people make at the
school where Mary Martin teaches. Complete
each request with *ask* or *tell*.

1. If you see Mary, can you _____ her that she
   left her phone in my car?
2. If you see Mary, could you _____ her
   whether or not she is coming to the
   teachers' meeting?
3. If you see Ms. Martin, can you _____ her if
   she's graded our tests yet?
4. If you see Mary, please _____ her not to
   forget the students' reports.
5. If you see Mary, could you _____ her to find
   me in the cafeteria after her meeting?
6. If you see Ms. Martin, would you _____
   her what time I can talk to her about my
   homework?

B Who do you think made each request?
the school coordinator? another teacher?
a student?

# 10 GRAMMAR FOCUS

▶ **Indirect requests**

| Statements | Indirect requests introduced by *that* |
|---|---|
| Mary, you left your phone in my car. → | Could you tell Mary **(that) she left her phone in my car**? |
| **Imperatives** | **Indirect requests using infinitives** |
| Mary, don't forget the students' reports. → | Can you tell Mary **not to forget the students' reports**? |
| **Yes/No questions** | **Indirect requests introduced by *if* or *whether*** |
| Ms. Martin, have you graded our tests? → | Can you ask her **if she's graded our tests yet**? |
| Mary, are you coming to the meeting? → | Could you ask her **whether or not she is coming to the meeting**? |
| **Wh-questions** | **Indirect requests introduced by a question word** |
| Mary, where are you having lunch? → | Can you ask Mary **where she's having lunch**? |
| Ms. Martin, what time can I talk to you about my homework? → | Would you ask her **what time I can talk to her about my homework**? |

GRAMMAR PLUS *see page 134*

Read the things people want to say to Mary. Rewrite the sentences as indirect requests. Then compare with a partner.

1. Mary, did you get my message about your phone?
2. Mary, will you give me a ride to school tomorrow?
3. Ms. Martin, when is our assignment due?
4. Mary, why didn't you meet us at the cafeteria for lunch?
5. Ms. Martin, I won't be in class tomorrow night.
6. Mary, are you going to the school party on Saturday?
7. Mary, please return my call when you get your phone back.
8. Mary, have you received my wedding invitation?

> 1. Could you ask Mary if she got my message about her phone?

# 11 SPEAKING No problem.

**A** Write five requests for your partner to pass on to classmates.

> Would you ask Keith if he can turn off his phone in class?

**B CLASS ACTIVITY** Ask your partner to pass on your requests. Go around the class and make your partner's requests. Then tell your partner how people responded.

**A:** Would you ask Keith if he can turn off his phone in class?
**B:** No problem. . . . Keith, could you turn off your cell phone in class?
**C:** I'm sorry, but I can't! I'm expecting an important phone call.
**B:** Lee, Keith says he's expecting an important phone call.

# 10 GRAMMAR FOCUS

**Learning Objective:** use statements, imperatives, and *yes-no* questions to ask someone to make indirect requests

▶ **[CD 1, Track 26]**

- Books closed. To explain an indirect request, draw a picture on the board of Mary's coordinator passing a message to Mary via Mary's assistant:

Mary's coordinator    Mary's assistant    Mary

*Could you ask Mary whether or not she is coming to the teachers' meeting?*

- Tell Ss that we use indirect requests when we want someone to give a message to someone else.

- Books open. Present the direct requests on the left and the indirect requests on the right. Ask Ss to (a) work out the rule and (b) find examples in the Perspectives on page 19.

  **1. Statements**
  Can/Could you (*or* Please) tell + (Mary) + (that) + original statement?
  (Examples from the Perspectives: message 1)
  Note: *That* is optional. Indirect requests can also use *would*.

  **2. Imperatives**
  Can/Could you tell/ask + (Mary) + (not) + infinitive?
  (Examples from the Perspectives: messages 4 and 5)

  **3. *Yes/No* questions**
  Can/Could you ask + (Mary) + if/whether + SVO statement?
  (Example from the Perspectives: messages 2 and 3)

  **4. *Wh-* questions**
  Can/Could you ask (Mary) + *wh-* word + SVO statement?
  (Example from the Perspectives: message 6)

- Point out to students that the last example in the Grammar Focus box shows a change in the indirect object pronoun. The direct question uses *can I talk to you* because the speaker is talking directly to the person; but in the indirect form, *you* changes to *her* since the speaker is now talking about a third person.

- Play the audio program. Remind Ss that direct requests are on the left and indirect requests on the right.

- ***Option:*** Point out that most indirect requests have rising intonation. Play the audio program again. Ask Ss to focus on the rising intonation. Ss practice.

- ***Option:*** Write indirect sentences on the board in the wrong order (e.g., *not tell to could Mary call you me?*). Ss put them in the correct order.

- Explain the task. Use the first sentence as an example. Ask a S to read the example answer.

- Ss complete the task individually. Ss change the direct requests to indirect requests. Go around the class and give help as needed.

- Check some early finishers' answers. Tell the Ss to write their answers on the board.

## Answers

1. Can/Could/Would you ask Mary if/whether she got my message about her phone?
2. Can/Could/Would you ask Mary if/whether she'll give me a ride to school tomorrow?
3. Can/Could/Would you ask Ms. Martin when our assignment is due?
4. Can/Could/Would you ask Mary why she didn't meet us at the cafeteria for lunch?
5. Can/Could/Would you tell Ms. Martin (that) I won't be in class tomorrow night?
6. Can/Could/Would you ask Mary if she's going to the school party on Saturday?
7. Can/Could/Would you ask/tell Mary to please return my call when she gets her phone back?
8. Can/Could/Would you ask Mary if/whether she (has) received my wedding invitation?

# 11 SPEAKING

**Learning Objective:** pass on and respond to indirect requests

**A**

- Explain the task. Read the example request.
- Ss complete the task individually. They write five requests. Go around the class and give help as needed.

**B** *Class activity*

- Explain the task. Ask three Ss to model the conversation.
- First, Ss work in pairs. They exchange requests from part A.

- Then Ss go around the class and make their partner's requests. They note how each person responds. Set a time limit of about ten minutes. Go around the class and listen in.

- Ss return to their partners and tell how each person responded.

- ***Option:*** Add one more person to the chain. Ss 2 and 3 are both messengers.

- Ask Ss to share some interesting requests they received and how they responded.

**Learning Objective:** scan, read for main ideas and details, and identify referents in an article

- Books closed. Ask the class to brainstorm things that are difficult to say to friends. Write some common suggestions on the board. Ask Ss if they have ever had this problem (where they wanted to say something to a friend but didn't want to hurt their feelings).

- Books open. Read the title. Tell Ss the article is about bringing up difficult subjects.

## A

- Go over the task. Ask: "What are the three problems these people are having?" Tell Ss to raise their hands when they find the answers. Elicit answers. (Answer: disliking someone's friends, someone wanting to copy homework, someone constantly asking for favors)

## B

- Ss read the article individually. Remind Ss to mark words they can't guess from context and continue reading.

- Elicit or explain any new vocabulary.

### Vocabulary

**bring up:** raise for discussion or consideration
**matter:** a subject or situation that you need to think about, discuss, or deal with
**tip:** a useful piece of information
**handle:** deal with
**get along:** like each other and be friendly to each other

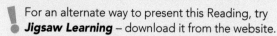 For an alternate way to present this Reading, try **Jigsaw Learning** – download it from the website.

- Ss complete the task individually. Ask Ss to mark the lines in the text where they find the answers to the questions.

- Ss go over their answers in pairs. Remind Ss to show each other where they found the answers. Go around the class to resolve any problems, or ask Ss to raise their hands if they have a question.

### Answers

1. She is spending time with people who Carly thinks are not good for her.
2. He is worried about putting his grades at risk/ getting in trouble.
3. She doesn't want to hurt her friend's feelings.
4. a Matt, b Dana, c Carly

## C

- Ss work individually. Ss find referents for nouns and noun phrases. Go around the class and give help as needed.

- **Option:** If Ss are having difficulty, they can work in pairs or small groups.

- Ss go over their answers in pairs. Then go over answers with the class.

### Answers

1. close friends
2. the fact that the new friends are a bad influence
3. school and studying
4. the situation of Matt's friend copying his homework
5. favors Dana's friend asks

## D Pair work

- Explain the task. Read the questions.

- Ss work in pairs. Ss talk about similar problems and give advice to the writers in the article.

- Ask Ss to tell the rest of the class some of the more interesting problems they discussed.

- **Option:** Ss can work in small groups, or this can be done with the whole class.

### TIP

Ask Ss how they are progressing with their self-study listening. Encourage Ss to share useful strategies and offer advice.

## End of Cycle 2

See the Supplementary Resources chart at the beginning of this unit for additional teaching materials and student activities related to this Cycle.

**A** Scan the article. What are the three problems?

# CAN YOU TELL IT LIKE IT IS?

**There are some things that are almost impossible to say to our close friends – especially if we want <u>them</u> to be our friends for life. Are you wondering what problems others have with bringing up difficult subjects? Read on.**

### 1. "I can't stand your other friends."

My best friend sometimes hangs out with some people that I really don't like. I think they have a bad influence on her, and she only spends time with them because they are "cool." Could you tell me if I should bring <u>the matter</u> up with her, or if it would be better for me to keep quiet? I don't want to lose her as a friend. – Carly

### 2. "I won't help you cheat."

My closest friend has lost interest in school and studying. He says he's bored with <u>the whole thing</u>, so he often asks me whether I'll do him a favor and let him copy my homework. So far I've said no, but he keeps asking me. I told him that I think we'll get in trouble, but he just laughed and told me not to worry. I don't want to put my grades at risk, but I'm afraid to confront my friend about <u>this</u>, so I just keep avoiding the topic. How can I get him to stop asking? I was wondering if you could give me some tips for handling my problem. – Matt

### 3. "No, I CAN'T do that for you!"

My best friend and I get along really well, but she is constantly asking me to do things for her. "Could you help me pick out some new clothes? Would you mind if I borrowed your car? Can you look after my apartment while I'm away?" And <u>these</u> are just a few examples. I've said yes so many times that now I'm afraid I'll hurt her feelings if I say no. Any ideas? – Dana

**B** Read the article. Then answer the questions.

1. Why is Carly concerned about her friend? _____
2. What is Matt most worried about? _____
3. Why is Dana afraid to say no to her friend? _____
4. Who is this advice best for?
   a. Say that you know your friend can handle the work himself. _____
   b. Agree to some requests, but only if your friend does something in return. _____
   c. Tell your friend there are more important things than being popular. _____

**C** What do the underlined words in the article refer to? Write the correct word(s).

1. them _____
2. the matter _____
3. the whole thing _____
4. this _____
5. these _____

**D** PAIR WORK Have you ever had similar problems with friends? How were the problems resolved? What advice would you give to Carly, Matt, and Dana?

# Unit 4 Supplementary Resources Overview

| | After the following SB exercises | You can use these materials in class | Your students can use these materials outside the classroom |
|---|---|---|---|
| **CYCLE 1** | **1 Snapshot** | | **GAME** Sentence Stacker (News categories) |
| | **2 Perspectives** | | |
| | **3 Grammar Focus** | | **SB** Unit 4 Grammar plus, Focus 1 <br> **SS** Unit 4 Grammar 1 <br> **GAME** Sentence Runner (Past continuous vs. simple past) |
| | **4 Pronunciation** | | |
| | **5 Listening** | | |
| | **6 Writing** | | **WB** Unit 4 exercises 1–4 |
| **CYCLE 2** | **7 Conversation** | | **SS** Unit 4 Speaking 1–2 |
| | **8 Grammar Focus** | **TSS** Unit 4 Grammar Worksheet <br> **TSS** Unit 4 Writing Worksheet | **SB** Unit 4 Grammar plus, Focus 2 <br> **SS** Unit 4 Grammar 2 <br> **GAME** Say the Word (Past continuous vs. simple past and past perfect) |
| | **9 Word Power** | **TSS** Unit 4 Vocabulary Worksheet <br> **TSS** Unit 4 Listening Worksheet <br> **TSS** Unit 4 Extra Worksheet | **SS** Unit 4 Vocabulary 1–2 <br> **GAME** Spell or Slime (Events) |
| | **10 Speaking** | | |
| | **11 Interchange 4** | | |
| | **12 Reading** | **TSS** Unit 4 Project Worksheet <br> **VID** Unit 4 <br> **VRB** Unit 4 | **SS** Unit 4 Reading 1–2 <br> **SS** Unit 4 Listening 1–3 <br> **SS** Unit 4 Video 1–3 <br> **WB** Unit 4 exercises 5–9 |

| With or instead of the following SB section | You can also use these materials for assessment |
|---|---|
| **Units 3–4 Progress Check** | **ASSESSMENT PROGRAM** Units 3–4 Oral Quiz <br> **ASSESSMENT PROGRAM** Units 3–4 Written Quiz |

**Key**

| | | | | | | | |
|---|---|---|---|---|---|---|---|
| **GAME:** | Online Game | **SB:** | Student's Book | **SS:** | Online Self-study | **TSS:** | Teacher Support Site |
| **VID:** | Video DVD | **VRB:** | Video Resource Book | **WB:** | Online Workbook/Workbook | | |

# My Plan for Unit 4

Use the space below to customize a plan that fits your needs.

| With the following SB exercises | I am using these materials in class | My students are using these materials outside the classroom |
|---|---|---|
| | | |
| | | |
| | | |
| | | |
| | | |
| | | |
| | | |
| | | |
| | | |
| | | |
| | | |
| | | |
| | | |

| With or instead of the following SB section | I am using these materials for assessment |
|---|---|
| | |
| | |
| | |

# 4 What happened?

▸ Describe past events
▸ Tell stories

## 1 SNAPSHOT

### NEWS
Several Streets Closed After "Suspicious Package" Was Found

### HEALTH
Why Weight Loss Isn't the Same as Being Healthy

### TRENDING TOPICS
The Earth Is Getting Warmer and the Signs Are Everywhere

### ARTS
The Top-Rated TV Shows You Need to Be Watching Right Now

### SCIENCE
Women Need More Sleep Than Men Because They Use More of Their Brains

### TECH
Here Are the Five Must-Have Apps for Runners

*Which story would you like to read? Why?*
*What types of stories do you usually read online?*
*Where do you get your news? What's happening in the news today?*

## 2 PERSPECTIVES  Listen up.

A  Listen to what people are listening to on their way to work. Which stories from Exercise 1 are they related to?

Hey, I just downloaded this incredible app. I used it this morning and I think you're going to love it. While I was working out, it calculated exactly how many calories I burned. The bad thing is, it tells me I still need to run about 4 miles to burn off last night's dinner.

As scientists were doing some research on the effects of sleep deprivation, they discovered that women need about 20 more minutes of sleep a night than men do. They think the reason is that women tend to do several tasks at once, which makes their brains work harder.

Hi, Jeff. We're canceling our meeting in the downtown office this morning. We just learned that the police have closed all the streets in the area. It seems that a man was looking for his lost cat when he found a suspicious package inside a trash can. In the end, it was just an old box of chocolates.

B  Which is a message from a co-worker? a message from a friend? a podcast?

# 4 What happened?

**Cycle 1, Exercises 1–6**

In this unit, students focus on storytelling and describing past events. By the end of Cycle 1, students will be able to describe past events using the simple past and past continuous. By the end of Cycle 2, students will be able to tell stories using the past perfect tense.

## 1 SNAPSHOT

**Learning Objective:** discuss different types of stories

- **Option:** Hold a brief discussion about news. Ask: "Who follows the news? How do you get your news? What news do you find interesting? How important is it to keep up-to-date?"

- Books closed. Brainstorm with Ss about online newspapers. Ask what sections, or categories, they contain. Ask Ss to write their ideas on the board.

**TIP**
To introduce a new unit, ask Ss motivating questions and elicit information related to the unit topic. If possible, bring – or ask Ss to bring – realia to class (e.g., for this unit, printouts or screen shots of online newspapers, local and/or international).

- Books open. Say that this Snapshot lists popular categories of online news. Read the categories. Ss circle categories that match the ones they brainstormed.

- Elicit or explain any new vocabulary.

**Vocabulary**
**top-rated:** very popular or successful
**must-have:** an object that many people want to own

- **Option:** Ss look through printouts of online newspapers or view them online. Ask Ss to find the categories listed in the Snapshot. Encourage Ss to note any others they find.

- Read the questions.

- Ss discuss the focus questions in pairs or small groups. Set a time limit of about five minutes.

## 2 PERSPECTIVES

**Learning Objective:** identify different types of stories that use the past continuous and simple past in context

▶ **A** *[CD 1, Track 27]*

- Books closed. Explain the task.

- Play the audio program. Ss listen to three things people are listening to. Ss decide which story in Exercise 1 each item relates to. Pause after each item to give Ss time to write down key words about each one.

- Elicit answers from the class. For each item, ask: "Which words told you the answer?"

**Answers**
1. Here Are the 5 Must-Have Apps for Runners
2. Women Need More Sleep Than Men Because They Use More of Their Brains
3. Several Streets Closed after "Suspicious Package" Was Found

- Books open. Play the audio program again. Ss listen and read.

- Elicit or explain any new vocabulary.

**Vocabulary**
**incredible:** extremely good
**work out:** exercise to improve the strength or appearance of your body
**burn:** exercise to work off calories that you have eaten
**sleep deprivation:** a situation in which you do not sleep
**look for:** try to find someone or something
**suspicious:** making you feel that something illegal is happening or that something is wrong

**B**

- Focus Ss' attention on the title of the exercise: "Listen up." Explain that this phrasal verb is an informal way to make people listen to you.

- Explain the task. Ask a S to read the first story aloud. Elicit the answer from the class. (Answer: a friend)

- Ss work individually for a few minutes. Elicit the answers from the class. Ask "Why do you think it's from a friend, a podcast, or a co-worker?"

**Answers**
1. a friend          2. a podcast          3. a co-worker

# 3 GRAMMAR FOCUS

**Learning Objective:** use the past continuous and simple past to describe past events

▶ **[CD 1, Track 28]**

### Past continuous vs. simple past

- Draw two pictures on the board. One picture shows a man working out. The second shows the man looking at his smartphone.

1.                    2.

- Focus Ss' attention on the Perspectives on page 22. Ask Ss to find the sentence that fits the pictures. Write it on the board. Underline and label the sentence like this:

  While I <u>was working out</u>, it <u>calculated</u> how many calories I burned.
      past continuous   simple past

- To help Ss see the relationship between the tenses, ask questions like these:
  1. [*point to first picture*] What was the man doing here? Is *working out* a "continued" action that lasted for some time?
  2. Was the action of *working out* interrupted by another action?

- Say that the past continuous (*was working out*) describes an ongoing action in the past. The simple past (*calculated*) is a shorter complete action. It takes place at one moment and interrupts the ongoing action.

- Ask Ss to look for past continuous and simple past verbs in the Perspectives on page 22. Tell Ss to underline past continuous verbs and put a circle around simple past verbs. (Answers: Past continuous verbs: *was working out, were doing, was looking for*; simple past verbs: *downloaded, used, calculated, burned, discovered, learned, found, was*)

- Focus Ss' attention on the Grammar Focus box. Point out the adverb clauses with *while* and *as*. Say that these clauses cannot stand alone as a sentence. When an adverb clause comes before the main clause, it has a comma.

# 4 PRONUNCIATION

**Learning Objective:** use correct intonation to sound more natural when using complex sentences

▶ **A [CD 1, Track 29]**

- Point out that each clause has a falling intonation pattern. This helps the listener follow the two groups of ideas in a long sentence.

---

- Next, point out the clause with *when* in the second column. When an adverb clause comes after the main clause, it does not have a comma.

- Play the audio program. Ss listen and read or repeat.

⚠ To practice the sentences, try the activity **Split Sentences** – download it from the website.

**A**

- Explain the task.

- Ss complete the task individually. Tell Ss to read each story once before filling in the blanks. This will help Ss understand which action was ongoing and which action interrupted it.

- Elicit or explain any new vocabulary (e.g., *thrift shop* is a shop in which a charity or a small business sells used goods given by the public).

⚠ To help Ss with vocabulary in this exercise, try the **Vocabulary Mingle** – download it from the website.

- Ss work in pairs to compare answers.

### Answers

1. Marcia Murphy **donated** her old pants to a thrift shop. As she **was walking** home, she **remembered** she left $20 in her pants pocket.
2. Jason Clark **was walking** home one day, when he **saw** a little puppy crying on the sidewalk, so he **stopped** to help. As he **was picking** him up, a woman **came** from nowhere screaming: "Stop that guy. He's trying to steal my puppy." Jason **ended** up spending three hours at the police station.
3. On her birthday last year, Diane Larson **was driving** to work when she **had** a bad accident. This year, just to be safe, she decided to stay home on her birthday. Unfortunately, that night while she **was sleeping** in her apartment, the floor of her living room **collapsed** and she **fell** into her neighbor's apartment.

### B *Group work*

- Explain the task.

- Ss work in groups of three. Ask each S to reread a different story from Part A and note four or five key words or phrases. Ss use their notes to retell the story. Remind Ss to add new information or a new ending.

- Play the audio program. Ss listen and repeat.

### B *Pair work*

- Explain the task. Ss work in pairs to make complex sentences with *while* or *as* and the past continuous. Ss take turns starting and finishing the sentences using falling intonation.

# 3 GRAMMAR FOCUS

## Past continuous vs. simple past

Use the past continuous for an ongoing action in the past.
Use the simple past for an event that interrupts that action.

| *Past continuous* | *Simple past* |
|---|---|
| While I **was working** out, | it **calculated** how many calories I burned. |
| As scientists **were doing** research, | they **discovered** that women need more sleep than men. |
| A man **was looking** for his cat | when he **found** a suspicious package inside a trash can. |

GRAMMAR PLUS *see page 135*

A Complete the stories using the past continuous or simple past forms
of the verbs. Then compare with a partner.

1. **Bad memory, bad luck:** Marcia Murphy
   _____ (donate) her old pants to
   a thrift shop. As she _____ (walk)
   home, she _____ (remember) she
   _____ (leave) $20 in her pants pocket.

2. **Good intentions, bad interpretation:** Jason Clark
   _____ (walk) home one day, when he
   _____ (see) a little puppy crying on the
   sidewalk, so he _____ (stop) to help.
   As he _____ (pick) him up, a woman
   _____ (come) from nowhere screaming:
   "Stop that guy. He's trying to steal my puppy." Jason
   _____ (end) up spending three hours at the
   police station.

3. **A bad ride, a bad fall:** On her birthday last year,
   Diane Larson _____ (drive) to work
   when she _____ (have) a bad accident.
   This year, just to be safe, she decided to stay home
   on her birthday. Unfortunately, that night while she
   _____ (sleep) in her apartment, the floor
   of her living room _____ (collapse) and she
   _____ (fall) into her neighbor's apartment.

B **GROUP WORK** Take turns retelling the stories in part A. Add your own
ideas and details to make the stories more interesting!

# 4 PRONUNCIATION Intonation in complex sentences

A Listen and practice. Notice how each clause in a complex sentence has
its own intonation pattern.

As Marcia was walking home, she remembered she left $20 in her pants pocket.

A man was looking for his cat when he found a package.

B **PAIR WORK** Use your imagination to make complex sentences. Take turns
starting and finishing the sentences. Pay attention to intonation.

A: As Lee was coming to school today . . .
B: . . . he saw a parade coming down the street.

## 5 LISTENING Crazy but true!

▶ **A** Listen to three news stories. Number the pictures from 1 to 3. (There is one extra picture.)

▶ **B** Listen again. Take notes on each story.

|  | Where did it happen? | When did it happen? | What happened? |
|---|---|---|---|
| 1. |  |  |  |
| 2. |  |  |  |
| 3. |  |  |  |

## 6 WRITING A personal account

**A** Think of a story that happened to you or to someone you know. Choose one of the titles below, or create your own.

A Scary Experience          I'll Never Forget That Day
I Was Really Lucky          I Can't Believe It Happened

**B** Write your story. First, answer these questions.

Who was involved?          Where did it happen?
When did it happen?          What happened?

> <u>I Was Really Lucky</u>
>
> Last year, I took a trip to see my grandparents. I was waiting in the airport for my flight when a storm hit, and all the flights were cancelled. Luckily, I . . .

**C** GROUP WORK Take turns telling your stories. Other students ask questions. Who has the best story?

# 5 LISTENING

**Learning Objective:** listen for and take notes on the details of stories in the simple past

## ▶ A [CD 1, Track 30]

- Ask: "Who watched the news on TV today or yesterday?" Encourage the class to tell any interesting stories they heard.
- Have Ss look at the pictures and describe what they see.
- Explain the task. Ss will listen to the audio and number the pictures in the order that they hear the matching news stories in the audio. Make sure Ss understand that there is one extra picture.
- Play the audio program. Ss complete the task individually.
- Allow pairs to compare answers. Then go over answers with the class.

### Answers

X 2
3 1

## ▶ B [CD 1, Track 31]

- Read the questions in the chart aloud.
- Explain the task. Ss will listen to the audio and answer the questions in the chart for each news story.
- Play the audio program. Pause after each news event. Give Ss time to complete the chart. Ask Ss to write their answers on the board.
- **Option:** Ask: "Which story did you find most interesting? Why?" Elicit Ss' ideas.

### Audio script

See page T-170.

### Answers

1. Australia; Saturday; bull ran onto soccer field and started chasing a soccer player
2. Missouri; last Thursday; tornado carried 19-year-old boy over 1,300 feet and dropped him in an abandoned field
3. Ontario; early Tuesday morning; A thief rescued two police officers after they lost control of their vehicle and drove into a river while chasing the thief.

For more practice with events and vocabulary, play **Prediction Bingo** – download it from the website.

# 6 WRITING

**Learning Objective:** write a story using the past continuous and simple past

## A

- Explain the task. Go over the titles.
- Ss work individually to think about and plan their stories. Explain that they can choose a title or create a new one.

## B

- Explain the task. Tell Ss that the questions should help them guide the story, but they should provide more information.
- Ss work individually to write their news stories. Ask them to write one or two paragraphs and to come up with an interesting ending.

### TIP
If Ss struggle to find ideas, remind them of the 5 Ws and H questions used by journalists: *who*, *what*, *where*, *when*, *why*, and *how*.

## C Group work

- Ss read or tell their stories in small groups.
- The group votes on the best story.

### End of Cycle 1

See the Supplementary Resources chart at the beginning of this unit for additional teaching materials and student activities related to this Cycle.

# 7 CONVERSATION

**Learning Objective:** use the past perfect in a conversation about past events

## ▶ A *[CD 1, Track 32]*

- Ss cover the text. Play the audio program. Ss take notes.

- Ss compare notes in pairs. Then Ss use their notes to write three comprehension questions.

- Each pair joins another pair. They take turns asking and answering their questions.

- Tell Ss to uncover the text. Play the audio program. Ss listen and read. Then they practice the conversation in pairs.

## ▶ B *[CD 1, Track 33]*

- Read the focus questions. Play the second part of the audio program. Elicit Ss' answers.

### Audio script

See page T-171.

### Answer

Milo once had his carry-on bag stolen, with his wallet, his credit card, and his phone. He was overseas, waiting for a bus to take him to the airport.

# 8 GRAMMAR FOCUS

**Learning Objective:** correctly use the past continuous, simple past, or past perfect to describe past events

## ▶ *[CD 1, Track 34]*

### *Past perfect*

- Explain that the past perfect is *had* + past participle. Focus Ss' attention on the Conversation. Elicit sentences with the past perfect. Write them on the board in a chart:

| 1 | 2 | 3 | 4 |
|---|---|---|---|
| I | had | parked | my bike on the street. |
| Someone | had | stolen | my bike. |
| I | 'd | forgotten | to lock it up. |

- Explain that when we are talking about *two events* in the past, we use the past perfect to express the earlier one. Write an example on the board:

  from 12:00-1:00 P.M.          at 11:45 A.M.
  I was having lunch with a friend, and I <u>had parked</u> it on the street.

- Next, write these sentences on the board:

  I came back.     Someone stole my bike.

- Ask: "Which event happened 'earlier'?" (Answer: Someone stole my bike.) Elicit a sentence with the cues and the past perfect. (Answer: When I came back, someone had stolen my bike.)

- Play the audio program.

## A

- Ss complete the task individually.

- Allow pairs to compare answers. Then go over answers with the class.

### Answers

1. I **took** a trip to London last year. I was a bit scared because I **hadn't traveled** abroad before, but everything was perfect.
2. I **was visiting** the British Museum one afternoon when I **ran** into an old school friend who I **hadn't seen** for over 10 years.
3. One weekend, we **were driving** to Liverpool when we **ran** out of gas on the highway because we **had forgotten** to fill up the tank before leaving. Fortunately, a truck driver **stopped** and **helped** us.
4. On the last day, as I **was going** up to my hotel room, I **got** stuck in the elevator. After I **had been** stuck for an hour, someone **started** it again.

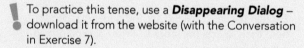
To practice this tense, use a **Disappearing Dialog** – download it from the website (with the Conversation in Exercise 7).

## B *Pair work*

- Ss work in pairs to complete the task.

- Allow pairs to compare answers with another pair. Ss share some of their sentences with the class.

## 7 CONVERSATION  That's terrible!

 **A** Listen and practice.

 **CAROL** Guess what? Someone stole my new bike yesterday!

**MILO** Oh, no! What happened?

 **CAROL** Well, I was having lunch with a friend, and I had parked it on the street, just like I always do. When I came back, someone had stolen it. I guess I'd forgotten to lock it up.

 **MILO** That's terrible! Did you report the theft to the police?

 **CAROL** Yes, I did. And I also listed it on that site for stolen and lost bikes. But I doubt I'll ever get it back.

**B** Listen to the rest of the conversation. What did Milo have stolen once? Where was he?

## 8 GRAMMAR FOCUS

### Past perfect

Use the past perfect for an event that occurred before another event in the past.

| Past event | Past perfect event |
| --- | --- |
| I **was having** lunch with a friend, | and I **had parked** my bike on the street. |
| When I **came back**, | someone **had stolen** it. |
| They **were able** to steal it | because I **had forgotten** to lock it up. |

GRAMMAR PLUS *see page 135*

**A** Write the correct verbs to complete the sentences. Then compare with a partner.

1. I _____ (took/had taken) a trip to London last year. I was a bit scared because I _____ (didn't travel/hadn't traveled) abroad before, but everything was perfect.

2. I _____ (visited/was visiting) the British Museum one afternoon when I _____ (ran/had run) into an old school friend who I _____ (didn't see/hadn't seen) for over 10 years.

3. One weekend, we _____ (were driving/had driven) to Liverpool when we _____ (ran/were running) out of gas on the highway because we _____ (forgot/had forgotten) to fill up the tank before leaving. Fortunately, a truck driver _____ (stopped/had stopped) and _____ (helped/had helped) us.

4. On the last day, as I _____ (was going/had gone) up to my hotel room, I _____ (got/had gotten) stuck in the elevator. After I _____ (was/had been) stuck for an hour, someone _____ (started/had started) it again.

**B** PAIR WORK  Complete the sentences with your own ideas.

Until last year, I had never . . .

One day, as I was . . .

## 9 WORD POWER Exceptional events

**A** Match the words in column A with the definitions in column B.

**A**

1. coincidence _____
2. dilemma _____
3. disaster _____
4. emergency _____
5. lucky break _____
6. mishap _____
7. mystery _____
8. triumph _____

**B**

a. an unexpected event that brings good fortune
b. a situation that involves a difficult choice
c. something puzzling or unexplained
d. an event that causes suffering or destruction
e. a great success or achievement
f. an accident, mistake, or unlucky event
g. a sudden, dangerous situation that requires quick action
h. a situation when two similar things happen at the same time for no reason

**B** PAIR WORK Choose one kind of event from part A. Write a situation for it.

> A man bought an old house for $10,000. As he was cleaning the attic of his new home, he found an old painting by a famous painter. He had never collected art, but when he took it to a museum, he found out it was worth almost one million dollars. (lucky break)

**C** GROUP WORK Read your situation. Can others guess which kind of event it describes?

## 10 SPEAKING It's a story about . . .

GROUP WORK Have you ever experienced the events in Exercise 9, part A? Tell your group about it. Answer any questions.

A: It's a story about a coincidence.

B: What happened?

A: My sister bought a new dress for her graduation party. She had saved for months to buy it. When she got to the party, another girl was wearing the exact same dress!

C: Wow! That's more than a coincidence. It's a disaster! And what did she do?

## 11 INTERCHANGE 4 Spin a yarn

Tell a story. Go to Interchange 4 on page 117.

# 9 WORD POWER

## A

- Explain the task. Model the first word as an example.
- **Option:** Model the word stress of each noun. Ss listen and repeat.
- Ss work individually or in pairs. Ss match words with definitions. Tell Ss to check their dictionaries only after they finish.
- Go over answers with the class.

### Answers

| | | | |
|---|---|---|---|
| 1. h | 3. d | 5. a | 7. c |
| 2. b | 4. g | 6. f | 8. e |

## B *Pair work*

- Explain the task. Read aloud the example for *lucky break*.
- Ss work in pairs. Ss choose one event from part A. Then they write a situation for it. Go around the class and briefly check sentences.

## C *Group work*

- Explain the task. Two or three pairs work in a group. Ss take turns reading their situations without saying the kind of event. Others in the group guess the event.

# 10 SPEAKING

Learning Objective: tell stories using various past tenses

## Group work

- Read the instructions. Ask three Ss to model the conversation.
- Explain the task. Give Ss time to read the events in Exercise 9 and think of a situation they would like to talk about.
- **Option:** If Ss appear reluctant or embarrassed to talk about a personal situation, allow them to tell a story about a friend or someone they heard about in the news.
- Ss work in small groups. They take turns talking about the situations. Tell Ss to talk about the events in any order. Encourage Ss to ask follow-up questions.

### TIP
A fluency activity is designed to challenge Ss to do their best with whatever language abilities they have. It's best to give help only if asked directly.

### TIP
To ensure that all Ss ask four follow-up questions, ask each S to take out four small coins (or paper clips) and put them in a pile. As they ask a follow-up question, they can remove a coin from the pile.

- **Option:** As a follow-up, two groups form a large group to swap stories, or do this as a whole class activity.

For a different way to use this activity, try the **Chain Game** – download it from the website.

# 11 INTERCHANGE 4

See page T-117 for teaching notes.

**Learning Objectives:** skim and read news articles for specific information; identify the meaning of words in context

### A

Note: If possible, bring several satirical articles from the Internet to class and pass them around.

- Books closed. Ask: "Is everything you read or see on the Internet true? Why or why not? Where do you go to find trustworthy information?"
- Books open. Go over the task. Read the questions.
- Give Ss time to skim the article themselves. Ss work individually to find the answer to the question.
- Elicit the answer from the class. (Answer: false)

! To introduce new vocabulary and have Ss predict the stories, try **Cloud Prediction** – download it from the website.

### B

- Ss read the article individually.

> **TIP**
> Tell Ss not to look up any words as they read. Instead, they should underline or circle words they don't know and keep reading.

- Then Ss work in small groups. Each S shares words he or she underlined. If group members know the word, they explain it. If no one in the group knows the word, Ss look at the context and as a group write one or two guesses about its meaning.
- **Option:** Each group says what words they chose and what their guesses were. Each group gets one point for making a guess and two points for a correct guess.
- Elicit or explain any new vocabulary.

> **Vocabulary**
> **trustworthy:** able to be trusted
> **spread:** to cover, reach, or have an effect on a wider or increasing area
> **lice:** small insects that live on the skin of mammals and birds and cause itching
> **outbreak:** a time when a disease or something dangerous suddenly begins
> **"ick" factor:** an amount of shock or dislike that makes you feel sick

- Explain the task.
- Ss complete the task individually or in pairs. Ss scan the article to find the words. Then they guess the meaning. Point out that this exercise will help Ss confirm their previous guesses and remember the words.
- Ss go over answers in pairs. Ss may use their dictionaries to check the meaning of words to be matched to the ones in italics.
- Go over answers with the class.

> **Answers**
> 1. not exact or true
> 2. humorously critical
> 3. public opinion of someone
> 4. very large
> 5. hard to fight against
> 6. proof of truth

### C  *Pair work*

- Ask a S to read the questions out loud.
- Ss work in pairs to discuss the questions. Encourage Ss to share opinions about the story presented in the article and false information found on the web. Go around the class and listen.

### D  *Group work*

- Read the focus questions.
- Ss work in groups. Ss describe a story they know. Encourage Ss to give specific details and to ask each other follow-up questions.
- **Option:** Groups share one particularly interesting thing they talked about.

## End of Cycle 2

See the Supplementary Resources chart at the beginning of this unit for additional teaching materials and student activities related to this Cycle and for assessment tools.

**A** Skim the article. Was the story about lice true or false?

Menu    Articles    Community    Search                    Sign in / Sign up

# Believing More Than We Should

Is everything you read on the Internet true? If your answer is "no," you are absolutely right. Many stories and even photos are not to be trusted. And don't believe that because a good friend or a well-known news source has posted something that it is necessarily trustworthy.

There are many reasons for the spread of inaccurate content on the Internet. One reason is that satirical websites can create very believable stories, which they invent in order to make a point or to make people laugh. Other reasons might be an attempt to gain more readers, a desire to damage someone's reputation, or simple curiosity about how far a fake story can spread.

One story that spread throughout the media before anyone had checked the facts involved teenagers, selfies, and head lice. The article claimed that when teenagers were posing together for selfies, their heads often touched and the tiny insects were jumping from head to head. The article went on to say that this was causing a massive outbreak of lice. Some major websites and news outlets picked up the story, not even bothering to consult the experts. It turned out that some entrepreneurs who were marketing a new treatment for head lice had made up the story and posted it. Their motivation was to get attention and more business.

The spread of this story is understandable. It involved one epidemic (selfies) causing another (lice), and the "ick" factor was irresistible. Because there is so much false information online, there are now websites, such as *Snopes* and *Factcheck*, which exist specifically to find out if stories are true or not. So the next time you see a story that sounds too good to be true, at least you have somewhere to turn for verification before you spread false information to all your friends.

**B** Read the article. Find the words in italics in the article. Then check (✓) the meaning of each word.

| | | | | |
|---|---|---|---|---|
| **1.** *inaccurate* | ☐ | not exact or true | ☐ | shocking or disgusting |
| **2.** *satirical* | ☐ | humorously critical | ☐ | completely factual |
| **3.** *reputation* | ☐ | hurtful news about someone | ☐ | public opinion of someone |
| **4.** *massive* | ☐ | small | ☐ | very large |
| **5.** *irresistible* | ☐ | hard to prove | ☐ | hard to fight against |
| **6.** *verification* | ☐ | proof of truth | ☐ | another opinion |

**C** PAIR WORK  Discuss these questions.

Do you think you would have believed the story about selfies and head lice?

Do you think the creation of the story was justified or not?

Who do you think is most responsible for the story being so popular?

Do you think there should be a penalty for spreading false information? If so, what should it be?

**D** GROUP WORK  Have you ever read a story that turned out to be false? How did you find out the truth?

## SELF-ASSESSMENT

How well can you do these things? Check (✓) the boxes.

| I can . . . | Very well | OK | A little |
|---|---|---|---|
| Discuss favors (Ex. 1) | ☐ | ☐ | ☐ |
| Leave messages with requests (Ex. 2) | ☐ | ☐ | ☐ |
| Tell a story, making clear the sequence of events (Ex. 3, 5) | ☐ | ☐ | ☐ |
| Understand the sequence of events in a story (Ex. 4) | ☐ | ☐ | ☐ |

## 1 ROLE PLAY Save the date!

*Student A:* You are planning a class party at your house. Think of three things you need help with. Then call a classmate and ask for help.

*Student B:* Student A is planning a party. Agree to help with some things, but not everything.

"Hi, Martina. I'm calling about the party. Would you mind . . . ?"

Change roles and try the role play again.

## 2 DISCUSSION Who said it?

**A GROUP WORK** Take turns reading each request. Then discuss the questions and come up with possible answers.

> Tell Rita that I'm going to be a half hour late for our meeting. Ask her to wait for me in her office.

> Tell your officers that he's white and wears a blue collar with his name on it – Rex. Please call if you find him.

> I'm sorry to bother you, but I really need it back for the office party on Friday. Please ask Sue to bring it over before that.

1. What is the situation?
2. Who is the request for? Who do you think received the request and passed it on?
3. Give an indirect request for each situation.

   "Could you tell Rita . . . ?"

**B CLASS ACTIVITY** Compare your answers. Which group has the most interesting answers for each message?

# Progress check

## *SELF-ASSESSMENT*

**Learning Objectives:** reflect on one's learning; identify areas that need improvement

- Ask: "What did you learn in Units 3 and 4?" Elicit Ss' answers.

- Ss complete the Self-assessment. Explain to Ss that this is not a test; it is a way for them to evaluate what they've learned and identify areas where they need additional practice. Encourage them to be honest, and point out they will not get a bad grade if they check (✓) "a little."

- Ss move on to the Progress check exercises. You can have Ss complete them in class or for homework, using one of these techniques:
  1. Ask Ss to complete all the exercises.
  2. Ask Ss: "What do you need to practice?" Then assign exercises based on their answers.
  3. Ask Ss to choose and complete exercises based on their Self-assessment.

## 1 ROLE PLAY

**Learning Objective:** demonstrate one's ability to make requests with modals, *if* clauses, and gerunds

- Explain the task.
- Divide the class into pairs, and assign A/B roles. Student As are planning a party. Student Bs are asked to help. Ask a S to model the request.

- Ss role-play in pairs. To set the scene for a telephone conversation, ask Ss to sit back-to-back. Remind Student Bs to agree to some things, but not others.

- Ss change roles and repeat the role play.

## 2 DISCUSSION

**Learning Objective:** demonstrate one's ability to make indirect requests

### A *Group work*

- Explain the task. Ask different Ss to read the requests and focus questions.

- Ss work in groups of three. Ss take turns reading aloud a request and discussing the questions. In groups, Ss answer questions about the situation and the people involved. Then Ss write an indirect request for each situation.

- Go around the class and give help as needed.

### B *Class activity*

- Explain the task. Ask a S to share each group's answers with the class.

- Take a vote to see who has the most interesting answers.

## 3 SPEAKING

**Learning Objective:** demonstrate one's ability to tell a story using the past continuous and simple past

### A Pair work

- Explain the task. Ask a S to read the types of events in the box.
- Ss work in pairs. Remind Ss to choose only the type of event and write a title.

### B Pair work

- Explain the task. Ask a S to read the example story. Elicit *who, what, where, when, why,* and *how* questions and answers for the example.

- Pairs exchange titles with another pair. Then pairs discuss how to answer the questions about the other pair's title. Point out that the stories do not have to be true.
- Pairs can take notes on their ideas or write out the story. Only one S needs to write, but both Ss should contribute equally. Ask the S who didn't write to check for errors.

### C

- Explain the task. Ss tell their stories to the pair who wrote the title.
- Ask: "Were you surprised at the way the story turned out?"
- Ask some Ss to tell their stories to the class.

## 4 LISTENING

**Learning Objective:** demonstrate one's ability to listen and understand sequence in the past

▶ **[CD 1, Track 35]**

- Explain the task. Give Ss time to read all of the sentences.
- Tell Ss to listen and number the events in each situation from 1 to 3. Play the audio program. Pause after each event.
- Play the audio program as many times as needed. Elicit answers.

### Audio script

See page T-171.

### Answers

1. 1. She went on vacation. 2. She got sick.
   3. She went back to work.
2. 1. I changed phone numbers. 2. John called me. 3. I didn't get the message.
3. 1. I was very nervous. 2. I left the office.
   3. I felt relieved.
4. 1. I was watching a movie. 2. My cousin stopped by. 3. We went out.

## 5 DISCUSSION

**Learning Objective:** demonstrate one's ability to describe events using the past perfect

### Group work

- Explain the task. Read the beginnings and endings. Ask four Ss to model the example story chain.
- Ss work in small groups. Ss choose any beginning and any ending. They discuss events that could link the two. Point out that Ss can decide the story as they do the task.

- The first S reads the sentence the group chose and then adds a sentence of his or her own. Ss take turns adding sentences to the story. Remind Ss to keep the ending in mind when they add a sentence.
- The story ends when a S is able to use the group's ending.
- **Option:** Ss change groups and repeat the exercise. This time Ss write the story. Ss pass a sheet of paper around the group. Each S adds a sentence to the story.

## WHAT'S NEXT?

**Learning Objective:** become more involved in one's learning

- Focus Ss' attention on the Self-assessment again. Ask: "How well can you do these things now?"

- Ask Ss to underline one thing they need to review. Ask: "What did you underline? How can you review it?"
- If needed, plan additional activities or reviews based on Ss' answers.

## 3 SPEAKING And then . . . ?

**A** PAIR WORK Choose a type of event from the box. Then make up a title for a story about it. Write the title on a piece of paper.

| disaster | emergency | lucky break | mystery | triumph |

**B** PAIR WORK Exchange titles with another pair. Discuss the questions *who, what, where, when, why,* and *how* about the other pair's title. Then make up a story.

**C** Share your story with the pair who wrote the title.

> The Mystery of the Message in a Bottle
>
> I was walking on the beach when I saw a bottle with a message inside. The bottle looked very old, and it was hard to open it. Inside there was a message: "My beloved Catherine, I hope you . . ."

## 4 LISTENING What happened first?

▶ Listen to each situation. Number the events from 1 to 3.

| | | | | | |
|---|---|---|---|---|---|
| **1.** ☐ She got sick. | | ☐ She went on vacation. | | ☐ She went back to work. |
| **2.** ☐ John called me. | | ☐ I didn't get the message. | | ☐ I changed phone numbers. |
| **3.** ☐ I was very nervous. | | ☐ I left the office. | | ☐ I felt relieved. |
| **4.** ☐ We went out. | | ☐ My cousin stopped by. | | ☐ I was watching a movie. |

## 5 DISCUSSION Beginning, middle, and end

GROUP WORK Choose the beginning of a story from column A and an ending from column B. Discuss interesting or unusual events that could link A to B. Then make up a story.

**A**

*Once, I . . .*
accepted an interesting invitation.
was asked to do an unusual favor.
received an unexpected phone call.
owed someone a big apology.

**A:** Once, I accepted an interesting invitation.
**B:** Let's see. . . . I was biking home when I got a text from an old friend.
**C:** I hadn't seen him in over five years.
**D:** I was really surprised, but . . .

**B**

*Believe it or not, . . .*
I got home, and there were 30 people in my living room!
I had no idea where I was.
when I got there, everyone had left.
it was the star of my favorite TV show!

## WHAT'S NEXT?

Look at your Self-assessment again. Do you need to review anything?

# Unit 5 Supplementary Resources Overview

| | After the following SB exercises | You can use these materials in class | Your students can use these materials outside the classroom |
|---|---|---|---|
| **CYCLE 1** | 1 **Perspectives** | | |
| | 2 **Word Power** | **TSS** Unit 5 Vocabulary Worksheet | **SS** Unit 5 Vocabulary 1–3<br>**GAME** Say the Word (Culture shock) |
| | 3 **Grammar Focus** | **TSS** Unit 5 Listening Worksheet | **SB** Unit 5 Grammar plus, Focus 1<br>**SS** Unit 5 Grammar 1<br>**GAME** Sentence Stacker (Noun phrases containing relative clauses) |
| | 4 **Pronunciation** | | |
| | 5 **Discussion** | **TSS** Unit 5 Extra Worksheet | **WB** Unit 5 exercises 1–3 |
| **CYCLE 2** | 6 **Snapshot** | | |
| | 7 **Conversation** | | **SS** Unit 5 Speaking 1–2 |
| | 8 **Grammar Focus** | **TSS** Unit 5 Grammar Worksheet | **SB** Unit 5 Grammar plus, Focus 2<br>**SS** Unit 5 Grammar 2<br>**GAME** Word Keys (Expectations)<br>**GAME** Sentence Runner (Expectations) |
| | 9 **Listening** | | |
| | 10 **Speaking** | | |
| | 11 **Writing** | **TSS** Unit 5 Writing Worksheet | |
| | 12 **Interchange 5** | | |
| | 13 **Reading** | **TSS** Unit 5 Project Worksheet<br>**VID** Unit 5<br>**VRB** Unit 5 | **SS** Unit 5 Reading 1–2<br>**SS** Unit 5 Listening 1–3<br>**SS** Unit 5 Video 1–3<br>**WB** Unit 5 exercises 4–7 |

**Key**

| | | | | | | | |
|---|---|---|---|---|---|---|---|
| **GAME:** | Online Game | **SB:** | Student's Book | **SS:** | Online Self-study | **TSS:** | Teacher Support Site |
| **VID:** | Video DVD | **VRB:** | Video Resource Book | **WB:** | Online Workbook/Workbook | | |

# My Plan for Unit 5

Use the space below to customize a plan that fits your needs.

| With the following SB exercises | I am using these materials in class | My students are using these materials outside the classroom |
|---|---|---|
|  |  |  |
|  |  |  |
|  |  |  |
|  |  |  |
|  |  |  |
|  |  |  |
|  |  |  |
|  |  |  |
|  |  |  |
|  |  |  |
|  |  |  |
|  |  |  |
|  |  |  |

| With or instead of the following SB section | I am using these materials for assessment |
|---|---|
|  |  |
|  |  |
|  |  |

# Expanding your horizons

▸ Discuss living in a foreign country
▸ Describe cultural expectations and differences

## 1 PERSPECTIVES Challenges of living abroad

▶ **A** Listen to people talk about moving to a foreign country.
Check (✓) the concerns you think you would share.

☐ "One thing that I'd really miss is hanging out with my friends." _____
☐ "Something that I'd be worried about is the local food. I'm a picky eater."
   _____
☐ "Getting used to a different culture might be difficult at first." _____
☐ "I'd be worried about not knowing how to get around in a new city." _____
☐ "The people that I'd miss the most are my parents. We're very close."
   _____
☐ "Not knowing the local customs is something I'd be concerned about."
   _____
☐ "I'd be nervous about getting sick and not knowing how to explain
   my symptoms." _____
☐ "Communicating in a foreign language could be a challenge." _____

**B** Rate each concern from 1 (not worried at all) to 5 (really worried).
What would be your biggest concern? Why?

## 2 WORD POWER Mixed feelings

**A** These words are used to describe how people sometimes feel when they
live in a foreign country. Which are positive (**P**)? Which are negative (**N**)?
Write P or N.

| anxious | _____ | embarrassed | _____ | insecure | _____ |
| comfortable | _____ | enthusiastic | _____ | nervous | _____ |
| confident | _____ | excited | _____ | uncertain | _____ |
| curious | _____ | fascinated | _____ | uncomfortable | _____ |
| depressed | _____ | homesick | _____ | worried | _____ |

**B** GROUP WORK Tell your group about other situations in which you
experienced the feelings in part A. What made you feel that way?
How do you feel about the situations now?

**A:** I felt very embarrassed yesterday. I fell down the stairs in a restaurant.
**B:** How did it happen?
**A:** I think I slipped on something.
**C:** Did you get hurt?
**A:** Just a couple of bruises, but the restaurant manager was worried,
so he convinced me to go to the hospital.

confident

# 5 Expanding your horizons

## Cycle 1, Exercises 1–5

In this unit, Ss discuss living in a foreign country and describe cultural expectations and differences. By the end of Cycle 1, students will be able to discuss living abroad using noun phrases and relative clauses. By the end of Cycle 2, students will be able to describe expectations using *when* and *if* clauses.

## 1 PERSPECTIVES

**Learning Objectives:** respond to concerns about living abroad; identify noun phrases containing relative clauses in context

▶ **A** *[CD 1, Track 36]*

- Books closed. Explain that Ss will hear people talking about concerns they would have about living abroad.
- Ask Ss to brainstorm concerns they would have about living abroad and things they would miss. Write Ss' ideas on the board like this:

  *I'd worry about: the food, the climate, getting sick . . .*
  *I'd miss: my mom's cooking, my friends, my dog . . .*

- Books open. Play the audio program.

- **Option:** Books closed. Ss listen and write the sentences they hear, like a dictation. Books open. Ss check their answers.

  For an alternative dictation, try the **Running Dictation** – download it from the website.

- Ss compare their ideas on the board with those in the book.

**B**

- Explain the task. Read the first sentence in part A aloud. Model the task by rating the concern as it is appropriate for you.
- Ss work individually to rate the concerns.
- Ask several Ss to tell the class their biggest concerns. Ask: "Does anyone agree?" Take a class vote.

## 2 WORD POWER

**Learning Objective:** describe positive and negative feelings about living abroad

**A**

- Read the exercise title aloud. Elicit that *mixed feelings* means you feel both pleased and not pleased about a situation at the same time.
- Explain the task. Focus Ss' attention on the photograph and caption. Ask: "How does the person feel? Is *confident* a positive or negative feeling?" (Answer: positive) Model the task by writing *P* next to *confident*.
- Ss complete the task individually or in pairs. Ask Ss to try the task first without a dictionary. Go around the class and give help as needed.
- Elicit or explain any new vocabulary.

  Vocabulary
  **anxious:** feeling nervous
  **confident:** certain about one's ability to do things well
  **curious:** wanting to know or learn about something
  **depressed:** low in spirits; sad
  **enthusiastic:** energetically interested in something
  **fascinated:** being completely interested; showing complete attention to something
  **homesick:** longing for home and family while absent from them
  **insecure:** not confident or sure
  **uncertain:** lacking clear knowledge or a definite opinion

- To check answers, write two columns on the board: negative and positive. Ss come up to the board and write their answers in the correct column.

### Answers

| | | | | | |
|---|---|---|---|---|---|
| anxious | N | embarrassed | N | insecure | N |
| comfortable | P | enthusiastic | P | nervous | N |
| confident | P | excited | P | uncertain | N |
| curious | P | fascinated | P | uncomfortable | N |
| depressed | N | homesick | N | worried | N |

- **Option:** Model the pronunciation of the adjectives on the list. Ss practice.

**B** *Group work*

- Explain the task. Read the focus questions aloud. Read the example with two Ss.
- Ss work in small groups. Ss take turns talking about their feelings. Remind Ss to use the adjectives in part A.
- When time is up, ask: "What did you have in common with other Ss in your group?" Elicit ideas.

  To practice the new vocabulary, play **Tic-Tac-Toe** – download it from the website.

## 3 GRAMMAR FOCUS

**Learning Objective:** use noun phrases containing relative clauses to discuss living in a foreign country

▶ **[CD 1, Track 37]**

- Write these four phrases on cards:

  | | |
  |---|---|
  | one thing | I'd really miss |
  | is | hanging out with my friends |

- Write *one thing* and *is* in another color.
- Ask two Ss to come to the front of the class. Ask them to hold up these two cards: *I'd really miss* and *hanging out with my friends*.
- Explain that we can say the same thing in a different way. Ask two more Ss to come to the front. Give them the other two cards.
- Now the four Ss stand facing the class, holding up their cards in this order:

  S1: *one thing*    S2: *I'd really miss*
  S3: *is*    S4: *hanging out with my friends*

- Say that *one thing I'd really miss* is a noun phrase. It is made up of a noun (*one thing*) and a relative clause (*I'd really miss*). The noun phrase can go before or after *be*. Here it is before the verb *be*. It is the subject.
- Next, show the noun phrase after *be*. Ss rearrange themselves so that they are holding up this sentence:

  S4: *hanging out with my friends*    S3: *is*
  S1: *one thing*    S2: *I'd really miss*

- Point out that the noun phrase is now the object. It is after the verb *be*.
- Finally, explain that all three example sentences have the same meaning. Note: If needed, ask Ss to show the class the three sentences again.
- Play the audio program. Point out that the words in parentheses can be omitted. Remind Ss to use *who* with people.

### A

- Ask Ss to read the list of phrases. Use the picture to model the first sentence.
- Ss work individually. Tell Ss to write their sentences on a separate piece of paper. Ss will use these sentences again in part B of Exercise 4.
- Go around the class and give help as needed. Ask Ss to write their answers on the board.

**Possible answers**

1. Trying new foods
2. learning about a different culture.
3. My grandmother's cooking
4. my family and my friends.
5. feeling like an outsider.
6. Getting sick
7. speaking a foreign language.
8. My friends
9. not understanding people.
10. Being away from home and getting lost in a new city

### B

- Explain the task. Ss complete three sentences in part A with their own information. Encourage Ss to use their own ideas and feelings.

### C *Group work*

- Explain the task. Ss work individually to change the order of each sentence in part A. Read the example answer for number 1.
- Ss work in groups. They take turns reading their sentences. After about five minutes, ask groups to share the sentences that most of them agreed with.

## 4 PRONUNCIATION

**Learning Objective:** sound more natural when using word stress in sentences

▶ **A [CD 1, Track 38]**

- Write a sentence like this on the board:

  Uruguay is a country that I'd like to live in.

- Explain that we stress the key words in a sentence.
- Elicit the three key words in the sentence. Underline them. (Answer: *Uruguay, country, live*) Read the sentence aloud, stressing those words. Ss repeat.
- Play the audio program. Ss listen and notice which words are stressed.

- Play the audio program again. Ss listen and repeat.
- **Option:** Ss tap their desk with a pencil each time they hear a stressed word.

### B *Pair work*

- Explain the task. Ss mark the key words in the sentences they wrote in part A of Exercise 3.
- Then pairs take turns reading their sentences aloud. Remind Ss to pay attention to the stress on key words. Go around the class and help with stress as needed.

! To practice word stress in a fun and useful way, use **Walking Stress** – download it from the website.

## 3 GRAMMAR FOCUS

**Noun phrases containing relative clauses**

| | |
|---|---|
| **Something (that) I'd be worried about** is the local food. | The local food **is something (that) I'd be worried about.** |
| **One thing (that) I'd really miss** is hanging out with my friends. | Hanging out with my friends is **one thing (that) I'd really miss.** |
| **The people (who/that) I'd miss the most** are my parents. | My parents are **the people (who/that) I'd miss the most.** |

GRAMMAR PLUS *see page 136*

**A** Complete the sentences about living in a foreign country. Use the phrases below. Then compare with a partner.

| | | | |
|---|---|---|---|
| my friends | trying new foods | being away from home | getting lost in a new city |
| my family | feeling like an outsider | my grandmother's cooking | not understanding people |
| getting sick | making new friends | speaking a foreign language | learning about a different culture |

1. . . . is something I'd be very enthusiastic about.
2. The thing I'd probably be most excited about is . . .
3. . . . is something I'd really miss.
4. Two things I'd be homesick for are . . .
5. Something I'd get depressed about is . . .
6. . . . is one thing that I might be embarrassed about.
7. The thing I'd feel most uncomfortable about would be . . .
8. . . . are the people who I'd miss the most.
9. One thing I'd be insecure about is . . .
10. . . . are two things I'd be anxious about.

**B** Now complete three sentences in part A with your own information.

> 1. *Going to different festivals is something I'd be very enthusiastic about.*

**C** GROUP WORK Rewrite your sentences from part B in another way. Then compare. Do others feel the same way?

> 1. *I'd be very enthusiastic about going to different festivals.*

## 4 PRONUNCIATION Word stress in sentences

**A** Listen and practice. Notice that the important words in a sentence have more stress.

Uruguay is a country that I'd like to live in.

Speaking a foreign language is something I'd be anxious about.

Trying new foods is something I'd be curious about.

**B** PAIR WORK Mark the stress in the sentences you wrote in Exercise 3, part A. Then practice the sentences. Pay attention to word stress.

## 5 DISCUSSION  Moving to a foreign country

**GROUP WORK**  Read the questions. Think of two more questions to add to the list. Then take turns asking and answering the questions in groups.

What country would you like to live in? Why?

What country wouldn't you like to live in? Why?

Who is the person you would most like to go abroad with?

What is something you would never travel without?

Who is the person you would email first after arriving somewhere new?

What would be your two greatest concerns about living abroad?

What is the thing you would enjoy the most about living abroad?

**A:** What country would you like to live in?

**B:** The country I'd most like to live in is Zimbabwe.

**C:** Why is that?

**B:** Well, I've always wanted to work with wild animals. Besides, . . .

## 6 SNAPSHOT

# ETIQUETTE TIPS FOR INTERNATIONAL TRAVELERS

**CANADA:** Always bring a small gift for the host when invited to a meal at a Canadian home.

**RUSSIA:** Do not turn down offers of food or drink.

**JAPAN:** Take off your shoes before entering a house.

**FRANCE:** When eating, don't rest your elbows on the table.

**CHINA:** Never point your chopsticks at another person.

**BRAZIL:** You can arrive between 15 to 30 minutes late for a party at a Brazilian friend´s home.

**THAILAND:** Never touch a person's head.

**ETHIOPIA:** Don't eat anything with your left hand.

*Does your culture follow any of these customs?*

*Do any of these customs seem unusual to you? Explain.*

*What other interesting customs do you know?*

## 5 DISCUSSION

**Learning Objective:** discuss living in a foreign country using noun phrases containing relative clauses

### Group work

- Explain the task. Ask different Ss to read each question aloud. Ask three Ss to model the conversation.
- **Option:** Use the questions to practice pronunciation, intonation, and word stress. Read each question. Ss listen and repeat.
- Ss work individually to write two more questions. Go around the class and give help as needed.
- Ss work in small groups.

---

**TIP**
To form groups, go around the class and assign each S an adjective (e.g., *confident, curious, enthusiastic*, etc.). Ask all the "confident" Ss to form a group together, all the "curious" Ss together, etc.

---

- Ss take turns asking and answering the questions. Remind Ss that one-word answers are not allowed!

**TIP**
To increase student talking time, introduce challenging rules (e.g., answers must have more than three words; each S must ask three follow-up questions) and rewards (e.g., Ss earn one point for each question they ask).

---

- Set a time limit of about ten minutes. Go around the class and listen in discreetly. Make note of problems, especially with noun phrases and relative clauses.
- When time is up, write some of the problems on the board. Elicit Ss' suggestions on how to correct them.

Try the discussion activity in a different way, using the **Onion Ring** technique – download it from the website.

### End of Cycle 1

See the Supplementary Resources chart at the beginning of this unit for additional teaching materials and student activities related to this Cycle.

---

## Cycle 2, Exercises 6–13

## 6 SNAPSHOT

**Learning Objective:** discuss customs from various countries

- Books closed. To introduce the topic of etiquette tips for international travelers, brainstorm with the class. Write Ss' ideas on the board:
  - U.S.: Say "Excuse me" if you bump into or touch someone accidentally.
  - Indonesia: Wear proper clothes when visiting temples.
- Write this chart on the board. Ask Ss to guess the answers and match the country and custom:

| Custom | Country |
|---|---|
| Arrive a little late for a meal. | Thailand |
| Never touch anyone on the head. | Brazil |
| Bring a small gift for the host. | Canada |

- Books open. Ss read the information in the Snapshot and check their answers. Encourage Ss to use a dictionary to check unfamiliar words.
- Read the questions.
- Ss discuss the questions in small groups. (Try to put Ss from different countries or regions together in each group.)
- **Option:** Play **Earthlings have some strange customs!** Ss imagine they are from another planet and have just landed on Earth. Pairs describe five strange customs on Earth (e.g., *Human females around 14 years old – called "girls" – start to paint their lips red or pink. The males don't do this at any age.*). Ss share their observations.

# 7 CONVERSATION

**Learning Objective:** use *if* and *when* clauses in a conversation about expectations

▶ **A** *[CD 1, Track 39]*

- Tell Ss to cover the text and look only at the picture.
- Ss discuss the picture in pairs and create a story about it. Tell Ss there is no correct answer.
- Set the scene. Klaus is going to dinner at someone's house and is asking his friend Olivia for advice about visiting someone's home. Tell Ss to listen to find out who invited Klaus to dinner.
- Play the opening line of the audio program. Elicit the answer. (Answer: his boss)
- Write these statements on the board:

  *Klaus asks Olivia:*
  - *what kind of gift he should take to his boss*
  - *what time he should arrive*
  - *whether it's all right to bring the kids along*

- Tell Ss to listen to find out which question Klaus does *not* ask Olivia.

- Play the rest of the audio program. Elicit Ss' answers. (Answer: Klaus doesn't ask the second question.)
- Play the audio program again. Ss listen and read. Elicit the customs that Olivia mentions. (Answers: It's the custom to bring a small gift. If you want to bring your kids, you're expected to ask if it's OK.)
- Ss practice the conversation in pairs.

! For a new way to practice this Conversation, try the **Disappearing Dialog** – download it from the website.

▶ **B** *[CD 1, Track 40]*

- Explain the task. Read the focus questions aloud. Use them to elicit Ss' responses around the class. (Answers: You are expected to arrive on time. You can bring flowers, but not red roses, chrysanthemums, carnations, or lilies.)

### Audio script

See page T-171.

# 8 GRAMMAR FOCUS

**Learning Objective:** use *if* and *when* clauses to describe expectations

▶ *[CD 1, Track 41]*

- Point out that there are several ways to describe expectations. Play the audio program for the Grammar Focus box. Ss listen, read, and repeat.
- Elicit or explain any new vocabulary.

> **Vocabulary**
> **expectations:** feelings or beliefs about the way something should be or how someone should behave
> **be supposed to:** should
> **host:** the person giving a party or dinner
> **be acceptable:** considered to be socially correct

- Explain that statements with *when* and *if* clauses can be used to describe a custom or something that is expected or normally done.
- Write these sentences on the board:

  I'm going to Brazil this summer. _____ I go to Brazil, I'll visit my family there.
  I might go to Brazil this summer. _____ I go to Brazil, I'll visit my family there.

- Elicit which set of sentences should use *when* and which should use *if*. (Answer: The first set should use *when*. The second should use *if*).
- Explain that we use *when* for things that are sure to happen and *if* for things that will possibly happen.

**A**

- Explain the task. Ss match up information about some customs in the United States and Canada. Ask a S to model the first one.
- Ss complete the task individually. Then Ss compare answers in pairs. Go around the class and give help as needed. Ask early finishers to write their answers on the board.

### Answers

| | | | | | |
|---|---|---|---|---|---|
| 1. e | 2. a | 3. f | 4. b | 5. c | 6. d |

**B Group work**

- Read the question aloud.
- Ss work in groups to discuss the customs in part A.

**C**

- Explain the task. Ask one or more Ss to complete the first sentence.
- Ss work individually. Encourage Ss to be creative.

🎲 To practice sentences with *if* and *when*, Ss play **Sculptures** – download it from the website.

- Ss work in pairs. They take turns reading their sentences aloud.
- Ask Ss to share some of their sentences with the class.

## 7 CONVERSATION  Bring a small gift.

▶ **A** Listen and practice.

**Klaus:** My boss invited my wife and me to dinner at his house.

**Olivia:** Oh, how nice!

**Klaus:** Yes, but what do you do here when you're invited to someone's house?

**Olivia:** Well, here in the U.S., it's the custom to bring a small gift.

**Klaus:** Like what?

**Olivia:** Oh, maybe some flowers or chocolates.

**Klaus:** And is it all right to bring our kids along?

**Olivia:** Well, if you want to bring them, you're expected to ask if it's OK first.

▶ **B** Listen to the rest of the conversation. If you are invited to someone's house in Germany, when are you expected to arrive? What can you bring as a gift?

## 8 GRAMMAR FOCUS

▶
| Expectations | |
| --- | --- |
| When you visit someone, | it**'s the custom to** bring a small gift. |
| | you **aren't supposed to** arrive early. |
| If you want to bring others, | you**'re expected to** ask if it's OK first. |
| | you**'re supposed to** check with the host. |
| | it**'s not acceptable to** bring them without asking. |

GRAMMAR PLUS *see page 136*

**A** Match information in columns A and B to make sentences about customs in the United States and Canada. Then compare with a partner.

**A**
1. If someone sends you a gift, _____
2. If you plan to visit someone at home, _____
3. When you go out with friends for dinner, _____
4. If the service in a restaurant is acceptable, _____
5. When you meet someone for the first time, _____
6. When you receive an invitation, _____

**B**
a. you're supposed to call first.
b. it's the custom to leave a tip.
c. you aren't supposed to kiss him or her.
d. you're expected to respond to it quickly.
e. you're expected to thank the person.
f. it's acceptable to share the expenses.

**B** GROUP WORK  How are the customs in part A different in your country?

**C** Complete these sentences with information about your country or a country you know well. Then compare with a partner.

1. In . . . , if people invite you to their home, . . .
2. When you go out on a date, . . .
3. If a friend is in the hospital, . . .
4. When you receive a gift, . . .
5. If you're staying at someone's home, . . .
6. When someone has a baby, . . .

## 9 LISTENING Different cultures

▶ **A** Listen to people describe customs they observed abroad. Complete the chart.

|  | Where was the person? | What was the custom? | How did the person react? |
|---|---|---|---|
| **1.** Carla |  |  |  |
| **2.** Nate |  |  |  |
| **3.** Shauna |  |  |  |

**B** PAIR WORK Which custom would you have the most trouble adapting to? Why?

## 10 SPEAKING Local customs

**A** PAIR WORK What should a visitor to your country know about local customs? Make a list. Include these points.

greeting and addressing someone
eating or drinking in public
taking photographs
giving gifts

dressing appropriately
visiting someone's home
using public transportation
tipping

> When you ride in a cab, you're supposed to tip the driver.

**B** GROUP WORK Compare your lists with another pair. Then share experiences in which you (or someone you know) *didn't* follow the appropriate cultural behavior. What happened?

**A:** Once, when traveling abroad, I took a cab, and I didn't give the driver a tip.

**B:** What happened?

**A:** Well, he looked kind of angry. Then my friend gave the guy a tip, and I realized my mistake. It was a little embarrassing. . . .

## 11 WRITING A tourist pamphlet

**A** GROUP WORK Choose five points from the list you made in Exercise 10. Use them to write and design a pamphlet for tourists visiting your country or city.

### WE HOPE YOU ENJOY YOUR STAY.

When you visit Italy, there are some important things you should know. For example, you can't buy a bus ticket on the bus in most big cities. Actually, you are supposed to . . .

**B** CLASS ACTIVITY Present your pamphlets. Which of the points were the most useful? What other information would a tourist need to know?

## 12 INTERCHANGE 5 Cultural dos and taboos

Compare customs in different countries. Go to Interchange 5 on page 118.

# 9 LISTENING

**Learning Objective:** listen for and identify key information in descriptions of living abroad discussed using *if* and *when* clauses

**▶ A [CD 1, Track 42]**

- Write this famous saying on the board:

  *When in Rome, do as the Romans do.*

- Ask: "What do you think this means? Should a person living abroad follow *all* the customs of the country? Would you celebrate different holidays? Wear different clothes?" Elicit Ss' ideas.

- Explain the task. Ask Ss to read the questions and the names in the chart.

- Play the audio program once or twice. Ss listen and complete the chart.

**Audio script**

See page T-171.

- Ss compare answers in groups of three.

**Answers**

1. Carla: Saudi Arabia; women cover their whole body and head; she felt uncomfortable but then started to like it
2. Nate: Spain; people eat late in the evening; he found it difficult for work the next day
3. Shauna: South Korea; people slurp soup and make noise; it bothered her but she got used to it

**B Pair work**

- Ss discuss their reactions to the Listening in pairs. How would they feel about each of those customs?

# 10 SPEAKING

**Learning Objective:** discuss local customs using *if* and *when* clauses

## A Pair work

- Explain the task. Read the focus question aloud. Then read the points. Elicit other situations Ss could give advice on. Write Ss' suggestions on the board.

- Show how to set up a "do's and don'ts" list on the board:

  <u>Some do's and don'ts when visiting my country</u>
  <u>Do's</u>
  When you visit . . . , you're supposed to . . .
  If you are invited to someone's home, it's the custom to . . .
  You're also expected to . . . when you meet someone for the first time.

<u>Don'ts</u>
If you *go* to a movie or play, it's not acceptable to . . .
You aren't expected to . . . when someone invites you out.
People aren't supposed to . . . when driving.

- Ss work in pairs. Try to match up Ss from the same country or from similar ethnic or cultural areas. Set a time limit of about ten minutes. Go around the class and give help as needed.

## B Group work

- Explain the task. Read the example with a S. Explain or elicit that in some countries, it's customary to tip the taxi driver.

- Tell pairs to select three customs from their lists and present them to the rest of the class. Note: Tell Ss to keep their lists to use in Exercise 11.

# 11 WRITING

**Learning Objective:** write a tourist guide about local customs using *if* and *when* clauses

## A Group work

- Explain the task. Ask a S to read the model paragraph.

- Remind Ss to include at least five points. Encourage Ss to write two or three paragraphs.

## B Class activity

- Explain the task. Read the focus question aloud.

- Ss present their pamphlets to the class. Ss discuss anything they feel is missing from each other's pamphlets.

- Ss revise their pamphlets, incorporating the suggestions (as they wish) and their own ideas. Then they present them to the class.

# 12 INTERCHANGE 5

See page T-118 for teaching notes.

## 13 READING

**Learning Objective:** scan and identify main ideas and details in a blog about cultural differences

### A

- Books closed. Ask: "Do you or your friends post anything on social media when you travel? What kinds of information do people post?" Elicit Ss' responses around the class.
- Books open. Read the question. Ask Ss to scan the text quickly to determine the kinds of culture shock the writer experienced.
- Elicit answers. (Answers: She finds that the streets are much quieter at night / there is less night life, that American students are quieter and ask fewer questions in class, and that certain people in the U.S. use a Spanish-style greeting, though it isn't common.)
- *Option:* Elicit the similarities and differences between a personal journal (or diary) and an online post. Ask: "Why do some people like to write about their experiences online?"
- *Option:* Ask if anyone writes a blog or keeps a journal. If someone says yes, let the class ask that S questions (e.g., *How often do you write in it or post entries? How long have you had it? What kinds of things do you write about?*). If many Ss keep blogs or journals, this can be done in small groups.
- *Option:* If your class has students from Spain, ask them to predict what differences the Spanish student found between Seville and Seattle. Write Ss' guesses on the board.
- Elicit or explain any new vocabulary.

> **Vocabulary**
> **eye-opener:** something that surprises you and teaches you new facts about life, people, etc.
> **air-kissing:** an action similar to kissing someone without touching them with your lips
> **greeting:** a polite word or sign of welcome

### B

- Ss read the blog individually. Ask them to notice where vocabulary they just learned occurs.
- Explain the task. Point out that the three titles express the main ideas of the paragraphs. Explain that *meeting and greeting* refers to what you do when you meet people, for the first time or not.
- Ss reread the post individually. Then Ss match the entries to the titles.
- Go over answers with the class.

> **Answers**
> January 15: Where's the party?
> January 22: Class contrasts
> February 8: Meeting and greeting

### C

- Explain the task. Ask Ss to read the statements. Explain that Ss need to find the information in the post and check if the statements are true or false.
- Ss complete the exercise individually. Ss can cross out the incorrect information and write the correct information next to each statement or copy the correct sentences in their notebooks.
- Ask Ss to compare answers in pairs.
- Go over answers by asking Ss the questions.

> **Answers**
> 1. F; The writer became nervous because there were so few people in the streets.
> 2. T
> 3. F; Touching cheeks is the usual greeting among friends in Spain.
> 4. F; The writer will continue to greet people with handshakes and hugs.

### D *Pair work*

- Read the questions. Ss work in pairs. (Mix nationalities if possible.) First tell Ss to talk about the online post's situations in their own cities (greeting people, nightlife, and classroom customs).
- Ss compare their cities to Seville and Seattle. Encourage Ss to discuss other differences as well. Ss can work orally or can take notes about differences.
- *Option:* Ss talk about differences between their cities and other cities they know about, not just Seville and Seattle.
- Call on Ss to tell the whole class some of the interesting or surprising things they learned from their partner.
- *Option:* Ss role-play. S1 interviews the person who wrote the journal (played by S2) about his or her experiences living abroad.

> To recycle information Ss have learned from the Reading and the unit, play **True or False?** – download it from the website.

## End of Cycle 2

See the Supplementary Resources chart at the beginning of this unit for additional teaching materials and student activities related to this Cycle.

# 13 READING

**A** Scan the blog. What kinds of culture shock did the writer experience?

## CULTURE SHOCK

I'm an exchange student from Spain navigating life in the United States. *Lucia M.*

PROFILE | PHOTOS | BLOG | COMMUNITY

### JANUARY 15 _____

My hometown of Seville, Spain is a city with active, passionate people and a lively nightlife, so coming to Seattle, in the United States, has been quite an eye-opener. Americans think of Seattle as an exciting city, but the first time I went out with friends on a Saturday night, there was hardly anybody out in the streets. I actually thought something was wrong! Then my friend explained that most of their social life takes place indoors. In Seville, people fill the streets year-round, and Saturday nights are like a big celebration.

### JANUARY 22 _____

After a couple of weeks of classes, I've begun to notice some differences between Spanish students and American students. In Spain, students talk a lot during class, and it's not always related to the lesson. On the other hand, when Spanish students are enthusiastic about a lesson, they often ask unusual questions, and it's common to stay after class to talk to the teacher. American students are expected to talk less and listen more, and many of them take detailed notes. Most of them leave the room as soon as the class ends, though, and are already focused on the next lesson.

### FEBRUARY 8 _____

Before I came to the United States, a friend who had studied here told me that American friends don't greet each other like we do in Spain, where we touch cheeks and make kissing sounds. Americans often hug each other, but kissing is not common, and I've gotten used to that. So imagine my surprise when I was introduced to a new girl, and she immediately gave me the Spanish-style double kiss. When I asked my friend about this later, she explained that the girl was from a family of actors, and that "air-kissing" was a usual greeting for artistic people. My friend also said that some outgoing people greet their friends or family this way, but that it would make other people feel uncomfortable. I think I'll stick to handshakes and hugs while I'm here!

**B** Read the blog. Then add the correct title to each entry.

Meeting and greeting    Where's the party?    Class contrasts

**C** Check (✓) True or False for each statement. Then correct the false statements.

|  | True | False |  |
|---|---|---|---|
| 1. The writer was nervous because the Seattle streets were crowded at night. | ☐ | ☐ | |
| 2. Spanish students often stay after class to ask questions. | ☐ | ☐ | |
| 3. Hugging is a usual greeting among friends in Spain. | ☐ | ☐ | |
| 4. The writer plans to change the way she greets American friends. | ☐ | ☐ | |

**D** PAIR WORK How do things in your city compare with Seville? with Seattle?

# Unit 6 Supplementary Resources Overview

| | After the following SB exercises | You can use these materials in class | Your students can use these materials outside the classroom |
|---|---|---|---|
| **CYCLE 1** | 1  Snapshot | | |
| | 2  Perspectives | **TSS** Unit 6 Extra Worksheet | |
| | 3  Grammar Focus | | **SB** Unit 6 Grammar plus, Focus 1<br>**SS** Unit 6 Grammar 1<br>**GAME** Sentence Stacker (Describing problems) |
| | 4  Listening | | |
| | 5  Role Play | | **WB** Unit 6 exercises 1–2 |
| **CYCLE 2** | 6  Conversation | | **SS** Unit 6 Speaking 1–2 |
| | 7  Grammar Focus | **TSS** Unit 6 Grammar Worksheet<br>**TSS** Unit 6 Listening Worksheet | **SB** Unit 6 Grammar plus, Focus 2<br>**SS** Unit 6 Grammar 2<br>**GAME** Word Keys (Describing problems)<br>**GAME** Speak or Swim (Describing problems)<br>**GAME** Name the Picture (Describing problems) |
| | 8  Word Power | **TSS** Unit 6 Vocabulary Worksheet | **SS** Unit 6 Vocabulary 1–2 |
| | 9  Pronunciation | | |
| | 10  Listening | | |
| | 11  Writing | **TSS** Unit 6 Writing Worksheet | |
| | 12  Interchange 6 | | |
| | 13  Reading | **TSS** Unit 6 Project Worksheet<br>**VID** Unit 6<br>**VRB** Unit 6 | **SS** Unit 6 Reading 1–2<br>**SS** Unit 6 Listening 1–3<br>**SS** Unit 6 Video 1–3<br>**WB** Unit 6 exercises 3–7 |

| With or instead of the following SB section | You can also use these materials for assessment |
|---|---|
| **Units 5–6 Progress Check** | **ASSESSMENT PROGRAM** Units 5–6 Oral Quiz<br>**ASSESSMENT PROGRAM** Units 5–6 Written Quiz |

Key  **GAME:** Online Game    **SB:** Student's Book    **SS:** Online Self-study    **TSS:** Teacher Support Site
　　 **VID:** Video DVD    **VRB:** Video Resource Book    **WB:** Online Workbook/Workbook

# My Plan for Unit 6

Use the space below to customize a plan that fits your needs.

| With the following SB exercises | I am using these materials in class | My students are using these materials outside the classroom |
|---|---|---|
|  |  |  |
|  |  |  |
|  |  |  |
|  |  |  |
|  |  |  |
|  |  |  |
|  |  |  |
|  |  |  |
|  |  |  |
|  |  |  |
|  |  |  |
|  |  |  |
|  |  |  |
|  |  |  |

| With or instead of the following SB section | I am using these materials for assessment |
|---|---|
|  |  |
|  |  |
|  |  |

# That needs fixing.

▸ Describe problems and make complaints
▸ Discuss what needs fixing

## 1 SNAPSHOT

## Some common complaints

**Banking**
The credit card company bills you for something you didn't buy.

**Online shopping**
The store sends you an incorrect size.

**Internet providers**
The Internet connection is not reliable, and you hardly ever get the speed you pay for.

**Restaurants**
The server rushes you to leave as soon as you finish your meal.

**Vehicles**
Your new car consumes too much gas.

**Repair services**
Your TV breaks again, a week after it was repaired.

**Parking garage**
Someone damages your car.

*Have you ever had any of these problems? Which ones?*
*What would you do in each of these situations?*
*What other complaints have you had?*

## 2 PERSPECTIVES  That's not right!

▸ **A** Listen to people describe complaints. Check (✓) what you think each person should do.

**1.** "I got a new suitcase, but when I arrived home, I noticed the lining was torn."
☐ take it back to the store          ☐ ask the store to send you a new one

**2.** "My father sent me a coffee mug with my favorite team's logo, but when it arrived, it was chipped."
☐ tell your father about it          ☐ contact the seller yourself

**3.** "I lent my ski pants to a friend, but when he returned them, there was a big stain on them."
☐ clean them yourself          ☐ ask him to have them cleaned

**4.** "My boss borrowed my camera for a company event, and now the lens is scratched."
☐ talk to him or her about it          ☐ say nothing and repair it yourself

**5.** "I bought a new washing machine just a month ago, and it's leaking already."
☐ ask for a refund          ☐ send it back and get a new one

**B** Have you ever had similar complaints? What happened? What did you do?

# 6 That needs fixing.

**Cycle 1, Exercises 1–5**

In this unit, students practice describing problems, making complaints and discussing what needs fixing. By the end of Cycle 1, students will be able to describe problems using nouns and past participles as adjectives. By the end of Cycle 2, students will be able to discuss what needs fixing using *need* with passive infinitives and gerunds, and *keep* with gerunds.

## 1 SNAPSHOT

**Learning Objective:** discuss common complaints

- To introduce the topic of complaints, write this well-known joke on the board:

  *Customer: Waiter, waiter! There's a fly in my soup! Waiter: Well, don't shout about it, or the other customers will want one, too.*

- Elicit the meaning of *complaint*. (Answer: a criticism about a problem) Ask Ss to brainstorm typical complaints about restaurants (e.g., *The waiter was rude. The food was cold*.).

- **Option:** Label each of seven sheets of paper with a situation from the Snapshot. Put the sheets around the classroom walls. Ss write typical complaints on each sheet.

- Tell Ss to skim through the list of situations and complaints in the Snapshot.

- Elicit or explain any new vocabulary.

  **Vocabulary**
  **bill:** charge; ask for payment
  **reliable:** able to be trusted or believed
  **hardly ever:** almost never
  **rush:** make someone or something hurry or move quickly somewhere
  **consume:** to use something such as a product, energy, or fuel

- Read the questions. Ss discuss the questions in pairs or small groups.

- **Option:** Have a class discussion about services and complaints in the Ss' country(ies). Recycle language from Unit 5 by asking questions such as: "Is it the custom to complain in writing? Is it acceptable to ask to see the manager?" etc.

## 2 PERSPECTIVES

**Learning Objective:** give opinions about complaints that use past participles as adjectives in context

### ▶ A *[CD 1, Track 43]*

- Books closed. Set the scene. People are describing complaints about some items they bought, received, or lent.

- Tell Ss to listen first for what *item* each of the five people is talking about. Ask Ss to write down the items.

- Play the audio program. Elicit the answers. (Answers: 1. a suitcase 2. a coffee mug 3. ski pants 4. camera 5. washing machine)

- Books open. Play the audio program again. Ss listen and read or repeat.

- Elicit or explain any new vocabulary.

  **Vocabulary**
  **lining:** the inside material in clothing or other items
  **torn:** having a hole or a rip in fabric
  **chipped:** with a small piece broken off
  **stain:** a mark from something
  **scratched:** having small cuts from something rough or sharp
  **leak:** escape as a liquid or gas from a hole or crack

**TIP**
To help Ss remember the new vocabulary, ask Ss to draw each item and problem in their vocabulary notebook.

- Model the task. Read the first complaint. Ask a S to read the two possible solutions.

- Ask Ss what advice they would give. Make sure Ss understand that both answers are possible. Ss check (✓) the option they prefer.

- Find out which options are most popular. Ss put up their hands if they checked the option.

### B

- Explain the task.

- In pairs or small groups, Ss discuss similar complaints of their own. Ss share what their complaint was, what they did to resolve it, and what the result was.

- Ss share their responses with the class.

# 3 GRAMMAR FOCUS

**Learning Objective:** describe problems with past participles as adjectives and with nouns

## ▶ [CD 1, Track 44]

- Explain that the two sets of sentences have more or less the same meaning (e.g., *We can say that something is torn or has a tear in it.*).

- Focus Ss' attention on the sentences on the left of the Grammar Focus box. Elicit the rule:
  subject + *be* + past participle as adjective
  Note: *is leaking* is the present continuous form.

- Then do the same with the right column:
  subject + *have* + noun OR *there is/there are* + noun

- Play the audio program to present the sentences in the Grammar Focus box. Ss listen and read or repeat.

- **Option:** Write this chart on the board. Ask Ss to complete the chart with the verbs *stain*, *scratch*, and *leak*. Tell Ss to copy the chart into their notebooks. As Ss learn new words in part B, add them to the chart:

| Verb | Participle/Adjective | Noun |
|------|---------------------|------|
| tear | torn | a tear |
| damage | damaged | some damage |
| chip | chipped | a chip |

### A

- Explain the task. Model the first item with *This one is cracked./This one has a crack in it.*

- Ss work individually to complete each sentence two ways. Go around the class and give help as needed.

- Ss go over their answers in pairs or small groups.

- Draw two columns on the board. Label them *Past participles* and *Nouns*. Ask Ss to write examples for each item on the board.

### Answers

1. Could we have another water pitcher? This one is **cracked**. This one **has a crack** (**in it**).
2. The valet was very careless. My car **is dented**. My car **has a dent** (**in it**).
3. The toilet is dirty. And the sink **is leaking**. And the sink **has a leak**.
4. This tablecloth isn't very clean. It **is stained**. It **has a stain** (**on it**).
5. Would you bring me another glass? This glass **is chipped**. This glass **has a chip** (**in it**).
6. The table looks pretty dirty. The wood **is scratched**, too. The wood **has** (**a lot of**) **scratches**, too.
7. The server needs a new shirt. The one he's wearing **is torn.** The one he's wearing **has a tear** (**in it**).
8. The walls really need paint. And the ceiling **is damaged**. And the ceiling **has some damage**.

## B Pair work

- **Option:** Explain the words in the box. Show how the words are collocated, using a chart like this on the board:

|  | dent | crack | scratch | stain | tear | leak | break |
|--|------|-------|---------|-------|------|------|-------|
| 1. vase |  | ✓ |  |  |  |  | ✓ |
| 2. ceiling |  | ✓ |  |  |  | ✓ |  |
| 3. chair |  |  |  | ✓ | ✓ |  |  |
| 4. car | ✓ |  | ✓ |  |  |  |  |

- Explain the task. Read the words in the box. Focus Ss' attention on the pictures.

- Ask two Ss to model the conversation.

- Ss work in pairs and take turns making two different sentences about each picture. Ask Ss to write down their answers. Go around the class and give help as needed.

- Ask a few Ss to read their answers for the class. Ask if anyone has a different answer (e.g., *The vase is cracked.*).

### Possible answers

1. The vase is broken. It has lots of cracks.
2. There is a leak in the ceiling. / The ceiling is leaking.
3. The chair is torn and stained.
4. The car is dented. The paint is scratched.

## C Group work

- Explain the task. Read the example sentence. Ss find problems in the classroom.

- Ss work individually. Set a time limit of about ten minutes. Ss move around the room, if necessary.

- Then in groups of three, Ss compare notes. They take turns describing the problems they found. Ask which group found the most problems.

⚃ To practice the new language, play **Picture It!** – download it from the website.

# 3 GRAMMAR FOCUS

| With past participles as adjectives | With nouns |
|---|---|
| The suitcase lining is **torn**. | It has **a tear** in it./There's **a hole** in it. |
| The car is **damaged**. | There is **some damage** on the bumper. |
| The coffee mug is **chipped**. | There is **a chip** in it. |
| My pants are **stained**. | They have **a stain** on them. |
| The camera lens is **scratched**. | There are **a few scratches** on it. |
| The washing machine **is leaking**.* | It has **a leak**. |

*Exception: is leaking *is a present continuous form.*

GRAMMAR PLUS *see page 137*

**A** Read the comments from customers in a restaurant. Write sentences in two different ways using forms of the word in parentheses. Then compare with a partner.

1. Could we have another water pitcher? This one . . . (crack)
2. That valet was so careless. My car . . . (dent)
3. The toilet is dirty. And the sink . . . (leak)
4. This tablecloth isn't very clean. It . . . (stain)
5. Would you bring me another glass? This glass . . . (chip)
6. The table looks pretty dirty. The wood . . . , too. (scratch)
7. The server needs a new shirt. The one he's wearing . . . (tear)
8. The walls really need paint. And the ceiling . . . (damage)

> 1. This one is cracked.
>    It has a crack.

**B PAIR WORK** Describe two problems with each thing below. Use forms of the words in the box. You may use the same word more than once.

| break | crack | damage | dent | leak | scratch | stain | tear |
|---|---|---|---|---|---|---|---|

**A:** The vase is broken.
**B:** Yes. And it has a crack, too.

**C GROUP WORK** Look around your classroom. How many problems can you describe?

"The floor is scratched, and the window is cracked. The desks are . . ."

## 4 LISTENING I'd like a refund.

**A** Listen to three customers return items they purchased. Complete the chart.

|  | Did the store give a refund? | Why or why not? |
|---|---|---|
| **1.** Evie |  |  |
| **2.** Darren |  |  |
| **3.** Gisela |  |  |

**B** GROUP WORK How is your culture similar or different in terms of refunds and customer service?

## 5 ROLE PLAY How can I help you?

*Student A*: You are returning an item to a store. Decide what the item is and explain why you are returning it.

*Student B*: You are a salesperson. A customer is returning an item to the store. Ask these questions:

What exactly is the problem?    When did you buy it?
Can you show it to me?    Do you have the receipt?
Was it like this when you bought it?    Would you like a refund or a store credit?

Change roles and try the role play again.

## 6 CONVERSATION It needs to be adjusted.

**A** Listen and practice.

**MR. LEROY**  Hello?

**HEATHER**  Hello, Mr. Leroy. This is Heather Forman.

**MR. LEROY**  Uh, Ms. Forman . . .

**HEATHER**  In Apartment 12C.

**MR. LEROY**  Oh, yes. What can I do for you? Does your refrigerator need fixing again?

**HEATHER**  No, it's the oven this time.

**MR. LEROY**  Oh. So, what's wrong with it?

**HEATHER**  Well, I think the temperature control needs to be adjusted. The oven keeps burning everything I try to cook.

**MR. LEROY**  Really? OK, I'll have someone look at it right away.

**HEATHER**  Thanks a lot, Mr. Leroy.

**MR. LEROY**  Uh, by the way, Ms. Forman, are you sure it's the oven and not your cooking?

**B** Listen to another tenant's call with Mr. Leroy. What's the tenant's problem?

# 4 LISTENING

**Learning Objective:** listen for main ideas and details in complaints

▶ **A** *[CD 1, Track 45]*

- Books closed. Ask: "Have you ever returned anything to a store? What happened? Did you get a refund or an exchange?" Encourage discussion.
- Books open. Explain the task.
- Play the audio program. Ss listen to find out what each person is returning and what the problem is. They complete the first two columns of the chart.
- Play the audio program again. Ss listen to find out if the store will exchange the item. Ss complete the chart.

## Audio script

See page T-171.

- Elicit answers.

## Answers

1. Evie: yes; her dress ripped and she had a receipt
2. Darren: no; he didn't have a receipt and the coffeemaker was 4 years old
3. Gisela: no; she was at the wrong store

## B *Group work*

- Read the question. If possible, form groups with Ss from different nationalities. Ss discuss how their culture is similar or different according to the information they heard in the Listening.

# 5 ROLE PLAY

**Learning Objective:** make a complaint using past participles as adjectives

- Focus Ss' attention on the title and explain that "How can I help you?" is usually what the salesperson says when a customer enters a store.
- Assign A/B roles. Explain the task. Student A is the customer who is returning something to the store. Student B is the salesperson.
- Student As work in pairs. Tell them to brainstorm some items they could return and the problems each item might have (e.g., *a pair of jeans - too big/ stained/torn*).
- Student Bs work in pairs. They read the questions a salesperson might ask. Ss add questions to the list.

- Divide the class into A/B pairs. Set a time limit of three or four minutes. Tell Student Bs to begin. Encourage Ss to use humor and have fun!
- Ss change roles and try the role play again.

!  To carry out the Role Play in a new way, try **Time Out!** – download it from the website.

## End of Cycle 1

See the Supplementary Resources chart at the beginning of this unit for additional teaching materials and student activities related to this Cycle.

## Cycle 2, Exercises 6–13

# 6 CONVERSATION

**Learning Objective:** use *keep* and *need* with gerunds and *need* with passive infinitives in a conversation about problems

▶ **A** *[CD 1, Track 46]*

- Focus Ss' attention on the picture. Ss describe the picture in pairs.
- Books closed. Set the scene. A tenant, Heather, is calling the building manager, Mr. Leroy. Write focus questions like these on the board:

  *Which household appliance isn't working?* (Answer: the oven)

  *What is the problem?* (Answer: Everything gets burned.)

  *What does Mr. Leroy think the real problem is?* (Answer: her cooking)

- Play the audio program. Ss listen and answer the focus questions.

- Books open. Play the audio program again. Ss listen and read.
- Then Ss practice the conversation in pairs.

▶ **B** *[CD 1, Track 47]*

- Explain the task. Read the focus question.
- Play the second part of the audio program. Ss listen. Elicit answers.

## Audio script

See page T-172.

## Answer

The lights keep going off and coming back on again.

# 7 GRAMMAR FOCUS

**Learning Objective:** use *keep* and *need* with gerunds and *need* with passive infinitives to describe problems

▶ *[CD 1, Track 48]*
## Keep + gerund

- Focus Ss' attention on the Conversation on page 38. Ask: "What's the problem with the oven?" Elicit the answer and write it on the board:

  *The oven keeps burning everything.*

- Explain that a gerund follows the verb *keep* when it refers to a repetitive action. Write sentence stems like these on the board:

  *My coffee mug keeps . . . (leaking)*
  *My jeans keep . . . (shrinking)*
  *My parents keep . . . (telling me to get married)*

- Ask Ss to complete the sentences with their own ideas.

## Need + gerund or passive infinitive

- Explain that a gerund also follows the verb *need* (e.g., *The oven needs fixing.*).

- Say that *need* with a passive infinitive (e.g., *to be fixed*) means the same thing. Write on the board:

  *The oven needs fixing. = The oven needs to be fixed.*

- Ask Ss to look around the classroom and make sentences using the two structures with *need* (e.g., *These chairs need fixing. This desk needs to be repaired.*).

- Play the audio program. Ss listen and read or repeat.

## A

- Explain the task. Focus Ss' attention on the picture. Ask different Ss to read the eight items and the example sentences.

- Elicit or explain any new vocabulary.

> ### Vocabulary
> **adjust:** to make a change so that something works better
> **replace:** to change for something new
> **fix:** to repair something

- Ss complete the task individually or in pairs.

- Draw two columns on the board: (1) *need* + gerund, (2) *need* + passive infinitive. Ask Ss to write one sentence in either column. Then go over answers.

> ### Answers
> 1. The cupboards **need to be cleaned/need cleaning.**
> 2. The fire alarm **needs to be adjusted/needs adjusting.**
> 3. The lights **need to be replaced/need replacing.**
> 4. The plants **need to be watered/need watering.**
> 5. The oven **needs to be fixed/needs fixing.**
> 6. The ceiling **needs to be painted/needs painting.**
> 7. The window **needs to be washed/needs washing.**
> 8. The light switch **needs to be changed/needs changing.**

## B *Pair work*

- Explain the task. Read the questions. Model the activity with improvements you would like to make.

- Ss discuss their plans in pairs.

# 8 WORD POWER

**Learning Objective:** describe things that can go wrong with electronic items

## A

- Explain the task. Read the verbs in bold. Model the task with the first sentence.

- Ss complete the task individually.

- Elicit or explain any new vocabulary.

> ### Vocabulary
> **flickering:** flashing on and off
> **crashing:** failing, used for computers
> **skipping:** moving from one place to another suddenly
> **freezing:** stopping completely
> **dying:** suddenly no longer working
> **dropping:** (describing phone calls) ending unexpectedly because of a technical problem
> **jamming:** not moving
> **sticking:** not moving

- Ss compare answers in pairs.

> ### Answers
> | | | |
> |---|---|---|
> | 1. flickering | 4. crashing | 7. freezing |
> | 2. skipping | 5. dropping | 8. sticking |
> | 3. dying | 6. jamming | |

## B *Group work*

- Explain the task. Read the example sentence.

- Ss work in small groups. Ss take turns describing their problems. Remind Ss not to say what the item is! The rest of the group guesses the item.

! For more practice with this vocabulary, try *Tic-Tac-Toe* – download it from the website. Add one more verb, e.g., *getting stuck.*

## 7 | GRAMMAR FOCUS

### ▶ Describing problems 2

| *Need* + gerund | *Need* + passive infinitive | *Keep* + gerund |
|---|---|---|
| The oven **needs adjusting**. | It **needs to be adjusted**. | Everything **keeps burning**. |
| The alarm **needs fixing**. | It **needs to be fixed**. | The alarm **keeps going off**. |

GRAMMAR PLUS *see page 137*

**A** What needs to be done in this apartment? Write sentences about these items using *need* with gerunds or passive infinitives.

1. the cupboards (clean)
2. the fire alarm (adjust)
3. the lights (replace)
4. the plants (water)

5. the oven (fix)
6. the ceiling (paint)
7. the window (wash)
8. the light switch (change)

1.   *The cupboards need cleaning.*
     *OR*
1.   *The cupboards need to be cleaned.*

**B** PAIR WORK  Think of five improvements you would like to make in your home. Which improvements will you most likely make? Which won't you make?

"First, the bedroom walls need painting. There are some small cracks. . . ."

## 8 | WORD POWER  Problems with electronics

**A** Circle the correct gerund to complete the sentences. Then compare with a partner.
1. My TV screen goes on and off all the time. It keeps **flickering / sticking**.
2. The music player app jumps to the next song every 20 seconds. It keeps **crashing / skipping**.
3. The battery in my new camera doesn't last long. It keeps **freezing / dying**.
4. Something is wrong with my computer! It keeps **crashing / jamming**.
5. I can't talk for long on my new phone. It keeps **dying / dropping** calls.
6. This printer isn't making all the copies I want. It keeps **jamming / flickering**.
7. My computer needs to be replaced. It keeps **dropping / freezing**.
8. The buttons on the remote control don't work well. They keep **skipping / sticking**.

**B** GROUP WORK  Describe a problem with an electronic item you own. Don't identify it! Others will try to guess the item.

"Some keys on my device keep sticking, and some are loose. . . ."

That needs fixing. **39**

## 9 PRONUNCIATION Contrastive stress

▶ **A** Listen and practice. Notice how a change in stress changes the meaning of each question and elicits a different response.

Is the bedroom window cracked?    (No, the kitchen window is cracked.)

Is the bedroom window cracked?    (No, the bedroom door is cracked.)

Is the bedroom window cracked?    (No, it's stuck.)

▶ **B** Listen to the questions. Check (✓) the correct response.

**1. a.** Are my jeans torn?
☐ No, they're stained.
☐ No, your shirt is torn.

**b.** Are my jeans torn?
☐ No, they're stained.
☐ No, your shirt is torn.

**2. a.** Is the computer screen flickering?
☐ No, it's freezing.
☐ No, the TV screen is flickering.

**b.** Is the computer screen flickering?
☐ No, it's freezing.
☐ No, the TV screen is flickering.

## 10 LISTENING A throwaway culture

▶ **A** Listen to a conversation between two friends. Answer the questions.

**1.** What is wrong with Hayley's phone? _____

**2.** What is Hayley's solution? _____

**3.** What is Aaron's solution? _____

**4.** Why doesn't Hayley like Aaron's solution? _____

▶ **B** Listen again. What is a "throwaway culture"?

**C** GROUP WORK Do you agree that electronics aren't made as well as they used to be? Give an example to support your opinion.

## 11 WRITING A critical online review

**A** Imagine that you ordered a product online, but when you received it, you were unhappy with it. Write a critical online review. Explain all of the problems with the product and why you think others shouldn't buy it.

> ### Best 4U promises a lot, delivers nothing.
>
> I ordered a phone from Best 4U's website for my son's birthday. First, it took six weeks for the company to send it, and it arrived two weeks after his birthday. Now, the battery keeps dying very fast when he's just watching a movie or . . . READ MORE

**B** GROUP WORK Read your classmates' reviews. What would you do if you read this critical online review and worked for the company that sold the product?

## 12 INTERCHANGE 6 Home makeover

Do you have an eye for detail? Student A, go to Interchange 6A on page 119; Student B, go to Interchange 6B on page 120.

# 9 PRONUNCIATION

**Learning Objective:** sound more natural when using contrastive stress

### A [CD 1, Track 49]

- Explain the concept of contrastive stress. If we want to call attention to a word or contrast it with something said earlier, we give it stronger stress. Give Ss these examples:

  A: Do you want *to borrow* a **pen**?
  B: No, I want *to borrow* a **pencil**.
  A: Do you want *to* **borrow** a pen?
  B: No, I want *to* **buy** a pen.

- Play the audio program to present the three sentences. Point out the different responses.

### B [CD 1, Track 50]

- Explain the task.
- Play the audio program. Ss listen and check (✓) the correct answer to the questions.

**Answers**

1. a. No, your shirt is torn.
   b. No, they're stained.
2. a. No, it's freezing.
   b. No, the TV screen is flickering.

- Ss work in pairs. S1 reads the questions in part B, stressing a different word each time. S2 chooses the correct response.

# 10 LISTENING

**Learning Objective:** listen for main ideas and details in descriptions of problems and repairs discussed using *keep* and *need* with gerunds and *need* with passive infinitives

### A [CD 1, Track 51]

- Books closed. Ask: "When something you own is not working properly, do you repair it, or just buy a new one?" "What do you think *a throwaway culture* means?"
- Books open. Explain the task. Ask Ss to read the questions.
- Next, ask Ss to listen and write the answers to the questions. Play the audio program once or twice. Pause after each speaker. Then elicit Ss' responses.

**Audio script**

See page T-172.

**Answers**

1. The phone keeps freezing and the camera isn't working.
2. to buy a new phone
3. to fix the damaged phone
4. She doesn't trust repair technicians.

### B [CD 1, Track 52]

- Ask Ss to talk about what a *throwaway culture* is, based on the Listening conversation. Write Ss' ideas on the board. Play the audio program. Elicit answers.

**Answer**

A "throwaway culture" is one where people throw products away instead of repairing them.

### C Group work

- Divide Ss into groups to discuss the question. One S takes notes and then shares with the class.

# 11 WRITING

**Learning Objective:** write a critical review of a product using *keep* and *need* with gerunds and *need* with passive infinitives

### A

- Read the scenario. Then read the example review.
- Ss choose a product and make notes individually.
- Ss use their notes to write a critical online review. Remind Ss to include: (a) the problem with the item (and possibly with the online store), and (b) why they think others shouldn't buy the item.
- Ss revise their reviews.

### B Group work

- Explain the task. Ss read reviews and discuss what they could do about the critical reviews.
- Ss pass around their reviews and read as many as possible in about five minutes.
- Ss talk about reviews they read. Each S should say what the classmate bought, what happened, and why others shouldn't buy it.
- Ask Ss to pretend that they work for the company that sold the product and say what they would do about the critical review.

# 12 INTERCHANGE 6

See page T-120 for teaching notes.

**Learning Objective:** skim and identify main ideas and specific information in an advice column about solutions to problems

- Books closed. Ask Ss if they know what ride-sharing services are. Explain that they are services that allow people to get a ride from someone who shares his or her car commercially.

## A

- Go over the task. Remind Ss that *skimming* means reading quickly just to find the answer, not carefully concentrating on each word.
- Ss skim individually for the answer. Ss should raise their hands to let you know they are finished.

### TIP
Seeing their classmates' hands raised will remind others to skim quickly instead of reading slowly.

- Elicit answers. (Answers: The reader did not know he/she would be charged for canceling a ride. The writer suggests that the company should make the rule more obvious and that riders should get a notification when they cancel.) Praise any correct answers.

## B

- Ss read the article individually. Ask Ss to underline vocabulary they are not sure about but not to look up words in the dictionary.
- **Option:** Play *I know, I think I know:*
  1. Write vocabulary from the box below on the board (without definitions). Tell each S to organize the vocabulary into three lists: *I know, I think I know,* and *I don't know.* Ss should also add words they underlined to the appropriate list.
  2. Ss work in small groups to share their words. If other Ss can explain unknown words, the S moves the words to the *I think I know* or *I know* columns. Ss change groups at least once and repeat.
- Elicit or explain any remaining new vocabulary.

### Vocabulary
**book:** to arrange to use or do something at a particular time in the future
**pick-up:** an act of collecting a person or thing from a location
**spot:** to see or notice something or someone
**state:** to officially say or write something
**highlight:** to emphasize something or make people notice something

- Explain the task.
- Ss complete the task individually.
- Elicit answers from different Ss.

### Answers
1. state that something will happen
2. act of stopping something
3. person who speaks for a company
4. rules of an agreement
5. act of giving information

- **Option:** Have Ss work in pairs to role-play a conversation between a reader and a journalist. The reader chooses a product or a service to talk about and the journalist comments on the issue presented by the reader.

## C

- Explain the task. Elicit that *Not given* means the information does not appear in the article.
- Ss complete the task individually.
- Then Ss work in pairs to compare answers. Ss should be able to show their partners where they found the answers.
- Go over answers with the class.

### Answers
| | | |
|---|---|---|
| 1. False | 3. True | 5. Not given |
| 2. True | 4. Not given | 6. True |

## D

- Read the questions aloud. Ss work in groups to discuss the questions. Encourage Ss to ask follow-up questions and give additional information.
- To recycle vocabulary from Units 5 and 6, play **Vocabulary Tennis** – download it from the website. Use categories (e.g., Adjectives) to describe broken things, and adjectives (e.g., anxious) to describe feelings.

## End of Cycle 2

See the Supplementary Resources chart at the beginning of this unit for additional teaching materials and student activities related to this Cycle and for assessment tools.

**A** Skim the advice column. What problem did the reader have? How does the writer suggest solving the problem?

Home | Local | World | Entertainment | Advice column     🔍

## Ask the Fixer!

*Our problem-solver Marci Davis addresses a common problem with ride-sharing services.*

*After a meeting downtown, I used my phone to book a ride with a private car service in order to get home. As soon as the pick-up was confirmed, a friend came out of the building, spotted me, and offered me a ride home. I immediately canceled the car. But the next day I got an alert on my phone – the car service had charged my credit card $10! I contacted the service, and they said it was for a late cancellation. I didn't realize they were going to charge me for that! Can you fix this? – Lawrence, New York City*

The fact is, Lawrence, that you need to read the terms of your ride-sharing app. It states clearly – somewhere in all those thousands of words – that when you cancel your ride less than ten minutes before your car is scheduled to arrive, you have to pay a fee. After all, the driver has already refused other possible passengers and is driving in your direction, so it's a loss when you cancel.

On the other hand, I do think something needs to be fixed. Do you know anyone who reads all the way through the terms of use for any app? There isn't enough time in the day! I talked to a representative at your ride-sharing company and made two suggestions. First, they need to highlight their cancellation policy at the beginning of the terms, where people will see it. Then, when you cancel a ride, a notification needs to be sent that tells you about the cancellation charge. That way, riders won't keep getting this annoying surprise. Let's hope the company pays attention.

*What do you think? Post your comments, suggestions, complaints, and anecdotes.*

**B** Read the advice column. Find the words in italics in the article. Then check (✓) the meaning of each word.

1. *confirm*
   - ☐ make something available
   - ☐ state that something will happen
2. *cancellation*
   - ☐ act of stopping something
   - ☐ act of delaying something
3. *representative*
   - ☐ person who speaks for a company
   - ☐ person who owns a company
4. *terms*
   - ☐ rules of an agreement
   - ☐ features of an app
5. *notification*
   - ☐ act of giving information
   - ☐ act of asking a question

**C** For each statement, check (✓) True, False, or Not given.

|  | True | False | Not given |
|---|---|---|---|
| 1. Lawrence booked a ride by mistake. | ☐ | ☐ | ☐ |
| 2. Lawrence did not expect to be charged for his ride. | ☐ | ☐ | ☐ |
| 3. The cancellation rule is available to read on the app. | ☐ | ☐ | ☐ |
| 4. Marci Davis thinks the cancellation fee is too expensive. | ☐ | ☐ | ☐ |
| 5. The company representative apologized for what happened. | ☐ | ☐ | ☐ |
| 6. Marci says ride-sharing agreements should be more clear. | ☐ | ☐ | ☐ |

**D** Have you ever used a ride-sharing service? What do you think of this type of service?

# Units 5–6 Progress check

## SELF-ASSESSMENT

How well can you do these things? Check (✔) the boxes.

| I can . . . | Very well | OK | A little |
|---|---|---|---|
| Talk about feelings and expectations (Ex. 1) | ☐ | ☐ | ☐ |
| Discuss cultural differences (Ex. 2) | ☐ | ☐ | ☐ |
| Understand problems and complaints (Ex. 3) | ☐ | ☐ | ☐ |
| Describe problems (Ex. 4) | ☐ | ☐ | ☐ |
| Discuss what needs to be improved (Ex. 5) | ☐ | ☐ | ☐ |

## 1 SPEAKING Facing new challenges

**PAIR WORK** Choose a situation. Then ask your partner questions about it using the words in the box. Take turns.

moving to another city      starting a new job
going to a new school      getting married

| | |
|---|---|
| anxious | excited |
| curious | insecure |
| embarrassed | nervous |
| enthusiastic | worried |

**A:** If you were moving to another city, what would you be nervous about?
**B:** One thing I'd be nervous about is not having any friends around. I'd be worried about feeling lonely!

## 2 SURVEY Cultural behavior

**A** What do you think of these behaviors? Complete the survey.

| Is it acceptable to . . . ? | Yes | No | It depends |
|---|---|---|---|
| give money as a gift | ☐ | ☐ | ☐ |
| call older people by their first names | ☐ | ☐ | ☐ |
| greet friends with a kiss on the cheek | ☐ | ☐ | ☐ |
| ask how old someone is | ☐ | ☐ | ☐ |
| put your feet on the furniture | ☐ | ☐ | ☐ |

**B** **GROUP WORK** Compare your opinions. When are these behaviors acceptable? When are they unacceptable? What behaviors are never acceptable?

**A:** It's not acceptable to give money as a gift.
**B:** Oh, I think it depends. I think it's OK to give money to kids and teens, and as a wedding gift, but . . .

# Progress check

## SELF-ASSESSMENT

**Learning Objectives:** reflect on one's learning; identify areas that need improvement

- Ask: "What did you learn in Units 5 and 6?" Elicit Ss' answers.

- Ss complete the Self-assessment. Explain to Ss that this is not a test; it is a way for them to evaluate what they've learned and identify areas where they need additional practice. Encourage them to be honest, and point out they will not get a bad grade if they check (✓) "a little."

- Ss move on to the Progress check exercises. You can have Ss complete them in class or for homework, using one of these techniques:
  1. Ask Ss to complete all the exercises.
  2. Ask Ss: "What do you need to practice?" Then assign exercises based on their answers.
  3. Ask Ss to choose and complete exercises based on their Self-assessment.

## 1 SPEAKING

**Learning Objective:** demonstrate one's ability to describe emotions using noun phrases containing relative clauses

### Pair work

- Explain the task. Read the situations. Ask two Ss to model the conversation.

- Ss work in pairs. They take turns interviewing each other.

- Then Ss change partners and repeat the exercise.

## 2 SURVEY

**Learning Objective:** demonstrate one's ability to talk about customs and expectations

### A

- Explain the task. Ask different Ss to read the survey items.

- Ss complete the survey individually. Ss can answer with what's acceptable to them, in their family, or in their country.

### B Group work

- Explain the task. Read the questions. Ask two Ss to model the conversation.

- Ss work in small groups. Try to mix nationalities, ages, and genders. Ss take turns offering opinions. Set a time limit of five minutes.

- When time is up, read each survey item, and tell Ss to share the group's opinion with the class.

- If time allows, ask some Ss to explain their answers.

## 3 LISTENING

**Learning Objective:** demonstrate one's ability to listen to and understand complaints

▶ **A** *[CD 1, Track 53]*

- Explain the task. Elicit or explain *tenant* (someone who rents a house or apartment) and *building manager* (someone who takes care of an apartment building for the owner).
- Play the audio program two or three times. Pause after each conversation. Ss listen and complete the chart. Ss may compare answers in pairs.

### Audio script

See page T-172.

- Go over answers with the class.

### Answers

1. the light keeps flickering and needs changing; building manager gives a light bulb and the tenant's son changes the bulb
2. the neighbor's dog keeps barking; building manager will call the neighbor and ask if he can keep his dog quiet
3. the kitchen window is jammed shut and won't open; tenant will call her cousin who's a weightlifter to look at it

**B** *Group work*

- Explain the task. Read the questions.
- Ss work in small groups to discuss solutions.
- Ask a S from each group to share some of the solutions.

## 4 ROLE PLAY

**Learning Objective:** demonstrate one's ability to describe problems using nouns and past participles as adjectives

- Explain the task. Elicit or explain that *haggling* means "bargaining."
- Divide the class into pairs, and assign A/B roles. Student As are the car buyers. Students Bs are the car sellers. Ask two Ss to model the conversation.
- Student As work in small groups to discuss problems with the car. Student Bs work in small groups to discuss a price and good features of the car.

- Ss role-play in A/B pairs. Ss negotiate the price of the car. Encourage Ss to find a price they can both agree on.
- Ss change roles and repeat the role play. If needed, Student As and Bs can work in small groups again to prepare.
- Take a class poll: Who paid the most for the car? Which car was in the best condition? Which car was in the worst condition?

## 5 DISCUSSION

**Learning Objective:** demonstrate one's ability to describe problems with gerunds and passive infinitives

**A** *Group work*

- Explain the task. Elicit or explain that a *school improvement committee* is a group of elected student leaders that makes suggestions to the school administrators. Ask two Ss to model the conversation.
- Ss work in small groups. Remind Ss to decide on five improvements.

**B** *Class activity*

- Explain the task. Ask the secretaries to read their group's lists.
- Write all the ideas on the board. Then ask the class to vote on the three most important.
- Ask the class to suggest ways to make the improvements.
- **Option:** Ss can first discuss how to make the improvements in their groups.

## WHAT'S NEXT?

**Learning Objective:** become more involved in one's learning

- Focus Ss' attention on the Self-assessment again. Ask: "How well can you do these things now?"

- Ask Ss to underline one thing they need to review. Ask: "What did you underline? How can you review it?"
- If needed, plan additional activities or reviews based on Ss' answers.

## 3 LISTENING I have a problem.

A Listen to three tenants complain to their building manager. Complete the chart.

|   | Tenant's complaint | How the problem is solved |
|---|---|---|
| 1. | | |
| 2. | | |
| 3. | | |

B GROUP WORK Do you agree with the solutions? How would you solve the problems?

## 4 ROLE PLAY Haggling

*Student A:* You want to buy this car from Student B, but it's too expensive. Describe the problems you see to get a better price.

*Student B:* You are trying to sell this car, but it has some problems. Make excuses for the problems to get the most money.

**A:** I'm interested in this car, but the door handle is broken. I'll give you $ . . . for it.

**B:** That's no big deal. You can fix that easily. How about $ . . . ?

**A:** Well, what about the windshield? It's . . .

**B:** You can't really see that. . . .

Change roles and try the role play again.

## 5 DISCUSSION School improvements

A GROUP WORK Imagine you are on a school improvement committee. You are discussing changes to your school. Decide on the five biggest issues.

**A:** The Wi-Fi connection needs to be improved. It keeps disconnecting, and it's not fast enough.

**B:** Yes, but it's more important to replace the couch in the student lounge. It has a big hole and stains.

B CLASS ACTIVITY Share your list with the class. What are the three most needed improvements? Can you think of how to accomplish them?

## WHAT'S NEXT?

Look at your Self-assessment again. Do you need to review anything?

# Unit 7 Supplementary Resources Overview

| | After the following SB exercises | You can use these materials in class | Your students can use these materials outside the classroom |
|---|---|---|---|
| **CYCLE 1** | 1 **Snapshot** | | |
| | 2 **Perspectives** | | |
| | 3 **Grammar Focus** | **TSS** Unit 7 Extra Worksheet | **SB** Unit 7 Grammar plus, Focus 1<br>**SS** Unit 7 Grammar 1<br>**GAME** Sentence Runner (Passive with prepositions) |
| | 4 **Pronunciation** | | |
| | 5 **Listening** | | |
| | 6 **Word Power** | **TSS** Unit 7 Vocabulary Worksheet | **SS** Unit 7 Vocabulary 1–2<br>**GAME** Spell or Slime (World problems)<br>**GAME** Name the Picture (Global challenges)<br>**WB** Unit 7 exercises 1–4 |
| **CYCLE 2** | 7 **Conversation** | | **SS** Unit 7 Speaking 1–2 |
| | 8 **Grammar Focus** | **TSS** Unit 7 Grammar Worksheet<br>**TSS** Unit 7 Listening Worksheet | **SB** Unit 7 Grammar plus, Focus 2<br>**SS** Unit 7 Grammar 2<br>**GAME** Sentence Stacker (Infinitive clauses and phrases) |
| | 9 **Discussion** | **TSS** Unit 7 Writing Worksheet | |
| | 10 **Interchange 7** | | |
| | 11 **Writing** | | |
| | 12 **Reading** | **TSS** Unit 7 Project Worksheet<br>**VID** Unit 7<br>**VRB** Unit 7 | **SS** Unit 7 Reading 1–2<br>**SS** Unit 7 Listening 1–3<br>**SS** Unit 7 Video 1–3<br>**WB** Unit 7 exercises 5–8 |

**Key**  **GAME:** Online Game    **SB:** Student's Book    **SS:** Online Self-study    **TSS:** Teacher Support Site
**VID:** Video DVD    **VRB:** Video Resource Book    **WB:** Online Workbook/Workbook

# My Plan for Unit 7

Use the space below to customize a plan that fits your needs.

| With the following SB exercises | I am using these materials in class | My students are using these materials outside the classroom |
|---|---|---|
|  |  |  |
|  |  |  |
|  |  |  |
|  |  |  |
|  |  |  |
|  |  |  |
|  |  |  |
|  |  |  |
|  |  |  |
|  |  |  |
|  |  |  |
|  |  |  |
|  |  |  |

| With or instead of the following SB section | I am using these materials for assessment |
|---|---|
|  |  |
|  |  |
|  |  |

# What can we do?

▸ Discuss environmental problems
▸ Compare solutions to social problems

## 1 SNAPSHOT

### WHAT A WASTE!

 The United States generates **254 million** tons of waste a year. The average American produces almost **2** kilograms of waste a day.

 Americans throw away around **130 million** cell phones a year. Much of this e-waste ends up in landfills.

 **Fifteen hundred** plastic bottles are consumed every second in the United States. It takes at least **500** years for a plastic bottle to decompose.

 In the U.S., **30–40%** of the food supply is wasted. That could feed **millions** of hungry people.

*How could we reduce the waste of each of these items?*
*What do you throw away? What do you tend to recycle?*
*What are two other environmental problems that concern you?*

## 2 PERSPECTIVES  Vote for a better city!

▶ **A** Listen to an announcement from an election campaign. What kinds of problems does Grace Medina want to fix?

### VOTE FOR GRACE MEDINA FOR CITY COUNCIL

> Grace Medina's ideas for Riverside!

Have you noticed these problems in our city?
• Our fresh water supply is being contaminated by toxic chemicals.
• The roads aren't being repaired due to a lack of funding.
• Our community center has been closed because of high maintenance costs.
• Our city streets are being damaged as a result of heavy traffic.
• Many public parks have been lost through overbuilding.
• Low-income families are being displaced from their homes due to high rental prices.

**GRACE MEDINA – THE CHANGE WE NEED**

**B** Which of these problems affect your city? Can you give specific examples?

# What can we do?

## Cycle 1, Exercises 1–6

In this unit, students discuss environmental problems and solutions to social problems. By the end of Cycle 1, students will be able to discuss environmental problems using the present continuous and present perfect passive tenses and prepositions of cause. By the end of Cycle 2, students will be able to discuss what they can do about problems using infinitive clauses and phrases.

## 1 SNAPSHOT

**Learning Objective:** discuss environmental problems

- Books closed. Write the word *environment* on the board. Elicit the meaning. (Answer: the land, water, and air in which people, animals, and plants live)

- Books open. Ask: "How much trash did you see on the way to class today? What kinds of trash? Where?"

- Ss read the Snapshot individually. Ask: "Which fact was the most surprising to you?" Elicit answers through a show of hands.

- Read the questions aloud.

- Ss discuss the questions in pairs or small groups.

## 2 PERSPECTIVES

**Learning Objective:** identify environmental problems that use present continuous and present perfect passive tenses and prepositions of cause in context

### ▶ A [CD 2, Track 1]

- Books closed. Set the scene. Grace Medina wants to be elected to the city council. In her campaign announcement, she describes problems in her city. Elicit or explain the meaning of *election campaign*. (Answer: an organized series of activities to get people to vote someone into an official position)

- Write questions like these on the board. Ask Ss to listen for the answers.

  In the city of Riverside, what or who is . . .
  contaminated?       damaged?
  not repaired?       lost?
  closed?             displaced?

- Explain any vocabulary that Ss don't know (without giving away the answers!).

- Show Ss how to predict an answer (e.g., *contaminated? Let's see. That could be water or air.*). Ss predict the others. Write Ss' ideas on the board.

- Play the audio program. Ss listen for the answers.

- Books open. Ss go over their answers in pairs. (Answers: water, roads, community center, streets, parks, low-income families being displaced) Discuss how accurate Ss' predictions were.

- Point out that Grace Medina also talked about the *cause* of each problem. Elicit the words she used to describe the cause (e.g., *by, due to, as a result of, through, because of*).

- Ask Ss to read and underline the cause of each problem. Model the first sentence with the class. Tell Ss to underline <u>by toxic chemicals</u>.

- Ss complete the task in pairs.

- Elicit or explain any new vocabulary.

### Vocabulary
**repair:** to fix
**overbuilding:** putting up too many buildings in an area
**displaced:** forced out

- Play the audio program again. Ss listen and read.

- For a new way to teach this vocabulary, try **Vocabulary Mingle** – download it from the website.

### B

- Explain the task. Read the questions.

- Elicit examples of how these problems affect Ss' city.

- **Option:** Ss discuss these questions: *If you were mayor of your city, which of the problems would you try to fix first? How would you solve them?*

**Learning Objectives:** use the present continuous passive and the present perfect passive to describe problems; use *by*, *because of*, *due to*, *through*, and *as a result of* to describe causes

▶ *[CD 2, Track 2]*

### Present continuous passive

- Focus Ss' attention on the Perspectives on page 44. Ask Ss to find examples with *is being* or *are being*. Write the examples on the board, in columns, like this:

| 1 | 2 | 3 |
|---|---|---|
| Our fresh water supply | is being | contaminated |
| Our city streets | are being | damaged |
| The roads | aren't being | repaired |

- Elicit or explain how to form the present continuous passive:
  subject + *is/are being* + past participle

- Point out that the present continuous passive describes an action that is in progress right now. Write an example on the board:

  Too many trees <u>are being cut down</u> right now/these days.

- Focus Ss' attention on the examples in the Grammar Focus box. Elicit a few more sentences from the class.

### Present perfect passive

- Focus Ss' attention on the Perspectives on page 44. Ask Ss to find examples with *has been* or *have been*. Write them on the board in columns. (Answers: *Our community has been closed, Many public parks have been lost*)

- Elicit or explain how to form the present perfect passive: subject + *has/have been* + past participle

- Point out that the present perfect passive describes something that started before the present (the exact time isn't important). Write an example on the board:

  Too many trees <u>have been cut down</u> recently/in the last few years.

- Play the audio program. Ss listen and repeat.

- Remind Ss to use *by*, *because of*, *due to*, *through*, and *as a result of* before the cause. Explain that these words have similar meanings.

### A Pair work

- Books open. Tell Ss to look at the six photos. Elicit words to describe the pictures (e.g., *sheep, farm, livestock*). Write Ss' ideas on the board.

- Explain the task. Model the task with the first photo.

- Ss complete the task in pairs. They match the photos with the sentences. Elicit Ss' responses to check answers.

**B**

- Explain the task. Show Ss how to change an active sentence into a passive sentence. Model it on the board. Use different colors if possible.
  (a) Write the cause, the verb, and the object. Underline them and number them:

      1                    2
  <u>Air pollution</u> is threatening <u>the health of people</u>.

  (b) Exchange 1 and 2 (the object and the cause). Then write a preposition (e.g., *by*) before the cause:

      2                    1
  <u>The health of people</u> (verb) by <u>air pollution</u>.

  (c) Identify the original tense (present continuous) and write the verb *be* in that tense (e.g., *is/are being*). Take the original verb (e.g., *threaten*) and make it a past participle:

  present continuous: <u>*is/are being + threatened*</u>

- Repeat the steps above with a present perfect passive sentence.

- Ss complete the task individually. Go around the class and give help as needed. Tell Ss to keep their sentences to use in Exercise 4.

> **TIP**
> If Ss finish early, check their work and ask them to join other Ss. Tell early finishers to help the slower Ss by giving them clues, not by telling them the answers.

### C Pair work

- Explain the task. Model the activity with a S.

- Ss work in pairs to take turns describing and guessing pictures. Go around the room and take notes on errors with passives. Write any errors you hear on the board. Elicit corrections from Ss.

## Passive with prepositions

**Present continuous passive**

| | |
|---|---|
| Our water supply **is being contaminated** | **by** toxic chemicals. |
| Our city streets **are being damaged** | **as a result of** heavy traffic. |
| The roads **aren't being repaired** | **due to** a lack of funding. |

**Present perfect passive**

| | |
|---|---|
| Our community center **has been closed** | **because of** high costs. |
| Many public parks **have been lost** | **through** overbuilding. |

GRAMMAR PLUS *see page 138*

**A** **PAIR WORK** Match the photos of environmental problems with the sentences below.

  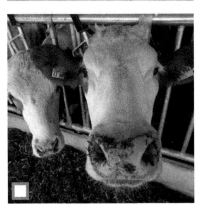

1. High emissions of carbon dioxide are causing climate changes. (by)
2. Rapid urbanization is depleting our natural resources. (through)
3. Water pollution has threatened the health of people all over the world. (due to)
4. Livestock farms have contaminated the soil and underground water. (because of)
5. The destruction of rain forests is accelerating the extinction of plants and wildlife. (as a result of)
6. Oil spills are harming birds, fish, and other marine life. (through)

**B** Rewrite the sentences in part A using the passive and the prepositions given.
Then compare with a partner.

> 1.   *Climate changes are being caused by high emissions of carbon dioxide.*

**C** **PAIR WORK** Cover the sentences in part A above. Take turns describing
the environmental problems in the pictures in your own words.

## 4 PRONUNCIATION Reduction of auxiliary verbs

▶ **A** Listen and practice. Notice how the auxiliary verb forms **is**, **are**, **has**, and **have** are reduced in conversation.

Food ~~is~~ being wasted.

Streets ~~are~~ being damaged.

Our community center ~~has~~ been closed.

Parks ~~have~~ been lost.

**B** PAIR WORK Practice the sentences you wrote in Exercise 3, part B. Pay attention to the reduction of **is**, **are**, **has**, and **have**.

## 5 LISTENING Saving the environment

▶ **A** Listen to three people describe some serious environmental problems. Check (✓) the problem each person talks about.

|  | Problem | | What can be done about it? |
|---|---|---|---|
| **1.** Morgan | ☐ landfills | ☐ poor farmland | |
| **2.** Dalton | ☐ electricity | ☐ e-waste | |
| **3.** Kendall | ☐ air pollution | ☐ water pollution | |

▶ **B** Listen again. What can be done to solve each problem? Complete the chart.

**C** GROUP WORK Which problem above worries you the most? What is being done to fix it?

## 6 WORD POWER Global challenges

**A** PAIR WORK How concerned is your partner about these problems? Check (✓) his or her answers.

| Problems | Very concerned | Fairly concerned | Not concerned |
|---|---|---|---|
| unemployment | ☐ | ☐ | ☐ |
| famine | ☐ | ☐ | ☐ |
| global warming | ☐ | ☐ | ☐ |
| government corruption | ☐ | ☐ | ☐ |
| infectious diseases | ☐ | ☐ | ☐ |
| political unrest | ☐ | ☐ | ☐ |
| poverty | ☐ | ☐ | ☐ |
| recession | ☐ | ☐ | ☐ |
| violence | ☐ | ☐ | ☐ |

**B** GROUP WORK Share your partner's answers with another pair. Which problems concern your group the most? What will happen if the problem isn't solved?

**A:** Many people have been affected by the high rates of unemployment.

**B:** We need to create more jobs and invest in education.

**C:** I agree. If we don't, young people won't have any opportunities in the future.

# 4 PRONUNCIATION

**Learning Objective:** sound more natural by using reduced auxiliary verbs

### ▶ A [CD 2, Track 3]

- Ask Ss to listen for the auxiliaries. Play the audio program. Model the difference between the full auxiliaries and the reductions.
- Play the audio program again. Pause after each sentence. Ss practice.

- **Option:** Ask Ss to stand in a line, facing the class. Each S represents a word in the example sentence. If the word is unstressed, the S sits or crouches down. Then they say their sentence aloud.

### B *Pair work*

- Explain the task.
- Ss work in pairs. They take turns reading the sentences from part B of Exercise 3 on page 45.
- Go around the class and listen for reductions.

# 5 LISTENING

**Learning Objective:** listen for main ideas and take notes about environmental problems

### ▶ A [CD 2, Track 4]

- Explain the task. Go over the information in the chart. Elicit or explain *e-waste* (electronic or electrical devices that people have thrown away).
- Tell Ss to listen and put a check next to the environmental problems that the speakers talk about. Remind Ss to listen for key phrases.
- Play the audio program. Pause after each description to give Ss time to write their answers. Then check Ss' responses.

#### Audio script

See page T-173.

#### Answers

1. landfills
2. e-waste
3. water pollution

### ▶ B [CD 2, Track 5]

- Explain the task. Read the question.
- Tell Ss to listen and write down the solutions. Remind Ss to listen for key phrases.
- Play the audio program. Pause after each description to give Ss time to write their answers.
- Then elicit Ss' answers.

#### Answers

1. do more recycling
2. dispose of it responsibly; take products to e-waste processing centers and reuse parts
3. treat all waste products more carefully

### C *Group work*

- Read the questions. Explain the task.
- Ss work in small groups. Tell Ss to first agree on the problem that worries them the most. Then Ss list what is being done to fix that problem. Set a time limit of about five minutes. Go around the class and give help as needed.
- Groups share their answers with the rest of the class.

# 6 WORD POWER

**Learning Objective:** discuss world problems

### A *Pair work*

- Explain the task. Read the question and the chart headings. Point out that there are no right or wrong answers.
- Model the task with a S:

  T: What does *unemployment* mean?

  S: Isn't it when people don't have jobs?

  T: Yes, that's right. How concerned are you about it?

  S: Oh, I worry about it a lot! What about you? Are you concerned about it?

- Ss work in pairs. Set a time limit of about ten minutes. Go around the class and give help as needed.

- Go over any unfamiliar vocabulary.

### B *Group work*

- Read the questions. Ask three Ss to model the conversation.
- Each pair from part A joins another pair to discuss the problems.

#### End of Cycle 1

See the Supplementary Resources chart at the beginning of this unit for additional teaching materials and student activities related to this Cycle.

# 7 CONVERSATION

**Learning Objective:** use infinitive clauses and phrases in a conversation about solutions to problems

### A [CD 2, Track 6]

- Tell Ss to cover the text and look only at the picture. Ask Ss to make notes about the problems they can see in the picture.
- Ask: "What environmental issue do you think Otis and Cindy are talking about?" Write Ss' suggestions on the board.
- Play the audio program. Then ask the class which topics on the board were "correct guesses." Circle them. (Answer: water pollution)
- Elicit any additional problems Ss heard. Add them to the board.
- Give Ss a few minutes to read the conversation. Then ask Ss to compare the conversation with their notes.
- Elicit or explain any new vocabulary.

> ### Vocabulary
> **pumping:** moving liquid from one place to another with a machine (a pump)
> **against the law:** illegal
> **ignore:** not pay attention to someone or something; disregard
> **management:** the people who are in charge of a company
> **run a story:** report about a recent event in a newspaper, on TV, or on the radio
> **bad publicity:** negative attention that someone or something gets from a news story
> **top executives:** the highest level of managers in a company

- Play the audio program again. Ask Ss to pay attention to the intonation. Then Ss practice the conversation in pairs.

> For fun and good intonation practice, encourage Ss to use the activity **Say It With Feeling!** – download it from the website.

### B Class activity

- Explain the task. Read the question. Have a brief class discussion about the question. Write Ss' suggestions on the board.

### C [CD 2, Track 7]

- Read the focus question aloud.
- Play the second part of the audio program. Ss listen and take notes.

> ### Audio script
> See page T-173.

- Check answers. Find out if Ss' suggestions in part B match what Cindy and Otis decide to do.

> ### Answer
> They decide to monitor the situation by taking pictures of the river and taking water samples (to see how bad the situation is).

# 8 GRAMMAR FOCUS

**Learning Objective:** use infinitive clauses and phrases to describe solutions to problems

### [CD 2, Track 8]

- Play the audio program.
- Elicit how to form the sentences:
  *(One way/Another way)* + infinitive + *is/are* + infinitive
- Ask Ss to generate more example sentences. Write their sentences on the board. Make corrections with the class.

### A

- Explain the task. Ss match problems and solutions individually or in pairs.
- Ss go over their answers in pairs. Then go over answers with the class.

> ### Possible answers
> | | | |
> |---|---|---|
> | 1. b | 3. b/d/f | 5. a/g |
> | 2. c | 4. e/h | 6. e/h |

### B Group work

- Explain the task. Read the question.
- Ss work in small groups. Tell Ss to first take turns giving their opinion on each solution in part A. Then Ss discuss new solutions. Set a time limit of about five minutes. Go around the class and give help as needed.
- Groups share one or two of their more interesting ideas with the rest of the class.

## 7 CONVERSATION What if it doesn't work?

▶ **A** Listen and practice.

**Cindy:** Did you hear about the dead fish that were found floating in the Bush River this morning?

**Otis:** Yeah, I read something about it. Do you know what happened?

**Cindy:** Well, there's a factory outside town that's pumping chemicals into the river.

**Otis:** How can they do that? Isn't that against the law?

**Cindy:** Yes, it is. But a lot of companies ignore those laws.

**Otis:** That's terrible! What can we do about it?

**Cindy:** Well, one way to change things is to talk to the company's management.

**Otis:** What if that doesn't work?

**Cindy:** Well, then another way to stop them is to get a news station to run a story on it.

**Otis:** Yes! Companies hate bad publicity. By the way, what's the name of this company?

**Cindy:** Believe it or not, it's called Green Mission Industries.

**Otis:** Really? My uncle is one of their top executives.

**B** CLASS ACTIVITY What else could Cindy and Otis do?

▶ **C** Listen to the rest of the conversation. What do Cindy and Otis decide to do?

## 8 GRAMMAR FOCUS

▶ **Infinitive clauses and phrases**

| | |
|---|---|
| One way **to change** things is | **to talk** to the company's management. |
| Another way **to stop** them is | **to get** a news station to run a story. |
| The best ways **to fight** unemployment are | **to create** more jobs and invest in education. |

GRAMMAR PLUS *see page 138*

**A** Find one or more solutions for each problem. Then compare with a partner.

**Problems**

1. The best way to fight poverty is _____
2. One way to reduce government corruption is _____
3. One way to reduce unemployment is _____
4. The best way to stop global warming is _____
5. One way to help the homeless is _____
6. One way to improve air quality is _____

**Solutions**

a. to provide more affordable housing.
b. to create more jobs.
c. to make politicians accountable for decisions.
d. to have more vocational training programs.
e. to increase the use of cleaner energy.
f. to provide education to all children.
g. to build more public shelters.
h. to reduce deforestation.

**B** GROUP WORK Can you think of two more solutions for each problem in part A? Agree on the best solution for each.

## 9 DISCUSSION What should be done?

**A GROUP WORK** Describe the problems shown in the photos.
Then make suggestions about how to solve these problems.

What can be done . . . ?

**1.** to reduce crime

**2.** to keep our water supplies safe

**3.** to improve children's health

**4.** to improve traffic and mobility

**A:** Our cities are being taken over by criminals.

**B:** Well, one way to fight crime is to have more police on the streets.

**C:** That's not enough. The best way to stop it is . . .

**B CLASS ACTIVITY** Share your solutions. Which ones are the most innovative?
Which ones are most likely to solve the problems?

## 10 INTERCHANGE 7 Take action!

Brainstorm solutions to some local problems. Go to Interchange 7 on page 121.

## 11 WRITING A post on a community website

**A** Choose one of the problems from the unit or use one of your own ideas.
Write a message to post on a community website.

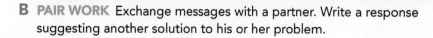

**NO MORE JUNK FOOD!**

Our schools are serving poor quality food to our children. School cafeterias offer
mostly fast food and soda to students. This has to change. One way to change this is . . .

**B PAIR WORK** Exchange messages with a partner. Write a response
suggesting another solution to his or her problem.

# 9 DISCUSSION

Learning Objective: discuss problems and solutions and give opinions using infinitive clauses and phrases

## A Group work

- Focus Ss' attention on the pictures. Ask Ss to describe the pictures.

- Explain the task. Ask a S to read the question and the cues. Ask two Ss to model the conversation. Encourage them to continue with additional suggestions and follow-up questions.

- **Option:** Ss earn one point for every follow-up question they ask or for every solution they suggest.

---

**TIP**
To provide variety and challenge, make sure Ss work with different partners. If possible, put Ss of a similar ability together for oral fluency activities.

---

- Ss work in groups. Remind Ss to make suggestions for each problem. Set a time limit of about five minutes. Go around the class and discreetly listen in. Make note of grammar or vocabulary problems.

- When time is up, write the common errors you noticed on the board. Elicit corrections from Ss.

- For a new way to develop oral fluency, play **Just One Minute** – download it from the website.

## B Class activity

- Explain the task. Read the questions. Elicit that *innovative* refers to something that is new or different (e.g., an idea, a method, a solution).

- Act as the discussion monitor. Present each problem. Elicit each group's solutions. Ask a S to record solutions on the board, using key phrases.

- Take a class vote (through a show of hands) on which solutions were the most innovative.

- **Option:** Follow up with a class debate. Elicit topics for the debate. Show Ss how to debate in teams.

---

**TIP**
To give Ss of all levels confidence that they are progressing, remind them regularly of what they have learned in the last few exercises. For example, say, "Now you know how to talk about problems and give solutions."

---

# 10 INTERCHANGE 7

See page T-119 for teaching notes.

# 11 WRITING

Learning Objective: write a description of a problem and offer a solution using infinitive clauses and phrases

## A

- Explain the task. Ask a S to read the model post. Point out that the first paragraph should present the problem. Later paragraphs should outline solutions.

- Ask Ss to brainstorm and make notes.

---

**TIP**
To help Ss brainstorm, set a time limit and ask them to write continuously for that time. "Free writing" is a useful way of writing fluently to generate ideas.

---

- Ss organize their ideas and draft their post.

- **Option:** Assign the task for homework.

- **Option:** Ss can take turns coming up to you for a mini-conference on their organization and content. If there is time, point out vocabulary or grammar problems Ss need to correct.

---

**TIP**
Use a correction code rather than correct Ss' work yourself. Write symbols on the page to indicate what needs fixing (e.g., *P* = punctuation, *Sp* = spelling, *WO* = word order, *Aux* = auxiliary, *WW* = wrong word, *MW* = missing word). Ss correct their own work.

---

## B Pair work

- Explain the task. Ss work in pairs. Set a time limit of about ten minutes for this task.

- Ss read each other's messages. Then Ss pretend to be a reader of the community website and write back to their partner proposing another solution to the problem.

- Ss exchange messages again. Ss read the messages and comment on the alternate solutions. They can comment in writing or discuss the solutions together.

- **Option:** Display the messages on the bulletin board or around the room, with a piece of blank paper beneath each one. Ss read the messages and choose three to respond to. They write their responses and alternative solutions beneath the message, as if responding to posts on a discussion forum.

**Learning Objectives:** skim and identify main ideas in an article about an environmental problem; identify causes and results

Note: You might want to bring a world map to show the location and size of St. Lucia, and a picture of a coral reef.

## A

- Books closed. Ask: "What do you know about coral reefs? What do you know about commercial fishing?" Elicit ideas. If a S seems to know quite a bit, put him or her on the "hot seat." The rest of the class asks questions to get more information.
- Books open. Go over the task.
- Ask Ss to skim the article to find out the problem for the people of St. Lucia. (Answer: The problem was an invasion of destructive fish. They decided to fish for and cook the fish.)

## B

- Explain the task.
- Ss read the article individually. Remind Ss to mark words or phrases they can't guess from context. When Ss finish, they can use their dictionaries to check words they marked.
- Ss answer the questions individually. Check the answers orally with the class.
- Elicit or explain any new vocabulary.

### Vocabulary
**destructive:** causing damage
**ecosystem:** all the living things in an area and the way they affect each other and the environment
**species:** a group of plants or animals that share similar characteristics
**dive:** swim under water, usually with breathing equipment
**coral:** a hard, rock-like substance in the ocean produced by vast numbers of very small animals
**coral reef:** a line of rocks or sand near the surface of the sea; the home to many forms of sea life
**trap:** catch an animal using a trap
**poison:** try to kill something by giving it a dangerous substance to drink or eat
**hunt:** chase and kill wild animals
**sting:** If an insect, plant, etc. stings you, it causes pain by putting poison into your skin.
**treat:** something special that you get or do for someone else

- Ss work individually or in pairs to answer the questions.
- Ss go over their answers with a partner or another pair. Ss should show where they found their answers.
- Go over answers with the class.

### Answers
1. The lionfish are a concern because they can destroy the natural habitat/coral reefs by eating the native fish that maintain the reefs.
2. St. Lucia has many coral reefs that tourists enjoy.
3. They reproduce very quickly.
4. They have encouraged both tourists and locals to catch and eat the lionfish.
5. They have slowed the growth of the lionfish population, though they haven't solved the problem.

- **Option:** Ss work in groups of three or four. Each group writes at least five comprehension questions with *how, what, why, where,* or *when.* Groups exchange questions and answer the other group's questions – if possible, from memory!

## C *Group work*
- Explain the task. Read the question.
- Ss work in small groups. Ss take turns giving their opinions.

## End of Cycle 2

See the Supplementary Resources chart at the beginning of this unit for additional teaching materials and student activities related to this Cycle.

**A** Skim the article. What problem did the island face? What solution did the inhabitants come up with?

● ● ●

Home | News | Feature stories | Sign in | Community

# TURNING AN INVASION INTO AN ADVANTAGE

Lionfish are beautiful creatures. They are also one of the most invasive and destructive sea creatures on the planet, causing particularly serious problems in the Caribbean Sea. Their numbers have increased dramatically in a few years there, and they have already caused a great deal of damage to the ecosystem.

St. Lucia is a Caribbean island where action is being taken against the invasive species. The island is famous for its clear blue waters, and many tourists enjoy diving in order to explore the wonders of the extensive coral reefs. Unfortunately, lionfish eat the native fish that keep the reefs clean and healthy, putting the reefs at risk. It is estimated that lionfish can eat up to 80% of the small fish in a coral reef in five weeks, and because the invasive fish reproduce very quickly the problem could easily get worse in no time.

Instead of trying to trap or poison the destructive fish, islanders are turning the lionfish invasion to their advantage. They realized that one way to reduce the population of lionfish was to hunt them for sport and business, and then use them for food. Although the fish have a very poisonous sting, they can be prepared so they are safe to eat. And Caribbean cooks were sure to find a way to turn these unwelcome fish into an unforgettable treat.

Unfortunately, the lionfish population has not been reduced by much, but at least the fish have been kept from multiplying too quickly. Jobs have also been provided for unemployed fishermen, who were unable to fish for other types of sea life in the protected waters. The lionfish are still a problem, but the islanders are making the best of a bad situation – and they are making a living from it, too!

**B** Read the article. Answer the questions.

1. Why are the lionfish a concern?
2. Why is it important to protect the area around St. Lucia?
3. What characteristic makes the lionfish hard to control?
4. What solutions have the islanders come up with?
5. What have the results of the islanders' efforts been?

**C GROUP WORK** What environmental threats exist where you live? Can you think of any creative or unusual ways to deal with them?

# Unit 8 Supplementary Resources Overview

| After the following SB exercises | You can use these materials in class | Your students can use these materials outside the classroom |
|---|---|---|
| **CYCLE 1** | | |
| 1 **Snapshot** | | |
| 2 **Perspectives** | | |
| 3 **Pronunciation** | | |
| 4 **Grammar Focus** | **TSS** Unit 8 Writing Worksheet | **SB** Unit 8 Grammar plus, Focus 1<br>**SS** Unit 8 Grammar 1<br>**GAME** Sentence Runner (*Would rather* and *would prefer*)<br>**GAME** Speak or Swim (*Would rather* and *would prefer*) |
| 5 **Listening** | **TSS** Unit 8 Listening Worksheet | |
| 6 **Speaking** | **TSS** Unit 8 Extra Worksheet | |
| 7 **Interchange 8** | | **WB** Unit 8 exercises 1–5 |
| **CYCLE 2** | | |
| 8 **Conversation** | | **SS** Unit 8 Speaking 1–2 |
| 9 **Grammar Focus** | **TSS** Unit 8 Grammar Worksheet | **SB** Unit 8 Grammar plus, Focus 2<br>**SS** Unit 8 Grammar 2<br>**GAME** Sentence Stacker (*By* + gerund to describe how to do things) |
| 10 **Discussion** | | |
| 11 **Word Power** | **TSS** Unit 8 Vocabulary Worksheet | **SS** Unit 8 Vocabulary 1–2<br>**GAME** Spell or Slime (Personal qualities) |
| 12 **Writing** | | |
| 13 **Reading** | **TSS** Unit 8 Project Worksheet<br>**VID** Unit 8<br>**VRB** Unit 8 | **SS** Unit 8 Reading 1–2<br>**SS** Unit 8 Listening 1–2<br>**SS** Unit 8 Video 1–3<br>**WB** Unit 8 exercises 6–9 |

| With or instead of the following SB section | You can also use these materials for assessment |
|---|---|
| **Units 7–8 Progress Check** | **ASSESSMENT PROGRAM** Units 7–8 Oral Quiz<br>**ASSESSMENT PROGRAM** Units 7–8 Written Quiz<br>**ASSESSMENT PROGRAM** Units 1–8 Test |

**Key**

| | | | |
|---|---|---|---|
| **GAME:** Online Game | **SB:** Student's Book | **SS:** Online Self-study | **TSS:** Teacher Support Site |
| **VID:** Video DVD | **VRB:** Video Resource Book | **WB:** Online Workbook/Workbook | |

# My Plan for Unit 8

Use the space below to customize a plan that fits your needs.

| With the following SB exercises | I am using these materials in class | My students are using these materials outside the classroom |
|---|---|---|
| | | |
| | | |
| | | |
| | | |
| | | |
| | | |
| | | |
| | | |
| | | |
| | | |
| | | |
| | | |
| | | |
| | | |

| With or instead of the following SB section | I am using these materials for assessment |
|---|---|
| | |
| | |
| | |

# Never stop learning.

▸ Discuss personal preferences
▸ Discuss ways of learning and life skills

## 1 SNAPSHOT

### Learning: Anywhere, Anytime, for Any Reason

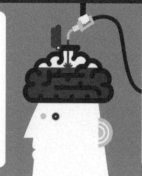

**LEARNING PATHS**

go to college
take online courses
take traditional training classes
study on your own
set up a study group
attend conferences
watch filmed lectures

**LEARNING BENEFITS**

get a degree
meet people and expand your network
change jobs or career path
get a raise or promotion at work
get a professional license or certification
learn something that makes your life easier
have fun

*Which learning paths have you tried? How was your experience?*
*Which learning benefits do you consider the most important? Why?*
*Are you planning to learn anything new this year? What?*

## 2 PERSPECTIVES  A survey

▶ **A** Listen to a survey that a school is conducting about student preferences.
Check (✓) the student's answers.

### Springfield Center for Continuing Education

New courses survey

1. Would you rather study on your own or join a study group?
   ☐ a. I'd rather study on my own.
   ☐ b. I'd rather join a study group.
   ☐ c. I'd rather do both.

2. Would you rather take an art course or a professional course?
   ☐ a. I'd rather take an art course.
   ☐ b. I'd rather take a professional course.
   ☐ c. I'd rather not take either. I'd rather <u>take a language course</u>.

3. Would you prefer to take an online course or a traditional course?
   ☐ a. I'd prefer to take an online course.
   ☐ b. I'd prefer to take a traditional course.
   ☐ c. I'd prefer not to take either. I'd prefer to <u>hire a private tutor</u>.

**B PAIR WORK** Take the survey. You can change the underlined information.
Discuss your answers with a partner.

# Never stop learning.

In this unit, students discuss personal preferences, ways of learning, and personal qualities. By the end of Cycle 1, students will be able to discuss personal preferences using *would rather* and *would prefer*. By the end of Cycle 2, students will be able to discuss ways to learn and personal qualities using *by* + gerund for manner.

## 1 SNAPSHOT

**Learning Objective:** discuss ways of learning and their benefits

- Books closed. Ask: "How do you like to learn new things? What are some studying methods that you know? Which do you prefer? Why?" Write some of the suggestions on the board.
- Books open. Have some Ss read the information in the Snapshot.
- Encourage Ss to use their dictionaries to check any unfamiliar words or expressions.
- Elicit or explain any remaining new vocabulary.

### Vocabulary
**path:** a particular way of doing something over a period of time
**on your own:** alone
**study group:** a group of people who meet to study a particular subject
**conference:** a large, formal meeting, often lasting a few days, where people discuss their work, politics, subjects they are studying, etc.
**lecture:** a formal talk given to a group of people in order to teach them about a subject
**degree:** a qualification given for completing a university course

**network:** use social events to meet people who might be useful for one's business
**raise:** an increase in the amount of money that one earns
**professional license:** a legal document giving a person the right to perform a business service

- Read the questions. Ss work in pairs or small groups to discuss the questions. Then ask Ss to share ideas around the class.

! To introduce the topic of learning, give the class a fun warm-up activity using **Vocabulary Tennis** – download it from the website. Ss name as many school subjects as they can.

## 2 PERSPECTIVES

**Learning Objective:** discuss and take a survey using *would rather* and *would prefer* in context

▶ **A** *[CD 2, Track 9]*
- Explain that a school is interviewing people in order to find out their preferences.
- Explain the task. Ask Ss to listen and find out the student's preferences.
- Play the audio program. Ss listen and read. Check answers. (Answers: 1. join a group, 2. neither; he'd rather take a language course, 3. an online course)

### Audio script
See page T-174.

**B** *Pair work*
- Explain the task. To help Ss complete question 2, ask Ss to brainstorm some classes they would add to the curriculum. To help Ss complete question 3, ask Ss to brainstorm some alternative ways to learn.

- Ss complete the survey individually. Then Ss discuss their answers in pairs.
- Tally the survey results as a class. Draw this chart on the board:

| study alone | study group | both |
|---|---|---|
| ____ | ____ | ____ |
| art course | professional course | language course |
| ____ | ____ | ____ |
| online | traditional | private tutor |
| ____ | ____ | ____ |

- Ask a S to come to the board. The S counts the number of Ss who raise their hand for each one. Remind Ss to vote for only one in each group. The S writes the totals on the board.

## 3 PRONUNCIATION

**Learning Objective:** identify intonation in questions of choice and sound more natural when asking them

▶ **[CD 2, Track 10]**

- Play the audio program. Point out the intonation patterns. Explain that when we ask someone to choose between two things, we use rising intonation on the word before *or* and falling intonation on the word after it. Also, point out the slight pause before *or*.

- Play the audio program again. Pause after each question to let Ss practice several times.

| **Tip** |
| --- |
| To demonstrate rising and falling intonation, ask Ss to stand up and rise or fall with their bodies. Alternatively, Ss can hum and use their hands to indicate rising and falling. |

- Ss work in pairs. They take turns asking each other the questions. Ask Ss to answer with real information.

- **Option:** Ss practice reading the questions of choice in the Perspectives on page 50.

## 4 GRAMMAR FOCUS

**Learning Objective:** use *would rather (not)* and *would prefer (not)*

▶ **[CD 2, Track 11]**

- Focus Ss' attention on the Perspectives on page 50. Ask Ss to find examples of *I'd rather* and *I'd prefer*. Elicit that *I'd* is the contraction of *I would*.

- Point out *would rather* and *would prefer* mean the same thing. Both are used with choices.

- Ask Ss to look at the examples in the Perspectives. Ask Ss to find one difference between *would rather* and *would prefer*. Elicit the answer. (Answer: *Would prefer* takes the infinitive; *would rather* takes the base form.)

- Write the following on the board:

  1. would rather + (not) + base form of verb:
     I'd rather learn . . .
     I'd rather (not) study . . .

  2. would prefer + (not) + infinitive:
     I'd prefer to learn . . .
     I'd prefer (not) to study . . .

- Focus Ss' attention on the right-hand column of the Grammar Focus box and ask: "How do you form a short answer?" (Answer: I'd rather [not]; I'd prefer [not] to.)

- Play the audio program. Ss listen and practice.

- **Option:** Elicit additional examples of questions and responses from around the class.

**A**

- Explain the task. Model the task with the first conversation. Ask different Ss to complete the answers.

- Ss complete the task individually. Go around the class and give help as needed. Check Ss' responses.

| **Answers** |
| --- |
| 1. A: **Would** you rather **take** a technical course or an art course?<br>B: I would prefer **to take** an art course. I'd like to learn to paint.<br>2. A: **Would** you prefer **to get** a promotion or a new job?<br>B: Actually, I'm not very happy at my present job, so I'd rather **get** a new job.<br>3. A: **Would** you prefer **to learn** something fun or something practical?<br>B: I guess I'd prefer **to study** something practical, like personal finance.<br>4. A: **Would** you rather **learn** English in England or Canada?<br>B: To tell you the truth, I'd prefer **not to study** in either place. I'd rather **go** to Australia because it's warmer there.<br>5. A: If you decided to learn to play an instrument, **would** you prefer **to attend** a class or **have** a private tutor?<br>B: I'd rather **take** a class than **hire** a tutor.<br>6. A: **Would** you rather **have** a job in an office or **work** outdoors?<br>B: I'd definitely rather **have** a job where I'm outdoors. |

| **Tip** |
| --- |
| To keep working on a specific pronunciation feature, make it the "pattern (or sound) of the week" and focus on it for the next few classes. |

**B** *Pair work*

- Explain the task. Ask two Ss to model the first conversation in part A.

- Ss work in pairs. They take turns asking the questions in part A. Remind Ss to give their own information and to pay attention to intonation. Go around the class and give help as needed.

- **Option:** Ss write a survey like the one in the Perspectives. They use their own information and a different setting if they wish (e.g., *English classes*).

❗ For more practice, try **Question Exchange** – download it from the website. Ss write their own questions.

Listen and practice. Notice the intonation in questions of choice.

Would you prefer to study online or at a school?

Would you rather learn something fun or useful?

# **4** GRAMMAR FOCUS

### *Would rather* and *would prefer*

*Would rather* takes the base form of the verb. *Would prefer* usually takes an infinitive. Both are followed by *not* in the negative.

**Would** you **rather take** an art course or
a professional course?
   **I'd rather take** an art course.
   **I'd rather not take either.**
   **I'd rather take** a language course than study art.

**Would you prefer to take** an online course or
a traditional course?

**I'd prefer to take** an online course.

Let's join a study group.
   **I'd rather not join** a group.
   **I'd rather not.**
   **I'd prefer not to join** a group.
   **I'd prefer not to.**

**I'd prefer not to take** either.

GRAMMAR PLUS *see page 139*

**A** Complete the conversations with *would* and the appropriate forms of the verbs in parentheses. Then practice with a partner.

1. **A:** _____ you rather _____ (take) a technical course or an art course?
   **B:** I would prefer _____ (take) an art course. I'd like to learn to paint.

2. **A:** _____ you prefer _____ (get) a promotion or a new job?
   **B:** Actually, I'm not very happy at my present job, so I'd rather _____ (get) a new job.

3. **A:** _____ you prefer _____ (learn) something fun or something practical?
   **B:** I guess I'd prefer _____ (study) something practical, like personal finance.

4. **A:** _____ you rather _____ (learn) English in England or Canada?
   **B:** To tell you the truth, I'd prefer _____ (not study) in either place. I'd rather _____ (go) to Australia because it's warmer there.

5. **A:** If you decided to learn to play an instrument, _____ you prefer _____ (attend) a class or _____ (have) a private tutor?
   **B:** I'd rather _____ (take) a class than _____ (hire) a tutor.

6. **A:** _____ you rather _____ (have) a job in an office or _____ (work) outdoors?
   **B:** I'd definitely rather _____ (have) a job where I'm outdoors.

**B** PAIR WORK  Take turns asking the questions in part A. Pay attention to intonation. Give your own information when responding.

## 5 LISTENING Do what you love.

▶ **A** Listen to a conversation between a student and his guidance counselor.
Check (✓) the suggestions the guidance counselor gives.

☐ talking to professors     ☐ volunteer work     ☐ more classes
☐ job shadowing     ☐ informational interviews     ☐ internships

**B PAIR WORK** If you could learn more about a job, what job would it be?
Why? Which options above would you use?

## 6 SPEAKING Learn something new

**A GROUP WORK** Think of a personal or professional skill you would like to learn
or improve. Discuss how you are planning to learn it. Use the ideas from
the Snapshot on page 50, or use your own ideas.

**A:** I want to speak Italian. I think I'm going to take an online course.
**B:** It's hard to learn a language online. I think you should go to a language school.
**A:** I don't know. I'm really shy. I'd rather not have classes with other people.
**C:** You could . . .

**B CLASS ACTIVITY** Share your ideas with your classmates. Who is going to learn
something unusual? How are they going to learn it?

## 7 INTERCHANGE 8 Making choices

What would you most like to learn? Take a survey. Go to Interchange 8 on page 122.

## 8 CONVERSATION It works for me.

▶ **A** Listen and practice.

**Marta:** So how's your Mandarin class going?
**Kevin:** Harder than I expected, actually. I'm finding the
pronunciation very difficult.
**Marta:** Well, I imagine it takes a while to get it right.
You know, you could improve your accent by
watching movies.
**Kevin:** That's a good idea. But how do you learn new
vocabulary? I always seem to forget new words.
**Marta:** I learn new English words best by writing them
down and reviewing them many times. I've been
using this vocabulary-building app. It really works
for me. Look.
**Kevin:** Hmm. Maybe I should try something like that!

▶ **B** Listen to two other students, Rick and Nia, explain how
they learn new words. Who uses technology to study?
Who organizes words by category?

**C CLASS ACTIVITY** How do you learn new words in a
foreign language?

# 5 LISTENING

**Learning Objective:** listen for main ideas and details of personal experiences discussed using *would rather* and *would prefer*

▶ **A** *[CD 2, Track 12]*

- Explain the task. Tell Ss to check only the suggestions that the guidance counselor gives.
- Play the audio program. Ss listen and check (✓) the suggestions.
- Elicit the answers.

**B** *Pair work*

- Explain the task. Read the focus question.
- Ss discuss which jobs they would learn more about and why.

# 6 SPEAKING

**Learning Objective:** use *would rather* and *would prefer* to discuss making a choice

**A** *Group work*

- Explain the task. Tell Ss to choose a skill they would like to learn. Then they decide how they would prefer to learn it. Tell Ss to go back to the Snapshot on page 50 to review some learning paths.

- Ss work in small groups. Ss take turns talking about their skill. The other Ss offer advice on the best way to learn the skill.

**B** *Class activity*

- Explain the task. Have Ss present their skill to the class and how they have decided to learn it.

# 7 INTERCHANGE 8

See page T-122 for teaching notes.

See the Supplementary Resources chart at the beginning of this unit for additional teaching materials and student activities related to this Cycle.

**End of Cycle 1**

**Cycle 2, Exercises 8–13**

# 8 CONVERSATION

**Learning Objective:** use *by* + gerund in a conversation about giving advice

▶ **A** *[CD 2, Track 13]*

- Set the scene. Two students, Marta and Kevin, are talking about ways to improve language learning.
- Write these focus questions on the board:

  Who is taking Mandarin classes? (Kevin)
  . . . finds pronunciation difficult? (Kevin)
  . . . writes new words on pieces of paper? (Marta)

- Play the audio program. Ss listen for the answers.

▶ **B** *[CD 2, Track 14]*

- Explain the task. Read the focus questions.
- Play the second part of the audio program. Elicit Ss' responses.

**C** *Class activity*

- Read the question. Discuss the question with the class. Give extra suggestions if possible.

# 9 GRAMMAR FOCUS

**Learning Objective:** use *by* + gerund to describe how to do things

▶ **[CD 2, Track 15]**

- Write the following on the board. Focus Ss' attention on the Conversation on page 52. Ask Ss to complete these sentences from the conversation.

  *You could improve your accent by . . . (watching movies.)*
  *I learn new English words best by . . . (writing them down and reviewing them many times.)*

- Point out the *by* + gerund structure in each sentence. Explain that *by* + gerund is used:

  1. to say how something can happen: *You could improve your accent **by watching** movies.*

  2. to describe how something is done: *I learn new words best **by writing** them down.*

  3. to describe how something could be done: *The best way to learn slang is not **by watching** the news but **by watching** TV series.*

- Explain the negative form *not . . . but* (e.g., *The best way to learn slang is **not** by watching the news **but** by watching TV series.*).

- Play the audio program. Ss listen and read or repeat.

- Elicit additional ways to complete Marta's advice using *by* + gerund. Write Ss' ideas on the board.

**A**

- Explain the task.

- Ss complete the task individually. Then Ss compare answers in pairs. Check Ss' answers.

**Answers**

1. A good way to learn idioms is **by watching** American sitcoms.
2. The best way to practice what you have learned is **by using** it in messages or conversation.
3. Students can become better writers **by reading** more.
4. You can learn to use grammar correctly **by doing** grammar exercises online.
5. The best way to develop self-confidence in communication is **by talking** with native speakers.
6. You can improve your accent **by listening** to songs and singing along.
7. A good way to memorize new vocabulary is **by playing** vocabulary games.
8. You could become a more fluent reader **by reading** something you're interested in every day.

**B Group work**

- Explain the task. Ss complete the statements in part A with their own ideas. Have two Ss read the example dialog.

- Ss work individually. Ask Ss to write down at least eight statements.

- Ss work in small groups and take turns sharing their suggestions. The group chooses the best suggestion for each item. Set a time limit of about ten minutes.

- Ss change groups and share their best suggestion for each item with the new group.

# 10 DISCUSSION

**Learning Objective:** discuss ways of learning using *by* + gerund

▶ **A [CD 2, Track 16]**

- Explain the task. Ask a S to read the two skills listed in the chart. Explain that an *effective public speaker* is a person who is able to give a good presentation to an audience. Tell Ss they are going to hear two people discussing these skills. Tell Ss to write down key words and phrases in note form in the chart.

- Play the audio program.

**Audio script**

See page T-174.

**Answers**

1. James: took a public speaking course and exercises before speaking
   Sophia: started organizing her ideas better
2. James: his dad taught him to drive on a busy street the first day
   Sophia: her mom took her outside the city to learn because parking was impossible in New York City

**B Group work**

- Explain the task. Write some useful phrases on the board:

  *I think a good way to learn to drive is by . . . Another way I learned to drive is by . . . The best way to learn to drive is by . . .*

- Ss discuss their ideas in small groups.

**C Group work**

- Explain the task and read the list of skills. Model the task with a S.

- Ss work in small groups. They take turns discussing the best way to learn each skill.

# 9 GRAMMAR FOCUS

> ▶ *By + gerund to describe how to do things*
>
> You could improve your accent **by watching** movies.
> I learn new words best **by writing** them down and **reviewing** them many times.
> The best way to learn slang is not **by watching** the news but **by watching** TV series.
>
> GRAMMAR PLUS *see page 139*

**A** How can you improve your English? Complete the sentences with *by*
and the gerund forms of the verbs. Then compare with a partner.

1. A good way to learn idioms is _____ (watch) American sitcoms.
2. The best way to practice what you have learned is _____ (use) it in messages or conversation.
3. Students can become better writers _____ (read) more.
4. You can learn to use grammar correctly _____ (do) grammar exercises online.
5. The best way to develop self-confidence in communication is _____ (talk) with native speakers.
6. You can improve your accent _____ (listen) to songs and singing along.
7. A good way to memorize new vocabulary is _____ (play) vocabulary games.
8. You could become a more fluent reader _____ (read) something you're interested in every day.

**B** GROUP WORK Complete the sentences in part A with your own ideas.
What's the best suggestion for each item?

**A:** In my opinion, a good way to learn idioms is by talking to native speakers.
**B:** I think the best way is not by talking to native speakers but by watching TV shows.

# 10 DISCUSSION Learning styles

**▶ A** Listen to James and Sophia describe how they developed two skills.
How did they learn? Complete the chart.

|  | James | Sophia |
|---|---|---|
| 1. become an effective public speaker |  |  |
| 2. learn to drive |  |  |

**B** GROUP WORK How would *you* learn to do the things in the chart?

**C** GROUP WORK Talk about different ways to learn to do each of these activities. Then agree on the most effective method.

take professional-looking photos
manage your time
cook
become a good conversationalist
break dance
swim
play a musical instrument

## 11 WORD POWER Life skills

**A PAIR WORK** How do we learn each of these things? Check (✓) your opinions.

|  | From parents | From school | On our own |
|---|---|---|---|
| communication skills | ☐ | ☐ | ☐ |
| competitiveness | ☐ | ☐ | ☐ |
| concern for others | ☐ | ☐ | ☐ |
| cooperation | ☐ | ☐ | ☐ |
| creativity | ☐ | ☐ | ☐ |
| money management | ☐ | ☐ | ☐ |
| perseverance | ☐ | ☐ | ☐ |
| problem solving | ☐ | ☐ | ☐ |
| self-confidence | ☐ | ☐ | ☐ |
| self-discipline | ☐ | ☐ | ☐ |
| time management | ☐ | ☐ | ☐ |
| tolerance | ☐ | ☐ | ☐ |

**B GROUP WORK** How can you develop the skills in part A? Use the activities in the box or your own ideas.

**A:** You can develop communication skills by taking a public speaking class.

**B:** You can also develop them by trying to be a better listener.

**some activities**

using a daily planner
volunteering in a hospital
taking a public speaking class
performing in a play
going to museums
learning a martial art
playing a team sport
making a budget

## 12 WRITING Something I learned

**A** Think of a skill you have learned. Read these questions and take notes. Then use your notes to write about what you learned.

What is required to be successful at it?
What are some ways people learn to do it?
How did you learn it?
What was difficult about learning it?

> I used to have serious problems managing my finances, and I never paid my bills on time. I have to admit I had very poor money management skills. Some people learn to manage their money at home or by taking courses at school, but I didn't.
>
> When a friend told me about a personal finance course, I decided to take it. I first learned to keep track of my expenses by recording every penny I spent. Then . . .

**B GROUP WORK** Share your writing. Have any of your classmates' experiences inspired you to learn a new skill?

# 11 WORD POWER

## A *Pair work*

- Ask Ss to read the list of life skills.

- Give Ss some time to work in pairs to discuss the meanings of any new words in the list. If needed, let Ss check their dictionaries.

- Elicit or explain any remaining new vocabulary.

### Vocabulary
**competitiveness:** the desire to win
**concern for others:** caring feelings for other people
**cooperation:** the act of working together to achieve a common goal
**creativity:** the use of the imagination or original ideas, especially in the production of an artistic work
**perseverance:** steady or continued action or belief
**self-confidence:** strong belief in one's powers and abilities
**time management:** the ability to use one's time effectively or productively
**tolerance:** the state of accepting differences in other people and/or their opinions

### Tip
Create a Vocabulary Box, using a transparent container (so that Ss can see how many words they have learned) or a shoe box. As new words are taught, ask a S to write each one on a slip of paper and put it in the box.

- Explain the task. Model one or two items in the chart. Tell Ss how you learned each thing.

- Ss work in pairs. They take turns talking about each skill. Tell Ss that there are no right or wrong answers. Also remind Ss to check (✓) the appropriate boxes in their charts.

- Ss think of three more things we learn from parents, from school, and on our own.

## B *Group work*

- Explain the task. Ask a S to read the activities in the box. Ask two Ss to model the conversation. Elicit additional suggestions from Ss.

- Ss work in small groups. Ss take turns sharing their opinions and ideas. Set a time limit of about ten minutes. Go around the class and give help as needed. Make note of difficulties Ss have with grammar or vocabulary.

- When time is up, share some of the problems with the class. Elicit Ss' solutions.

- *Option:* Ss work in pairs to write a conversation. Tell Ss to model their conversation after the one on page 52 and to include suggestions using *by* + gerund.

### Tip
To review vocabulary, pull out words from your Vocabulary Box. Write a check (✓) on the slip of paper if Ss were able to recall the word. When a slip has three checks, take it out of the box.

For more practice, play **Bingo** – download it from the website.

# 12 WRITING

**Learning Objective:** write a paragraph about a skill one has learned using *by* + gerund

## A

- Explain the task. Ask different Ss to read the four questions and the model paragraphs. Elicit the focus of each of the model paragraphs. (Answers: Paragraph 1 explains the writer's money management skills; paragraph 2 explains how the writer learned it.).

- First, ask Ss to brainstorm skills learned in recent years. Write Ss' suggestions on the board:
  *Skills: cooking, playing golf, speaking English*

- Then Ss work individually to choose a topic. Ss use the questions to make notes. Go around the class and give help as needed.

- Then Ss use their notes to write at least two paragraphs.

- *Option:* The paragraphs can be completed for homework.

## B *Group work*

- Explain the task. Ss share their writing in small groups. They can read aloud or sit in a circle and take turns passing their writing to another person.

- Encourage Ss to ask each other follow-up questions about their group members' skills.

- Groups discuss whether they feel inspired to learn a new skill.

For another way to practice giving a speech, try **Look Up and Speak!** – download it from the website.

## A

- Books closed. Use the pre-reading questions for a discussion about where the best places to study are.

- Books open. Ss read the article individually. Ask Ss to read without dictionaries because they will be working with vocabulary in part B.

- Ask Ss to summarize in one or two sentences what they read.

## B

- Explain the task. Use the first word to model the task.

- Ss work individually or in pairs. Ss scan the article for the words in italics and match the words with their meanings. Remind Ss to use the other words in the sentence and the sentences before and after as clues.

- Go over answers with the class.

### Answers

1. e    2. c    3. a    4. d    5. b

- **Option:** To reinforce new vocabulary, ask each pair or group to write one original sentence with each word. Ask Ss to read their sentences aloud or write them on the board. Correct as needed.

- Ss work on additional vocabulary from the article. Ss can check their dictionaries at this time, if needed.

- Elicit or explain any remaining new vocabulary.

### Vocabulary
**whereas:** in contrast or comparison with the fact that
**surround:** be all around (someone or something)
**on the other hand:** a phrase used to present factors that are opposed
**constantly:** frequently
**claim:** state or assert that something is the case
**on the move:** in the process of moving from one place to another

## C

- Explain the task. Ss complete the summary by adding the missing words. Point out that there may be more than one way to make the sentence correct.

- Ss complete the task individually. Then Ss compare answers in pairs.

- Go over answers by asking Ss to read the summary aloud. Ask if other Ss corrected them in a different way.

### Possible answers

Kelly and Maria are friends who have a lot **in common**, but they can't study together because they have **different habits**. Kelly likes a **clean place** which is very quiet, and she can **work/ sit still** for a long time. Maria prefers a space that is **cluttered/messy**, and she likes to **move around**. Studies show that neither way of studying is **better** than the other. Noise can help some people **concentrate/focus**, for example. Despite their different habits, Kelly and Maria are both **excellent** students, and it is interesting that the friends have **almost identical/similar** plans for the future.

## D *Group work*

- Explain the task. Ss work in small groups to discuss whose studying style is most like their own. Ss give reasons to support their answers. Encourage Ss to ask follow-up questions.

- Set a time limit of about five minutes. Go around the class and give help as needed.

## End of Cycle 2

See the Supplementary Resources chart at the beginning of this unit for additional teaching materials and student activities related to this Cycle and for assessment tools.

# 13 READING

**A** Have you ever had trouble focusing when you're studying? What did you do about it?

## Are you studying the "right" way?

Home | News | Articles | Sign in | Community    Search 🔍

**You may study differently from your friends, but your study habits are probably not wrong!**

Kelly and Maria are best friends with a lot in common. They love doing things together, such as going to movies and concerts, shopping, or just sitting at a local café. Since they take a lot of the same school subjects, they would love to study together, but they find this impossible. Their working styles are so completely different that they can't be in the same room while they are studying!

Kelly would rather study in a clean, open space, whereas Maria works best by surrounding herself with books, papers, and other clutter. Kelly prefers to study in a totally silent room, but Maria loves to play music or even have the TV on. Kelly can sit for hours without moving, and often gets all of her homework done in one sitting. Maria, on the other hand, is constantly getting up, and claims that she thinks best when she's on the move.

You might be asking yourself, which way of studying gets better results? Many people assume that a silent, uncluttered setting is the way to go, but it seems that is not necessarily the case. Some research has even shown that outside noise and clutter help some people concentrate because it makes them form a mental "wall" around what they are doing and improves their focus. So, if you're a student who chooses to study while sitting at a table in a busy shopping mall, don't worry about it. And if you work in total silence, that's OK, too. Judging from Kelly and Maria's study habits, the best way to study is the way that works for you. With their very different approaches, both of them do extremely well in school, and both finish their work in about the same amount of time as well.

One curious fact about the two friends: Despite their opposing studying styles, they have almost identical ambitions. Both are planning to go to law school – Kelly with the idea of becoming a human rights attorney and Maria hoping to become a public defender. But will they be study buddies? Not a chance!

**B** Read the article. Find the words in *italics* in the article. Then match each word with its meaning.

1. *clutter* _____
2. *sitting* _____
3. *concentrate* _____
4. *approach* _____
5. *identical* _____

a. focus attention on something
b. exactly the same
c. period of activity without a break
d. way of doing something
e. objects in a state of disorder

**C** Complete the summary with information from the article. Use one or two words in each blank.

Kelly and Maria are friends who have a lot _____, but they can't study together because they have _____. Kelly likes a _____ that is very quiet, and she can _____ for a long time. Maria prefers a space that is _____, and she likes to _____. Studies show that neither way of studying is _____ than the other. Noise can help some people _____, for example. Despite their different habits, Kelly and Maria are both _____ students, and it is interesting that the friends have _____ plans for the future.

**D** **GROUP WORK** Whose studying style is closest to yours, Kelly's or Maria's? Why?

## SELF-ASSESSMENT

How well can you do these things? Check (✓) the boxes.

| I can . . . | Very well | OK | A little |
|---|---|---|---|
| Describe environmental problems (Ex. 1) | ☐ | ☐ | ☐ |
| Discuss solutions to problems (Ex. 2) | ☐ | ☐ | ☐ |
| Understand examples of personal qualities (Ex. 3) | ☐ | ☐ | ☐ |
| Discuss personal preferences (Ex. 4) | ☐ | ☐ | ☐ |

## 1 SPEAKING Environmental issues

**PAIR WORK** Choose a probable cause for each of the problems and discuss possible solutions.

**PROBLEM**

- Forests are being destroyed.
- The quality of the air is being lowered.
- Marine life is being affected.
- Water is being contaminated.
- Landfills are overflowing.
- City streets are being damaged.

**CAUSE**

- the lack of recycling
- heavy traffic
- rapid urbanization
- climate changes
- fumes from cars
- factory waste

**A:** Forests are being destroyed because of rapid urbanization.
**B:** We need plans for urban development that don't . . .

## 2 DISCUSSION Tricky social situations

**A PAIR WORK** Read these problems that friends sometimes have with each other. Suggest solutions for each problem.

Your friend is always criticizing you and your other friends.
Your best friend never pays for his or her share at group dinners.
A friend is having a party and you weren't invited.

**B GROUP WORK** Agree on the best solution for each problem.

"The best thing to do is to talk to your friend and say how you feel."

| useful expressions |
|---|
| One thing to do is to . . . |
| Another way to help is to . . . |
| The best thing to do is . . . |

# Progress check

## SELF-ASSESSMENT

**Learning Objectives:** reflect on one's learning; identify areas that need improvement

- Ask: "What did you learn in Units 7 and 8?" Elicit Ss' answers.

- Ss complete the Self-assessment. Explain to Ss that this is not a test; it is a way for them to evaluate what they've learned and identify areas where they need additional practice. Encourage them to be honest, and point out they will not get a bad grade if they check (✓) "a little."

- Ss move on to the Progress check exercises. You can have Ss complete them in class or for homework, using one of these techniques:
  1. Ask Ss to complete all the exercises.
  2. Ask Ss: "What do you need to practice?" Then assign exercises based on their answers.
  3. Ask Ss to choose and complete exercises based on their Self-assessment.

## 1 SPEAKING

**Learning Objective:** demonstrate one's ability to describe problems using the passive with prepositions

### Pair work

- Explain the task. Ask Ss to read the problems. Elicit or explain any new vocabulary.

- Ask two Ss to model the conversation.

- Ss work in pairs to choose a cause for each problem.

- Spot-check by asking different Ss to read complete sentences.

- After you have checked the answers, tell students to think of possible solutions to the problems. When a S from the pair thinks of a solution, the other S should keep the conversation going.

**Possible answers**

Forests are being destroyed because of rapid urbanization.
The quality of the air is being lowered because of fumes from cars.
Marine life is being affected through climate changes.
Water is being contaminated by factory waste.
Landfills are overflowing due to the lack of recycling.
City streets are being damaged as a result of heavy traffic.

## 2 DISCUSSION

**Learning Objective:** demonstrate one's ability to offer solutions with infinitive clauses and phrases

### A Pair work

- Explain the task. Ask Ss to read the problems and useful expressions.

- Give Ss time to think of some solutions.

- Ss work in pairs to discuss solutions.

- **Option:** For added practice, ask one S to write down the solutions.

### B Group work

- Explain the task. Ask a S to read the example sentence.

- Each pair joins another pair, or Ss work in new small groups. Ss take turns sharing their solutions.

- Next, the group discusses and chooses the best solution. One S in each group should write down the best solution.

- Ask each group to share their best solutions.

## 3 LISTENING

**Learning Objective:** demonstrate one's ability to listen to and understand the meaning of personal qualities

▶ **A** *[CD 2, Track 17]*

- Explain the task. Tell Ss to listen first for the event or activity described.

- Play the audio program once or twice. Pause after each speaker for Ss to write. Remind Ss to write notes, not full sentences.

- Then read the qualities. Make sure Ss remember what each one means. If needed, ask other class members to explain or act out the meaning.

- Tell Ss to listen again for the qualities each speaker demonstrates.

- Play the audio program again. Ss check (✔) the boxes.

- Ss compare answers in pairs. If there are any disagreements, play the audio program again.

- Go over answers with the class.

### Audio script

See page T-175.

### Answers

1. Kate: got into the company she auditioned for; e, f
2. Mark: missed a goal and lost the game; b, d
3. Iris: saved money to take a painting class; a, c

**B** *Pair work*

- Divide Ss into pairs and explain the task. Remind them not to say which quality they are describing.

- Walk around the class, listen, and take notes of some mistakes you hear. Go over them with the class (don't point out who made the mistake).

## 4 QUESTIONNAIRE

**Learning Objectives:** demonstrate one's ability to ask about preferences using *would rather* and *would prefer*; demonstrate one's ability to talk about learning preferences with *by* + gerund

**A** *Pair work*

- Explain the task. Ask Ss to read the interview questions. Elicit or explain any new vocabulary. Ask a S to read the example answer.

- Ss interview each other in pairs. Encourage Ss to give reasons for their answers.

**B** *Group work*

- Explain the task. Ask three Ss to model the conversation.

- Each pair joins another pair. Tell Ss to discuss both options, even if all Ss chose the same option. Ask Ss to discuss other options.

- Ask each group to share their other options with the class.

## WHAT'S NEXT?

**Learning Objective:** become more involved in one's learning

- Focus Ss' attention on the Self-assessment again. Ask: "How well can you do these things now?"

- Ask Ss to underline one thing they need to review. Ask: "What did you underline? How can you review it?"

- If needed, plan additional activities or reviews based on Ss' answers.

**LISTENING** I got it!

▶ **A** Listen to people talk about recent events and activities in their lives. What events and activities are they talking about? What two qualities does each person's behavior demonstrate? Complete the chart.

**a.** money management
**b.** competitiveness

**c.** creativity
**d.** concern for others

**e.** perseverance
**f.** self-confidence

|   | Event or activity | Qualities |
|---|---|---|
| **1.** Kate |  | *e,* |
| **2.** Mark |  |  |
| **3.** Iris |  |  |

**B** PAIR WORK Describe a time when you demonstrated one of the qualities above. Can your partner guess the quality?

## 4

**QUESTIONNAIRE** Learning styles

**A** PAIR WORK Interview your partner. Circle the ways your partner prefers to improve his or her English.

1. When you don't understand a word, would you prefer to . . . ?
   **a.** look it up in a dictionary          or          **b.** try to guess the meaning

2. If you don't understand what someone says, would you rather . . . ?
   **a.** ask the person to repeat it          or          **b.** pretend you understand

3. When you hear a new word in English, would you rather . . . ?
   **a.** write it down          or          **b.** try to remember it

4. When you make a mistake in English, would you prefer someone to . . . ?
   **a.** correct it immediately          or          **b.** ignore it

5. When you meet a native English speaker, would you prefer to . . . ?
   **a.** try to talk to the person          or          **b.** listen while he or she speaks

6. When you have to contact someone in English, would you rather . . . ?
   **a.** call him or her on the phone          or          **b.** send him or her an email

"I'd prefer to try to guess the meaning of a new word."

**B** GROUP WORK Discuss the advantages and disadvantages of each option in part A. Are there better options for each situation?

**A:** When I try to guess the meaning of a new word, it takes less time, so I can read faster.

**B:** Yes, but if you look it up, you learn a new word.

**C:** I think the best way to deal with a new word is to try and guess the meaning, and then check if it makes sense.

## WHAT'S NEXT?

Look at your Self-assessment again. Do you need to review anything?

# Unit 9 Supplementary Resources Overview

| | After the following SB exercises | You can use these materials in class | Your students can use these materials outside the classroom |
|---|---|---|---|
| **CYCLE 1** | 1 Snapshot | **TSS** Unit 9 Vocabulary Worksheet | |
| | 2 Perspectives | | |
| | 3 Grammar Focus | **TSS** Unit 9 Extra Worksheet | **SB** Unit 9 Grammar plus, Focus 1<br>**SS** Unit 9 Grammar 1–2<br>**GAME** Sentence Stacker (*Get* or *have* something done) |
| | 4 Pronunciation | | |
| | 5 Discussion | | |
| | 6 Interchange 9 | | **WB** Unit 9 exercises 1–4 |
| **CYCLE 2** | 7 Word Power | | **SS** Unit 9 Vocabulary 1–2<br>**GAME** Spell or Slime (Three-word phrasal verbs)<br>**GAME** Sentence Runner (Three-word phrasal verbs) |
| | 8 Conversation | | **SS** Unit 9 Speaking 1 |
| | 9 Grammar Focus | **TSS** Unit 9 Grammar Worksheet | **SB** Unit 9 Grammar plus, Focus 2<br>**SS** Unit 9 Grammar 3<br>**GAME** Speak or Swim (Making suggestions) |
| | 10 Listening | **TSS** Unit 9 Listening Worksheet | |
| | 11 Speaking | | |
| | 12 Writing | **TSS** Unit 9 Writing Worksheet | |
| | 13 Reading | **TSS** Unit 9 Project Worksheet<br>**VID** Unit 9<br>**VRB** Unit 9 | **SS** Unit 9 Reading 1–2<br>**SS** Unit 9 Listening 1–3<br>**SS** Unit 9 Video 1–3<br>**WB** Unit 9 exercises 5–6 |

**Key**

| | | | | | | | |
|---|---|---|---|---|---|---|---|
| **GAME:** | Online Game | **SB:** | Student's Book | **SS:** | Online Self-study | **TSS:** | Teacher Support Site |
| **VID:** | Video DVD | **VRB:** | Video Resource Book | **WB:** | Online Workbook/Workbook | | |

# My Plan for Unit 9

Use the space below to customize a plan that fits your needs.

| With the following SB exercises | I am using these materials in class | My students are using these materials outside the classroom |
|---|---|---|
|  |  |  |
|  |  |  |
|  |  |  |
|  |  |  |
|  |  |  |
|  |  |  |
|  |  |  |
|  |  |  |
|  |  |  |
|  |  |  |
|  |  |  |
|  |  |  |
|  |  |  |

| With or instead of the following SB section | I am using these materials for assessment |
|---|---|
|  |  |
|  |  |
|  |  |

# 9 Getting things done

▸ Discuss professional services
▸ Make suggestions

## 1 SNAPSHOT

### Small Business Directory

Home    Advertise    Business reviews    Find a business    Quick search

**Automotive**
- Auto repair
- Car wash

**Computers and Electronics**
- Computer repair and data recovery
- Security systems repair

**Personal Services and Care**
- Carpet cleaning
- Home repairs

**Home and Garden**
- Laundry and dry cleaning
- Language tutoring

*Why would someone need these services? Have you ever used any of them?*
*How do you choose a company or person to do any of these services?*

## 2 PERSPECTIVES  Get the job done!

**A** Listen to an advertisement. Would you use a service like this? Why or why not?

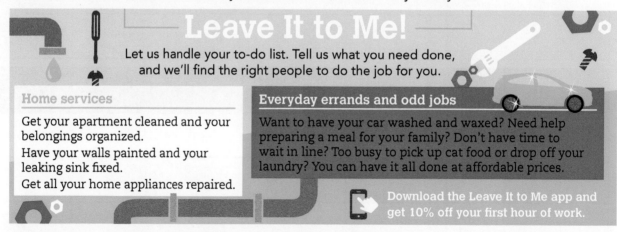

### Leave It to Me!

Let us handle your to-do list. Tell us what you need done, and we'll find the right people to do the job for you.

**Home services**

Get your apartment cleaned and your belongings organized.
Have your walls painted and your leaking sink fixed.
Get all your home appliances repaired.

**Everyday errands and odd jobs**

Want to have your car washed and waxed? Need help preparing a meal for your family? Don't have time to wait in line? Too busy to pick up cat food or drop off your laundry? You can have it all done at affordable prices.

Download the Leave It to Me app and get 10% off your first hour of work.

**B** What services do you need or want? What questions would you ask before hiring a person to do these services for you?

# 9 Getting things done

### Cycle 1, Exercises 1–6

In this unit, students discuss professional services and make suggestions. By the end of Cycle 1, students will be able to discuss professional services using causatives. By the end of Cycle 2, students will be able to use three-word phrasal verbs and make suggestions using a variety of structures.

## 1 SNAPSHOT

**Learning Objective:** discuss professional services

- To explain the concept of services, ask Ss about their haircuts. Ask: "Where do you get your hair cut? When you go to a hair salon or barber shop, do you leave with a product or a service?"

- Go over the information in the Snapshot. Point out that these are eight services that people commonly offer in the U.S.

- Elicit or explain any new vocabulary.

---

#### Vocabulary
**data recovery:** the process of getting information that had been erased from a computer
**tutoring:** working with one person to give extra help in a school subject

- Read the first two questions. Ss discuss the questions in small groups.

- Ss rank the usefulness of each service in the Snapshot using **Vocabulary Steps** – download it from the website.

- Read the last question. Then ask Ss to say different ways that services are offered in their own country (e.g., newspaper ads, Internet, recommendations). Then ask how they choose a service provider.

- Bring ads to class from service providers you can find online and discuss the ads with the class. Would they hire the people or companies in the ads?

## 2 PERSPECTIVES

**Learning Objective:** discuss professional services using *get* or *have something done*

### ▶ A [CD 2, Track 18]

- Books closed. Explain that some people offer a variety of services. You can find similar ads in the newspaper or on the Internet.

- Write these services on the board:

  | | |
  |---|---|
  | music lessons | laundry and dry cleaning |
  | home cleaning | car washing |
  | painting | repairs |
  | meal preparation | pet food |

- Books open. Read the questions.

- Play the audio. Ss listen and read. Have them answer the questions as a class.

### B

- Explain the task. Introduce *have something done* with questions like these: "What can you have done in a beauty salon? at a computer store? by a handyman? by an optician?" Write ideas on the board:

  | | |
  |---|---|
  | have your hair cut | have your house painted |
  | have your computer fixed | have your eyes tested |

- Read the first question. Write a model conversation on the board:

  A: What *do you need to have done?*
  B: Well, I *need to have my eyes tested, and I want to have my computer upgraded. What about you?*

- Model the conversation with a S. Tell Ss to think of at least five things they need to have done.

- Ss discuss the question in pairs. Go around the class and give help as needed. Then ask Ss to share ideas with the class.

- Read the second question. Elicit Ss' ideas (e.g., *How much do you charge for . . .? What beauty services do you offer? Do you pick up and drop off the laundry? Where can I get my car repaired?*).

# 3 GRAMMAR FOCUS

**Learning Objective:** use *get* or *have something done* to talk about professional services

▶ **[CD 2, Track 19]**
### Active

- Write these words on nine cards:

| you can | get | have |
|---|---|---|
| a plumber | your sink | by |
| to fix | fix | fixed |

- Ask five Ss to come to the front of the class. Give each S a card. Ask Ss to face the class, holding up their cards in this order:

  S1: you can    S2: have    S3: a plumber
  S4: fix          S5: your sink

- Explain that we can say the same sentence another way. Give S2 and S4 new cards. Now all five Ss face the class, holding up their cards in this order:

  S1: you can    S2: get     S3: a plumber
  S4: to fix      S5: your sink

- Elicit the rules and write them on the board:

  <u>Active</u>
  You can have a repair shop fix your computer.
      <u>have</u> + <u>someone</u> + <u>base form verb</u>
  You can get a repair shop to fix your computer.
      <u>get</u> + <u>someone</u> + <u>infinitive verb</u>

- Write two cues on the board. Elicit examples from the Perspectives exercise on page 58:

  You can have your car washed . . .
  You can get someone to . . .

### Passive

- Ask six Ss to hold up cards:

  S1: you can    S2: have   S3: your sink
  S4: fixed      S5: by     S6: a plumber

- Explain that we can say the same thing another way. Replace S2's card. Then ask Ss to hold up cards:

  S1: you can    S2: get    S3: your sink
  S4: fixed      S5: by     S6: a plumber

- Elicit the rules and write them on the board:

  <u>Passive</u>
  You can have/get your sink fixed (by a plumber).
      <u>have/get</u> + <u>object</u> + <u>past participle</u> (at/by)

- Focus Ss' attention on the Perspectives on page 58. Ask Ss to underline the active examples and circle the passive examples.

- Play the audio program. Ss listen and practice.

## A

- Explain the task. Ask a S to read the first item.
- Ss complete the task individually.

### Answers

1. My parents didn't paint their house before they moved in. They **had it painted**.
2. I didn't repair my own laptop. I **got it repaired** at the electronics store.
3. Many people don't wash their cars. They **have them washed**.
4. My bedroom carpet is very dirty, but I'm not cleaning it. I**'m getting it cleaned** next week.
5. My brother isn't repairing his bike. He**'s having it repaired**.

### B *Pair work*

- Explain the task. Read the example. Ask Ss which picture it describes.
- Ss work in pairs. Ss take turns describing the services in the pictures with the passive of *have* or *get*. (Answers: 1. Jessica is having her nails done. 2. Peter is getting / having his hair cut. 3. Zoe is having / getting her car repaired. 4. Tricia is having / getting her clothes dry cleaned.)

### C *Pair work*

- Explain the task. Model the activity by saying something you've had done for you recently and asking a S what he or she has had done.
- Ss work in pairs to discuss recent services they've had. Go around the room and listen for the passive of *have* or *get*. Take notes on errors you hear.
- Write any errors on the board. Elicit corrections from the class.

# 4 PRONUNCIATION

**Learning Objective:** sound more natural when using sentence stress

▶ **A [CD 2, Track 20]**

- Play the audio program. Ss listen. Elicit that stressed words carry the most important information. Point out that we don't usually stress pronouns.
- Play the audio program again. Ss practice both chorally and individually.

! To practice sentence stress, try the activity **Walking Stress** – download it from the website.

### B *Group work*

- Explain the task. Each S decides on three things he or she wants to have done.
- Ss work in small groups and take turns asking and answering questions.

# 3 GRAMMAR FOCUS

▶ **Get or have something done**

*Use get or have, the object, and the past participle of the verb to describe a service performed for you by someone else.*

| Do something yourself | Get/have something done for you |
|---|---|
| I **clean** my house every week. | I **get** my house **cleaned** (by a cleaner) every week. |
| He **is painting** his bedroom. | He **is having** his bedroom **painted**. |
| They **fixed** the sink. | They **got** the sink **fixed**. |
| Did you **paint** your bedroom? | Did you **have** your bedroom **painted**? |
| Where can I **wash** my car? | Where can I **have** my car **washed**? |

GRAMMAR PLUS *see page 140*

**A** Complete the sentences to express that the services are performed by someone else.

1. My parents didn't paint their house before they moved in. They _had it painted_. (have)
2. I didn't repair my own laptop. I _____ at the electronics store. (get)
3. Many people don't wash their cars. They _____. (have)
4. My bedroom carpet is very dirty, but I'm not cleaning it. I'm _____ next week. (get)
5. My brother isn't repairing his bike. He _____. (have)

**B** PAIR WORK Take turns describing the services in the pictures.

1. Jessica     2. Peter     3. Zoey     4. Tricia

"Jessica is having her nails done."

**C** PAIR WORK Tell your partner about three things you've had done for you recently. Ask and answer questions for more information.

# 4 PRONUNCIATION Sentence stress

▶ **A** Listen and practice. Notice that when the object becomes a pronoun (sentence B), it is no longer stressed.

**A:** Where can I have my car washed?

**B:** You can have it washed at the auto shop.

**A:** Where can I get my nails done?

**B:** You can get them done at a salon.

**B** GROUP WORK Ask questions about three things you want to have done. Pay attention to sentence stress. Other students give answers.

## 5 DISCUSSION On demand

**PAIR WORK** Are these services available in your city? For those that aren't, do you think they would be a good idea?

Can you . . . ?

get groceries delivered to your door
have a five-star meal cooked at your home by a chef
have your home organized by a professional organizer
have your portrait drawn by a street artist
get your pet vaccinated at home
get your blood pressure checked at a pharmacy
have your shoes shined on the street
get your car washed for less than $15
have a suit made in under 24 hours
have pizza delivered after midnight

**A:** Can you get groceries delivered to your door?
**B:** Sure! You can have it done by . . .

## 6 INTERCHANGE 9 Absolutely not!

What do parents and teenagers usually argue about? Go to Interchange 9 on page 123.

## 7 WORD POWER Three-word phrasal verbs

**A** Match each phrasal verb in these sentences with its meaning. Then compare with a partner.

**Phrasal verbs**

1. Polly has **broken up with** her boyfriend. _____
2. Lin **came up with** a great idea for a new app for meeting people. _____
3. My brother is **looking forward to** getting married. He really loves his fiancée. _____
4. I can't **keep up with** all the new technology. It changes so fast. _____
5. Luisa doesn't **get along with** her roommate. They argue over every little thing. _____
6. My doctor says I'm overweight. I should **cut down on** sweets. _____
7. I can't **put up with** the noise on my street! I'll have to move. _____
8. I don't like to **take care of** my own finances. I have an accountant manage my money. _____

**Meanings**

a. reduce the quantity of
b. end a romantic relationship with
c. continue to learn about
d. tolerate
e. be excited for
f. have a good relationship with
g. be responsible for
h. think of; develop

**B PAIR WORK** Take turns making sentences with each phrasal verb in part A.

## 5 DISCUSSION

**Learning Objective:** discuss where to find services using causatives

### Pair work

- Explain the task. Focus Ss' attention on the picture and the first question. Have two Ss model the conversation.
- Give Ss some time to read the situations.
- Elicit or explain any new vocabulary.

**Vocabulary**
**groceries:** goods bought to be used in the home, such as food and cleaning products
**portrait:** a painting of a person or group of people

- Ss discuss the questions in pairs. If possible, form pairs with Ss from different countries.
- Encourage Ss to give opinions. For services that aren't available, Ss should discuss whether the service would be a good idea. Set a time limit of about ten minutes.

**TIP**
As you walk around the class, make note of any grammar problems. When time is up, write representative problems on the board and elicit corrections from Ss.

 For another way to practice the Discussion, try the **Onion Ring** technique – download it from the website.

## 6 INTERCHANGE 9

See page T-123 for teaching notes.

### End of Cycle 1

See the Supplementary Resources chart at the beginning of this unit for additional teaching materials and student activities related to this Cycle.

### Cycle 2, Exercises 7–13

## 7 WORD POWER

**Learning Objective:** discuss problems using three-word phrasal verbs

### A

- Read the first sentence. Ask Ss to find the meaning of *break up with* in the meanings column.
- Elicit that these are three-word phrasal verbs. Point out that Ss already know a lot of two-word phrasal verbs. Elicit examples and write them on the board. (Possible answers: *pick up, turn off, get up, think about* . . .)
- Explain that the meaning of the three parts together is different from the individual parts:
  base verb + adverb particle + preposition
      *break*          *up*          *with*
- Ss complete the task individually.
- Then Ss compare answers in pairs. Ask Ss to write the answers on the board. Ss check their own work.

**Answers**

1. b   2. h   3. e   4. c   5. f   6. a   7. d   8. g

- **Option:** Show Ss ways to organize and store new vocabulary in their notebooks (e.g., *break up with* can be recorded as a diagram or a picture):

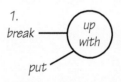

### B Pair work

- Explain the task. Ask a S to model the first phrasal verb in a sentence.
- Ss work in pairs. They take turns making sentences, preferably about their own lives.
- **Option:** Ask Ss to write a conversation or short story using the new vocabulary.

To review phrasal verbs, try the game **Sculptures** – download it from the website.

**Getting things done**   **T-60**

## 8 CONVERSATION

**Learning Objective:** make suggestions in a conversation about dating

 **A** *[CD 2, Track 21]*

- Books closed. To introduce the topic, ask: "How, when, and where did you meet your friend/partner?"

- Ss discuss the questions in pairs. Then elicit some interesting stories (e.g., *She was my next-door neighbor. One day . . .*).

- Books open. Ask Ss to cover the text and look only at the picture. Ask questions to set the scene (e.g., *How old are the two women? Are they friends?*).

- Ask Ss to listen to find out what Alice is upset about. Play the first line of the audio program. Elicit the answer. (Answer: She broke up with her boyfriend.)

- Next, ask Ss to take notes as they listen. Remind Ss to write down key words or phrases. Play the audio program once or twice.

- Ss compare notes in pairs. Ask Ss to share some of the things they heard discussed.

- Play the audio program again. Ss listen and read.

> **Vocabulary**
> **feel up to:** to have the energy to do something
> **I can't carry a tune to save my life:** I really can't sing well

! Pairs can practice the conversation using **Say It With Feeling!** – download it from the website.

**B** *Class activity*

- Read the question. Use the question to stimulate a short class discussion.

- **Option:** Tell Ss to imagine it is three weeks later and Alice has been to the running club. Ss write a follow-up conversation between Alice and Emma.

## 9 GRAMMAR FOCUS

**Learning Objective:** use gerunds, infinitives, modals + verbs, and negative questions to make suggestions

▶ *[CD 2, Track 22]*

- Focus Ss' attention on the previous Conversation. Ask Ss to underline examples of suggestions Emma makes.

- Point out the ways to make suggestions in the Grammar Focus box.

- Play the audio program. Ss listen and read or repeat.

- Go over the examples in the box again. Clarify which forms go together by writing this information on the board:

  *Making suggestions or giving advice*
  1. <u>Maybe you could</u> + base form verb . . .
  2. <u>Have you thought about</u> + gerund . . . ?
  3. <u>Why don't you</u> + base form verb . . . ?
  4. <u>One option is/It might be a good idea</u> + infinitive . . .

- Give Ss some additional situations. Elicit suggestions:
  T:   I'd like to lose some weight.
  S1:  One option is to walk everywhere.
  S2:  Have you thought about going on a diet?
  S3:  Why don't you join a health club?

**A**

- Explain the task. Ask Ss to read each problem and suggestion. Elicit or explain any new vocabulary.

- To model the task, read the first problem and suggestion. Elicit the answer. Elicit that *one option* is incorrect because it is not followed by the verb *be* + infinitive.

- Ss complete the task individually.

- Have Ss work in pairs to compare answers. Then go over the answers with the class.

> **Answers**
>
> 1. A: What can I do to keep up with all my assignments in college?
>    B: **Maybe** you could stay in on weeknights.
> 2. A: What can I do to get in shape?
>    B: **Have you thought about** working out at the gym?
> 3. A: How can I save money?
>    B: **Why don't you** come up with a budget?
> 4. A: How can I learn to dance?
>    B: **It might be a good idea** to take dance classes.
> 5. A: How can I build self-confidence?
>    B: **What about** participating in more social activities?

**B** *Group work*

- Explain the task. Ask two or three Ss to model the activity by making suggestions for the first problem in part A.

- Ss work in small groups. Set a time limit of about five minutes. Go around the class and give help as needed.

- **Option:** Ask one S in each group to disagree with everything (e.g., *No, that doesn't work! I've already tried it!*).

## 8 CONVERSATION  I can't carry a tune.

▶ **A** Listen and practice.

**Emma:** Are you going to Lina's party tonight?

**Alice:** No, I don't think so. I don't really feel up to it.

**Emma:** You haven't been going out much since you broke up with Carter.

**Alice:** I guess not. He's friends with all my friends, you know.

**Emma:** You need to meet new people. Have you thought about joining a running club? You love running.

**Alice:** I've thought about that, but they meet at 6 A.M. I'm not really a morning person.

**Emma:** Well . . . maybe you could take part in our singing group. I've made a lot of good friends there.

**Alice:** Um, I don't think so. Remember when we did karaoke? I can't carry a tune to save my life!

**Emma:** Yeah, I remember. . . . Well, I guess you'd better get used to waking up early. Just think of all the cute guys who go running in the park in the morning.

**B** CLASS ACTIVITY  What are some other good ways to meet people?

## 9 GRAMMAR FOCUS

▶ **Making suggestions**

| | |
|---|---|
| **With modals + verbs** | **With negative questions** |
| **Maybe you could** take part in a singing group. | **Why don't you** do some volunteer work? |
| **With gerunds** | **With infinitives** |
| **What about joining** a running club? | **One option is to join** a club. |
| **Have you thought about asking** your friends to introduce you around? | **It might be a good idea to check out** the cultural events at the university. |

GRAMMAR PLUS *see page 140*

**A** Circle the correct answers. Then practice with a partner.

1. **A:** What can I do to keep up with all my assignments in college?
   **B: Maybe / One option** you could stay in on weeknights.

2. **A:** What can I do to get in shape?
   **B: Why don't you / Have you thought about** working out at the gym?

3. **A:** How can I save money?
   **B: Why don't you / What about** come up with a budget?

4. **A:** How can I learn to dance?
   **B: Have you thought about / It might be a good idea** to take dance classes.

5. **A:** How can I build self-confidence?
   **B: What about / Why don't you** participating in more social activities?

**B** GROUP WORK  Take turns asking and answering the questions in part A.
Answer with your own suggestions.

## 10 LISTENING Resolutions

▶ **A** Listen to a conversation between three friends on New Year's Eve. Check (✓) the resolution each person makes and write their friends' suggestions.

|  | New Year's resolutions | | Suggestions |
|---|---|---|---|
| **1. Edward** | ☐ get a better job | ☐ start a project | |
| **2. Selena** | ☐ have more energy | ☐ go back to school | |
| **3. Hannah** | ☐ fix her relationship problems | ☐ spend more time on social media | |

**B** GROUP WORK Decide on your own suggestion for each person. Then vote as a class on the best suggestions.

## 11 SPEAKING Breaking a habit

GROUP WORK Make three suggestions for how to break each of these bad habits. Then share your ideas with the class. Which ideas are the most creative?

**How can I stop . . . ?**

drinking too much soda

biting my nails

spending more money than I can afford

"One thing you could do is carry a bottle of water with you all the time. And why don't you . . . ?"

## 12 WRITING Sound advice

**A** Read the posts from a question and answer website. Choose one of the posts below and make a list of suggestions. Then write a reply.

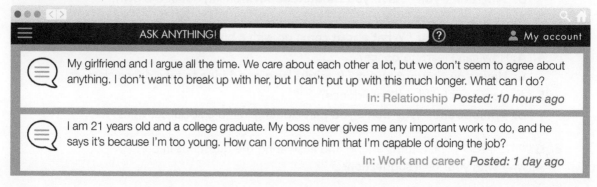

ASK ANYTHING!   ⑦   👤 My account

My girlfriend and I argue all the time. We care about each other a lot, but we don't seem to agree about anything. I don't want to break up with her, but I can't put up with this much longer. What can I do?

In: Relationship *Posted: 10 hours ago*

I am 21 years old and a college graduate. My boss never gives me any important work to do, and he says it's because I'm too young. How can I convince him that I'm capable of doing the job?

In: Work and career *Posted: 1 day ago*

**B** GROUP WORK Take turns reading your advice. Whose advice do you think will work? Why?

# 10 LISTENING

**Learning Objective:** listen for details in suggestions for solutions to problems

▶ **A** *[CD 2, Track 23]*

- Read the six resolutions in the chart. Ask: "Do you ever make New Year's resolutions? Have any of your resolutions been similar to these?" Elicit ideas.

- For more practice with predicting content, play **Prediction Bingo** – download it from the website.

- Explain the task. Ss will check the resolution mentioned in the audio and write the suggestion of a friend.

- Play the audio program. Pause after each speaker for Ss to write. Ss listen and write the suggestions.

- Play the audio program a second time so Ss can check their answers. Go over the answers with the class.

---

**TIP**
Listening should not be a memory test for Ss. If a Listening is long or contains many details, break it up into sections, pausing after each speaker. If helpful, mark in the script where you plan to pause, using the symbol //.

---

## Answers

1. start a project; cut down on distractions; go to the library for a few hours
2. have more energy; exercise at home with an app; do outdoor exercise like hiking, swimming, or jogging
3. fix her relationship problems; take a break from work; take a couple hours off from her phone every night

## Audio script

See page T-175.

**B** *Group work*

- Explain the task.

- Ss work in groups and think of a suggestion for each resolution. Walk around the class and help Ss with structure and vocabulary.

- Ask groups to share their answer with the class. Ss vote on the two or three best suggestions.

---

# 11 SPEAKING

**Learning Objective:** make suggestions

*Group work*

- Explain the task. Ask Ss to read the caption for each picture. Ss think of three suggestions for each habit. Ss should be able to explain why they are making the suggestion.

- Ss work individually to write down ideas.

- Then Ss work in groups. Ss take turns sharing suggestions. Remind Ss to ask follow-up questions.

**TIP**
To increase student talking time, introduce challenging rules (e.g., fewer than three-word answers are not acceptable, each S must ask three follow-up questions, or use at least three phrasal verbs).

---

- Go around the class and listen in. Note any problems and go over them later with the class.

- *Option:* Ss role-play one of the problems.

! For a new way to practice this exercise, try the **Substitution Dialog** with the Conversation on page 61 – download it from the website. Ss think of a new problem to discuss.

---

# 12 WRITING

**Learning Objective:** write a letter of advice making suggestions

**A**

- Explain the task. Ss imagine they are writing replies to people posting problems on a website.

- Give Ss a few minutes to read the posts and choose one. Set a time limit of about five minutes.

- Then Ss write a reply. Encourage Ss to give more than one suggestion for solving the problem.

**TIP**
To make writing assignments more challenging for higher-level Ss, increase the length of the assignment. You can also encourage them to use more new vocabulary and grammar.

---

**B** *Group work*

- Explain the task.

- Ss work in groups and take turns reading advice.

- Group members discuss which pieces of advice will work and why.

**Learning Objective:** identify main ideas, details, and examples in an article

**A**

- Books closed. Read the questions. Books open. Ss find the answers to the questions. (Answers: Jack Andraka; he developed a test for early-stage pancreatic cancer)

- See if Ss can also tell you why Jack Andraka decided to research pancreatic cancer testing. (Answer: A family friend died of the disease.)

**TIP**

Asking Ss a personal question related to a challenging or theoretical reading helps them to connect to the topic and encourages intrapersonal learning.

**B**

- Ss read the article. Tell Ss to mark any words they are unable to guess from context. Afterward, Ss can check their dictionaries for the meanings of any words they marked.

- Elicit or explain any new vocabulary.

**Vocabulary**

**disease:** an illness caused by an infection or by a failure of health and not by an accident
**deeply:** very much
**lethal:** able to cause death
**stage:** a period of development, or a particular time in a process
**endlessly:** continuing for a long time and never finishing, or never seeming to finish
**perseverance:** the quality of persisting when things are difficult
**prestigious:** respected and admired, usually because of being important
**after all:** a phrase used to add information that shows that what you have just said is true
**ground-breaking:** very new and a big change from other things of its type

- Explain the task. Ss will identify the main idea of each paragraph. Point out that the other sentences in the paragraph all support the main idea.

- Ss complete the task individually. Then they compare their answers in pairs.

- Go over answers with the class.

**Answers**

2 One doctor's help makes the unlikely become possible.
1 A personal experience creates a groundbreaking idea.
4 Family support and a passion for discovery can lead to great things.
3 Although he won a big prize, there's plenty of work ahead.

**C**

- Explain the task.

- Ss work individually to choose the correct answers.

- Then Ss compare their answers in pairs. Ask Ss to explain their reasons to their partner.

- Elicit answers from pairs.

**Answers**

1. Pancreatic cancer is so serious because **it is hard to diagnose early**.
2. Andraka was inspired to find a solution by **an upsetting experience**.
3. The response to Andraka's proposal was **largely negative**.
4. Andraka's test for pancreatic cancer is **being developed now**.
5. Andraka's family helped him by **encouraging him**.

**D** *Group work*

- Explain the task. Ss work in small groups to discuss the question. Remind Ss to ask follow-up questions and give additional suggestions.

- *Option:* Ask Ss to summarize their group members' ideas for the class.

## End of Cycle 2

See the Supplementary Resources chart at the beginning of this unit for additional teaching materials and student activities related to this Cycle.

**A** Scan the article. Who is the article about? What idea did he have?

# Improving the world
## – one idea at a time

[1] Jack Andraka was 15 when he came up with an idea for a new way to test for pancreatic cancer. When Andraka was 14, a family friend died of the disease, and this affected him deeply. This kind of cancer is particularly lethal because there is no test you can have done to find it in the early stages. By the time standard tests determine you have the disease, it is often too late. Realizing that this was the case, Andraka decided to try to develop a test that might catch problems at the earliest stages.

[2] The road ahead looked difficult for Andraka. He was still a high school student, and he wanted to create something that no one else had done. But Andraka read endlessly about the disease, wrote a proposal for his idea, and sent it out to 200 cancer researchers. Only one professor, Dr. Anirban Maitra, responded positively. Dr. Maitra agreed to work with Andraka on his idea, giving him guidance and access to a laboratory.

[3] The next big reward for Andraka's perseverance was winning the grand prize at the Intel International Science and Engineering Fair. This prestigious award is given to young innovators who have developed a world-changing idea. Developing the test is likely to take many years, but Andraka hopes the test will eventually improve people's lives – and maybe save them.

[4] Jack Andraka is not alone as a young innovator. After all, there were 1,499 other contestants for the Intel award, and all of them had ground-breaking ideas. For Andraka, having a family that loves science and encourages creative thinking gave him an advantage. But the key for Andraka is that reading, research, and discovery are just plain fun – and the chance to improve the world around him in the process makes it even better.

**B** Read the article. Write the number of each paragraph next to its summary sentence.

_____ One doctor's help makes the unlikely become possible.

_____ A personal experience creates a groundbreaking idea.

_____ Family support and a passion for discovery can lead to great things.

_____ Although he won a big prize, there's plenty of work ahead.

**C** Choose the correct answers.

1. Pancreatic cancer is so serious because **there is no treatment / it is hard to diagnose early**.
2. Andraka was inspired to find a solution by **an upsetting experience / reading about a disease**.
3. The response to Andraka's proposal was **fairly positive / largely negative**.
4. Andraka's test for pancreatic cancer is **in use now / being developed now**.
5. Andraka's family helped him by **encouraging him / working on his idea**.

**D** GROUP WORK If you could come up with an idea to help humanity, what would it be?

# Unit 10 Supplementary Resources Overview

| | After the following SB exercises | You can use these materials in class | Your students can use these materials outside the classroom |
|---|---|---|---|
| **CYCLE 1** | 1 Snapshot | | |
| | 2 Perspectives | | |
| | 3 Grammar Focus | **TSS** Unit 10 Listening Worksheet | **SB** Unit 10 Grammar plus, Focus 1 <br> **SS** Unit 10 Grammar 1 <br> **GAME** Say the Word (Referring to time in the past) |
| | 4 Pronunciation | **TSS** Unit 10 Extra Worksheet | |
| | 5 Word Power | **TSS** Unit 10 Vocabulary Worksheet | **SS** Unit 10 Vocabulary 1–2 <br> **GAME** Spell or Slime (Historic events) |
| | 6 Discussion | | |
| | 7 Writing | | |
| | 8 Interchange 10 | | **WB** Unit 10 exercises 1–4 |
| **CYCLE 2** | 9 Conversation | | **SS** Unit 10 Speaking 1–2 |
| | 10 Grammar Focus | **TSS** Unit 10 Grammar Worksheet <br> **TSS** Unit 10 Writing Worksheet | **SB** Unit 10 Grammar plus, Focus 2 <br> **SS** Unit 10 Grammar 2 <br> **GAME** Sentence Stacker (Predicting the future with *will*) <br> **GAME** Sentence runner (Predicting the future with *will*) |
| | 11 Listening | | |
| | 12 Discussion | | |
| | 13 Reading | **TSS** Unit 10 Project Worksheet <br> **VID** Unit 10 <br> **VRB** Unit 10 | **SS** Unit 10 Reading 1–2 <br> **SS** Unit 10 Listening 1–4 <br> **SS** Unit 10 Video 1–3 <br> **WB** Unit 10 exercises 5–8 |

| With or instead of the following SB section | You can also use these materials for assessment |
|---|---|
| **Units 9–10 Progress Check** | **ASSESSMENT PROGRAM** Units 9–10 Oral Quiz <br> **ASSESSMENT PROGRAM** Units 9–10 Written Quiz |

**Key**

| | | | | | | | |
|---|---|---|---|---|---|---|---|
| **GAME:** | Online Game | **SB:** | Student's Book | **SS:** | Online Self-study | **TSS:** | Teacher Support Site |
| **VID:** | Video DVD | **VRB:** | Video Resource Book | **WB:** | Online Workbook/Workbook | | |

# My Plan for Unit 10

Use the space below to customize a plan that fits your needs.

| With the following SB exercises | I am using these materials in class | My students are using these materials outside the classroom |
|---|---|---|
|  |  |  |
|  |  |  |
|  |  |  |
|  |  |  |
|  |  |  |
|  |  |  |
|  |  |  |
|  |  |  |
|  |  |  |
|  |  |  |
|  |  |  |
|  |  |  |
|  |  |  |

| With or instead of the following SB section | I am using these materials for assessment |
|---|---|
|  |  |
|  |  |
|  |  |

# 10 A matter of time

▶ Discuss important past events
▶ Make predictions

## 1 SNAPSHOT

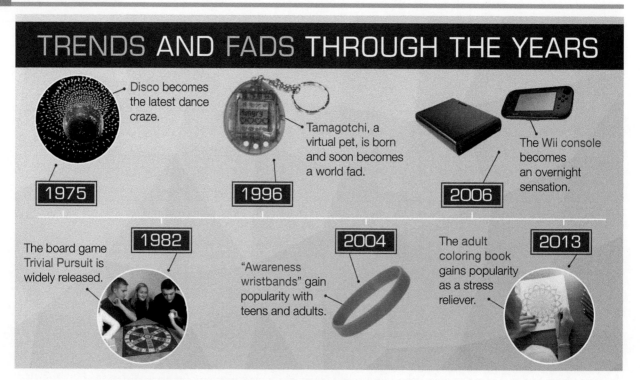

## TRENDS AND FADS THROUGH THE YEARS

Disco becomes the latest dance craze.

**1975**

Tamagotchi, a virtual pet, is born and soon becomes a world fad.

**1996**

The Wii console becomes an overnight sensation.

**2006**

The board game Trivial Pursuit is widely released.

**1982**

"Awareness wristbands" gain popularity with teens and adults.

**2004**

The adult coloring book gains popularity as a stress reliever.

**2013**

*Have any of these fads ever been popular in your country?*
*Can you think of other fads from the past or present?*
*Is there anything popular right now that you think is just a fad?*

## 2 PERSPECTIVES Quiz show

**A** Read the questions from a quiz show. Do you know the answers? Check (✓) your guesses.

1. **When was the first home video game console released?**
   ☐ **a.** in 1967     ☐ **b.** in 1972     ☐ **c.** in 1981

2. **How long has Washington, D.C., been the capital of the United States?**
   ☐ **a.** since 1776     ☐ **b.** since 1783     ☐ **c.** since 1800

3. **How long were the Beatles together?**
   ☐ **a.** for 8 years     ☐ **b.** for 10 years     ☐ **c.** for 15 years

4. **When did World War I take place?**
   ☐ **a.** during the 1910s     ☐ **b.** during the 1920s     ☐ **c.** during the 1940s

**B** Now listen and check your answers. What information is the most surprising?

64

# 10 A matter of time

## Cycle 1, Exercises 1–8

In this unit, students discuss important past events and make predictions. By the end of Cycle 1, students will be able to discuss important past events using time references. By the end of Cycle 2, students will be able to make predictions using a variety of structures.

## 1 SNAPSHOT

**Learning Objective:** discuss past trends

- Books closed. Write the following on the board. Elicit what each is. Ask Ss to match these things with the date they became popular:

  | | |
  |---|---|
  | Tamagotchi | 1975 |
  | Trivial Pursuit | 2006 |
  | Wii | 1982 |
  | Disco | 1996 |

- Books open. Point out that the Snapshot contains six trends in the U.S. through the years. Elicit or explain that a *trend* is something that is very popular or fashionable.
- Ss check their answers.
- Discuss the pictures. Give Ss a few minutes to read the Snapshot.

- Explain that these sentences are written in the present tense, but they refer to past events. This is sometimes called the *historical present*. It's occasionally used for special effect (as in newspaper headlines) or in informal conversation when narrating a past event.
- Elicit or explain any new vocabulary.
- Discuss the questions with the class.

### Vocabulary
**to be released:** to be published or put on the market for sale
**fad:** a style, activity, or interest that is very popular for a short period of time
**overnight sensation:** a sudden success

- Read the questions. Ss discuss the questions in small groups.

## 2 PERSPECTIVES

**Learning Objective:** use time references to talk about past events

### A

- Write the title on the board. Ask Ss: "Do you like trivia or quiz shows? Why or why not?"
- Explain the task. Ask Ss to read the quiz questions. Elicit Ss' guesses for each one, and ask them to write their answers.

### ▶ B [CD 2, Track 24]

- Play the audio program and Ss check their answers. Who got the most right?
- Play the audio program again. Ss listen and read.
- Discuss the questions with the class. Can they agree on which information is the most surprising?

- **Option:** Divide the class into two groups. Have Ss write five additional questions to quiz the other group.
- Discuss the correct answers.

### Answers
1. b    2. c    3. b    4. a

## 3 GRAMMAR FOCUS

**Learning Objective:** use adverbs and prepositions of time *during, in, from . . . to, since,* and *for* to refer to time in the past

▶ *[CD 2, Track 25]*

- Write the following on the board. Ask Ss to complete the blanks with the time references:

  *ago   during   for   from...to   in   since*
  1. The first video game console was released . . .
     _____ 1972 / _____ the 1970s
  2. Washington has been the capital of the U.S. . . .
     _____ 1800 / _____ over 200 years
  3. The Beatles were together . . .
     _____ 10 years / _____ 1960 _____ 1970

  ---
  **TIP**
  Let Ss try a task first, and then teach them what they don't know.
  ---

- Write the answers on the board. (Answers: 1. in, in/during 2. since, for 3. for, from . . . to)

### A point of time in the past (*in, ago, during*)
- Write on the board:

Rock 'n' roll became popular over 65 years **ago**.

Disco became a craze **in** 1975.

Rubik's Cubes were popular **during** the 1980s.

### A period of time that continues into the present (*since, for*)

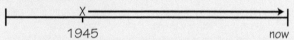

The United Nations has existed **since** 1945.
The United Nations has existed **for** over 70 years.
*since* + a point of time (e.g., *since last year/Tuesday*)
*for* + a length of time (e.g., *for two weeks/three hours*)

## 4 PRONUNCIATION

**Learning Objective:** use syllable stress to sound more natural when saying four- and five-syllable words

▶ **A** *[CD 2, Track 26]*

- Explain that in longer words, one syllable carries the main stress whereas another syllable carries the secondary stress.

- Tell Ss to focus on the main and secondary stress. Play the audio program. Ask Ss to tap or clap in time to the stress. Point out that the syllable before *-tion* is always stressed.

### A period of time in the past (*from . . . to, for*)

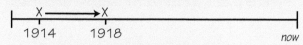

World War I lasted **from** 1914 **to** 1918.
World War I lasted **for** four years.

- Play the audio program. Ss listen and read or repeat.

**A**

- Focus Ss' attention on the pictures. Elicit what Ss know about the Olympic games.

- Explain the task. Ss use time words to complete the paragraphs. List the time words on the board.

- Ss complete the task individually.

- Ss compare answers in pairs.

---
**Possible answers**

1. The Olympic Games originated in ancient Greece about 3,000 years **ago**. **From** the eighth century BCE **to** the fourth century CE, the games took place in Olympia. The first modern Olympics were held **in** 1896 in Athens, with male participants from 14 nations. Women have only competed in the Olympics **since** 1900.
2. Although no one knows for sure, it's likely that the Chinese invented ice cream about 4,000 years **ago**. It was probably brought to Italy **in/during** the thirteenth century by Marco Polo, but the ice cream we enjoy today was probably created in Italy **in/during** the seventeenth century and spread through Europe **in/during** the eighteenth century. **Since** that time, different flavors have been created, but vanilla is still America's favorite.
---

**B** *Group work*

- Explain the task. Ask two Ss to model the conversation.

- Ss work individually. They write two true and two false statements about world events.

- Then Ss present their questions to the group. Others listen and correct the false statements.

▶ **B** *[CD 2, Track 27]*

- Explain the task.

- Play the second part of the audio program.

- Play the audio program again. Go over answers.

---
**Answers**

(main stress in boldface, secondary in italics)
*ca***tas**trophe        *rev*o**lu**tion        *as*sas**si**nation
ap**pre**ciate        *con*ver**sa**tion        *con*sider**a**tion
---

# 3 GRAMMAR FOCUS

▶ **Referring to time in the past**

**A point or period of time in the past**

When was the first video game console released?        How long were the Beatles together?
  **During** the 1970s. **In** the 1970s. Over 40 years **ago**.        **From** 1960 **to** 1970. **For** 10 years.

**A period of time that continues into the present**

How long has Washington, D.C. been the capital of the United States?
  **Since** 1800. **For** about 220 years.

GRAMMAR PLUS *see page 141*

**A** Complete the paragraphs with the **bold** words from the grammar box.
Then compare with a partner.

1. The Olympic Games originated in ancient
   Greece about 3,000 years _____. _____ the
   eighth century BCE _____ the fourth century CE,
   the games took place in Olympia. The first
   modern Olympics were held _____ 1896 in Athens,
   with male participants from 14 nations. Women
   have only competed in the Olympics _____ 1900.

2. Although no one knows for sure, it's likely that the
   Chinese invented ice cream about 4,000 years
   _____. It was probably brought to Italy _____
   the thirteenth century by Marco Polo, but the
   ice cream we enjoy today was probably created
   in Italy _____ the seventeenth century and spread
   through Europe _____ the eighteenth century.
   _____ that time, different flavors have been
   created, but vanilla is still America's favorite.

**B** GROUP WORK Write two true and two false statements about world events.
Then take turns reading your statements. Others give correct information for
the false statements.

**A:** The United Nations was founded about 50 years ago.
**B:** That's false. It was founded in 1945, after the end of World War II.

# 4 PRONUNCIATION Syllable stress

▶ **A** Listen and practice. Notice which syllable has the main stress in these four-
and five-syllable words. Notice the secondary stress.

• ● • •            ● • ● •            • ● • ● •
**identify**           **disadvantage**            **communication**

_____        _____          _____
_____        _____          _____

appreciate
assassination
catastrophe
consideration
conversation
revolution

▶ **B** Listen to the words in the box. Which syllable has the main stress?
Write the words in the correct column in part A.

## 5 WORD POWER Historic events

A Match each word with the best example. Then compare with a partner.

1. achievement _____
2. assassination _____
3. discovery _____
4. election _____
5. epidemic _____
6. natural disaster _____
7. revolution _____
8. terrorist act _____

a. In 2015, an earthquake hit Nepal and killed over 8,000 people.
b. Fidel Castro established a communist government in Cuba in 1959.
c. In 2015, scientists confirmed the existence of water on Mars.
d. Since the early 1980s, HIV has infected more than 70 million people.
e. Barack Obama became the first African American US president in 2009.
f. John Lennon was killed by a fan on December 8, 1980.
g. In 2003, scientists completed the Human Genome Project.
h. Two men invaded and killed the journalists of the *Charlie Hebdo* newspaper in Paris in 2015.

B PAIR WORK Give another example for each kind of event in part A.

"The invention of writing was a very important achievement for humankind."

## 6 DISCUSSION A major impact

GROUP WORK Choose two or three historic events (an election, an epidemic, an achievement, etc.) that had an impact on your country. Discuss the questions.

What happened (or what was achieved)? When did it happen?
What was the immediate effect on your country? the world? your family?
Did it change things permanently? How is life different now?

"The recent economic crisis has had a major impact on our lives . . ."

## 7 WRITING A biography

A Find information about a person who has had a major influence on the world or your country. Answer these questions. Then write a biography.

What is this person famous for?
How and when did he or she become famous?
What are his or her important achievements?

### MALALA YOUSAFZAI
Activist for Women and Children's Rights

Malala was born in 1997 in Pakistan where she spoke out for girls' right to education. When she was 15, she suffered an attack on her life and almost died. She was flown to England, recovered from her injuries, and continued her fight. When she was 17, she became the youngest winner of the Nobel Peace Prize . . .

B PAIR WORK Exchange biographies. What additional details can your partner add?

## 8 INTERCHANGE 10 History buff

Find out how good you are at history.
Student A, go to Interchange 10A on page 124; Student B, go to Interchange 10B on page 126.

## 5 WORD POWER

**Learning Objective:** discuss historical events

### A

- Explain the task. Model the task with the first word.
- Ss complete the task individually. Ss match words with definitions. Go around the class and give help as needed.
- Ss go over their answers in pairs. Then elicit Ss' answers. As you go over answers, help Ss with pronunciation and stress.

### Answers

1. g    2. f    3. c    4. e    5. d    6. a    7. b    8. h

### B Pair work

- Elicit two or three examples for each word or phrase.
- Explain the task. Ask a S to read the example sentence.
- Ss work in pairs to use the words from Part A in complete sentences.
- Then ask several pairs to write their best sentences on the board.
- **Option:** Ss write a story instead of sentences.
- To practice the vocabulary, play **Tic-Tac-Toe** – download it from the website. Add two more words from the unit.

## 6 DISCUSSION

**Learning Objectives:** discuss historic events using prepositions of time; discuss cause and effect in the past

### Group work

- Explain the task. Elicit the meaning of *had an impact on* (changed or greatly affected; the result could be either positive or negative).
- Read the questions aloud. Read the beginning of the example sentence aloud. Finish the sentence by explaining that the American economic crisis of 2008 was triggered by the decline of home prices and large amounts of unpaid debt. It had an impact on the U.S and many other countries. As a result of the crisis, many laws and regulations were changed.

- Ss work in small groups. First, they choose two or three historic events. Then they discuss the questions. Set a time limit of about ten minutes.
- Go around the class and give help as needed. Note any common errors.
- Elicit corrections orally to the common errors.
- When time is up, have one S from each group choose one event and tell the class what his or her group discussed.

## 7 WRITING

**Learning Objective:** research and write a biography of a famous person from the past using time references

### A

Note: Ss will need to do research ahead of time. This task can also be done for homework.

- Explain the task. Ask Ss to read the questions. Then read aloud the entry about Malala Yousafzai.
- Ask Ss to find the answers to the prewriting questions in the model paragraph. Elicit the answers. (Answers: speaking out for girls' education, she survived an attack when she was 15, youngest winner of Nobel Peace Prize)
- Then Ss work individually to choose an influential person and write a biography. Allow time for Ss to research answers to the prewriting questions.

### B Pair work

- Explain the task. Ss work in pairs to exchange biographies and suggest details to add.
- **Option:** Have pairs check each other's biographies for the correct use of time phrases.
- Have Ss revise their paragraphs to include new details, if possible, or make changes to time phrases, if necessary. Collect the biographies.
- **Option:** Post the biographies around the room or on a bulletin board and have Ss read them. Ask Ss which influential people and achievements were most memorable or interesting to them.

## 8 INTERCHANGE 10

See page T-124 for teaching notes.

See page T-124 for teaching notes.

See the Supplementary Resources chart at the beginning of this unit for additional teaching materials and student activities related to this Cycle.

### End of Cycle 1

# 9 CONVERSATION

**Learning Objective:** discuss predictions about the future using future tenses with *will* in context

## ▶ A [CD 2, Track 28]

- Ask Ss to cover the text and look only at the picture. Ask what is happening in the picture. (Answer: The woman is talking to her friend about space travel.)

- Write this prediction on the board:

  *In 50 years, we will spend vacations on Mars.*

- Now write these topics on the board. Ss discuss the topics in pairs. Ask Ss to make predictions about the future.

  *rocket technology       life on the moon*
  *Mars colony              Earth's destruction*

- Ask Ss to come to the board and write one prediction for each topic. Remind Ss to use *will*, not *be going to*, for predictions.

- Tell Ss to listen to find out if their predictions are mentioned. If their predictions aren't mentioned, elicit what they heard about each topic. Play the audio program.

- Text uncovered. Ask Ss to read the predictions.

- Elicit or explain any new vocabulary.

> **Vocabulary**
> **powerful:** having a lot of power
> **set up:** organized or arranged
> **colony:** a country or area controlled politically by a more powerful country that is often far away

## B *Class activity*

- Read the question. Ss discuss the question. Elicit ideas around the class.

# 10 GRAMMAR FOCUS

**Learning Objective:** use *will*, the future continuous, and the future perfect to make predictions

## ▶ [CD 2, Track 29]

- Explain that there are many ways to describe the future in English. Write the three future tenses on the board. Ask Ss to find examples in the previous Conversation. Write on the board:

  1. will/won't + base verb
     We <u>will spend</u> vacations in space.
     We <u>won't have</u> colonies on Mars.

  2. <u>future continuous: will be + present participle</u>
     Human beings <u>will be living</u> on another planet.
     We <u>won't be living</u> here.

  3. <u>future perfect: will have + past participle</u>
     We <u>will have set up</u> a research center on Mars.
     A company <u>will have built</u> a resort on the moon.

- Elicit or explain the differences among the structures. Ask: "Which describes an ongoing action? Which describes something that will be completed by a specific time?" Point out that the future perfect needs a date or time of completion (e.g., *within 20 years, by 2050*).

- Play the audio program. Ss listen and read or repeat.

## A

- Explain the task. Model the first sentence.

- Ss complete the task individually.

- Ss go over their answers in pairs. Then elicit Ss' responses around the class.

> **Answers**
> 1. Sometime in the future, buildings **will have** green walls and roof gardens to help retain carbon dioxide.
> 2. By the end of this century, half of the Amazon rain forest **will have been** deforested.
> 3. In 50 years, the world population **will reach/will have reached** 9 billion.
> 4. In the future, most of the population **will be living/will live** in cities.
> 5. Soon, computers **will become** more intelligent than humans.
> 6. In less than 20 years, scientists **will have discovered** a cure for cancer, but we **will suffer** from new diseases.

## 9 CONVERSATION I'll be their first guest!

▶ **A** Listen and practice.

**Hazel:** Would you want to spend a vacation in space?

**Oscar:** No, thanks. I'd rather go to the beach. Would you?

**Hazel:** Of course I would! I'd stay longer, too. Do you think we'll have colonies on Mars in 20 or 30 years?

**Oscar:** I don't know. Considering how fast we're destroying Earth, we won't be living here for much longer.

**Hazel:** I'm serious! You know, international space agencies are investing a lot of money in research to develop more powerful rockets.

**Oscar:** Well, I guess that within 50 years, we'll have set up a research center on Mars, but not a colony.

**Hazel:** You're probably right. But I'm sure some company will have built a resort on the moon by then. And I'll be their first guest!

**B** CLASS ACTIVITY Do you think Hazel and Oscar's predictions are correct?

## 10 GRAMMAR FOCUS

▶ **Predicting the future with *will***

Use ***will*** to predict future events or situations.

We **will spend** vacations in space. We **won't have** colonies on Mars.

Use future continuous to predict ongoing actions.

Human beings **will be living** on another planet. We **won't be living** here.

Use future perfect to predict actions that will be completed by a certain time.

Within 50 years, we **will have set up** a research center on Mars.

By 2050, a company **will have built** a resort on the moon.

GRAMMAR PLUS *see page 141*

**A** Complete these predictions with the correct verb forms. (More than one answer is possible.) Then compare with a partner.

1. Sometime in the future, buildings _____ (have) green walls and roof gardens to help retain carbon dioxide.

2. By the end of this century, half of the Amazon rain forest _____ (be) deforested.

3. In 50 years, the world population _____ (reach) 9 billion.

4. In the future, most of the population _____ (live) in cities.

5. Soon, computers _____ (become) more intelligent than humans.

6. In less than 20 years, scientists _____ (discover) a cure for cancer, but we _____ (suffer) from new diseases.

**B** GROUP WORK Discuss each prediction in part A. Do you agree or disagree?

**A:** Sometime in the future, buildings will have green walls and roof gardens to help retain carbon dioxide. What do you think?

**B:** Oh, I totally agree. That's also a good way to keep the temperature inside cooler in the summer.

**C:** I'm not so sure that will happen. Green walls are pretty expensive to maintain.

**C** CLASS ACTIVITY Discuss these questions.

**1.** What three recently developed technologies will have the greatest impact on our lives in the next 20 years?

**2.** What are the three most important changes that will have occurred on Earth by 2050?

**3.** Which three jobs will people *not* be doing in 50 years? Why?

## 11 LISTENING Not in our lifetime

▶ **A** Listen to people discuss changes that will affect these topics in the future. Write down two changes for each topic.

|  | Future changes | |
| --- | --- | --- |
| **1.** crime |  |  |
| **2.** space travel |  |  |
| **3.** environment |  |  |
| **4.** energy |  |  |
| **5.** money |  |  |

**B** PAIR WORK Which changes do you agree will happen? Which ones would most affect you? Why?

## 12 DISCUSSION Time will tell.

**A** Think about your dreams and goals for the future. Write down an idea for each category.

an activity you'd like to try          a city where you would like to live
an experience you'd like to have       a job you'd like to have
a skill you'd like to develop          a person you'd like to meet

**B** GROUP WORK Talk about these questions. Use your ideas from part A.

What do you think you'll be doing a year from now? five years from now?

Do you think you'll still be living in the same city? same country?

What are three things you think you'll have accomplished within the next 10 years?

What are three things you won't have done within the next 10 years?

In what ways do you think you'll have changed by the time you retire?

**A:** A year from now, I think I'll have a new hobby, like slacklining.

**B:** I'd like to try that, but I'm more interested in traveling.

**C:** Me too! I think in five years, I'll be living abroad.

## B Group work

- Explain the task. Ask three Ss to model the conversation. Point out that if Ss don't agree, they can say what they think will happen instead. Elicit expressions for agreeing/disagreeing.
- Ss discuss the predictions in small groups. Set a time limit of about five minutes. Go around the class and note any problems with future tenses.
- When time is up, write general problems on the board. Elicit Ss' corrections.

## C Class activity

- Explain the task. Read the questions.
- Ss discuss the questions as a class. Remind Ss to use the same tense as the one in each question.
- **Option:** Adapt the discussion into an **aquarium.** Divide the class into A and B groups. Group A sits in a circle, the aquarium, while Group B stands around the seated Group A. Group A begins the discussion. At any point, a Student B who wants to join the discussion can tap a Student A on the shoulder and the two exchange places.

!  For more speaking practice using future tenses, try **Just One Minute** – download it from the website.

# 11 LISTENING

**Learning Objective:** listen for details and take notes on a conversation about the future

## ▶ A [CD 2, Track 30]

- Point out the title "Not in our lifetime." Elicit Ss' ideas about what this means.
- Write the following on the board. Brainstorm future changes. Ask Ss to add their ideas.

  Changes in the future

  crime        space travel      environment
  energy       money

- Explain the task. Ss listen as people discuss future changes. Remind Ss to write only key words and phrases for two future changes for each topic.

### TIP
Discuss difficulties that Ss encounter while listening and strategies for overcoming them. Ask Ss to write their strategies on the board. Offer suggestions (e.g., *key words are usually stressed; try to predict what you will hear*).

- Play the audio program two or three times. First Ss listen. Then they listen and make notes. Pause after each topic to give Ss time to write their notes.
- Finally, Ss write their notes in the chart.

### Audio script
See page T-176.

### Answers

1. crime: there will be less street crime; crime will become more intelligent and digital; there will be more computer hacker criminals
2. space travel: people will be living on other planets within 100 years; humans will have traveled to other galaxies within the next 50 years
3. environment: in the next 20 years, we will have cleaned up all the trash in the oceans; in the next 30 years, we will have eliminated plastic and found better materials
4. energy: in 50 years, we will be using only green energy sources, like wind and solar energy; we will be able to charge electronics in just a few minutes
5. money: no one will use cash and everyone will have cards; everyone in the world will use the same currency

## B Pair work

- Explain the task.
- Ss work in pairs to answer the questions. For the changes they don't agree with, remind Ss to give reasons. Set a time limit of about five minutes. Then ask pairs to share the ones they think will affect them the most with the rest of the class. Take a poll and find out which change the class thinks will have the biggest impact on their lives.

# 12 DISCUSSION

**Learning Objective:** discuss one's own future using a variety of structures

## A

- Focus Ss' attention on the picture. Ask Ss to discuss the man's present and future.
- Explain the task and ask Ss to read all the categories. Check for any problems with vocabulary.
- Ss write down their ideas individually. Tell Ss to raise their hand if they need any help.

- **Option:** Have Ss work in pairs and use the categories to make questions to ask each other.

## B Group work

- Ss work in small groups. Ss take turns asking and answering the questions. Encourage Ss to ask questions of their own.

!  For another way to carry out the discussion, try the **Moving Dialog** – download it from the website.

## 13 READING

**Learning Objectives:** skim and summarize an article; identify main ideas and specific information

- Books closed. Ask Ss what they think will be different by the year 2050. Elicit examples in different areas like technology and housing.

### A

- Books open. Go over the task. Give Ss a few minutes to scan the article. Elicit the answer to the question. (Answer: Good Guesses About the Future)

### B

- Ss read individually. Ask Ss to mark words that they can't guess from context and to keep reading.

  ! For a new way to teach vocabulary, try **Vocabulary Mingle** – download it from the website. If you wish, you can join the activity. After you teach a S the meaning of a word, that S becomes a resource for other Ss to use.

- Elicit or explain any remaining new vocabulary.

---

#### Vocabulary

**futurist:** someone who studies social, political, and technical developments to understand what may happen in the future
**in order to:** with the aim of achieving something
**alter:** change something
**picture:** imagine how something looks
**target:** something to aim for; something you intend to achieve
**require:** need something or make something necessary
**speculation:** a guess without having enough information to be certain
**store:** put or keep things in a special place for use in the future
**eco-friendly:** products designed to do the least possible damage to the environment
**in store for (someone):** planned or likely to happen to

---

- Explain the task.
- Ss complete the task individually.
- Ss compare answers in pairs.
- Check answers by asking Ss to read the predictions the futurists made.

### Answers

Predictions they made: 2, 4, 6

### C *Group work*

- Explain the task. Ss work in small groups to discuss the questions. Remind Ss to give reasons for their answers and to ask follow-up questions. Ask one S in each group to write down the group's ideas.
- While the Ss discuss, go around the class and take notes of mistakes they make and go over them with the class.
- Discuss answers with the class and write the changes they would like to see on the board.

## End of Cycle 2

See the Supplementary Resources chart at the beginning of this unit for additional teaching materials and student activities related to this Cycle and for assessment tools.

**A** Skim the article. Which sentence below could be another title for the article? Why?

Professionals Who Can Change the Future          An Unhappy View of the Future
Good Guesses About the Future

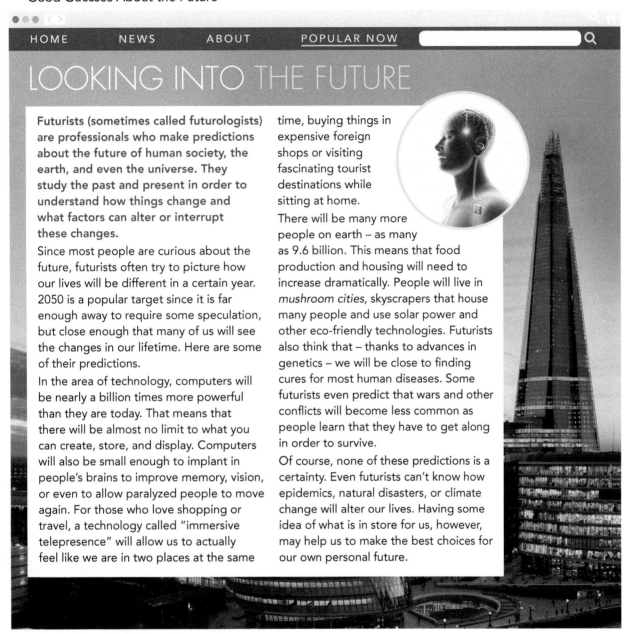

HOME          NEWS          ABOUT          <u>POPULAR NOW</u>          🔍

## LOOKING INTO THE FUTURE

Futurists (sometimes called futurologists) are professionals who make predictions about the future of human society, the earth, and even the universe. They study the past and present in order to understand how things change and what factors can alter or interrupt these changes.

Since most people are curious about the future, futurists often try to picture how our lives will be different in a certain year. 2050 is a popular target since it is far enough away to require some speculation, but close enough that many of us will see the changes in our lifetime. Here are some of their predictions.

In the area of technology, computers will be nearly a billion times more powerful than they are today. That means that there will be almost no limit to what you can create, store, and display. Computers will also be small enough to implant in people's brains to improve memory, vision, or even to allow paralyzed people to move again. For those who love shopping or travel, a technology called "immersive telepresence" will allow us to actually feel like we are in two places at the same time, buying things in expensive foreign shops or visiting fascinating tourist destinations while sitting at home.

There will be many more people on earth – as many as 9.6 billion. This means that food production and housing will need to increase dramatically. People will live in *mushroom cities*, skyscrapers that house many people and use solar power and other eco-friendly technologies. Futurists also think that – thanks to advances in genetics – we will be close to finding cures for most human diseases. Some futurists even predict that wars and other conflicts will become less common as people learn that they have to get along in order to survive.

Of course, none of these predictions is a certainty. Even futurists can't know how epidemics, natural disasters, or climate change will alter our lives. Having some idea of what is in store for us, however, may help us to make the best choices for our own personal future.

**B** Read the article. Check (✔) the predictions futurists made about the year 2050.

1. ☐ Computers will be as powerful as they are today.
2. ☐ Tiny computers will help people with physical problems.
3. ☐ Travel will be faster than it is now.
4. ☐ People will be able to explore places without leaving home.
5. ☐ People will need less food.
6. ☐ Many people will live together in eco-friendly buildings.
7. ☐ People will not get sick anymore.
8. ☐ People will fight with each other over food and water.

**C** **GROUP WORK** Do you agree that the predictions in the article are likely? What changes would you like to see in the future?

## SELF-ASSESSMENT

How well can you do these things? Check (✓) the boxes.

| I can . . . | Very well | OK | A little |
|---|---|---|---|
| Discuss professional services (Ex. 1) | ☐ | ☐ | ☐ |
| Give advice and make suggestions (Ex. 2) | ☐ | ☐ | ☐ |
| Understand and discuss historic events (Ex. 3) | ☐ | ☐ | ☐ |
| Make predictions about the future (Ex. 4) | ☐ | ☐ | ☐ |

## 1 DISCUSSION  Professional services

**GROUP WORK** Take turns asking questions about these services. When someone answers "yes," find out why and when the service was performed, and who performed it.

have a piece of clothing tailor-made for you
get your carpet cleaned
have your home redecorated or remodeled
get something translated
have your cell phone repaired

**A:** Have any of you ever had a piece of clothing tailor-made for you?
**B:** Yes, I have. I had a suit tailor-made when I got married.
**C:** Really? Why didn't you buy one in a store? . . .

## 2 ROLE PLAY  Advice needed

*Student A:*  Choose one of these problems. Decide on the details of the problem. Then tell your partner about it and get some advice.

I want to move to my own place, but I don't make enough money.
I never have time to do any of the things I enjoy doing. I'm always busy with . . .
I have a job interview in English, and I'm feeling nervous about it.
My in-laws are coming to dinner, but I can't cook at all.

*Student B:*  Your partner tells you about a problem.
Ask questions about it.
Then consider the situation and offer
two pieces of advice.

Change roles and choose another situation.

**useful expressions**

Have you thought about . . . ?
It might be a good idea to . . .
Maybe you could . . .
Why don't you . . . ?

# Progress check

## *SELF-ASSESSMENT*

**Learning Objectives:** reflect on one's learning; identify areas that need improvement

- Ask: "What did you learn in Units 9 and 10?" Elicit Ss' answers.

- Ss complete the Self-assessment. Explain to Ss that this is not a test; it is a way for them to evaluate what they've learned and identify areas where they need additional practice. Encourage them to be honest, and point out they will not get a bad grade if they check (✓) "a little."

- Ss move on to the Progress check exercises. You can have Ss complete them in class or for homework, using one of these techniques:
  1. Ask Ss to complete all the exercises.
  2. Ask Ss: "What do you need to practice?" Then assign exercises based on their answers.
  3. Ask Ss to choose and complete exercises based on their Self-assessment.

## 1 DISCUSSION

**Learning Objective:** demonstrate one's ability to talk about things people have or get done using the active and passive

### Group work

- Explain the task. Ask three Ss to model the conversation. Then ask different Ss to model the complete questions.

- Ss work in small groups. Ss take turns asking the questions. Remind Ss to ask follow-up questions with *why, when,* and *who.* Encourage Ss to ask other follow-up questions.

- Go around the class and give help as needed.

- Ask a S from each group to share a group member's experience.

## 2 ROLE PLAY

**Learning Objective:** demonstrate one's ability to make suggestions with gerunds, infinitives, modals, and negative questions

- Explain the task. Read the useful expressions.

- Divide the class into pairs, and assign A/B roles. Student As have a problem. Student Bs give advice.

- Ss role-play in pairs. Tell Student As to say whether or not they think the advice will work and why.

- Ss change roles and repeat the role play with another situation.

- Ask Ss to tell the class some of the best advice they got.

# 3 LISTENING

**Learning Objective:** demonstrate one's ability to listen to, understand, and refer to time in the past

## ▶ A [CD 2, Track 31]

- Explain the task. Ask Ss to read the questions.
- Play the audio program. Pause after each item for Ss to write. Play the audio program as many times as needed.

### Audio script

See page T-177.

- Go over answers with the class. If needed, play the audio program again. Ask Ss to focus on the correct answers.

### Answers

1. July 20, 1969
2. 1930
3. 1986
4. from 1909 to 1911 (two years)
5. December 26, 2004

## B Pair work

- Explain the task.
- Give Ss time to discuss the questions.
- Ss work in pairs. Remind them to give reasons for their answers.
- Elicit answers from the class.

## C Group work

- Give Ss time to write questions about historical events (e.g., achievements, disasters, or discoveries).
- Ss take turns asking and answering their questions. Remind Ss to use prepositions of time.
- Find out how many correct answers Ss came up with.

# 4 SURVEY

**Learning Objective:** demonstrate one's ability to predict the future with *will*, future continuous, and future perfect

## A Class activity

- Explain the task. Ask two Ss to model the conversation.
- Ask different Ss to read the survey items as questions. If Ss are having trouble, ask Ss to write the questions on the board. Leave the questions on the board during the activity.

- Ss work in small groups. Ss take turns asking the questions. Remind Ss to ask follow-up questions.
- Tell Ss to write down the number of "yes" and "no" answers in the group.

## B Group work

- Explain the task. Ask a S to read the example sentences.
- Give groups some time to make sentences about the results of their surveys.
- Ask each S in the group to report the results of at least one survey item to the class.

# WHAT'S NEXT?

**Learning Objective:** become more involved in one's learning

- Focus Ss' attention on the Self-assessment again. Ask: "How well can you do these things now?"
- Ask Ss to underline one thing they need to review. Ask: "What did you underline? How can you review it?"
- If needed, plan additional activities or reviews based on Ss' answers.

## 3 LISTENING Important world events

▶ **A** Listen to people discuss the questions. Write the correct answers.

1. What date did people first land on the moon? _____
2. When was the first World Cup? _____
3. When was the Chernobyl disaster? _____
4. How long did it take to build the *Titanic*? _____
5. When did the Indian Ocean tsunami occur? _____

**B** PAIR WORK Which of these events would you like to learn more about? Why?

**C** GROUP WORK Write three more questions about historic events. (Make sure you know the answers.) Then take turns asking your questions. Who has the most correct answers?

## 4 SURVEY What will happen?

**A** CLASS ACTIVITY How many of your classmates will have done these things in the next 5 years? Write down the number of "yes" and "no" answers. When someone answers "yes," ask follow-up questions.

| | "Yes" answers | "No" answers |
|---|---|---|
| 1. get a (new) job | | |
| 2. develop a new skill | | |
| 3. move to a new home | | |
| 4. learn another language | | |
| 5. travel abroad | | |
| 6. get a college or master's degree | | |

**A:** Five years from now, will you have moved to a new home?

**B:** Yes, I think I will be living in a new place.

**A:** Where do you think you'll be living?

**B:** I'd like to live in a bigger place. Our current apartment is too small.

**A:** Really? Would you rather live in a house or an apartment?

**B** GROUP WORK Tally the results of the survey as a group. Then take turns telling the class any additional information you found out.

"Most people think they will have moved to a new home. Only three people think they'll be living at their current address. One person thinks she'll be living in a big house in the suburbs, and . . . "

## WHAT'S NEXT?

Look at your Self-assessment again. Do you need to review anything?

# Unit 11 Supplementary Resources Overview

| | After the following SB exercises | You can use these materials in class | Your students can use these materials outside the classroom |
|---|---|---|---|
| **CYCLE 1** | **1 Snapshot** | | |
| | **2 Conversation** | | **SS** Unit 11 Speaking 1–2 |
| | **3 Grammar Focus** | | **SB** Unit 11 Grammar plus, Focus 1<br>**SS** Unit 11 Grammar 1<br>**GAME** Word Keys (Time clauses) |
| | **4 Listening** | | |
| | **5 Speaking** | **TSS** Unit 11 Extra Worksheet | |
| **CYCLE 2** | **6 Word Power** | **TSS** Unit 11 Vocabulary Worksheet<br>**TSS** Unit 11 Listening Worksheet | **SS** Unit 11 Vocabulary 1–2<br>**GAME** Name the Picture (Milestones) |
| | **7 Perspectives** | | |
| | **8 Grammar Focus** | **TSS** Unit 11 Grammar Worksheet | **SB** Unit 11 Grammar plus, Focus 2<br>**SS** Unit 11 Grammar 2<br>**GAME** Spell or Slime (Personal characteristics)<br>**GAME** Speak or Swim (Expressing regret and hypothetical situations) |
| | **9 Interchange 11** | | |
| | **10 Pronunciation** | | |
| | **11 Listening** | | |
| | **12 Writing** | **TSS** Unit 11 Writing Worksheet | |
| | **13 Reading** | **TSS** Unit 11 Project Worksheet<br>**VID** Unit 11<br>**VRB** Unit 11 | **SS** Unit 11 Reading 1–2<br>**SS** Unit 11 Listening 1–3<br>**SS** Unit 11 Video 1–3<br>**WB** Unit 11 exercises 1–7 |

**Key**  **GAME:** Online Game  **SB:** Student's Book  **SS:** Online Self-study  **TSS:** Teacher Support Site
**VID:** Video DVD  **VRB:** Video Resource Book  **WB:** Online Workbook/Workbook

# My Plan for Unit 11

Use the space below to customize a plan that fits your needs.

| With the following SB exercises | I am using these materials in class | My students are using these materials outside the classroom |
| --- | --- | --- |
|  |  |  |
|  |  |  |
|  |  |  |
|  |  |  |
|  |  |  |
|  |  |  |
|  |  |  |
|  |  |  |
|  |  |  |
|  |  |  |
|  |  |  |
|  |  |  |
|  |  |  |

| With or instead of the following SB section | I am using these materials for assessment |
| --- | --- |
|  |  |
|  |  |
|  |  |

# 11 Rites of passage

▸ Discuss life events and milestones
▸ Describe regrets and hypothetical situations

## 1 SNAPSHOT

### UNFORGETTABLE FIRSTS

*Some moments that matter*

- ☐ first sleepover
- ☐ losing your first tooth
- ☐ first day at school
- ☐ first pet
- ☐ first swim in the ocean
- ☐ first crush

- ☐ first trip with friends
- ☐ high school graduation
- ☐ first paycheck
- ☐ getting your driver's license
- ☐ entering college
- ☐ first heartbreak

a sleepover

*Which of these first experiences were important for you?
Check (✓) them.
How did you feel when you had these experiences?
What other first experiences have you had that you will never forget?*

## 2 CONVERSATION  I was so immature.

▶ **A** Listen and practice.

**Jim:** Congratulations, graduate! What's next for my favorite nephew?

**Luke:** I'm your *only* nephew, Uncle Jim!

**Jim:** But you're still my favorite! Anyway, what *are* your plans?

**Luke:** I'm looking for a job, so I can make some money before I go to college.

**Jim:** Ah! After *I* graduated, I went to Alaska to work as a fisherman. It was a tough job, but it helped me grow up.

**Luke:** How do you mean?

**Jim:** Until I started working, I'd never had any important responsibilities. I was so immature. But once I moved away from home, I learned to take care of myself.

**Luke:** So you became independent.

**Jim:** Yeah, but not for very long, actually. After two months, I moved back home . . . and got a job at your grandfather's store.

**Luke:** Hey, I think my search just ended. I'm going to talk to Grandpa about a job.

▶ **B** Listen to the rest of the conversation. What was an important turning point for Jim? for Luke?

# 11 Rites of passage

## Cycle 1, Exercises 1–5

In this unit, students discuss life events and milestones and describe regrets and hypothetical situations. By the end of Cycle 1, students will be able to discuss milestones in their lives using a variety of time clauses. By the end of Cycle 2, students will be able to discuss regrets using *should have* + past participle and *if* clauses in the past perfect.

## 1 SNAPSHOT

**Learning Objective:** discuss important life events

To introduce the topic, play **Line Up!** – download it from the website. Ss line up according to a major life event (e.g., their birthday, when they got married, etc.).

- Books closed. Ask: "What are some important events in a person's life?" Then ask Ss to open their books and compare their ideas with the Snapshot. Point out that *unforgettable first* refers to an important life event that happened for the first time.

- **Option:** Books closed. With Ss, brainstorm some major events or milestones. Then tell Ss to open their books and quickly scan pages 72 to 74. Which of their guesses were mentioned in their books?

- Elicit or explain any new vocabulary.

### Vocabulary
**sleepover:** a party when a group of young people stay at a friend's house for the night
**crush:** a strong but temporary feeling of love for someone

- Read the first question. Ss work individually to check the moments that were important to them.

- Then Ss compare their answers in pairs. If possible, pair Ss who are from different countries.

- Read the next two questions. Have Ss discuss them in pairs. If possible, pair Ss who are from different countries.

- Have Ss tell the class two things they learned from their partner.

## 2 CONVERSATION

**Learning Objective:** use time clauses in a conversation about becoming an adult

### A [CD 2, Track 32]

- Tell Ss to cover the text and look only at the picture. Ask: "Where are they? What do you think they are talking about?" Ss discuss the picture in pairs.

- Set the scene. Uncle Jim and Luke are talking about Luke's future. They are talking about Uncle Jim's experience after he graduated. Write this on the board:

  *What was Uncle Jim like before he graduated?*
  *What life event changed him?*

- Ss listen for answers to the questions on the board. Play the audio program. Ask two Ss to write the answers on the board. (Answers: Uncle Jim didn't have important responsibilities; a fishing job in Alaska)

- Text uncovered. Play the audio program again. Ss listen and read.

- Elicit or explain any new vocabulary.

### Vocabulary
**tough:** difficult
**immature:** not completely grown or developed

- To elicit the humor, ask: "How much has Uncle Jim really changed? Was he independent later? Why not?" (Answer: Uncle Jim was probably not as independent as he imagined because he was working for his grandfather.)

### B [CD 2, Track 33]

- Explain the task. Read the focus questions.

- Tell Ss to listen and to take notes. Play the second part of the audio program.

### Vocabulary
**turning point:** a time when an important change starts to happen

### Audio script

See page T-177.

- Ss compare notes in pairs. Then check answers around the class.

### Answers

A turning point for Jim was when he became a parent. A turning point for Luke was when he joined the basketball team.

- **Option:** In pairs, Ss discuss what they were like as kids and how they have changed.

**Learning Objective:** use time clauses and subordinating conjunctions to describe life experiences

▶ **[CD 2, Track 34]**

### Time clauses

- Write the first time clause on the board. Label the subject (S) and verb (V), like this:

       S     V

  Before I graduated from high school, . . .

- Remind Ss of some important facts about clauses:

  1. All clauses require a subject and a verb.
  2. A time clause is a dependent clause. It can't stand alone; it must be connected to a main clause.
  3. The time clause can come before or after the main clause.
  4. When the time clause comes before the main clause, a comma separates the two clauses.

- Ask Ss to read the sentences in the Grammar Focus box. Tell Ss to underline the clauses.

- Play the audio program. Ss listen and repeat, focusing on intonation.

### Conjunctions

- Go over the subordinating conjunctions in the Grammar Focus box. Elicit or explain the meanings as needed. Provide examples on the board.

  once/as soon as: when one event happens, another event happens soon afterward

  Once Sarah learned a little Spanish, she was able to talk to her neighbors, the Delgados.

  As soon as you're hired for your first job, you feel more confident.

  the moment: a particular point of time when two events happen together

  The moment John got married, he felt like an adult.

  until: to that time and then no longer

  Until I met Donna, I hadn't known what friendship was.

  by the time: one event is completed before another event

  By the time I graduated, I had already found a good job

- Point out the past perfect in the main clauses with until and by the time. This shows that two events occurred in the past, but meeting Donna (action #1) happened before knowing what friendship was (action #2).

- Elicit additional examples from Ss around the class.

! For another way to practice time clauses, try **Substitution Dialog** – download it from the website.

### A

- Explain the task. Point out the time clauses in column A and the main clauses in column B. Model the task with the first sentence.

- Ss complete the task individually. Go around the class and give help as needed.

- Ss work in pairs. Ss take turns reading aloud the sentences to compare answers.

- Elicit Ss' responses around the class.

| Possible answers |
| --- |

| 1. e | 2. h | 3. a | 4. b | 5. f | 6. c | 7. d | 8. g |
| --- | --- | --- | --- | --- | --- | --- | --- |

### B

- Explain the task. Have a S read the example sentence. Model sentences about yourself:

  T: I can make a sentence with number 1: "Until I went to college, I had never really studied very hard." Can you relate that to your life, Sandra?

  S: Yes, I can relate that one to my life: "Until I went to college, I had never had a loan."

- Ss write sentences. Go around the class and spot-check verb tenses.

- Then Ss compare sentences with a partner.

### C Group work

- Explain the task. Ask Ss to read the events. Read the example sentence.

- Ask: "What else happens after you move in with roommates?" Elicit suggestions.

- First, Ss work individually to write sentences. Remind Ss to use time clauses in the present with you. Point out that you here means "people in general;" it doesn't refer to any specific person.

- Then write a model conversation on the board:

  S1: After you move in with roommates, you have more freedom.

  S2: That is true, but you also have to share responsibilities.

  S3: So, what kind of things do you become accountable for?

  S2: Well, first you have to do your share of chores, like cooking and cleaning . . .

- Ss work in small groups. Ss take turns reading their sentences and discussing their ideas. Remind Ss to refer to the model on the board.

> **TIP**
> Encourage Ss to use natural discourse markers when speaking, e.g., well, so, you know, you see, actually, etc. Ask Ss to look at previous Conversations and dialogs for examples.

# 3 GRAMMAR FOCUS

## Time clauses

**Before** I graduated from high school, I had never worked.

**After** I graduated, I went to Alaska to work as a fisherman.

**Once** I moved away from home, I learned to take care of myself.

**The moment** I moved away from home, I felt like a different person.

**As soon as** I got my own bank account, I started to be more responsible.

**Until** I moved to Alaska, I had never been away from home.

**By the time** I went to college, I had already lived away from home.

GRAMMAR PLUS *see page 142*

A Match the clauses in column A with appropriate information
in column B. Then compare with a partner.

**A**

**1.** Until I went to college, _____

**2.** Before I became a parent, _____

**3.** Once I joined a sports team, _____

**4.** The moment I had a car accident, _____

**5.** As soon as I got my first paycheck, _____

**6.** By the time I was 15, _____

**7.** After I began a relationship, _____

**8.** Until I left home, _____

**B**

**a.** I learned the importance of teamwork.

**b.** I understood why you shouldn't text and drive.

**c.** I realized that I wasn't a child anymore.

**d.** I learned that love can hurt!

**e.** I had never taken school very seriously.

**f.** I began to understand the value of money.

**g.** I had never cooked a real meal.

**h.** I had never worried about the future.

B Which of the clauses in column A can you relate to your life? Add your own
information to those clauses. Then compare with a partner.

"Until I left home, I had never bought my own clothes."

C GROUP WORK What do you think people
learn from these events? Write sentences
using time clauses in the present. Then take
turns reading and talking about them.

**1.** moving in with roommates

**2.** buying your own home

**3.** having a pet

**4.** getting a credit card

**5.** getting your first paycheck

**6.** getting your driver's license

**7.** getting married

**8.** becoming a parent

1.   "Once you move in with roommates,
     you have to learn to work together."

## 4 LISTENING Turning points

A Listen to three people describe important events in their lives. Complete the chart.

| | Turning point | How it affected him or her |
|---|---|---|
| **1.** Nari | | |
| **2.** Anthony | | |
| **3.** Karina | | |

B Listen again. What do these three people have in common?

C PAIR WORK What has been a turning point in your life? Discuss with a partner.

## 5 SPEAKING Milestones

A PAIR WORK In your country, how old are people when these things typically happen?

get a first job          graduate from college
get a driver's license   get married
move out of their parents' home   retire

B GROUP WORK Choose three milestones. What do you think life is like before and after each one? Join another pair and discuss.

"Before you get a job, you depend on your family for everything. The moment you get your first paycheck, you . . ."

## 6 WORD POWER Personal characteristics

A PAIR WORK At what age do you think people possess these traits? Check (✓) one or more ages for each trait.

| | In their teens | In their 20s | In their 30s | In their 40s | In their 60s |
|---|---|---|---|---|---|
| ambitious | ☐ | ☐ | ☐ | ☐ | ☐ |
| argumentative | ☐ | ☐ | ☐ | ☐ | ☐ |
| carefree | ☐ | ☐ | ☐ | ☐ | ☐ |
| dependable | ☐ | ☐ | ☐ | ☐ | ☐ |
| naive | ☐ | ☐ | ☐ | ☐ | ☐ |
| pragmatic | ☐ | ☐ | ☐ | ☐ | ☐ |
| rebellious | ☐ | ☐ | ☐ | ☐ | ☐ |
| sophisticated | ☐ | ☐ | ☐ | ☐ | ☐ |
| wise | ☐ | ☐ | ☐ | ☐ | ☐ |

B GROUP WORK Use the words in part A to describe people you know. "My mother is dependable. I can always count on her when I need help."

# 4 LISTENING

**Learning Objective:** listen for main ideas and take accurate notes about events in people's lives discussed using time clauses

## ▶ A *[CD 2, Track 35]*

- Books closed. Write these questions on the board. Ask Ss to discuss them in small groups:

  *What event has been very important in your life? Why? How did it affect you or change you?*

- Books open. Ss listen for each event and how it affected each person. Play the audio program. Pause after each speaker for Ss to write in the chart.

### Audio script

See page T-177.

## ▶ B *[CD 2, Track 36]*

- Play the audio program again. Ss listen to find out what the three people have in common.

### Answers

Parts A and B
1. Nari: she bought a cell phone; she knew she was going to be OK with her English and get her dream job in Boston
2. Anthony: he started getting his own clients; he became serious about working for himself
3. Karina: her aunt's illness; she knew she wanted to be a doctor and help people like her.
Their turning points all helped their careers.

## C *Pair work*

- Have Ss work in pairs to discuss the question. Ask them to think of important moments in their lives. Go around the class to help with vocabulary and structure.

# 5 SPEAKING

**Learning Objective:** discuss important life events using a variety of time clauses

## A *Pair work*

- Explain the task. Read the question. Point out the expression "in their (teens)" in the Word Power.

- Focus Ss' attention on the picture and the first event. Model a discussion with two Ss.

- Ss discuss the events in pairs.

## B *Group work*

- Explain the task. Read the example sentence.

- In pairs, discuss the events in part A and what changes after these events.

- Each pair joins another pair. Set a time limit of about ten minutes. Go around the class and listen in.

### End of Cycle 1

See the Supplementary Resources chart at the beginning of this unit for additional teaching materials and student activities related to this Cycle.

## Cycle 2, Exercises 6–13

# 6 WORD POWER

**Learning Objective:** discuss behavior and personality

## A *Pair work*

- Explain the task. Give Ss some time to read the list of adjectives. Model with *ambitious*.

- Elicit or explain any new vocabulary. Also model stress or pronunciation if needed.

### Vocabulary

**ambitious:** having a strong desire to be successful
**argumentative:** liking to argue or disagree
**dependable:** able to be trusted and very likely to do what people expect you to do
**naive:** lacking experience or knowledge
**pragmatic:** practical; making decisions based on facts rather than ideas

**rebellious:** reacting against rules or traditions
**sophisticated:** confident, socially mature, and having knowledge about many subjects
**wise:** using knowledge and experience to make good decisions and give good advice

- Ss complete the task in pairs.

## B *Group work*

- Model the task.

- Ss complete the task in small groups. As a final check, elicit Ss' responses around the class.

- For more practice, play **Bingo** – download it from the website. Recycle vocabulary from pages 3 and 30 to describe people and people's feelings.

# 7 PERSPECTIVES

**Learning Objectives:** respond to descriptions of regrets using *should have* and *if* in context

## ▶ A [CD 2, Track 37]

- Ss cover the text and look only at the pictures. Set the scene. Two friends have graduated from college and are complaining about all the things they should or shouldn't have done.
- Play the audio program. Ss listen and read. Pause after each regret. Ask different Ss to summarize each one in their own words (e.g., *I could have interned at a company, but I didn't.*).
- Elicit similar regrets from individual Ss.

## B Group work

- Explain the task. Read the question.
- Ss discuss the question in small groups.
- **Option:** Ss role-play the graduates' session with their advisor. The advisor's goal is to suggest possible solutions for the graduates' regrets.

# 8 GRAMMAR FOCUS

**Learning Objective:** use *have* + past participle and *if* clauses in the past perfect to express regrets and hypothetical situations

## ▶ [CD 2, Track 38]

### Should have + past participle

- Focus Ss' attention on the Perspectives. Ask Ss to find two sentences with *should have*. Write them on the board:

| 1 | 2 | 3 | 4 | 5 |
|---|---|---|---|---|
| I | should | have | done | an internship... |
| I | shouldn't | have | taken out | a student loan... |

- Elicit the rule:

  subject + *should have*/'ve + past participle

- Explain that we use *should have* to speculate about or imagine things that did or didn't happen (e.g., *He took out a student loan, but now he realizes that he shouldn't have. Now he regrets it.*).
- Encourage Ss to make up their own examples.
- **Option:** To practice *should have*, do part A now.

### If + past perfect (or third conditional)

- Repeat the steps above for *If I'd*... Elicit examples from the Perspectives. Write them on the board.
- Elicit the rule: *If* + subject + *had* + past participle, subject *could/would have* + past participle
- Explain that this structure describes hypothetical situations in the past. The *could/would have* clause shows what didn't happen.
- Encourage Ss to make up their own examples.
- Play the audio program. Ss listen and practice.

## A

- Explain the task. Read the example.
- Ss complete the task individually. Go around the class and spot-check Ss' responses.

### Possible answers

1. I should have played sports when I was younger.
2. I should have been more careful with money when I was a teenager.
3. I should have stayed in touch with my friends after I graduated.
4. I shouldn't have been so naive/should have been less naive when I first started working.
5. I should have studied hard in school.

- Then Ss work in pairs. They talk about which statements are true about their own lives.

## B

- Explain the task. Model how to do number 1. Then have Ss complete the task individually.
- Ss compare answers in pairs. Elicit answers around the class.

### Answers

1. c   2. d   3. e   4. b   5. a

## C

- Explain the task. Read number 1 in part B. Ask Ss to complete the clause.
- Ss work individually to complete the task. Go around the class and spot-check Ss' answers.
- Ss compare answers in small groups. Accept any answers that are both grammatical and logical.
- **Option:** Ss save their sentences for the Pronunciation on page 76.

# 7 PERSPECTIVES That was a mistake.

▶ **A** Listen to two recent college graduates talk about their regrets.
Do you have any similar regrets?

1 I should have done an internship while I was in college.

2 If I'd been more ambitious in college, I could have learned to speak another language.

3 If I hadn't been so irresponsible, I could have gotten better grades.

4 I shouldn't have taken out a student loan to pay for college.

5 If I'd listened to my professors, I would have taken some additional courses.

6 If I hadn't wasted so much money last year, I would have saved enough to start graduate school.

**B** GROUP WORK What advice would you give to these recent grads?

# 8 GRAMMAR FOCUS

▶ **Expressing regret and describing hypothetical situations**

Use *should have* + the past participle to express regret.
**I should have done** an internship while I was in college.
**I shouldn't have taken out** a student loan.

Use *would have* + the past participle to express probable outcomes in hypothetical situations.
Use *could have* + the past participle to express possible outcomes.
**If I'd listened** to my professors, I **would have taken** additional courses.
**If I hadn't been** so irresponsible, I **could have gotten** better grades.

GRAMMAR PLUS *see page 142*

**A** For each statement, write a sentence expressing regret. Then talk with a partner about which statements are true for you.

1. I didn't play any sports when I was younger.
2. I was carefree with money when I was a teenager.
3. I didn't stay in touch with my school friends after I graduated.
4. I was naive when I first started working.
5. I didn't study hard in school.

1. I should have played sports when I was a teenager.

**B** Match the clauses in column A with appropriate information in column B.

| A | B |
|---|---|
| 1. If I hadn't gone to so many parties, _____ | **a.** I would have been nicer to my parents. |
| 2. If I'd been more careful, _____ | **b.** I wouldn't have borrowed money for a new car. |
| 3. If I'd been wiser, _____ | **c.** I would have done better in school. |
| 4. If I'd listened to my financial advisor, _____ | **d.** I wouldn't have lost all my documents. |
| 5. If I hadn't been so rebellious, _____ | **e.** I wouldn't have argued with my boss. |

**C** Add your own information to the clauses in column A. Then compare in groups.

## 9 INTERCHANGE 11 Good choices, bad choices

Imagine if things were different. Go to Interchange 11 on page 125.

## 10 PRONUNCIATION Reduction of *have* and *been*

**A** Listen and practice. Notice how **have** and **been** are reduced in these sentences.

I should **have been** less selfish when I was younger.
If I'd **been** more ambitious, I could **have** gotten a promotion.

**B PAIR WORK** Complete these sentences and practice them. Pay attention to the reduced forms of **have** and **been**.

I should have been . . . when I was younger.    If I'd been more . . ., I could have . . .
I should have been . . . in school.    If I'd been less . . ., I would have . . .

## 11 LISTENING My biggest regret

**A** Listen to a conversation between three friends about regrets. Write two regrets that each person has.

|  | Regrets | |
|---|---|---|
| **1.** Ariana |  |  |
| **2.** Ray |  |  |
| **3.** Kira |  |  |

**B** Listen again. Which friend feels differently about regrets? How does he or she feel?

**C PAIR WORK** Do you agree with the attitude about regrets in part B? Why or why not?

## 12 WRITING An apology

**A** Think about something you regret doing that you want to apologize for. Consider the questions below. Then write a message of apology.

What did you do? What were the consequences?
Is there any way you can undo those consequences?

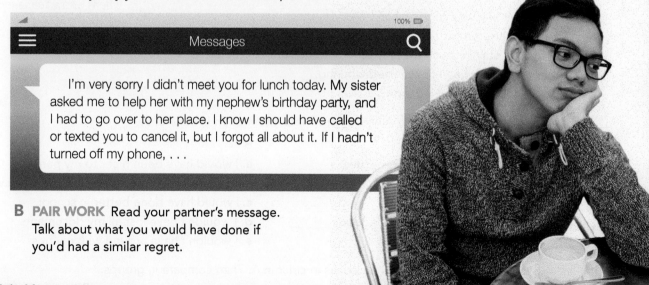

Messages    100% 🔋

I'm very sorry I didn't meet you for lunch today. My sister asked me to help her with my nephew's birthday party, and I had to go over to her place. I know I should have called or texted you to cancel it, but I forgot all about it. If I hadn't turned off my phone, . . .

**B PAIR WORK** Read your partner's message. Talk about what you would have done if you'd had a similar regret.

## 9 INTERCHANGE 11

See page T-126 for teaching notes.

## 10 PRONUNCIATION

**Learning Objective:** sound more natural by using reductions of *have* and *been*

▶ **A [CD 2, Track 39]**

- Remind Ss that we stress key words. Words such as pronouns and auxiliary verbs are reduced. When *have* follows a modal (e.g., *should, could, would*), it is reduced to /əv/ (it sounds like the word *of*). The word *been* is reduced to /bɪn/.
- Ask Ss to listen for the reductions. Play the audio program. Ss listen and read.

- Play the audio program again. Ss listen and repeat.

**B Pair work**

- Explain the task. Model a few sentences with words from the Word Power on page 74 and others of your own.
- Ss complete the sentences in pairs. Then Ss practice the reductions.

🎲 For more practice with reductions, have Ss work in groups and play the **Chain Game** – download it from the website.

## 11 LISTENING

**Learning Objective:** listen for main ideas and summarize descriptions of regrets discussed using *should have* + past participle and *if* clauses in the past

▶ **A [CD 2, Track 40]**

- Explain the task. Draw the chart on the board.
- Tell Ss to listen the first time for the regret. Play the audio program. Pause after each speaker for Ss to complete the chart.

### Answers

1. Ariana: she should've spent more time with her grandma; she shouldn't have waited so long to start learning Arabic
2. Ray: he should've talked to the bully; he should've been more confident
3. Kira: she should've been more ambitious in high school; she could've done more volunteer work and helped people more in her spare time

❗ For another way to set the scene, try **Cloud Prediction** – download it from the website.

▶ **B [CD 2, Track 41]**

- Explain the task. This time Ss listen to find out who feels differently.

- Play the audio program once or twice.
- Elicit Ss' responses.

**TIP**
To check answers, draw the chart on the board and ask Ss to complete it. This way, those who are weak at listening will be able to see the answers.

### Audio script

See page T-178.

### Answer

Kira; There are no regrets in life, just lessons learned. She has learned lessons from her mistakes and become a better person.

🎲 For more practice with recognizing the grammar structures, play **Stand Up, Sit Down** – download it from the website. Use Variation 1.

**C Pair work**

- Ss work in pairs to discuss the question. Remind them to ask follow-up questions.

## 12 WRITING

**Learning Objective:** write a message of apology using *should have* + past participle and *if* clauses in the past

**A**

- Focus Ss' attention on the picture. Ask what is happening. Then ask Ss to read the message of apology.
- Explain the task. Read the questions.
- Give Ss time to make some notes.

- Ss use their notes to write a first draft.

❗ For a new way for Ss to think of and plan their content, try **Pass the Paper** – download it from the website.

**B Pair work**

- Explain the task. Ss work in pairs. They exchange messages and discuss what they would have done in a similar situation.

**Learning Objective:** skim and identify main ideas in an advice column

## A

- Go over the task. Give Ss several minutes to skim the advice column. Elicit the answers. (Answers: Paul accidentally deleted a file on his friend's computer and caused a division between the two of them. He wants to know if he should apologize.)
- *Option:* Elicit or have Ss write questions about regrets using *who, what, when, where, why,* and *how.* When they read the column again, they can see if the column answers any of their questions.
- 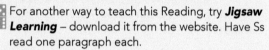 For another way to teach this Reading, try ***Jigsaw Learning*** – download it from the website. Have Ss read one paragraph each.

> **TIP**
> Remind Ss that an effective reader does not need to know the meaning of every word to understand the main ideas of a text. Encourage Ss to guess the meaning of words from context. Tell Ss to mark new words as they read and check the definitions only after they have finished reading.

## B

- Ss read the column quickly and silently. Ask Ss to summarize Paul's problem in one or two sentences.
- Elicit or explain any new vocabulary.

> **Vocabulary**
> **look something up:** check a fact or get information about something
> **essay:** a short piece of writing on a particular subject, especially one done by students as part of the work for a course
> **somehow:** in a way or by some means that is not known or is not stated
> **yell:** shout something, usually when you are angry, in pain, or excited
> **on purpose:** intentionally, not by accident
> **act cold towards (someone):** be indifferent; unfriendly
> **be able to tell:** be able to see or understand
> **two-way discussion:** a discussion where the two people have a voice and can talk equally and openly
> **blame:** say that someone or something did something wrong

- *Option:* Assign the advice column for homework. Ask Ss to read the column once or twice and mark unfamiliar vocabulary. Also tell Ss to make a list of the words, check definitions in a dictionary, and write the definitions. During the next class, Ss work in groups to discuss and compare their lists.
- Explain the task. Read the list of words on the left.
- Ss re-read the advice column individually and look for the words. Then they match the words to their definitions.
- Ss compare answers in pairs. Encourage Ss to say where they found the information in the column.
- Check Ss' answers around the class.

| Answers |
| --- |
| 1. b   2. d   3. e   4. a   5. c |

## C

- Explain the task. Point out that the true statements can be found in the advice column. Do the first item together as a class.
- Ss work individually to check *True, False,* or *Not given.*
- Ss compare their charts in pairs. Then elicit answers from the class.

| Answers | | | |
| --- | --- | --- | --- |
| 1. NG | 3. F | 5. NG | 7. T |
| 2. T | 4. T | 6. F | 8. NG |

- *Option:* Have Ss work in pairs to correct the false statements.

## D *Pair work*

- Explain the task. Read the focus questions.
- Ss discuss the questions in pairs.
- *Option:* Each pair joins another pair. Ss take turns telling the others what their partner said. The partner makes corrections if needed.
- *Option:* Each S writes a paragraph about a problem they had with a friend, using the text as a model.

## End of Cycle 2

See the Supplementary Resources chart at the beginning of this unit for additional teaching materials and student activities related to this Cycle.

## 13 READING

**A** Skim the advice column. What is Paul's problem? What does he ask Stella?

# STELLA'S ANSWERS

HOME ABOUT ADVICE ASK STELLA COMMUNITY FOLLOW STELLA

Dear Stella,
I have a problem, and I'm not sure what to do about it. I was studying with my friend Karl, and he let me use his laptop for a minute to look something up. He had been busy typing an essay, so I opened the document again when I was done. But somehow I hit the wrong button, and I deleted the document. All of his work was gone. It was a total accident, and I did say, "Sorry," just so he wouldn't yell at me. But he got really angry and accused me of doing it on purpose. Now Karl is acting really cold towards me, and I can tell he's still angry. It really wasn't my fault, but I still feel bad. Should I apologize anyway just to make him feel better?

*Paul in Philadelphia*

Dear Paul,
When you've done something that hurt a friend, even by accident, it can be really uncomfortable. You obviously feel bad about deleting Karl's essay, and you didn't mean for it to happen. Unfortunately, it sounds like Karl has a pretty short fuse. Sure, if you'd apologized better at the time, and if you had offered to help him recover his work, it might have smoothed things over. After being accused of sabotage, however, I understand why you didn't apologize again.
What should you do now? First, ask yourself if an apology is necessary. If you don't feel you did anything wrong, it wouldn't mean very much. An apology has to be sincere and heartfelt to be effective. Second, if someone stops treating you like a friend because you made a mistake – which is a form of emotional blackmail – they probably won't believe your apology anyway. Third, a two-way discussion is often more effective than an apology. I think you need to sit down with Karl, tell him how badly you feel, avoid making excuses or trying to blame him, and get on with your friendship. If he still won't forgive you after that, maybe he's not such a great friend after all.

**B** Read the advice column. Find the words in *italics* in the text. Match the definitions to the words.

1. *short fuse* _____
2. *sabotage* _____
3. *heartfelt* _____
4. *blackmail* _____
5. *forgive* _____

a. act of demanding something from someone in exchange for a benefit
b. quick or violent temper
c. decide not to be angry at someone
d. act of destroying something to get an advantage
e. very sincere

**C** Check (✓) True, False, or Not given for each statement.

|  | True | False | Not given |
|---|---|---|---|
| 1. The two boys are best friends from childhood. | ☐ | ☐ | ☐ |
| 2. Paul mistakenly deleted some of Karl's work. | ☐ | ☐ | ☐ |
| 3. Karl reacted very calmly at the time. | ☐ | ☐ | ☐ |
| 4. Stella thinks Paul could have improved the situation at the time. | ☐ | ☐ | ☐ |
| 5. Stella believes that both friends need to apologize. | ☐ | ☐ | ☐ |
| 6. Stella thinks even an insincere apology is helpful. | ☐ | ☐ | ☐ |
| 7. Karl's behavior shows that he is not very forgiving. | ☐ | ☐ | ☐ |
| 8. Stella says that Paul and Karl's friendship is over. | ☐ | ☐ | ☐ |

**D** PAIR WORK Do you agree with the advice Stella gave Paul? If not, what advice would you give him?

# Unit 12 Supplementary Resources Overview

| After the following SB exercises | You can use these materials in class | Your students can use these materials outside the classroom |
|---|---|---|
| **CYCLE 1** | | |
| 1 Snapshot | | |
| 2 Perspectives | | |
| 3 Pronunciation | | |
| 4 Grammar Focus | | **SB** Unit 12 Grammar plus, Focus 1<br>**SS** Unit 12 Grammar 1<br>**GAME** Sentence Stacker (Describing purpose) |
| 5 Word Power | **TSS** Unit 12 Extra Worksheet | **SS** Unit 12 Vocabulary 1–2<br>**GAME** Name the Picture (Qualities for success) |
| 6 Role Play | | **WB** Unit 12 exercises 1–4 |
| **CYCLE 2** | | |
| 7 Conversation | | **SS** Unit 12 Speaking 1 |
| 8 Grammar Focus | **TSS** Unit 12 Vocabulary Worksheet<br>**TSS** Unit 12 Grammar Worksheet | **SB** Unit 12 Grammar plus, Focus 2<br>**SS** Unit 12 Grammar 2<br>**GAME** Speak or Swim (Giving reasons and qualities of success)<br>**GAME** Say the Word (Giving reasons) |
| 9 Listening | **TSS** Unit 12 Listening Worksheet | |
| 10 Interchange 12 | | |
| 11 Discussion | | |
| 12 Writing | **TSS** Unit 12 Writing Worksheet | |
| 13 Reading | **TSS** Unit 12 Project Worksheet<br>**VID** Unit 12<br>**VRB** Unit 12 | **SS** Unit 12 Reading 1–2<br>**SS** Unit 12 Listening 1–3<br>**SS** Unit 12 Video 1–3<br>**WB** Unit 12 exercises 5–8 |

| With or instead of the following SB section | You can also use these materials for assessment |
|---|---|
| **Units 11–12 Progress Check** | **ASSESSMENT PROGRAM** Units 11–12 Oral Quiz<br>**ASSESSMENT PROGRAM** Units 11–12 Written Quiz |

Key    **GAME:** Online Game      **SB:** Student's Book       **SS:** Online Self-study       **TSS:** Teacher Support Site
          **VID:** Video DVD          **VRB:** Video Resource Book     **WB:** Online Workbook/Workbook

# My Plan for Unit 12

Use the space below to customize a plan that fits your needs.

| With the following SB exercises | I am using these materials in class | My students are using these materials outside the classroom |
| --- | --- | --- |
|  |  |  |
|  |  |  |
|  |  |  |
|  |  |  |
|  |  |  |
|  |  |  |
|  |  |  |
|  |  |  |
|  |  |  |
|  |  |  |
|  |  |  |
|  |  |  |
|  |  |  |

| With or instead of the following SB section | I am using these materials for assessment |
| --- | --- |
|  |  |
|  |  |
|  |  |

# 12 Keys to success

▸ Give personal views and describe qualities for success
▸ Give reasons

## 1 SNAPSHOT

### HOW SOME MAJOR COMPANIES GOT THEIR NAMES

**Nike** The company got its name from the ancient Greek goddess of victory.

**Google** Google comes from *googol*, which is the math term for the number 1 followed by 100 zeros.

**Facebook** The name was taken from the term for a list with students' names and photos found at American universities.

**Samsung** In Korean, *sam* means "three" and *sung* means "star," so the name means "three stars." It represents the idea that the company should be everlasting, like stars in the sky.

**Skype** The original concept for the name was Sky-Peer-to-Peer, which became Skyper, and then Skype.

**Häagen-Dazs** The name of the American ice cream brand was invented to sound Danish and traditional, but it has no meaning in any language.

**Pepsi** The soft drink got its name from the word *dyspepsia*, which means indigestion, because its inventor believed it helped treat an upset stomach.

*Which of these brands exist in your country? Are they successful?*
*Do you know the origin of the names of other companies or brands?*

## 2 PERSPECTIVES Business strategies

▸ **A** Listen to the survey. What makes a business successful? Number the choices from 1 (most important) to 3 (least important).

## What makes a business successful?

1. **In order for an app to succeed, it has to be:**
   ☐ easy to use     ☐ inexpensive     ☐ original

2. **To attract talented professionals, a company should offer:**
   ☐ competitive salaries     ☐ flexible working schedules     ☐ a good career plan

3. **For a small company to be profitable, it should have:**
   ☐ a good marketing plan     ☐ a great product     ☐ excellent professionals

4. **To build a successful start-up, it's important to:**
   ☐ have a great product     ☐ have a clear business plan     ☐ control costs

5. **In order to finance a new business, it's a good idea to:**
   ☐ try a crowd-funding platform     ☐ get a bank loan     ☐ borrow money from family

6. **For people to work from home, they need to have:**
   ☐ self-discipline     ☐ a separate working space     ☐ a daily schedule

**B GROUP WORK** Compare your answers. Do you agree on the most important success factors?

# 12 Keys to success

## Cycle 1, Exercises 1–6

In this unit, students give personal views and describe qualities for success, as well as give reasons for things. By the end of Cycle 1, students will be able to express personal views and describe qualities for success using infinitive clauses and phrases. By the end of Cycle 2, students will be able to describe features and give reasons using *because, since, because of, for, due to,* and *the reason*.

## 1 SNAPSHOT

**Learning Objective:** discuss successful businesses

- Books closed. Give Ss or elicit a list of international companies. Elicit products that the companies make. For example:

| International company | Product |
|---|---|
| Nike | Athletic clothes |
| Google | Search engine |
| Facebook | Social media |
| Samsung | Electronics |
| Skype | Internet communication |
| Häagen-Dazs | Ice cream |
| Pepsi | Soft drinks |

- Books open. Ask Ss to read the Snapshot. Ss may use their dictionaries.
- Ask Ss if any of the facts surprise them. Why?

- Elicit or explain any remaining new vocabulary.

  Vocabulary
  **goddess:** a female god
  **everlasting:** lasting forever or for a long time
  **Danish:** from the country of Denmark
  **upset stomach:** a feeling of mild sickness

- *Option:* Read aloud the main products and facts (omitting the name of each). Ss listen and guess the company.
- Read the questions.
- Ss discuss the questions in pairs, small groups, or as a class.
- *Option:* If your class is made up of business Ss, have several Ss give a brief presentation (or "snapshot") of their company.

## 2 PERSPECTIVES

**Learning Objective:** describe personal views using infinitive clauses and phrases in context

  TIP
  To show Ss the purpose of activities, write the objectives on the board. As you finish each activity, check off the objective so that Ss know where they are. Then at the end of the class, tell Ss what they have achieved.

### ▶ A [CD 3, Track 1]

- Books closed. With Ss, brainstorm some factors that make an app successful. Ask Ss to write their suggestions on the board, like this:

  <u>What makes an app successful?</u>

  - free
  - innovative
  - good marketing

- Books open. Tell Ss to look at the first sentence. How similar were the Ss' opinions to the ones listed on the board?
- *Option:* Find out what Ss know about surveys. Ask: "What is a survey? Has anyone answered a real survey before? Why do businesses conduct surveys?"

- Explain the task. Point out the three options and explain the numbering system.
- Then ask the class to complete the first three boxes. To make sure that Ss understand the task, take a class vote. Which of the three options do Ss think is the most important?
- Ss complete the task individually. Go around the class and give help as needed. Write new words or expressions on the board in your vocabulary column.
- Play the audio program. Ss listen and read. Ask Ss to raise their hands when they hear a success factor they rated *most important.*

### B *Group work*

- Explain the task.
- Ss work in small groups. Ss discuss the most important factor in each case. Ask Ss to find out whose answers are most similar to theirs.
- Then elicit Ss' ideas. How well do they agree?
- *Option:* Ss add one more success factor to each sentence.

## 3 PRONUNCIATION

**Learning Objective:** sound more natural by using reduced forms

▶ **A** *[CD 3, Track 2]*

- Point out that structure words such as *a, an, and, for,* and *to* are rarely stressed. The vowel in these words is usually reduced to /ə/. Explain that /ə/ is the most common sound in English.
- Play the audio program to present the reduced forms. Ss listen and read.
- Play the audio program again. Ss listen and repeat.

## 4 GRAMMAR FOCUS

**Learning Objective:** use infinitive clauses to describe purpose

▶ *[CD 3, Track 3]*

- Write these sentences on the board. Ask Ss to fill in the blanks (answers in parentheses):

  *Describing purpose with infinitive clauses*

  1. _____ attract talented professionals, a company should offer competitive salaries. (To)
  2. _____ _____ _____ finance a new business, it's a good idea to get a bank loan. (In order to)
  3. _____ a small company _____ profitable, it should have a good marketing plan. (For, to be)
  4. _____ _____ _____ an app to succeed, it has _____ be easy to use. (In order for, to)

- Explain the different types of infinitive clauses. Elicit or explain how sentences 1 and 2 are similar:

  (*In order*) + infinitive

  <u>In order to</u> finance a new business, it's a good idea to . . .

      <u>To</u> attract talented professionals, . . .

- Point out that sentences 3 and 4 both use *for.*

  (*In order*) + *for* + noun + infinitive

  <u>In order for</u> an app to succeed, . . .

      <u>For</u> a small company to be profitable, . . .

- Elicit additional examples. Write some of the Ss' suggestions on the board.

- For more practice, play the **Chain Game** – download it from the website. Start with: "For a coffee shop to succeed, . . ."

- Play the audio program. Ss listen and read or repeat.

**B** *Pair work*

- Explain the task. Ss practice reading the sentences in Perspectives on page 78.
- **Option:** Play the audio program for Perspectives again. Ss listen and repeat.
- Ss work in pairs and take turns reading their first choices aloud. Go around the class and listen discreetly. Note: Ss will have additional practice using reduced forms in part A of Exercise 4.

**A**

- Explain the task.
- Ss work individually and match goals with suggestions. Go around the class and give help as needed.
- Go over answers with the class. If Ss have different answers, ask them to explain their choices. Accept any answers that are logical and grammatically correct.
- Then Ss work in pairs. They take turns reading their sentences. Remind Ss to use the reduced forms they practiced in Exercise 3.

| Possible answers | | |
|---|---|---|
| 1. c, d, e | 3. b, c, d, e | 5. a, d, e |
| 2. c, d, e | 4. a, b, d | |

**B** *Pair work*

- Explain the task.
- Ss work in pairs. They add one more suggestion for each goal in part A. Go around the class and give help as needed.
- Ask different Ss to write their suggestions on the board. Accept any answers that are logical and grammatically correct.

**C** *Group work*

- Explain the task. Ask three Ss to model the conversation.
- Ss work in small groups to discuss the kinds of businesses they would like to have and give suggestions on how to make them succeed. Remind Ss to use infinitive clauses.

- For more practice, try **Vocabulary Tennis** – download it from the website. Choose a business (e.g., a movie theater) and have teams take turns calling out success factors. Instead of words, Ss use sentences with infinitive clauses.

# 3 PRONUNCIATION Reduced words

▶ **A** Listen and practice. Notice how certain words are reduced in conversation.

In order **før** ~~a~~ hotel **tø** be successful, it needs **tø** have friendly service **ånd** reasonable prices.

**Før ån** entrepreneur **tø** be successful, they have **tø** invest in ~~a~~ good marketing campaign.

**B** PAIR WORK Take turns reading the sentences in Exercise 2 aloud. Use your first choice to complete each sentence. Pay attention to reduced words.

# 4 GRAMMAR FOCUS

▶ **Describing purpose**

**Infinitive clauses**

| | |
|---|---|
| **To attract** talented professionals, | a company should offer competitive salaries. |
| **(In order) to finance** a new business, | it's a good idea to get a bank loan. |

**Infinitive clauses with** *for*

| | |
|---|---|
| **For** a small company **to be** profitable, | it should have a good marketing plan. |
| **(In order) for** an app to succeed, | it has to be easy to use. |

GRAMMAR PLUS *see page 143*

**A** Match each goal with a suggestion. Then practice the sentences with a partner. (More than one answer is possible.)

**Goals**

1. To run a popular convenience store, _____
2. In order to run a profitable clothing boutique, _____
3. To establish a successful language school, _____
4. In order for a health club to succeed, _____
5. For a restaurant to attract more customers, _____

**Suggestions**

a. it has to offer friendly service.
b. it's a good idea to know the competition.
c. you need to choose the right location.
d. you have to train your staff well.
e. it's important to understand your customers' needs.

**B** PAIR WORK Give another suggestion for each goal in part A.

**C** GROUP WORK What kind of business would you like to have? Talk to your classmates and get suggestions on how to make your business successful.

**A:** I think I'd like to set up a coffee shop.

**B:** For a coffee shop to succeed, it's important to choose a good location.

**C:** And in order to attract customers, you have to offer some tasty desserts, too.

## 5 WORD POWER Qualities for success

**A** PAIR WORK What qualities are important for success?
Rank them from 1 to 5.

| A personal trainer | A politician | A news website |
|---|---|---|
| ☐ athletic | ☐ clever | ☐ affordable |
| ☐ passionate | ☐ charming | ☐ attractive |
| ☐ industrious | ☐ knowledgeable | ☐ entertaining |
| ☐ muscular | ☐ persuasive | ☐ informative |
| ☐ experienced | ☐ tough | ☐ well written |

**B** GROUP WORK Add one more adjective to each list.

"For a personal trainer to be successful, he or she needs to be . . ."

## 6 ROLE PLAY The job is yours!

**Student A:**

Interview two people for one of these jobs. What
qualities do they need for success? Decide who is
more qualified for the job.

**Students B and C:**

You are applying for the same job. What are your
best qualities? Convince the interviewer that you
are more qualified for the job.

sales associate at a trendy boutique     public relations specialist     tour guide

**A:** To be a good sales associate, you need to be persuasive. Are you?
**B:** Oh, yes. I'm very good at convincing people. And I'm industrious.
**C:** I've worked at other stores before, so I'm experienced. And I'm fashionable, too.

## 7 CONVERSATION It's always packed.

▶ **A** Listen and practice.

**Kyle:** What's your favorite club, Lori?
**Lori:** The Firefly. They have fabulous music, and it's never
crowded, so it's easy to get in.
**Kyle:** That's funny. There's always a long wait outside my
favorite club. I like it because it's always packed.
**Lori:** Why do you think it's so popular?
**Kyle:** Well, it just opened a few months ago, everything is
brand-new and modern, and lots of trendy people
go there. It's called the Dizzy Lizard.
**Lori:** Oh, right! I hear the reason people go there is
just to be seen.
**Kyle:** Exactly! Do you want to go some night?
**Lori:** I thought you'd never ask!

**B** CLASS ACTIVITY What are some popular places in your
city? Do you ever go to any of these places? Why or
why not?

## 5 WORD POWER

**Learning Objective:** discuss the qualities needed for success

### A Pair work

- Focus Ss' attention on the picture. With Ss, brainstorm some qualities that are important for a personal trainer to be successful. Write Ss' ideas on the board.
- Ask Ss to read the adjectives in each list. Elicit or explain any new vocabulary.

#### Vocabulary
**industrious:** hardworking
**knowledgeable:** knowing a lot
**persuasive:** able to influence other people
**tough:** strong; able to deal with difficult conditions
**affordable:** having a reasonable price
**entertaining:** amusing and interesting
**well written:** written in an effective or interesting way

- Ss work in pairs and rank the adjectives from 1 to 5. Remind Ss that 1 is most important. Encourage Ss to give reasons for their rankings and to try to come to an agreement.
- Go around the room and offer help as needed.
- Elicit examples of the most important quality (ranked number 1) for success for each item.

### B Group work

- Explain the task.
- Ss work in small groups to add one more adjective to each list.
- Elicit the new adjectives from each group. Encourage groups to explain their reason for adding that to the list.

## 6 ROLE PLAY

**Learning Objective:** use infinitive clauses in a job interview

- Explain the task. Ask three Ss to model the conversation.
- Students work in groups of three. Student A is the interviewer. He or she chooses a job from the list. Students B and C are applicants. Each tries to convince the interviewer that he or she is best for the job. Remind Ss to use vocabulary from the Word Power, as well as to recycle vocabulary from pages 3, 30, and 74.

- Set a time limit of about seven minutes. Go around the class and give help as needed.
- Ss change roles and do the role play again.

### End of Cycle 1

See the Supplementary Resources chart at the beginning of this unit for additional teaching materials and student activities related to this Cycle.

## Cycle 2, Exercises 7–13

## 7 CONVERSATION

**Learning Objective:** use various ways of giving reasons in a conversation about a successful business

### ▶ A [CD 3, Track 4]

- Tell Ss to cover the text and look only at the picture. Elicit details about the picture.
- Set the scene. Two friends, Kyle and Lori, are talking about their favorite nightclubs. Tell Ss to listen to find out how the clubs are different.
- Play the audio program. Ss listen and take notes.

- Text uncovered. Tell Ss to read the conversation. Ask them to check the accuracy of their notes.
- Ask: "Which club would you rather go to? Why?"
- Ss practice the conversation in pairs.

  For another way to practice this Conversation, try the **Musical Dialog** – download it from the website.

### B Class activity

- Explain the task. Read the questions. Hold a class discussion about "in" places. Ss compare and evaluate clubs they know.

# 8 GRAMMAR FOCUS

**Learning Objective:** use *because, since, because of, for, due to,* and *the reason* to give reasons

▶ *[CD 3, Track 5]*

- Focus Ss' attention on the Grammar Focus box. Explain that the phrases in boldface are used for giving reasons. Present the following information and examples:

**1. because *and* since**

- They mean the same, although *since* is more formal.
- *Because* and *since* are followed by a subject and verb:
  subject + verb
  I like the Dizzy Lizard **because** <u>it's</u> always <u>packed</u>.

- Ask Ss to underline the subject + verb phrases with *because* and *since* in the Grammar Focus box.

  - *Because* or *since* can begin or end a sentence. When the clause is at the beginning, it is followed by a comma.
    **<u>Since</u>** <u>it's always so packed</u>, there's a long wait outside the club. OR
    There's a long wait outside the club **<u>since</u>** <u>it's always so packed</u>.
  - The clause with *because* or *since* is a subordinate clause, not a main clause.

**2. because of *and* due to**

- They mean the same, although *due to* often has a negative connotation.
- *Because of* and *due to* are followed by a noun or noun phrase.
  It's popular **because of** <u>the trendy people</u>.

- Ask Ss to underline the noun/noun phrases used with *because of* and *due to* in the Grammar Focus box.

  - *Because of* or *due to* can begin a sentence. When the clause is at the beginning, it is followed by a comma.
    **<u>Due to</u>** the crowds, the Dizzy Lizard is difficult to get into. OR
    It's difficult to get into the Dizzy Lizard due to the crowds.
  - The clause with *because of* or *due to* is a subordinate clause, not a main clause.

**3. for**

  **for** + noun (or noun phrase)
  The Firefly is famous **<u>for</u>** <u>its fantastic music</u>.

**4. the reason (that/why) . . . is . . .**

  **<u>The reason (that/why)</u>** people go there **<u>is</u>** just to be seen.

- Play the audio program. Ss listen and read or repeat.
- **Option:** Ss choose a popular restaurant or club in their city and write sentences using the six patterns in the Grammar Focus box. Tell Ss to give reasons for the place's success. Go around the class and give help as needed.

## A

- Books closed. Draw a circle on the board. Write *Apple* inside it. Ask: "What do you know about Apple? Do you own any of its products? Why is it so popular?" Ss come to the board to add their ideas to the mind map.
- Books open. Explain the task. Point out that more than one answer is possible.
- Ss complete the paragraphs individually.
- Ss compare answers in pairs. Check Ss' responses around the class.

### Answers

1. Apple is considered one of the most innovative companies in the world. The company is known **for** introducing original products, but it's also admired **because of/for** its ability to predict what the market will need in the future. **The reason why** Apple has been so successful is that it has become a symbol of status and high-end technology.
2. McDonald's is popular worldwide **because** customers know what to expect when they eat there. Whether you're in Florida or in France, your Big Mac is the same. The company is also known **for** its ability to adapt to different markets. **Because/Since** the company adjusts some items to local tastes, you can eat pineapple pie in Thailand, or a shrimp burger in Japan.

## B *Pair work*

- Explain the task. Model the first sentence with the class.
- Ss complete the task in pairs and add two more reasons. Then check Ss' responses.

### TIP
If a S finishes the task early, check his or her work, and send the S to work with another person. Alternatively, ask the S to start writing the answers on the board.

### Answers

| | | | | | | | |
|---|---|---|---|---|---|---|---|
| 1. b | 2. f | 3. e | 4. a | 5. h | 6. d | 7. c | 8. g |

## C *Group work*

- Ss work in groups to answer the questions. Elicit responses from the class.
- **Option:** Ask Ss to write one idea each on the board. Use those suggestions to go over any problems Ss may still have with these structures.

For more practice with giving reasons, try **Just One Minute** – download it from the website. Ss describe a business, TV show, or product, and the reasons for its success.

## ▶ Giving reasons

The Firefly is famous **for** its fantastic music.

I like the Dizzy Lizard **because** it's always packed.

**Since** it's always so packed, there's a long wait outside the club.

It's popular **because of** the trendy people.

**Due to** the crowds, the Dizzy Lizard is difficult to get into.

**The reason** (**that/why**) people go there **is** just to be seen.

GRAMMAR PLUS *see page 143*

A  Complete the paragraphs with *because, since, because of, for, due to,* and *the reason*. Then compare with a partner. (More than one answer is possible.)

1.  Apple is considered one of the most innovative companies in the world. The company is known _____ introducing original products, but it's also admired _____ its ability to predict what the market will need in the future. _____ Apple has been so successful is that it has become a symbol of status and high-end technology.

2.  McDonald's is popular worldwide _____ customers know what to expect when they eat there. Whether you're in Florida or in France, your Big Mac is the same. The company is also known _____ its ability to adapt to different markets. _____ the company adjusts some items to local tastes, you can eat a pineapple pie in Thailand or a shrimp burger in Japan.

B  **PAIR WORK**  Match the situations with the reasons for success. Compare ideas with a partner. Then give two more reasons for each success.

**Situation**

1.  FedEx is famous _____
2.  Samsung is a successful company _____
3.  Online stores are becoming very popular _____
4.  Netflix has expanded quickly _____
5.  People buy Levi's jeans _____
6.  Many people like Amazon _____
7.  Nike is known _____
8.  People everywhere drink Coca-Cola _____

**Reason**

a.  because of its ability to attract new customers.
b.  for its fast and reliable service.
c.  for its innovative athletic wear.
d.  for its wide selection of products.
e.  since prices are generally more affordable.
f.  due to its high investment in research.
g.  since it's advertised worldwide.
h.  because they appeal to people of different ages and lifestyles.

**A:** FedEx is famous for its fast and reliable service.

**B:** I think another reason why FedEx is famous is . . .

C  **GROUP WORK**  What are some successful companies in your country? Why are they successful?

## 9 LISTENING What have you got to lose?

▶ **A** Listen to radio commercials for three different businesses. What are two special features of each place?

|  | Fitness For Life | Beauty To Go | Like-New Repair Services |
|---|---|---|---|
| **1.** |  |  |  |
| **2.** |  |  |  |

▶ **B** Listen again. Complete the slogan for each business.

1. "Fitness For Life, where _____."
2. "Beauty To Go. When and where you want, beauty _____."
3. "Like-New Repair Services. Don't let your phone _____."

**C** GROUP WORK Which business do you think would be the most successful in your city? Why?

## 10 INTERCHANGE 12 Advertising taglines

How well do you know the slogans companies use for their products? Go to Interchange 12 on page 127.

## 11 DISCUSSION Ads and commercials

GROUP WORK Discuss these questions.

When you watch TV, do you pay attention to the commercials? Why or why not?
When you're online, do you click on any ads that you see?
   What ads attract your attention?
What are some effective commercials or ads you remember?
   What made them effective?
What is the funniest commercial you've ever seen? the worst? the most shocking?
Which celebrities have been in commercials or ads?
   Has this affected your opinion of the product?
   Has it affected your opinion of the celebrity?

## 12 WRITING A commercial

**A** Choose one of your favorite products. Read the questions and make notes about the best way to sell it. Then write a one-minute TV or online commercial.

What's good or unique about the product?
Why would someone want to buy or use it?
Can you think of a clever name or slogan?

**B** GROUP WORK Take turns presenting your commercials. What is good about each one? Can you give any suggestions to improve them?

Do you want a car that is dependable and economical? Do you need more space for your family? The new Genius SUV has it all. Genius offers the latest safety technologies and . . .

# 9 LISTENING

**Learning Objective:** listen for specific information and take notes on commercials giving reasons to use businesses

## A *[CD 3, Track 6]*

- Explain the task. Then ask Ss to read the names of the businesses and predict what kind of business each is.
- Tell Ss to listen to the commercials for the special features. Remind Ss to write down only key words.
- Play the audio program. Ss listen and write the features. Were Ss' predictions correct?
- Elicit the answers.

### Audio script

See page T-178.

### Possible answers

Fitness For Life: free personal trainer for 21 days; qualified trainers; state-of-the-art fitness equipment; dynamic group classes; nutritional guidance
Beauty To Go: they go to your house; they bring all the equipment and products with them; you only have to go to their site and select what you want and where you live; they're cheaper
Like-New Repair Services: they diagnose the problem for free; if they can't fix it, you don't pay for it

## B *[CD 3, Track 7]*

- Play the audio program again. Ss listen and complete the slogan for each place. Then check Ss' answers.

### Answers

1. "Fitness For Life, where **you come first**."
2. "Beauty To Go. When and where you want, beauty **has never been this easy**."
3. "Like-New Repair Services. Don't let your phone **slow you down**."

For another way to teach this exercise, try *Jigsaw Learning* – download it from the website. Student A listens for the feature, Student B listens for the slogan.

## C *Group work*

- Ss answer the question in small groups. Remind them to ask follow-up questions and keep the conversation going.
- Ask groups to share their answers with the class. Accept any logical answer they give and go over any mistakes with the class.

### TIP

Don't interrupt the Ss while they are speaking. Instead, write down all the mistakes you hear and go over them after they have all finished.

# 10 INTERCHANGE 12

See page T-127 for teaching notes.

# 11 DISCUSSION

**Learning Objective:** discuss advertisements using various ways of giving reasons

Note: If possible, show some recordings of TV commercials in class.

## Group work

- Read the discussion questions. Explain the task. Encourage Ss to ask follow-up questions.

- Ss work in small groups to discuss the questions. Go around the room and offer help as needed.
- *Option:* Write each question on a card. Divide the class into five groups, if possible. Give each group a card with a question. Set a time limit of three minutes for groups to discuss the question. Then have groups pass their question on to another group, and repeat the process until groups have discussed all five questions.

# 12 WRITING

**Learning Objective:** write an advertisement using various ways of giving reasons

## A

- Explain the task. Read the questions. Explain that Ss can use them to help organize their ideas. Ask a S to read the example commercial.
- Ss work individually. Tell Ss to choose one product and make notes on how it could be advertised. Ss use their notes to write a first draft.
- *Option:* The first draft can be assigned for homework.

## B *Group work*

- Explain the task. Ss present their one-minute commercials to their group. The rest of the group offers feedback on the presentation.
- *Option:* Encourage Ss to include props and music.
- *Option:* Ss create a storyboard for their commercial and present it to the group or the class. The storyboard could show, using a comic-book style, the main scenes in the TV commercial.

**Learning Objective:** make predictions and inferences about an article about market research

## A

- Read the question. Ask Ss what *sticky* means and have them give examples of things that are sticky. (Answer: *Sticky* means "easily attaching to something." Possible examples are tape, honey, and gum.)
- Elicit Ss' answers to the focus question. (Answer: An advertisement that is *sticky* is memorable, or "sticks" in people's minds.)
- Ask: "Do you know any ads that are sticky?"

## B

- Explain the task. Then go over ideas 1–6. Point out only three are mentioned in the article.
- Ss read the article individually. Tell Ss to guess the meanings of unfamiliar words while quickly reading for main ideas. Remind Ss to mark any words they don't understand.

! For another way to teach this reading, try **Reading Race** – download it from the website.

- Ss work in pairs or small groups to discuss vocabulary. Tell Ss to ask each other about words they still don't understand. Ss may use their dictionaries for a final check.
- Elicit or explain any remaining new vocabulary.

### Vocabulary

**barrage:** a large amount of something that comes very quickly at a person
**unforgettable:** something with a strong effect or influence on you that you cannot forget
**pick up the message:** understand a message
**split second:** a very short moment of time
**out of the ordinary:** unusual
**whether . . . or not:** it is not important if either of two conditions is true
**dive:** jump into water, especially with your head and arms going in first
**ever-changing:** constantly changing or developing
**grab:** attract the attention
**puzzle:** a situation that is difficult to understand
**time span:** a period of time between two fixed points

- Ss work individually or in pairs to choose the correct answers.
- Go over answers with the class.

### Answers

Correct ad concepts:
an uncomplicated concept
a sensual or emotional appeal
something unexpected or strange

## C

- Explain the task. Read the two ads.
- Ss work individually.
- Go over answers with the class.

### Possible answers

The first ad is sticky because it is simple and clear, easy to understand, and surprising.
The second ad is simple and easy, but it's not very sticky because there is nothing out of the ordinary.

## D *Pair work*

- Explain the task. Brainstorm products with memorable advertisements.
- Ss complete the task in pairs. Go around the class and give help as needed.

! For more practice, try **Twenty Questions** – download it from the website. Ss think of an advertisement.

## End of Cycle 2

See the Supplementary Resources chart at the beginning of this unit for additional teaching materials and student activities related to this Cycle and for assessment tools.

**A** Scan the article. What does "sticky" mean in the advertising world?

## BRAIN INVASION:
### WHY WE CAN'T FORGET SOME ADS

**Advertisements:** They're all over our social media pages; they arrive as text messages; they interrupt our favorite shows; and they bombard us in the streets. In order to survive the constant barrage of advertising, we learn to ignore most of what we see. But what is it that makes certain ads "sticky"? In other words, why do we remember some ads while managing to completely forget others?

According to advertising experts, an ad needs three key elements to make it unforgettable. In the first place, it needs to be clear and simple. TV commercials usually last about 30 seconds, so a complicated or confusing presentation will not do the job. For an ad to be "sticky," it has to be obvious enough that we can pick up the message in a split second.

More importantly, ads should appeal to our senses and emotions. When we really feel something, it tends to stick in our brains much longer than if we simply understand it. This is the reason why so much advertising depends on emotional music and images of family, romance, or success that relate directly to our own hopes and dreams.

One more element necessary to make an ad successful is surprise. When we see something out of the ordinary, it makes us take notice whether we want to or not. A talking animal, a beautifully dressed model diving into a swimming pool, a car zooming through an ever-changing landscape – these are the types of things that grab our attention.

But do "sticky" ads actually make us buy the products? That's another story. Sometimes the most memorable ads make people laugh or mention them to their friends, but they don't actually convince people to buy anything. Still, after watching a "sticky" ad, we usually remember the name of the company it promotes. And in a world with so many brands and products, that is almost as important as sales.

**B** Read the article. Check (✓) the three things that make an ad memorable.

- ☐ an uncomplicated concept
- ☐ a puzzle or mystery
- ☐ a short time span
- ☐ a sensual or emotional appeal
- ☐ a familiar scene or situation
- ☐ something unexpected or strange

**C** Read these descriptions of two ads. According to the article, are these "sticky" ads? Explain why.

A family of four is having breakfast together, and they're all looking tired. The father pours each of them a glass of "Super Juice," and as they all drink it, they are transformed into costumed superheroes. As they leave, the mother says, "Ready to save the world, team?"

A young couple are in a luxurious car; the woman is driving. They are driving quickly through lush countryside. They glance at other and smile. A voiceover says: "The Eternity: a car that feels like home."

**D** PAIR WORK Describe an advertisement that has stuck in your mind. Why do you think you remember it? Has it influenced what you buy in any way?

# Units 11–12 Progress check

## SELF-ASSESSMENT

How well can you do these things? Check (✓) the boxes.

| I can . . . | Very well | OK | A little |
|---|---|---|---|
| Describe important life events and their consequences (Ex. 1) | ☐ | ☐ | ☐ |
| Describe and explain regrets about the past (Ex. 2) | ☐ | ☐ | ☐ |
| Describe hypothetical situations in the past (Ex. 2) | ☐ | ☐ | ☐ |
| Understand and give reasons for success (Ex. 3, 4) | ☐ | ☐ | ☐ |
| Give reasons (Ex. 4) | ☐ | ☐ | ☐ |

## 1 SPEAKING  Important events

**A** What are two important events for each of these age groups?
Complete the chart.

| Children | Teenagers | People in their 20s | People in their 40s |
|---|---|---|---|
| | | | |
| | | | |

**B GROUP WORK** Talk about the events. Why is each event
important? What do people learn from each event?

**A:** Learning to drive is an important event for teenagers.
**B:** Why is learning to drive an important milestone?
**A:** Once they learn to drive, . . .

| useful expressions | |
|---|---|
| after | once |
| as soon as | before |
| the moment | until |
| by the time | |

## 2 GAME  Regrets

**A** Write three regrets you have about the past.

> 1.   I wish I hadn't argued with my boss.

**B GROUP WORK** What if the situations were different?
Take turns. One student expresses a regret. The next
student adds a hypothetical result, and so on, for as long
as you can.

**A:** I shouldn't have argued with my boss.
**B:** If you hadn't argued with your boss, she wouldn't
have fired you.
**C:** If she hadn't fired you, you could have . . .

# Progress check

## SELF-ASSESSMENT

**Learning Objectives:** reflect on one's learning; identify areas that need improvement

- Ask: "What did you learn in Units 11 and 12?" Elicit Ss' answers.

- Ss complete the Self-assessment. Explain to Ss that this is not a test; it is a way for them to evaluate what they've learned and identify areas where they need additional practice. Encourage them to be honest, and point out they will not get a bad grade if they check (✓) "a little."

- Ss move on to the Progress check exercises. You can have Ss complete them in class or for homework, using one of these techniques:
  1. Ask Ss to complete all the exercises.
  2. Ask Ss: "What do you need to practice?" Then assign exercises based on their answers.
  3. Ask Ss to choose and complete exercises based on their Self-assessment.

## 1 SPEAKING

**Learning Objective:** demonstrate one's ability to describe important events with time clauses

**A**

- Explain the task. Ss come up with important events at several points in people's lives.

- Ss work individually to complete the chart. Go around the class and give help with vocabulary.

**B Group work**

- Explain the task. Read the focus questions. Ask Ss to read the useful expressions. Ask two Ss to model the conversation.

- Ss work in small groups to discuss the events. Go around the class and note mistakes you hear. Also note time clauses you hear used correctly.

- After the discussion, write mistakes you heard on the board. Ask the class to correct them. Point out examples of time clauses you heard used correctly.

- Ask each group to share one or two of the important events they discussed.

## 2 GAME

**Learning Objectives:** demonstrate one's ability to talk about behavior and personality; demonstrate one's ability to express regrets about the past using past modals; demonstrate one's ability to describe hypothetical situations using *if* clauses

**A**

- Explain the task.

- Ss work individually to write three regrets. Remind Ss that they will be sharing these regrets, so they should avoid anything too personal to share.

- Go around the class to check grammar and give help as needed.

**B Group work**

- Explain the task. Ask three Ss to model the conversation.

- Ss work in small groups. Ss take turns talking about regrets. Group members add hypothetical results. Challenge Ss to think of several hypothetical results for each situation.

- **Option:** Ask Ss to write their sentences. Ss can read them aloud or turn them in to you to check.

## 3 LISTENING

**Learning Objective:** demonstrate one's ability to listen to, understand, and give reasons for success

### ▶ A *[CD 3, Track 8]*

- Explain that Ss are going to hear three factors necessary to work for yourself.

- Tell Ss to listen and write keywords for each factor they hear. Play the audio program once or twice. Elicit or explain any new vocabulary.

#### Audio script

See page T-179.

- Go over answers with the class.

#### Answers

Parts A and B
1. knowing your field; research is knowledge and knowledge is power; if your clients trust you, they will come back to you
2. networking; you never know who may be a potential client
3. establish small goals every week; you'll accomplish the goals and make progress

### ▶ B *[CD 3, Track 9]*

- Explain the task.

- Tell Ss to listen for the reasons each factor is important. Play the audio program again. Pause after each section for Ss to write. Remind Ss to answer in their own words. Play the audio program as many times as needed.

- Ss compare answers with a partner. If they have any disagreements, play the audio program again.

- Go over answers with the class.

- **Option:** Ss work in groups. They discuss the factors not mentioned in the audio program. Ask groups to share their ideas with the class.

### C *Pair work*

- Ss work in pairs to discuss the question. Ask them to write down at least one sentence each explaining what they would do and why.

- Walk around the class and help with structure and vocabulary. If you see any mistakes, go over them with the class.

- Ask Ss to share their ideas with the class.

## 4 DISCUSSION

**Learning Objectives:** demonstrate one's ability to give reasons for success; demonstrate one's ability to describe purpose with infinitive clauses and clauses with *for*

### A *Pair work*

- Explain the task. Ask Ss to read the list of businesses. Elicit or explain any new vocabulary.

- Ss work in pairs. First, Ss discuss the factors affecting success. Remind Ss to choose two businesses.

- Then Ss write three sentences describing the most important factors. Go around the class and give help as needed.

### B *Group work*

- Explain the task. Ask two Ss to model the conversation.

- Each pair joins another pair. Ss take turns sharing their ideas.

- Ask groups which ideas they agreed and disagreed about.

### C *Group work*

- Explain the task. Read the example sentence. Ask Ss to read the useful expressions.

- Ss work in the same groups or in different groups. Ss choose a successful business to discuss. Encourage Ss to name factors like the ones in Exercise 3.

- Ask groups to share ideas with the class.

## WHAT'S NEXT?

**Learning Objective:** become more involved in one's learning

- Focus Ss' attention on the Self-assessment again. Ask: "How well can you do these things now?"

- Ask Ss to underline one thing they need to review. Ask: "What did you underline? How can you review it?"

- If needed, plan additional activities or reviews based on Ss' answers.

## 3 LISTENING The road to success

▶ **A** Listen to a career coach discuss some factors necessary to work for yourself. Write down the three factors that you hear.

| | Factor | Why is it important? |
|---|---|---|
| **1.** | | |
| **2.** | | |
| **3.** | | |

▶ **B** Listen again. In your own words, write why each factor is important.

**C** PAIR WORK If you could work for yourself, what would you do? Why?

## 4 DISCUSSION Effective strategies

**A** PAIR WORK Choose two businesses and discuss what they need to be successful. Then write three sentences describing the most important factors.

☐ a convenience store    ☐ a dance club    ☐ a juice bar
☐ a gourmet supermarket    ☐ a beach hotel    ☐ a used clothing store

> In order for a convenience store to be successful, it has to be open 24 hours.

**B** GROUP WORK Join another pair. Share your ideas. Do they agree?

**A:** We think in order for a convenience store to be successful, it has to be open 24 hours.

**B:** Really? But many convenience stores close at midnight.

**C** GROUP WORK Now choose a popular business that you know about. What are the reasons for its success?

"I think Mark's Comics is successful because their comic books are affordable and they don't mind if people hang out there and read."

**useful expressions**

It's successful because (of) . . .
It's popular due to . . .
The reason it's successful is . . .
It's become popular since . . .
It's famous for . . .

## WHAT'S NEXT?

Look at your Self-assessment again. Do you need to review anything?

# Unit 13 Supplementary Resources Overview

| | After the following SB exercises | You can use these materials in class | Your students can use these materials outside the classroom |
|---|---|---|---|
| **CYCLE 1** | 1 Snapshot | | |
| | 2 Conversation | | **SS** Unit 13 Speaking 1–2 |
| | 3 Pronunciation | | |
| | 4 Grammar Focus | | **SB** Unit 13 Grammar plus, Focus 1<br>**SS** Unit 13 Grammar 1<br>**GAME** Speak or Swim (Past modals for degrees of certainty) |
| | 5 Listening | | |
| | 6 Speaking | **TSS** Unit 13 Extra Worksheet | |
| | 7 Interchange 13 | | **WB** Unit 13 exercises 1–4 |
| **CYCLE 2** | 8 Perspectives | | |
| | 9 Grammar Focus | **TSS** Unit 13 Grammar Worksheet<br>**TSS** Unit 13 Listening Worksheet | **SB** Unit 13 Grammar plus, Focus 1<br>**SS** Unit 13 Grammar 2<br>**GAME** Sentence Runner (Past modals for judgments and suggestions)<br>**GAME** Sentence Stacker (Past modals) |
| | 10 Word Power | **TSS** Unit 13 Vocabulary Worksheet | **SS** Unit 13 Vocabulary 1–2<br>**GAME** Say the Word (Reactions) |
| | 11 Listening | | |
| | 12 Discussion | **TSS** Unit 13 Writing Worksheet | |
| | 13 Writing | | |
| | 14 Reading | **TSS** Unit 13 Project Worksheet<br>**VID** Unit 13<br>**VRB** Unit 13 | **SS** Unit 13 Reading 1–2<br>**SS** Unit 13 Listening 1–3<br>**SS** Unit 13 Video 1–3<br>**WB** Unit 13 exercises 5–7 |

**Key**  **GAME:** Online Game  **SB:** Student's Book  **SS:** Online Self-study  **TSS:** Teacher Support Site
**VID:** Video DVD  **VRB:** Video Resource Book  **WB:** Online Workbook/Workbook

# My Plan for Unit 13

Use the space below to customize a plan that fits your needs.

| With the following SB exercises | I am using these materials in class | My students are using these materials outside the classroom |
| --- | --- | --- |
| | | |
| | | |
| | | |
| | | |
| | | |
| | | |
| | | |
| | | |
| | | |
| | | |
| | | |
| | | |
| | | |

| With or instead of the following SB section | I am using these materials for assessment |
| --- | --- |
| | |
| | |
| | |

# 13 What might have been

▸ Suggest explanations and reasons
▸ Give opinions and advice about past situations

## 1 SNAPSHOT

# PET PEEVES

### IT DRIVES ME CRAZY WHEN . . . .

- people push too close to me on the subway.
- someone borrows my things without asking.
- people keep interrupting me.
- a couple starts arguing in public.
- people don't pay for their share at a restaurant.

- a friend criticizes another friend.
- someone is late for no reason.
- people chew with their mouths open.
- a friend constantly asks me for favors.
- someone cuts in line in front of me.

*Which of the pet peeves do you have about people you know? Which one is the worst?*
*What other pet peeves do you have?*
*Do you do any of these things? When and why?*

## 2 CONVERSATION He might have gone out.

▶ **A** Listen and practice.

**Chris:** Didn't Tyler ask us to come at 7:30?

**Ava:** Yes, and it's almost 8:00 now. Why don't we ring the bell again? He must not have heard it.

**Chris:** That's impossible. We've been ringing the bell for more than 10 minutes.

**Ava:** He must have fallen asleep. You know Tyler has been working so hard on his new project.

**Chris:** Or he might have forgotten about our dinner and just gone out.

**Ava:** No, he couldn't have forgotten. I just talked to him about it this morning. Besides, the lights are on. He could have had an emergency. He might not have had time to call us.

**Chris:** Yeah, maybe. I'll call him and find out.

**Ava:** And?

**Chris:** He's not answering. . . . Now *I'm* getting worried.

▶ **B** Listen to the rest of the conversation. What happened?

# 13 What might have been

## Cycle 1, Exercises 1–7

In this unit, students give explanations, reasons, and suggestions, as well as give their opinions and advice about past situations. By the end of Cycle 1, students will be able to give explanations, reasons, and suggestions using past modals *must have*, *may have*, and *could have*. By the end of Cycle 2, students will be able to give opinions and advice with past modals *should have*, *could have*, and *would have*.

## 1 SNAPSHOT

**Learning Objective:** discuss annoying social habits

- Books closed. Write the title "Pet Peeves" on the board. List one or two pet peeves not shown in the Snapshot:

  *Why is it that some people:*

  – *always talk about how much things cost?*

  – *never help clean up after a party?*

  Note: Ss discuss their own pet peeves later.

- Elicit that *pet peeves* are things that always annoy you.

- Books open. Ask Ss to look at the Snapshot in pairs.

- Elicit or explain any new vocabulary.

### Vocabulary
**chew:** crush food between your teeth before you swallow it
**share:** a part of something that has been divided

- Read the questions.

- Ss discuss the questions in small groups. Remind Ss to use "I hate it when/It bothers me when," etc. from Unit 1.

- **Option:** Ss work in small groups. Each group writes ten rules for good manners (e.g., *People should always:*

  – *hold the door open for the next person*

  – *call if they're going to be late*).

- For more practice with the vocabulary, play **True or False?** – download it from the website. Ss cover the text and look at the picture for one minute. Then ask Ss to close their books and test their memory (e.g., *The man's shirt is blue [false]*).

## 2 CONVERSATION

**Learning Objective:** use past modals in a conversation about offering explanations

▶ **A** *[CD 3, Track 10]*

- Books closed. Set the scene. Two people are talking about a friend who is not answering the door.

- Write these questions on the board:

  *What time were Ava and Chris asked to come?*
  (Answer: 7:30)
  *What time is it now?* (Answer: almost 8:00)
  *What does Chris decide to do?* (Answer: call Tyler)
  *What happened on the phone call?* (Answer: Tyler didn't answer.)

- Tell Ss to listen for the answers. Play the audio program. Then elicit the answers. Ask: "What would you do in a similar situation?"

- Write these sentence starters on the board. Do not write the answers.

  *What has happened to Tyler?*
  Ava: He must not have _____ _____.
  (Answer: heard it)
  Ava: He must have _____ _____.
  (Answer: fallen asleep)
  Chris: He might have _____ _____
  _____ _____.
  (Answer: forgotten about our dinner)

- Tell Ss to listen for the answers. Play the audio program again.

- Ask Ss to come to the board to fill in the answers. Ask the class to correct answers if needed.

- Books open. Play the audio program. Ss listen and read or repeat.

▶ **B** *[CD 3, Track 11]*

- Explain the task. Tell Ss to listen to what really happened to Tyler. Play the second part of the audio program. Elicit Ss' responses.

### Audio script
See page T-179.

### Answer
Tyler locked himself out of his house. He walked to the gas station and called a locksmith.

## 3 PRONUNCIATION

**Learning Objective:** use reduced forms of *have* and *not* to sound more natural when using past modals

▶ **A** *[CD 3, Track 12]*

- Play the audio program. Ss listen. Point out that in past modals, *have* is reduced to /əv/. The reduced *have* sounds like *of*.
- Play the audio program again. Ss listen and repeat.

▶ **B** *[CD 3, Track 13]*

- Play the audio program. Ss listen and focus on the full form of *not*.
- Play the audio program again. Ss listen and repeat.

❗ For a different way to practice reductions, try **Walking Stress** – download it from the website. Ss identify key words first.

## 4 GRAMMAR FOCUS

**Learning Objective:** use past modals *must have, may have,* and *could have* to express degrees of certainty in explanations, reasons, and suggestions

▶ *[CD 3, Track 14]*

### Past modals of possibility (may/might/could have)

- Point out that we use *may, might,* and *could* when something is possible, but we don't know for sure. Write the rule on the board. Elicit other possible reasons for Tyler's lateness, using *may/might/could have*.

  subject + may/might/could + have + past participle
  He       may          have    gone out.

### Past modals of certainty (must/couldn't have)

- Ask Ss to find an example of *must (not) have* in the Conversation on page 86. Write it on the board.

- Tell Ss that we use *must not have* when we are almost certain. Remind Ss: Ava and Chris have been waiting for 10 minutes, so Tyler *must have fallen asleep*, because he is not answering the door.

- Explain that when we are more certain, we use *couldn't have*. Ask Ss to find the example of *couldn't have* in the Conversation. Write it on the board. (Answer: *No, he couldn't have forgotten.*)

- Play the audio program. Ss listen and read or repeat.

❗ For another way to practice past modals, try **Disappearing Dialog** – download it from the website, using the Conversation on page 86. Erase the past modals first.

**A**

- Explain the task. Read the situations and explanations. Elicit or explain any unfamiliar words.

- Ss complete the task individually. Go over answers with the class.

- Then Ss practice reading their answers in pairs. Remind Ss to use reduced forms.

| Answers |
|---------|
| 1. c   2. a   3. e   4. b   5. f   6. d |

**B** *Pair work*

- Explain the task.

- Ss work in pairs and take turns suggesting explanations for each situation.

## 5 LISTENING

**Learning Objectives:** make predictions and give explanations using past modals; listen and take notes on explanations

**A** *Group work*

- Explain the task. Ask Ss to form small groups.

- Invite Ss to give explanations for the events pictured. Remind Ss to use past modals.

▶ **B** *[CD 3, Track 15]*

- Explain the task. Remind Ss to take notes.

- Play the audio program. Then ask: "What *did* happen?" Elicit Ss' responses. Discuss how similar their part A explanations were to what really happened.

| Audio script |
|---------|
| See page T-179. |

| Answers |
|---------|
| 1. They woke up late, missed their flight, and had to catch the next plane. They arrived just as dinner started. |
| 2. His dog Sheba escaped because someone left the back gate open. The neighbor saw the dog on the street, rescued her, and took her back home. |

## 3 PRONUNCIATION  Reduction in past modals

▶ **A** Listen and practice. Notice how **have** is reduced in these sentences.

He may ~~have~~ fallen asleep.                    She might ~~have~~ gone out.

▶ **B** Listen and practice. Notice that **not** is not contracted or reduced in these sentences.

He might **not** have had time to call us.         She must **not** have heard the doorbell.

## 4 GRAMMAR FOCUS

▶ **Past modals for degrees of certainty**

| | |
|---|---|
| It's almost certain. | It's possible. |
| He **must have fallen** asleep. | He **may/might have gone** out. |
| He **must not have heard** the doorbell. | He **may/might not have had** time to call us. |
| It's not possible. | He **could have had** an emergency. |
| He **couldn't have forgotten** about it. | |

GRAMMAR PLUS see page 144

**A** Read each situation and choose the best explanation. Then practice with a partner.
(Pay attention to the reduced forms in past modals.)

**Situation**
1. Marcia seems very relaxed. _____
2. Claire is packing her things. _____
3. Jeff got a bad grade on his test. _____
4. Rodrigo looks very tired today. _____
5. Julia didn't talk to her friends in the cafeteria. _____
6. Ahmed got a call and looked worried. _____

**Explanation**
a. She must have gotten fired.
b. He might have worked late last night.
c. She may have just come back from vacation.
d. He couldn't have heard good news.
e. He might not have studied very hard.
f. She must not have seen them.

**B** PAIR WORK Suggest different explanations for each situation in part A.

## 5 LISTENING  What could have happened?

**A** GROUP WORK Look at the pictures. What do you think happened?
Offer an explanation for each event.

▶ **B** Listen to the explanations for the two events in part A and take notes.
What *did* happen? How similar were your explanations?

## 6 SPEAKING What's your guess?

**A** **PAIR WORK** What do you think were the reasons for these events? Suggest two different explanations for each.

1. The bride didn't show up for her wedding. She sent a bunch of flowers to the groom with a note: "Thank you."
2. A man arrived at the airport with a suitcase and saw his brother. He grabbed a cab and went back home.
3. It was a hot, sunny day. A man arrived home. He was soaking wet.

**B** **GROUP WORK** Each student thinks of two situations like the ones in part A. Others suggest explanations.

**A:** A man went around town and bought all the copies of the latest issue of a specific magazine.

**B:** Well, the magazine might have had an article about him.

## 7 INTERCHANGE 13 Think of the possibilities!

What's your best explanation for some unusual events? Go to Interchange 13 on page 128.

## 8 PERSPECTIVES I'm going nuts!

**A** Listen to a person complaining about her family members. Check (✓) the response you think is best for each problem.

*Last night, my sister borrowed my car without asking. She did call me a couple of times, but I was in a meeting and couldn't answer the phone. We had a big fight, and now we're not speaking.*

☐ She shouldn't have used your car without permission, no matter what.

☐ You could have been more understanding. After all, she tried to call you first.

*My nephew is so inconsiderate. He called me at 3:00 in the morning to talk about his problems with his best friend, and I had to get up very early to work. I was really mad.*

☐ You could have told him that you had to get up early the next day.

☐ Your nephew is always doing that. You shouldn't have answered his call.

*My brother came over for the weekend with his wife and three kids. They made such a mess of the apartment! I'll never invite them over again.*

☐ I would have asked them to help clean up the place.

☐ I wouldn't have invited them to spend the weekend. Having overnight guests can be really stressful.

**B** Do you talk about pet peeves with your friends? Do they give you advice?

## 6 SPEAKING

**Learning Objective:** offer explanations for hypothetical events using past modals

### A Pair work

- Explain the task. Focus Ss' attention on the picture.
- Read the first situation. Model the task with a S:

    T: I have an explanation. The woman could have had a problem and decided to change the date for the wedding. What do you think?

    S1: Well, she might have just decided not to get married.

- Read the other two situations. Elicit or explain that *soaking wet* means "very wet."
- Ss work in pairs. They take turns suggesting explanations. Tell Ss to be creative and to use past modals. Go around the class and give help as needed.
- Accept all logical answers.

### B Group work

- Explain the task. Ask two Ss to model the conversation. Elicit additional explanations.
- Ss work individually to think of situations like the ones in part A. Go around and give help as needed.
- Then Ss work in small groups. Ss read their situations. Group members offer explanations. Set a time limit of about ten minutes.

**TIP**
Ss like to receive feedback after Speaking activities. Include positive reinforcement on issues like creativity, accuracy, fluency, use of new language, and participation.

## 7 INTERCHANGE 13

See page T-128 for teaching notes.

### End of Cycle 1

See the Supplementary Resources chart at the beginning of this unit for additional teaching materials and student activities related to this Cycle.

### Cycle 2, Exercises 8–14

## 8 PERSPECTIVES

**Learning Objective:** listen and respond to people discussing problems using *should have, could have,* and *would have* in context

### ▶ A [CD 3, Track 16]

- Write these questions on the board. Ss discuss them in pairs.

    *Do you know someone who drives you crazy? What does he or she do? How do you react?*

- Set the scene. A woman is complaining about different situations.
- Ask Ss to read the three complaints. Then ask: "Who(m) is she complaining about? What's the problem?"

- Books closed. Explain the task.
- Play the audio program. Ss listen to three complaints. Pause after each complaint. Ss decide which response is best.
- Books open. Ss check their responses. Ask Ss which response they prefer, and why.

### B

- Explain the task. Read the questions.
- Ss discuss the questions in pairs or small groups.
- **Option:** Ask Ss how many of them share problems with their friends. Who shares more, men or women? Discuss possible reasons.

# 9 GRAMMAR FOCUS

**Learning Objective:** use past modals *should have*, *could have*, and *would have* to give judgments and suggestions

▶ *[CD 3, Track 17]*

### Judging past actions

- Explain that we use *should/shouldn't have* to give opinions. Focus Ss' attention on the Perspectives on page 88. Ask Ss to find two examples with *should(n't) have*. Write them on the board in columns:

| 1 | 2 | 3 | 4 | 5 |
|---|---|---|---|---|
| She | shouldn't | have | used | your car. |
| You | shouldn't | have | answered | his call. |

- Elicit or explain the examples:

  *She shouldn't have used your car.* (The person is giving an opinion. He/she thinks the sister should have gotten permission first.)

  *You shouldn't have answered his call.* (The person is giving an opinion. He/she thinks the nephew needs to not call so late.)

- Elicit the rule. Write it on the board:

  *subject + should (not) + have + past participle*

- Encourage Ss to think of more examples.

### Suggesting alternative past actions

- Repeat the above steps. Explain that we use *would have/could have* to suggest alternatives. Note: There are two examples of *would(n't) have* in the Perspectives.

- Explain the meaning *of would have* like this:

  *I wouldn't have invited them to spend the weekend.* (The person is imagining this [hypothetical] situation

happening to him/her and saying he/she would have done things differently.) Ask Ss to listen for the reduced form of *have* in past modals. Play the audio program. Ss listen and read or repeat.

### A

- Explain the task. Tell Ss to look at the picture as you model the first conversation.

- Ss complete the task individually. Ss use past modals to complete the conversations. Go around the class and give help as needed.

- Elicit or explain any new vocabulary.

> **Vocabulary**
> **make up an excuse:** give an explanation for not doing something
> **check:** a list that you are given in a restaurant showing how much your meal costs; the bill
> **get the hint:** understand an indirect message

- Go over answers with the class.

> **Answers**
> 1. could/should have made up; shouldn't have asked
> 2. should have paid; wouldn't have lent
> 3. wouldn't have paid; would have told; shouldn't have invited
> 4. shouldn't have stayed; could/should have started

- Ss practice the conversations in pairs.

### B Pair work

- Ss work in pairs to think of another suggestion or comment for each situation in part A.

# 10 WORD POWER

**Learning Objective:** discuss different types of reactions

### A

- Explain the task. Set the scene: Helena's boyfriend forgot their anniversary.

- Give Ss time to read the reactions and examples. Elicit or explain any vocabulary Ss ask about (without giving away the answers).

- Model the task with the first reaction. Elicit that *assumption* means "a jump to conclusions." Then ask Ss to find the example. (Answer: c)

- Ss complete the task individually. Ss may use a dictionary.

- Then Ss compare answers in pairs or small groups. Elicit Ss' responses to check answers.

> **Answers**
> 1. c   2. a   3. e   4. f   5. h   6. b   7. d   8. g

### B Group work

- Explain the task. Model the task making an assumption:

  T: Rob isn't in class today. He must have had a doctor's appointment.

- Ss work in small groups. Each group chooses a situation. Then Ss take turns giving examples of each reaction (1–8). Remind Ss to use past modals for opinions and advice.

▦ For more practice with the vocabulary, play **Tic-Tac-Toe** – download it from the website. Add one more reaction (e.g., a reason).

# 9 GRAMMAR FOCUS

## ▶ Past modals for judgments and suggestions

**Judging past actions**

You **should have asked** your sister to help.

He **shouldn't have used** your car.

**Suggesting alternative past actions**

You **could have told** her that you had to get up early.

I **would have asked** them to help clean up the place.

I **wouldn't have invited** them to spend the weekend.

GRAMMAR PLUS *see page 144*

**A** Complete the conversations using past modals with the verbs given. Then practice with a partner.

1. **A:** My boss asked me to help her choose a gift for her husband, and I ended up spending all day at the mall.

   **B:** You _____ (make up) an excuse not to help her. She _____ (not ask) for such a personal favor in the first place.

2. **A:** I lent my sister-in-law some money a year ago, and she never paid it back.

   **B:** She _____ (pay) it back already! Well, I _____ (not lend) money to her anyway. I never lend money to relatives.

3. **A:** Austin invited me out to dinner, but when the check came, he said he was broke!

   **B:** I _____ (not pay) for him. I _____ (tell) him to wash the dishes. He _____ (not invite) you if he didn't have enough money.

4. **A:** I can't believe my cousin came over and stayed until 1:00 in the morning!

   **B:** He _____ (not stay) so late. You _____ (start) yawning. Maybe he would have gotten the hint!

**B** PAIR WORK Think of another suggestion or comment for each situation above.

# 10 WORD POWER Reactions

**A** Helena's boyfriend forgot their anniversary. How does she react? Match each reaction with the best example.

**Reaction**

1. an assumption _____
2. a criticism _____
3. a demand _____
4. an excuse _____
5. a prediction _____
6. a suggestion _____
7. a suspicion _____
8. a warning _____

**Example**

a. "Sometimes you're so selfish."

b. "You could take me out to dinner."

c. "You must have wanted to break up with me."

d. "I bet you went out with your friends."

e. "Now you'll have to get me a really nice gift."

f. "I know you've been busy lately. It just slipped your mind."

g. "If you ever forget another important date, I'll never talk to you again."

h. "You'll probably forget my birthday, too!"

**B** GROUP WORK Imagine that someone was late for class, or choose another situation. Give an example of each reaction in the list above.

## 11 LISTENING What should they have done?

**A** Listen to descriptions of three situations. What would have been the best thing to do in each situation? Check (✓) the best suggestion.

1. ☐ Simon should have kept the ring for himself.
   ☐ He should have called the police.
   ☐ He did the right thing.

2. ☐ Jana shouldn't have mentioned her last job at all in her application.
   ☐ She should have been honest in her application and admitted she made a mistake.
   ☐ She did the right thing.

3. ☐ Martin should have reported what his boss did as soon as he found out.
   ☐ He should have withdrawn more money and blamed it on his boss.
   ☐ He did the right thing.

**B PAIR WORK** What would you have done in each situation in part A?

## 12 DISCUSSION How would you have reacted?

**GROUP WORK** Read each situation. Say what the person could have or should have done, and what you would have done.

> " It was my friend's birthday, and he had invited a few close friends out to celebrate. I forgot all about it, so I called him the next day and pretended I'd had to take my mother to the hospital. " –Warren

> " My sister got a new haircut, and I thought it looked a little dated. I didn't want to hurt her feelings, so I told her I liked it. " –Sonia

> " I didn't have any money to buy my cousin a birthday present, so I gave her something I had received previously as a gift. My brother told my cousin about my regifting, and now she's mad at me. " –Chase

> " I went to my in-laws' house for dinner last night. My husband thinks his mother is a great cook, but the food was awful! I didn't know what else to do, so I ate it. " –Fay

**A:** Warren should have told his friend the truth.
**B:** I agree. He could have taken his friend out to make up for it.
**C:** I think I would have . . .

## 13 WRITING A tricky problem

**A** Think of a complicated situation from your own experience. Write a paragraph describing the situation, but don't explain how you resolved it.

> I have a close friend who doesn't get along with my other friends. He's a nice guy, friendly and funny, but every time we all go out, he makes a fuss over how much everyone should pay. Last week, my friends were going to dinner, and he wanted to come along. I didn't want to hurt his feelings . . .

**B PAIR WORK** Exchange papers. Write a short paragraph about how you would have resolved your partner's situation.

**C PAIR WORK** Read your partner's resolution to your situation. Tell your partner how you resolved it. Whose resolution was better?

# 11 LISTENING

**Learning Objective:** listen for information in descriptions of situations and respond using past modals *should have*, *could have*, and *would have*

## ▶ A [CD 3, Track 18]

- Explain the task. Ss will listen to descriptions of three situations. Ask Ss to read the three suggestions for each situation.
- Elicit or explain any new vocabulary.

### Vocabulary
**withdraw:** to take money out of a bank account

- Tell Ss to listen and decide what would have been the best thing to do.
- Play the audio program. Pause after each situation. Ss check (✓) what they think is the best suggestion. Make sure Ss understand there are no "correct" answers.

### Audio script
See page T-179.

- Elicit Ss' responses around the class.

### TIP
To increase talking time, have Ss try the activity again. Be sure to give Ss a new challenge (e.g., *work with a new partner, focus on intonation, give longer answers*).

## B Pair work

- Explain the task. Model the task by encouraging Ss to explain their choices in part A. For example:

  T:    Kenita, what would you have done if you had been Simon (in number 1)?

  S1:  I would have called my mom to ask her for advice.

  S2:  Really? I think that would have taken too long. I would have . . .

- Ss discuss their ideas in pairs. Go around the class and give help as needed.

# 12 DISCUSSION

**Learning Objective:** give advice for complicated past situations using past modals *should have*, *could have*, and *would have*

## Group work

- Explain the task. Read the first situation. Ask three Ss to read the example responses. Ask Student C to complete the third sentence in the example.
- Have Ss work in groups of four, if possible. Ss take turns reading a situation from the box. The group members discuss opinions and advice for each complicated situation.

- Set a time limit of about ten minutes. Go around the class and listen in. Make note of common errors to go over after the activity. Remember to give positive feedback, too!
- **Option:** Ss work in groups. They think of three more problem situations. Suggest that Ss jot down each situation in note form. Set a time limit of five to eight minutes. Go around the class and give help as needed. Then Ss give their situations to another group to discuss.

### TIP
Tell Ss to make a "time out" signal (forming a T-shape with their hands) if they want to use their first language. Give Ss a limit for the number of time outs.

# 13 WRITING

**Learning Objective:** write a paragraph about a complicated situation in the past using past modals *should have*, *could have*, and *would have*

## A

- Explain the task.
- Ss write about a situation they personally experienced. Remind Ss not to write about how they resolved the problem.
- Encourage Ss to brainstorm or note ideas before starting their drafts. Go around the class and give help as needed.
- **Option:** The first draft can be assigned for homework.

## B Pair work

- Explain the task.
- Ss exchange papers in pairs. Then Ss work individually to write a response. Remind Ss to use past modals in their advice.

## C Pair work

- Explain the task. Ss return papers and read the advice.
- Then Ss tell each other how they actually resolved the problem. Finally, Ss discuss whose solution was better.

# 14 READING

**Learning Objectives:** identify main ideas and specific information in an article about strange phenomena; distinguish between fact and opinion

## A

- Read the question. Elicit Ss to skim the article to find the answer.
- Remind them not to focus on the words they don't know.

### Answer

They are both sounds/noises. (Also possible: Both are compared to musical instruments.)

## B

- Tell Ss to read the article. Remind Ss to mark any vocabulary they can't guess from context or with the help of the pictures.
- Ss work in pairs or groups to go over marked vocabulary. If no one knows the meaning of a certain word, then Ss may use their dictionaries.
- Elicit or explain any remaining new vocabulary.
- Explain the task. Read the five questions.
- Ss complete the task individually, in pairs, in small groups, or as a class. Ss can write their answers or give them orally. Encourage Ss to use their own words in their answers.
- If the activity is done individually, in pairs, or in groups, elicit Ss' answers around the class.

### Vocabulary
**take place:** happen
**trumpet:** a metal musical instrument that you play by blowing into it and pressing buttons to make different notes
**sci-fi:** short for science fiction
**spaceship:** a vehicle that can travel outside the Earth and into space, especially one which is carrying people
**flare:** a burst of bright light or energy, usually lasting a short time
**baffle:** If something baffles you, you cannot understand it at all.
**high-pitched:** describes a noise that is high and sometimes also loud or unpleasant
**squeal:** make a loud, high sound
**sewer:** a large underground system of pipes that carries away sewage
**flee:** leave a place quickly because you are in danger or are afraid
**leak:** a hole or crack that allows liquid or gas to come out when it should not

### TIP
If you are short of time, limit the number of words you explain. Ss choose the key words to ask you about, and look up the rest in a dictionary for homework.

### Answers

1. They have compared it to trumpets playing and sound effects from science-fiction movies.
2. People think that the end of the world is coming or that spaceships are landing.
3. It is a sound like a giant flute being badly played or a train or truck slowing down.
4. That it is a gas leak.
5. There would be a different kind of sound, and people would smell gas.

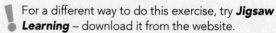 For a different way to do this exercise, try **Jigsaw Learning** – download it from the website.

## C

- Explain the task. Make sure Ss know the difference between a fact (something that can be proved to be true) and an opinion (someone's belief).
- Ss work individually to complete the exercise.
- Then Ss compare answers in pairs. Ask Ss to discuss any disagreements.
- Go over answers with the class.

### Answers

1. fact       5. fact
2. opinion    6. fact
3. opinion    7. fact
4. opinion

- **Option:** Ss role-play an interview between people who hear the noise and a journalist.

## D Pair work

- Explain the task. Read the questions.
- Ss discuss the questions in pairs. Set a time limit of five to ten minutes. Go around the class and give help as needed.
- Ask groups to share their ideas around the class. Take a class vote to find out which group's explanation is the most reasonable.

## End of Cycle 2

See the Supplementary Resources chart at the beginning of this unit for additional teaching materials and student activities related to this Cycle.

A Skim the article. What do the two unexplained events have in common?

## Messages from **Outer Space**, or a Leaking Pipe?

Home | Sciencenews | Technology | Articles | Blog | Community

**Even though we know so much about the world around us, unexplained events still take place. Read about these two events. What do you think may have happened?**

Since 2008, people around the world have been reporting a mysterious sound that seems to come from the sky. Some people say it sounds like trumpets playing. Others say it is like sound effects from sci-fi movies. The phenomenon has caused both fear and fascination, and many people have been looking for explanations. One popular idea is that the sound is an announcement of the end of the world, and another

suggests that it's the sound of spaceships. But there may be a more scientific explanation. It involves flares from the sun and energy from the center of the earth. Which explanation do you think might be right?

Of course, there are some strange events that still baffle both the general public and experts. Take the high-pitched noise that has been driving people crazy in Forest Grove, Oregon. To some people, it sounds like a giant flute being played very badly, and to others, it sounds like a train slowing down or truck brakes squealing. The sound is coming from under the street, but gas, water, and sewer inspectors have said there is nothing wrong down there. One resident was so sure it was a serious gas leak that he was ready to flee. However, experts say that a leak would make a different sound, and people would definitely smell gas. How would you explain this mysterious and annoying event?

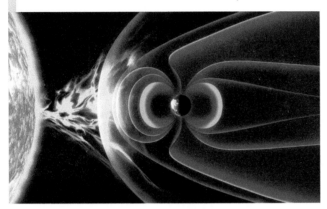

B Read the article. Then answer the questions.

1. To what two things have people compared the first sound?
2. What non-scientific explanations have been offered?
3. What sort of sound are people in Forest Grove hearing?
4. What explanation has been proven untrue?
5. If there had been a gas leak, what would be different?

C Which of these statements are facts? Which are opinions? Check (✓) Fact or Opinion.

|  | Fact | Opinion |
|---|---|---|
| 1. Science has not explained everything that happens. | ☐ | ☐ |
| 2. Some sounds mean the end of the world is coming. | ☐ | ☐ |
| 3. The first sound is caused by energy from planets. | ☐ | ☐ |
| 4. The sound in Forest Grove is very annoying. | ☐ | ☐ |
| 5. The Forest Grove sound comes from under the street. | ☐ | ☐ |
| 6. Gas lines and other systems in Forest Grove have no problems. | ☐ | ☐ |
| 7. No local problems can explain the Forest Grove noise. | ☐ | ☐ |

D PAIR WORK Which explanations of the events in the article do you think are the most likely? least likely? Can you think of any other possible explanations?

# Unit 14 Supplementary Resources Overview

| | After the following SB exercises | You can use these materials in class | Your students can use these materials outside the classroom |
|---|---|---|---|
| **CYCLE 1** | 1 Snapshot | | |
| | 2 Conversation | | **SS** Unit 14 Speaking 1–2 |
| | 3 Grammar Focus | | **SB** Unit 14 Grammar plus, Focus 1<br>**SS** Unit 14 Grammar 1<br>**GAME** Sentence Stacker (The passive to describe process)<br>**GAME** Sentence Runner (The passive to describe process) |
| | 4 Listening | **TSS** Unit 14 Extra Worksheet | |
| | 5 Speaking | | |
| | 6 Writing | | **WB** Unit 14 exercises 1–4 |
| **CYCLE 2** | 7 Word Power | **TSS** Unit 14 Vocabulary Worksheet<br>**TSS** Unit 14 Listening Worksheet | **SS** Unit 14 Vocabulary 1–2<br>**GAME** Name the Picture (Creative jobs) |
| | 8 Perspectives | | |
| | 9 Pronunciation | | |
| | 10 Grammar Focus | **TSS** Unit 14 Grammar Worksheet<br>**TSS** Unit 14 Writing Worksheet | **SB** Unit 14 Grammar plus, Focus 2<br>**SS** Unit 14 Grammar 2<br>**GAME** Word Keys (Relative clauses) |
| | 11 Interchange 14 | | |
| | 12 Reading | **TSS** Unit 14 Project Worksheet<br>**VID** Unit 14<br>**VRB** Unit 14 | **SS** Unit 14 Reading 1–2<br>**SS** Unit 14 Listening 1–3<br>**SS** Unit 14 Video 1–3<br>**WB** Unit 14 exercises 5–8 |

| With or instead of the following SB section | You can also use these materials for assessment |
|---|---|
| **Units 13–14 Progress Check** | **ASSESSMENT PROGRAM** Units 13–14 Oral Quiz<br>**ASSESSMENT PROGRAM** Units 13–14 Written Quiz |

Key
**GAME:** Online Game  **SB:** Student's Book  **SS:** Online Self-study  **TSS:** Teacher Support Site
**VID:** Video DVD  **VRB:** Video Resource Book  **WB:** Online Workbook/Workbook

# My Plan for Unit 14

Use the space below to customize a plan that fits your needs.

| With the following SB exercises | I am using these materials in class | My students are using these materials outside the classroom |
|---|---|---|
|  |  |  |
|  |  |  |
|  |  |  |
|  |  |  |
|  |  |  |
|  |  |  |
|  |  |  |
|  |  |  |
|  |  |  |
|  |  |  |
|  |  |  |
|  |  |  |
|  |  |  |

| With or instead of the following SB section | I am using these materials for assessment |
|---|---|
|  |  |
|  |  |
|  |  |

# 14 Creative careers

▸ Describe steps in a process
▸ Discuss jobs in entertainment and the media

## 1 SNAPSHOT

### MILESTONES IN CONTEMPORARY CINEMATOGRAPHY

THE FIRST . . .

- movie with **Dolby Digital** sound. – *Batman Returns* (1992)
- **computer-animated** feature film. – *Toy Story* (1995)
- major movie **shot entirely in digital video.** – *Star Wars Episode II: Attack of the Clones* (2002)
- computer-animated **motion-captured** film. – *The Polar Express* (2004)
- movie to be **released simultaneously** in theaters, on DVD, and on the Internet. – *EMR* (2005)
- **film directed by a woman** to win the Oscar for Best Picture. – *The Hurt Locker* (2008)
- full-length feature film **shot on a phone.** – *Olive* (2011)
- major movie **filmed at 48 frames per second,** instead of the standard 24 fps. – *The Hobbit: An Unexpected Journey* (2012)

*Have you seen any of these movies? Did you enjoy them?*
*What's the most popular movie playing right now? Have you seen it? Do you plan to?*
*Are there many movies made in your country? Name a few of your favorites.*

## 2 CONVERSATION I have more control.

▶ **A** Listen and practice.

**Clara:** Thanks for coming to the film festival! Directing this film was amazing, and I'm happy to answer your questions about it.

**Diego:** Yes, hi. What is it like to direct an animated movie? Is it different from live action?

**Clara:** Well, for one thing, I have a lot more control. There are no actors to argue with me!

**Diego:** I guess not! But how do you direct cartoon characters?

**Clara:** Well, after a screenplay is chosen, many drawings of the characters are presented to me . . .

**Diego:** And you get to choose which ones to use?

**Clara:** Even better: I can change them if I want. The characters have to be drawn just right – like I see them in my mind.

**Diego:** So you decide a lot about the characters early on.

**Clara:** Definitely. By the time the voice actors are picked, the characters feel like old friends!

▶ **B** Listen to the rest of the conversation. Who helps Clara choose the voice actors?

# 14 Creative careers

**Cycle 1, Exercises 1–6**

In this unit, students describe steps in a process and discuss jobs in the media. By the end of Cycle 1, students will be able to describe processes using the passive. By the end of Cycle 2, students will be able to discuss jobs using defining and non-defining relative clauses.

## 1 SNAPSHOT

**Learning Objective:** discuss entertainment industry firsts

- **Option:** Show a popular English-language movie during this unit. Use it to explain useful vocabulary and concepts.

- As a warm-up, Ss play **Line Up!** – download it from the website. Ss line up according to when they last saw a movie (on TV, DVD, video, or at a movie theater).

- Books closed. Explain that Ss are going to discuss some movie "firsts." Write this information on the board. Ask Ss to match the "first" with the date:

| | |
|---|---|
| The first film shot on a phone | 2002 |
| The first movie directed by a woman to win the Oscar for Best Picture | 2011 |
| The first movie shot in digital video | 2008 |

- Books open. Ss read the Snapshot individually. Tell Ss to check their "firsts" in the Snapshot.

- Elicit or explain any new vocabulary.

### Vocabulary
**full-length:** a book, film, etc. that is the complete length and not shortened
**feature film:** a full-length movie
**animated:** using cartoons rather than live actors
**simultaneously:** happening at the same time
**Dolby:** a sound-engineering company

- Read the questions. Ss discuss the questions in small groups.

## 2 CONVERSATION

**Learning Objective:** use the passive in a conversation about how something is done in the entertainment industry

### A [CD 3, Track 19]

- Ask Ss to cover the text and describe the picture.

- **Option:** Ask: "Have you ever seen how animated movies are made?" If a S has, the class asks the S questions.

- Set the scene. Clara works on animated movies. Diego is asking her how movies are made.

- Ask: "How is making animated movies different from making live action movies?" Elicit suggestions. Play the audio program. Ss listen and take notes.

- Ss compare notes in pairs.

- Tell Ss to read the conversation to check their notes.

- Elicit or explain any new vocabulary.

### Vocabulary
**live action:** action involving real people or animals, not models or images that are drawn or produced by a computer
**screenplay:** a story that is written for television or for a film
**pick:** choose

- Play the audio program again. Ss listen and read or repeat.

- Ss practice the conversation in pairs.

### TIP
To encourage Ss to look at each other while practicing Conversations, ask them to stand up and face each other. This also makes the conversation more active and natural.

- For another way to practice the conversation, try the **Onion Ring** technique – download it from the website.

- **Option:** Ask questions like these: "Did you just learn anything new about how animated movies are made? Would you like to visit a film studio? Would you like to work on movies? Why or why not?"

### B [CD 3, Track 20]

- Explain the task. Read the question.

- Tell Ss to listen for the answer. Play the second part of the audio program. Elicit answers.

### Audio script

See page T-180.

### Answer

a casting director

**Learning Objective:** use the passive to describe processes

▶ **[CD 3, Track 21]**

- Elicit that the basic passive is *be* + past participle. Review the reasons for using the passive:

  a. we don't know who does the action

  b. it's not important who does the action

### Passive with modals

- Write this clause on the board. Do not write the answer. Ask Ss to find the clause in the Conversation on page 92 and complete it:

  *The characters _____* (Answer: have to be drawn)

- Explain or elicit the rule. Write it on the board:

  *modal* + *be* + *past participle*

- Play the audio program. Ss listen and read or repeat.

**A**

- Explain the task. Model the first sentence.

- Ss complete the task individually or in pairs. Remind Ss to use *be* + past participle. Go around the class and give help as needed.

- Elicit or explain any new vocabulary.

### Vocabulary

**storyboard:** (in films and television) a series of drawings showing the planned order of images
**character:** a person in a book, film, etc.
**hire:** pay money in order to use something/ someone for a short time
**voice-over:** on a television program, film, or advertisement, the spoken words of a person that you cannot see
**scratch:** the starting point
**rehearse:** practice a play, dance, etc. in order to prepare for a performance

### Answers

*Storyboard and animation steps*
1. are drawn; be drawn
2. be placed
3. is completed; be hired
4. be created
5. is added; are populated
*Voice-over steps*
6. are recorded; are not replaced
7. are hired; be used
8. are rehearsed; is recorded
9. is chosen

### B Pair work

- Explain the task. Have a S model the example sentence.

- Suggest that Ss use the sequencing language from part A.

- Ss complete the task in pairs. Elicit responses.

❗ For more practice, have Ss act out the sentences using **Mime** – download it from the website.

# 4 LISTENING

**Learning Objective:** listen for specific details in a conversation using the passive

▶ **A [CD 3, Track 22]**

- Books open. Explain the task. Ss listen for the sequence of events in the movies. Play the audio program.

### Audio script

See page T-180.

### Answers

Parts A and B:
4. A new plan is put into action.
   *Luke planned to destroy the Death Star.*
   *The president sets a trap.*
2. A problem is presented.
   *Luke Skywalker has to save Princess Leia and fight Darth Vader.*
   *President has to fight enemy soldiers trying to take over the White House.*

3. Something bad happens, and all hope is lost.
   *Princess Leia's planet was destroyed.*
   *The bad guys kidnap the president's family.*
1. The main character is introduced.
   *Luke Skywalker*
   *The President of the United States*
5. The bad guy is defeated.
   *Darth Vader is spun off into space.*
   *The soldiers are sent to jail.*

▶ **B [CD 3, Track 23]**

- Explain the task. Ss listen for the examples. Play the audio program again. Check responses.

# 3 GRAMMAR FOCUS

**The passive to describe process**

| *is/are* + past participle | Modal + *be* + past participle |
|---|---|
| A screenplay **is chosen**. | The characters **have to be drawn** just right. |
| Many drawings **are presented**. | The drawings **might be changed** 10 times. |

GRAMMAR PLUS *see page 145*

**A** The sentences below describe how an animated movie is made. First, complete the sentences using the passive. Then compare with a partner.

**Storyboard and animation steps**

1. First, storyboards _____ (draw) by story artists. For some movies, over 200,000 storyboards might _____ (draw).

2. Next, the storyboards need to _____ (place) in order.

3. After the storyboarding process _____ (complete), technical directors must _____ (hire).

4. Then, the scenes and characters have to _____ (create) on the computer by the technical directors.

5. Finally, movement _____ (add) to the scenes by animators. In addition, the scenes _____ (populate) with background characters.

**Voice-over steps**

6. First, temporary "scratch" voices _____ (record). Sometimes scratch voices are so good that they _____ (not replace).

7. Later, professional actors _____ (hire) to record the character voices. For some movies, studios hire famous actors so their names can _____ (use) as a marketing tool.

8. The lines _____ (rehearse) and the same line _____ (record) in different ways.

9. Finally, the best recording _____ (choose) for the final movie.

**B PAIR WORK** What are some steps that happen after the animated movie is complete? Discuss with a partner.

"After all that, the movie is sent to theaters."

# 4 LISTENING It was too predictable.

**A** Listen to Casey and Grant talk about things that often happen in movies. Number the parts of a movie in the order they are mentioned.

| | Movie example |
|---|---|
| ☐ A new plan is put into action. | Luke planned to destroy the Death Star. |
| ☐ A problem is presented. | |
| ☐ Something bad happens, and all hope is lost. | |
| ☐ The main character is introduced. | |
| ☐ The bad guy is defeated. | |

**B** Listen again. For each movie part above, write an example from the movies the friends discuss.

## 5 SPEAKING Tutorials

**A PAIR WORK** What do you think is required to make a short movie? Put the pictures in order and describe the steps. More than one order may be possible. Use the vocabulary to help you.

☐ add titles and credits

☐ rehearse the lines

☐ shoot the movie

☐ find a location

☐ edit the movie

1 write the script

**A:** Making a short movie requires many steps. First, the script needs to be written.
**B:** Right! And after that, a location must be found.
**A:** I agree. Then . . .

**B PAIR WORK** Choose one of these topics. Come up with as many steps as you can.

preparing a school party     organizing a fundraising campaign     developing a mobile app
organizing a trip abroad     planning a wedding                     putting on a school musical

**C GROUP WORK** Share your information from part B with another pair.

## 6 WRITING Describing a process

**A** Write about one of the topics from Exercise 5, part B or use your own idea. Describe the different steps in the process.

> Developing a mobile app requires a lot of work. First, the objective of the app must be defined. Then, a prototype should be built. After that, the prototype can be tested by potential users or friends. Then a developer needs to be hired, and . . .

**B PAIR WORK** Read your partner's description. Can you think of any more steps?

# 5 SPEAKING

**Learning Objective:** describe steps in a process using the passive

## A *Pair work*

- Focus Ss' attention on the pictures, and ask Ss to explain what happens at each stage, using the passive and the vocabulary given.

### Vocabulary
**shoot:** to use a camera to record a film
**location:** a place suitable to the story
**script:** the words in a film, play, etc.

- Explain the task. Ask two Ss to help put the first two pictures in order. Remind Ss to use the passive to describe the process:

  T:  Look at the pictures. Which one probably comes first when making a short movie?

  S1: I think it's the last picture. The script is written.

  S2: Yes, I agree. After that, the location is found. That's the fourth picture.

  S1: Right. Then the next step is . . .

- Ss order the pictures in pairs. Allow Ss to add more steps to the process.
- Set a time limit of about five minutes. Go around the class and give help as needed. Note problems Ss are having, especially with passives.

- When time is up, write the more common problems on the board. Ask Ss to suggest corrections.
- Check the order. Then ask three Ss to model the conversation.

### Possible answers

(as pictured from left to right)
6. Titles and credits are added.
3. The lines are rehearsed.
4. The movie is shot.
2. A location is found.
5. The movie is edited.
1. The script is written.

## B *Pair work*

- Explain the task.
- Ss choose another event to discuss. Ss work in pairs to come up with as many steps as possible.

For another way to practice this activity, try **Just One Minute** – download it from the website. Ss take turns coming up with as many steps as possible.

## C *Group work*

- Each pair joins another pair. Ss take turns presenting their work. Ss discuss any missing steps.
- **Option:** Ask Ss to look at the pictures again. Then, without looking, Ss describe the steps from memory. Tell Ss to include any new steps.

# 6 WRITING

**Learning Objective:** write about steps in a process using the passive

## A

- Explain the task.
- Model the task.
- Point out the passives in the example. Also point out the sequence markers. Remind Ss to use these, as well as time clauses (see Exercise 3 on page 73). Write suggestions on the board:

  Sequence markers
  first, second, next, then, after that, afterward, finally

  Time clause markers
  before, once, after, as soon as

- Ss work individually to choose a topic. Remind Ss to brainstorm key words involved in the steps or process.

### TIP
To prevent Ss from copying the model paragraph too closely, ask Ss to close their books after reading it.

- Next, Ss write their first draft.
- **Option:** The brainstorming and draft can be done as homework.

## B *Pair work*

- Explain the task.
- Ss work in pairs to give each other feedback. Ss exchange papers and point out any missing steps.
- Ss write a final draft. Remind Ss to use their partner's suggestions if they wish and their own ideas.

## End of Cycle 1

See the Supplementary Resources chart at the beginning of this unit for additional teaching materials and student activities related to this Cycle.

# 7 WORD POWER

**Learning Objective:** discuss jobs in the media

## A

- Explain the task. Elicit that *compound nouns* are made up of two nouns (e.g., *film* + *editor*) or an adjective and a noun (e.g., *foreign* + *correspondent*).
- Ss work individually to complete the chart. Point out that more than one answer is possible.
- Go over answers with the class.

### Possible answers

**Film/TV:** storyboard artist, talk show host, stunt person
**Publishing:** editorial director, news photographer, web content manager
**Gaming:** game animator, gameplay programmer, quality assurance analyst
**Music:** band manager, club DJ, songwriter

## B *Group work*

- Explain the task. Read the example.
- Ss complete the task in groups. They write sentences to describe the occupations in part A.
- **Option:** Have Ss choose one of the jobs from the chart and do research online to find out more about it. Have Ss report back to their group or the class with three additional details about that job.

For more practice with the vocabulary, play **Twenty Questions** – download it from the website. Ss think of a media profession.

# 8 PERSPECTIVES

**Learning Objective:** use defining and non-defining relative clauses in context

## ▶ A [CD 3, Track 24]

- Books closed. Write the occupations on the board (news photographer, videographer, stunt person, talk show host). Ss work in pairs to guess what each person does.
- Set the scene. Ss will hear career questions from four people. As Ss hear each question, they think of an answer.

- Play the audio program.
- Books open. Play the audio program again. Ss write their answers. Go over answers with the class.

## B *Pair work*

- Explain the task. Ss choose the career they think would be most interesting. Encourage Ss to say *why* the jobs would be interesting.

For more practice with vocabulary for jobs, try **Vocabulary Steps** – download it from the website.

# 9 PRONUNCIATION

**Learning Objective:** sound more natural when saying compound nouns

## ▶ A [CD 3, Track 25]

- Explain the task. Remind Ss that the first word in a compound noun usually has stronger stress, but that there are some exceptions to this rule.
- Play the audio program. Have Ss mark the stress that they hear on each word.

- Elicit answers. Then play the audio program again. Ss listen and repeat.

**B**

- Explain the task. Ss identify the compound nouns in the sentences in Exercise 8.
- Ss read the sentences to a partner.
- Go around the class and have different Ss read their sentences aloud. Correct any pronunciation problems.

## 7 WORD POWER Creative jobs

**A** What kind of jobs are these? Complete the chart with the compound nouns.
(More than one answer is possible.)

| band manager | game animator | songwriter | talk show host |
| club DJ | gameplay programmer | storyboard artist | quality assurance analyst |
| editorial director | news photographer | stunt person | web content manager |

| Film/TV jobs | Publishing jobs | Gaming jobs | Music jobs |
| --- | --- | --- | --- |
|  |  |  |  |
|  |  |  |  |
|  |  |  |  |

**B** GROUP WORK Choose four jobs from part A. Describe each job.

"A band manager negotiates contracts for artists and helps promote their careers."

## 8 PERSPECTIVES Career questions

**A** Listen to the career questions that people have. How would you answer them?

I have a degree in journalism, and I'm an amateur photographer. I'm considering a career as a news photographer who covers conflicts around the world. Do you think that's too dangerous?

Videographers like me, who shoot weddings and other social events, often work evenings and weekends. I want to have a nine-to-five job, so I'm looking for a job with a major studio. Is that a good move?

I love movies and I love action, so I'm thinking of becoming a stunt person – you know, the person who takes the place of an actor in dangerous scenes. What do you think?

A talk show host, who interviews artists, politicians, and celebrities, gets to meet lots of people. I love to meet new people. Do you think that would be a good job for me?

**B** PAIR WORK Which of these careers do you think would be the most interesting? Why?

## 9 PRONUNCIATION Review of stress in compound nouns

**A** Listen and practice. Notice how the first word in a compound noun usually receives greater stress.

band manager    talk show host    game animator    news photographer    stunt person

**B** Practice the sentences in Exercise 8. Pay attention to the word stress in the compound nouns.

> ## Defining and non-defining relative clauses

Defining relative clauses are used to identify people.

I want to become a photographer.
I want to cover conflicts. → I want to become a photographer **who/that covers conflicts**.

Non-defining relative clauses give further information about people.

Videographers shoot weddings and social events. They work evenings and weekends. → Videographers, **who shoot weddings and social events**, work evenings and weekends.

GRAMMAR PLUS *see page 145*

**A** Do these sentences contain defining (**D**) or non-defining (**ND**) clauses? Write **D** or **ND**. Add commas to the non-defining clauses. Then compare with a partner.

1. The art editor who creates the look of a magazine should make it attractive. _____
2. A game programmer is the person who writes the computer code that runs and controls a game. _____
3. The extras are the people who appear in the background scenes. _____
4. The producer who is responsible for the budget is the big boss in an animation studio. _____

**B** Add the non-defining relative clauses in parentheses to the sentences.

1. A game designer works closely with the programmers. (who creates new games)

   _____
   _____

2. A lead vocalist is the main voice on stage. (who may also be a songwriter)

   _____
   _____

3. A news reporter collects information about news and events. (who should be impartial)

   _____
   _____

4. A photo editor selects the photos that go into magazines. (who is responsible for the quality and content of images)

   _____
   _____

**C** Write three sentences with relative clauses about jobs you know. Compare with a partner.

# 11 INTERCHANGE 14 Celebrities

Can you guess who the celebrities are? Go to Interchange 14 on page 129.

Learning Objective: use defining relative clauses to identify people and non-defining relative clauses to give further information about them

▶ **[CD 3, Track 26]**

***Defining and non-defining relative clauses***

- Focus Ss' attention on the Perspectives on page 95. Ask Ss to underline the relative clause (i.e., the part beginning with *who* or *that*) in each sentence.

- Explain that there are two types of relative clauses: defining and non-defining relative clauses. Point out the differences between them:

  **1. Defining relative clause:** The information in the clause is necessary. It shows us which person is being described or talked about.
  *The actor who starred in that movie is very talented.*

  **2. Non-defining relative clause:** The information isn't necessary. It is extra information that is added to the sentence.
  *Tom Cruise, who starred in that movie, is very talented.*

---

**TIP**

To help Ss remember the difference between two structures, write the two examples using different colored chalk or markers.

---

- Again focus Ss' attention on the Perspectives. Ss decide whether the clauses are necessary to the sentences (defining) or extra information (non-defining).

- Ask Ss to find each sentence containing a relative clause and label it Defining (**D**) or Non-defining (**ND**). (Answers: D – 1, 3; ND – 2, 4)

- Point out that commas are used before and after a non-defining relative clause.

- ***Option:*** To check Ss' comprehension, ask Ss to give a quick summary of the rules.

- Play the audio program. Ss listen and read or repeat.

▦ For more practice with relative clauses, play ***Run For It!*** – download it from the website. Read out sentences that contain defining and non-defining relative clauses.

## 11 INTERCHANGE 14

See page T-129 for teaching notes.

**A**

- Explain the task. Model the first sentence.

- Ss complete the task individually. They decide if clauses are defining or non-defining. Remind Ss to add commas to non-defining clauses. Go around the class and give help as needed.

- Go over answers with the class.

### Answers

1. ND: The art editor, who creates the look of a magazine, should make it attractive.
2. D
3. D
4. ND: The producer, who is responsible for the budget, is the big boss in an animation studio.

**B**

- Explain the task. Model the first sentence.

- Ss complete the task individually. They add non-defining relative clauses. Remind Ss to add commas in the correct places. Go around the class and give help as needed.

- Ask an early finisher to write the answers on the board. Go over answers with the class.

### Answers

1. A game designer, who creates new games, works closely with the programmers.
2. A lead vocalist, who may also be a songwriter, is the main voice on stage.
3. A news reporter, who should be impartial, collects information about news and events.
4. A photo editor, who is responsible for the quality and content of images, selects the photos that go into magazines.

**C**

- Explain the task.

- Ss work individually. Ss write three sentences with relative clauses about jobs they know. Point out that they do not have to be media jobs.

- Ss compare their sentences in pairs.

## 12 READING

Learning Objectives: scan an article about the entertainment industry; distinguish between main ideas and supporting ideas

### A

- Books closed. Ask if anyone knows what a film extra is. If anyone answers "yes," let the rest of the class ask questions.
- Books open. Ask Ss to look at the pictures. Go over the task. Tell Ss to scan the article to answer the questions. Elicit answers from the class.

### Answer

It was probably written for people who are curious about the movie business or about what being a film extra is like.

### B

- Ss read individually. Remind them to mark any words or expressions they want clarified.

! For another way to teach vocabulary, try the **Vocabulary Mingle** – download it from the website.

- Elicit or explain any new vocabulary.

### Vocabulary
**standard:** usual and not special
**rude:** behaving in a way that is not polite and upsets people
**crowd:** a large group of people who are together in one place
**all walks of life:** from many different places and backgrounds
**role:** a part in a play or film
**in-demand:** wanted or needed in large numbers
**deal:** take or have as a subject
**jury:** a group of people in a court of law who decide if someone is guilty or not
**clerk:** someone who sells things in a shop
**bright and early:** very early in the morning
**nonexistent:** doesn't exist
**challenging:** difficult to do in a way that tests your ability or determination
**beat:** defeat someone in a competition

- Explain the task. Model the task with the first question.
- Ss complete the task individually, then they compare answers in pairs.
- Go over answers with the class.

### Answers

1. Unlike many extras, I'm a trained actor.
2. I'm registered with an agency that deals exclusively with extras, so I get calls all the time.
3. I was one of a group of office workers . . .
4. I've beaten my high scores on all my phone games . . .

### C

- Explain the task. Model how to find the first word in the article.
- Ss complete the task individually.
- Then Ss compare answers in pairs.
- Go over answers with the class.

### Answers

1. come from all walks of life
2. in-demand
3. bright and early
4. nonexistent
5. challenging

- **Option:** Assign each S a paragraph. Ss change two facts in their paragraph. Then they read their "changed" text to the class. Ss try to spot the incorrect facts.

### D Pair work

- Explain the task. Read the questions.
- Remind Ss to give reason for their responses.
- **Option:** If no one would like to work in movies or TV, offer alternative discussion questions about movie types (e.g., *Do you like animated movies/science fiction movies/documentaries/musicals? Why or why not?*).
- Ss discuss the question in pairs or small groups. Remind Ss to ask follow-up questions and to add information.

## End of Cycle 2

See the Supplementary Resources chart at the beginning of this unit for additional teaching materials and student activities related to this Cycle and for assessment tools.

T-97 Unit 14

**A** Scan the title and first paragraph of the article. Who do you think it was written for? Why?

Home | News | Entertainment | Articles | Blog | Community

# THE TRUTH ABOUT BEING A FILM EXTRA
*by Anna Murphy*

When people discover that I work as a film and TV extra, they always ask me the same questions: *Is it easy to get work? Isn't it boring? Do you get to meet famous actors? Does it pay well?* My answers are pretty standard as well: yes, sometimes, once in a while, and . . . kind of. The life of an extra is both more interesting and more boring than you might imagine.

Extras, who play the people in crowds, on streets, or in the background of indoor scenes, can come from all walks of life. Unlike many extras, I'm a trained actor. I do get real speaking roles, but work can be hard to come by if you're not an in-demand star. I'm registered with an agency that deals exclusively with extras, so I get calls all the time. The agency explains who I'll be – someone in a crowd, a member of a jury, a clerk – and tells me where to go. Call time is usually bright and early, so I try to get to bed at a reasonable hour.

Sometimes being an extra is a "hurry up and wait" job. In my first extra role, I was one of a group of office workers who come out of a building just as a car explodes in the street. We waited for hours for the scene to be shot, and then went in and out of the building about fifty times, trying to act horrified by a nonexistent explosion. Then we had lunch, changed clothes, and spent the afternoon as customers in a department store.

It may sound like I don't enjoy the work, but I do. Being part of the background in a convincing way is challenging, and being on a film or TV set is always fascinating. A lot of famous actors don't even notice the extras, but the ones who do make the job a lot of fun for everyone. As for the money, it's nothing compared to what the big actors make, but it pretty much pays the bills. And, as a bonus, I've beaten my high scores on all my phone games, thanks to all the time I spend sitting around, waiting for something to happen.

**B** Read the article. Underline a sentence in the article that answers each question below.

1. What training has the writer had?
2. How does she get work as an extra?
3. What was her first role as an extra?
4. What unexpected advantage of the work does she mention?

**C** Find words or phrases in the article that mean the same as the following.

1. have very different jobs and life experiences  _____
2. wanted or needed by many people  _____
3. first thing in the morning  _____
4. imaginary  _____
5. difficult  _____

**D** PAIR WORK What job would you most like to have on a film or TV show? Why?

## SELF-ASSESSMENT

How well can you do these things? Check (✓) the boxes.

| I can . . . | Very well | OK | A little |
|---|:---:|:---:|:---:|
| Speculate about past events (Ex. 1) | ☐ | ☐ | ☐ |
| Give opinions and advice about past events (Ex. 2) | ☐ | ☐ | ☐ |
| Describe steps in processes (Ex. 3) | ☐ | ☐ | ☐ |
| Use relative clauses to give information about people (Ex. 4) | ☐ | ☐ | ☐ |

## 1 LISTENING Something's not right.

**A** Listen to three conversations. Where do you think each conversation takes place? What do you think might have happened? Take notes.

| | Location | What might've happened | What could've happened next |
|---|---|---|---|
| **1.** | | | |
| **2.** | | | |
| **3.** | | | |

**B PAIR WORK** Decide what happened with your partner. Then decide what could have happened next in each situation. Complete the chart.

## 2 DISCUSSION Bad moves

**A PAIR WORK** React to these situations. First, make a judgment or suggestion using a past modal. Then add another statement using the reaction in parentheses.

1. Samantha didn't get to work on time today. (a suggestion)
2. Pat took a vacation, and now he doesn't have money for rent. (a warning)
3. Jim didn't study for the test, but he got all the answers correct. (a suspicion)
4. Nick was driving too fast, and the police stopped him. (an excuse)
5. Carl spent the night playing his favorite game online. (a prediction)

"Samantha should have left home earlier. She could have set an alarm."

**B GROUP WORK** Join another pair and compare your comments. Who has the most interesting reaction to each situation?

# Progress check

## SELF-ASSESSMENT

**Learning Objectives:** reflect on one's learning; identify areas that need improvement

- Ask: "What did you learn in Units 13 and 14?" Elicit Ss' answers.

- Ss complete the Self-assessment. Explain to Ss that this is not a test; it is a way for them to evaluate what they've learned and identify areas where they need additional practice. Encourage them to be honest, and point out they will not get a bad grade if they check (✓) "a little."

- Ss move on to the Progress check exercises. You can have Ss complete them in class or for homework, using one of these techniques:
  1. Ask Ss to complete all the exercises.
  2. Ask Ss: "What do you need to practice?" Then assign exercises based on their answers.
  3. Ask Ss to choose and complete exercises based on their Self-assessment.

## 1 LISTENING

**Learning Objective:** demonstrate one's ability to listen to, understand, and express degrees of certainty using past modals

### ▶ A [CD 3, Track 27]

- Explain the task.

- Ss work individually to complete the first two columns of the chart. Play the audio program two or three times. Pause between conversations for Ss to write. Remind Ss to write notes, not complete sentences.

- Don't check answers before completing part B.

### Audio script

See page T-180.

- **Option:** For lower-level classes, ask Ss to listen first for "where" and then for "what."

### B *Pair work*

- Explain the task.

- Ss work in pairs to compare notes from part A and decide what happened. Then have Ss think about what could have happened next and complete the last column of the chart. Remind them to use modal expressions (e.g., *It could have taken place . . . They might have . . . She must have . . . He may have . . .*).

- Ask Ss to share ideas with the class.

### Possible answers

Parts A and B:
1. in an elevator: The man might've gotten stuck in an elevator. The manager must've helped him.
2. at home/in an office: The computer must've stopped working. It could have lost all their data.
3. at a restaurant/café: The waiter must've given bad service. The waiter must've been fired.

## 2 DISCUSSION

**Learning Objectives:** demonstrate one's ability to give opinions and advice using past modals; demonstrate one's ability to react to different situations

### A *Pair work*

- Explain the task.

- Read the example judgment and suggestion. Point out the past modals in the example. Elicit additional reactions from the class.

- Ss work in pairs to react to each situation. Go around the class to check use of past modals and give help as needed.

### B *Group work*

- Explain the task.

- Each pair joins another pair. Ss take turns reading their sentences. The other Ss comment on the opinions or advice.

- Ask groups to share comments with the class. Ss vote on who has the most interesting reaction.

## 3 GAME

**Learning Objective:** demonstrate one's ability to use the passive to describe process with *be* and modals

### A *Group work*

- Explain the task. Ask Ss to read the opening and closing sentences of each topic.
- Ss work in small groups. Ask each group to choose one process. Tell Ss to describe the entire process orally before they write.
- Ss write the steps in the process. Remind Ss to use passives and modals. Ss can use a separate sheet of paper if needed.
- Go around the class to check sentences and to give help as needed.

### B *Class activity*

- Explain the task. Ask: "Who has more than five steps? More than six steps?" until you find the group with the most steps. Ask that group to read the steps to the class.
- **Option**: Ask each group to read their steps. Award one point for each step that correctly uses the passive. The group with the most points "wins."
- **Option**: Ss form pairs. Each pair joins another pair. Ss in one pair take turns reading the steps in the process. Ss in the other pair mime the actions. Then the pairs switch roles.

## 4 SPEAKING

**Learning Objective:** demonstrate one's ability to describe people using defining and non-defining relative clauses

### A

- Explain the task. Model the task by completing two or three sentences about someone in your life.
- Ss work individually to write their statements. Go around the class and give help as needed.

### B *Pair work*

- Explain the task. Ask two Ss to model the conversation. Point out the follow-up question.
- Ss compare their answers in pairs.
- Ask Ss to share interesting things they learned about people in their partner's life.
- **Option**: Ss write a paragraph about one of the people in part A. Ss can exchange paragraphs, post them around the room, or hand them in for you to check.

## WHAT'S NEXT?

**Learning Objective:** become more involved in one's learning

- Focus Ss' attention on the Self-assessment again. Ask: "How well can you do these things now?"
- Ask Ss to underline one thing they need to review. Ask: "What did you underline? How can you review it?"
- If needed, plan additional activities or reviews based on Ss' answers.

## 3 GAME Step by step

**A GROUP WORK** Look at these topics. Set a time limit. Talk with your group and write as many steps as you can between the first and last parts of each process.

making a grilled cheese sandwich

organizing a party

First, the bread has to be sliced.

_____
_____
_____
_____

Finally, the sandwich is served on a plate.

First, the guests have to be chosen.

_____
_____
_____
_____

Finally, the guests are welcomed.

**B CLASS ACTIVITY** Compare your answers. Which group has the most steps?

## 4 SPEAKING Your social circle

**A** Complete these statements about people in your life.

My best friend is a person who _____.

My neighbor, who _____, always _____.

My mother is someone that _____.

My teacher, who _____, is _____.

_____ is a _____ who _____.

**B PAIR WORK** Compare your answers. Ask two follow-up questions about each of your partner's statements.

**A:** My best friend is a person who always listens to me when I have a problem.
**B:** Does she give you good advice?

## WHAT'S NEXT?

Look at your Self-assessment again. Do you need to review anything?

# Unit 15 Supplementary Resources Overview

| | After the following SB exercises | You can use these materials in class | Your students can use these materials outside the classroom |
|---|---|---|---|
| **CYCLE 1** | 1 Snapshot | | |
| | 2 Perspectives | | |
| | 3 Grammar Focus | | **SB** Unit 15 Grammar plus, Focus 1<br>**SS** Unit 15 Grammar 1<br>**GAME** Sentence Runner (Giving recommendations and opinions)<br>**GAME** Speak or Swim (Giving recommendations and opinions) |
| | 4 Discussion | | |
| | 5 Listening | **TSS** Unit 15 Listening Worksheet | |
| | 6 Interchange 15 | **TSS** Unit 15 Writing Worksheet | **WB** Unit 15 exercises 1–5 |
| **CYCLE 2** | 7 Word Power | **TSS** Unit 15 Vocabulary Worksheet | **SS** Unit 15 Vocabulary 1–2<br>**GAME** Name the Picture (Community issues) |
| | 8 Conversation | | **SS** Unit 15 Speaking 1–2 |
| | 9 Grammar Focus | **TSS** Unit 15 Grammar Worksheet | **SB** Unit 15 Grammar plus, Focus 2<br>**SS** Unit 15 Grammar 2<br>**GAME** Say the Word (Tag questions for opinions) |
| | 10 Pronunciation | **TSS** Unit 15 Extra Worksheet | |
| | 11 Listening | | |
| | 12 Writing | | |
| | 13 Reading | **TSS** Unit 15 Project Worksheet<br>**VID** Unit 15<br>**VRB** Unit 15 | **SS** Unit 15 Reading 1–2<br>**SS** Unit 15 Listening 1–3<br>**SS** Unit 15 Video 1–3<br>**WB** Unit 15 exercises 6–9 |

**Key**   **GAME:** Online Game    **SB:** Student's Book    **SS:** Online Self-study    **TSS:** Teacher Support Site
      **VID:** Video DVD    **VRB:** Video Resource Book    **WB:** Online Workbook/Workbook

# My Plan for Unit 15

Use the space below to customize a plan that fits your needs.

| With the following SB exercises | I am using these materials in class | My students are using these materials outside the classroom |
|---|---|---|
|  |  |  |
|  |  |  |
|  |  |  |
|  |  |  |
|  |  |  |
|  |  |  |
|  |  |  |
|  |  |  |
|  |  |  |
|  |  |  |
|  |  |  |
|  |  |  |
|  |  |  |
|  |  |  |

| With or instead of the following SB section | I am using these materials for assessment |
|---|---|
|  |  |
|  |  |
|  |  |

# 15 A law must be passed!

▶ Make recommendations about social issues
▶ Give opinions about laws and social issues

## 1 SNAPSHOT

### 8 UNUSUAL LAWS FROM AROUND THE WORLD

1. A law prohibits unmarried women from parachuting on Sunday in Florida.
2. In Switzerland, it's illegal to keep only one pet if it's a social animal.
3. It's against the law to feed the pigeons in Venice.
4. In some states in Australia, you may not leave the car keys inside an unattended vehicle.
5. In the U.K., women aren't allowed to eat chocolate on public transportation.
6. Businesses must provide rails for tying up horses in Canada.
7. In the state of Washington, it's illegal to pretend your parents are rich.
8. In Finland, taxi drivers must pay royalties if they play music for customers.

Adapted from www.dumblaws.com

Which of these laws would you like to have in your city or country? Why?
Can you think of reasons for these laws?
Do you know of any other unusual laws?

## 2 PERSPECTIVES  Rules and regulations

▶ A  Listen to people make recommendations at a city council meeting. Would you agree with these proposals if they were made in your community? Check (✓) your opinion.

### CITY OF BRISTOL

## MEETING NOTES

| | STRONGLY AGREE | SOMEWHAT AGREE | DISAGREE |
|---|---|---|---|
| 1. Clubs should be required to install soundproof walls. | ☐ | ☐ | ☐ |
| 2. Riding a bike on the sidewalk mustn't be permitted. | ☐ | ☐ | ☐ |
| 3. Pet owners shouldn't be allowed to walk dogs without a leash. | ☐ | ☐ | ☐ |
| 4. Something has got to be done about littering. | ☐ | ☐ | ☐ |
| 5. A law must be passed to control the pollution from vehicles. | ☐ | ☐ | ☐ |
| 6. Children ought to be required to wear a helmet when riding a bike. | ☐ | ☐ | ☐ |
| 7. Schools should only be permitted to serve organic food. | ☐ | ☐ | ☐ |

**B  GROUP WORK**  Compare your opinions. Try to get your classmates to agree with you.

# 15 A law must be passed!

**Cycle 1, Exercises 1–6**

In this unit, students practice making recommendations about social issues and giving opinions about laws and social issues. By the end of Cycle 1, students will be able to make recommendations using passive modals. By the end of Cycle 2, students will be able to express opinions using tag questions.

## 1 SNAPSHOT

**Learning Objective:** discuss laws

Note: If possible, bring in a world map to help Ss find the places mentioned in the Snapshot.

- Introduce the topic of laws by asking Ss some questions about laws on marriage, driving, ID cards, etc., in their country (e.g., *How old do you have to be in order to get married?*). Check Ss' use of *must* and *have to*.

- Explain that this Snapshot is about unusual laws.

- Ss read individually. Encourage Ss to use context to guess the meaning of new words. Ss may check their dictionaries if they wish.

- Elicit or explain any remaining new vocabulary.

### Vocabulary
**parachute:** jump from a plane wearing a piece of equipment made of a large piece of special cloth
**unattended:** not being watched or looked after

**rail:** a horizontal bar that you tie things to or hang things on
**tie up:** fasten something together using string, rope, etc.
**illegal:** not legal, against the law
**pretend:** act as if something is true when it is false
**royalties:** money that is paid to a musician (or other artist) each time their work is sold, played, or performed

- Elicit some useful expressions from the Snapshot (e.g., *It's against the law to, The law prohibits, It's illegal to*, etc.).

- Read the questions. Ss discuss the questions in groups. Model some imaginative answers:

    T:  Paul, why do you think it's an offense to flush a toilet after 10 P.M.?

    S1: Well, maybe because of the noise?

    S2: Yeah, or it could be because there is no water supply at night.

## 2 PERSPECTIVES

**Learning Objectives:** agree or disagree with recommendations that use passive modals in context; give reasons for one's opinions

### ▶ A [CD 3, Track 28]
- Books closed. Write these categories on the board. With Ss, brainstorm some problems associated with these people and places:

    | car owners | clubs | pet owners |
    | school cafeterias | people who litter | cyclists |

- Set the scene. Some people are discussing the problems on the board. They are making recommendations about what should be done.

- Ask Ss to copy the points on the board. Play the audio program. Ss listen and number the problems in the order they are discussed.

- Books open. Ss read the recommendations and check the order. Point out that sentences 2 and 6 are both about cyclists.

- Elicit or explain any remaining new vocabulary.

### Vocabulary
**leash:** a chain or leather strap used to lead a dog
**litter:** make (a place) untidy with trash

**helmet:** a hard, protective hat
**organic:** not using artificial chemicals to produce

### TIP
To avoid teaching words that Ss already know, let Ss *tell you* what they need to know. Also, make the most of your Ss' knowledge: elicit meanings from them whenever possible.

- Elicit the meaning of "strongly agree," "somewhat agree," and "disagree." Explain that Ss should check only one box for each recommendation.

- Ss work in pairs. Tell Ss to re-read the recommendations and check (✓) their own opinions. Set a time limit of about five minutes. Go around the class and give help as needed.

- Take a class poll. Play the sentences again and ask Ss to raise their hands. What do most Ss think about these issues?

### B Group work
- Explain the task. Ss work in small groups. Ss take turns trying to persuade the group to agree with their opinions.

## 3 GRAMMAR FOCUS

**Learning Objective:** use *ought to*, *should*, *have (got) to*, and *must* + passive to give recommendations and opinions

▶ **[CD 3, Track 29]**

- Focus Ss' attention on the Perspectives on page 100. Explain that passive modals were used for recommendations. If needed, remind Ss that a passive modal is modal + *be* + past participle.

- Ask Ss to underline the passive modal in each sentence.

- Point out that some opinions are stronger than others. Explain the following. Then write the chart on the board:

  1. We use *should* and *ought to* when we think something is a good idea.
  2. We use *must* and *have (got) to* when we think something is absolutely necessary. Note: It may even be a law.

| A good idea | Absolutely necessary |
|---|---|
| should | must |
| ought to | have to/have got to |

- Ask Ss to look at the Perspectives. Ask: "Which were considered 'absolutely necessary'?" (Answers: 2, 4, 5)

- Write these two sentences on the board. Ask if Ss can understand the difference:

  *Cyclists should be required to wear a helmet.*
  *Cyclists must be required to wear a helmet.*

- Play the audio program. Ss listen and read or repeat.

### A

- Explain the task. Ask Ss to describe what is happening in the picture.

- Tell Ss to look at the first sentence. Ask: "Who thinks young people *should* be permitted to vote before 21? Who thinks they shouldn't? Does anyone think it *mustn't* be allowed?" Elicit possible answers for number 1.

- Give Ss time to read the issues.

- Elicit or explain any new vocabulary.

**Vocabulary**
**offensive:** likely to make people angry or upset
**health care:** the set of services provided by a country or an organization for treating people who are sick
**citizen:** someone who lives in a particular country or city
**fur:** material made from animal hair and skin

- Ss complete the task individually. Check answers, accepting any that are logical and grammatically correct.

**Possible answers**

1. Young people **should be/must be permitted** to vote before age 21.
2. Laws **have got to be/must be passed** to protect people's online privacy.
3. People **ought not to be/shouldn't be allowed** to use offensive language in social media.
4. Governments **must be/should be required** to provide health care to all their citizens.
5. Children **mustn't be/shouldn't be allowed** to play violent video games.
6. Scientists **shouldn't be/mustn't be permitted** to use animals for research.
7. The sale of fur products **should be/must be prohibited.**
8. Something **has to be/ought to be done** to stop the pollution of rivers and oceans.

### B Group work

- Explain the task. Ask three Ss to model the conversation.

- Ss work in small groups. Ss take turns reading their statements. Remind Ss to say whether they agree or not and to give reasons for their opinions.

- For more practice with recommendations and opinions, play **Mime** – download it from the website.

## 4 DISCUSSION

**Learning Objective:** give and discuss opinions for and against issues using passive modals

### A Group work

- Explain the task. Read the topics. Model the conversation with a S.

- Ask Ss to read the phrases in the box. Explain that these are polite ways of disagreeing.

- Elicit or explain any new vocabulary.

- Ss work individually. Set a time limit of about five minutes.

- Ss discuss their ideas in groups. Remind Ss to use passive modals and phrases such as *due to, because of, because,* and *since.*

- **Option:** Adapt the discussion into an **aquarium.** See page T-68, Exercise 10, part C.

### B Class activity

- Explain the task. Ss share the group's ideas.

# 3 GRAMMAR FOCUS

▶ **Giving recommendations and opinions**

**When you think something is a good idea**

Clubs **should be required** to install soundproof walls.

Pet owners **shouldn't be allowed** to walk dogs without a leash.

People **ought (not) to be required** to wear a helmet when riding a bike.

**When you think something is absolutely necessary**

A law **must be passed** to control the pollution from vehicles.

Riding a bike on the sidewalk **mustn't be permitted**.

A rule **has to be made** to require bike lanes on city streets.

Something **has got to be done** to stop littering.

GRAMMAR PLUS *see page 146*

A Complete the sentences positively or negatively. Choose a modal that shows how strongly you feel about these issues.

**1.** Young people _____ (permit) to vote before age 21.

**2.** Laws _____ (pass) to protect people's online privacy.

**3.** People _____ (allow) to use offensive language in social media.

**4.** Governments _____ (require) to provide health care to all their citizens.

**5.** Children _____ (allow) to play violent video games.

**6.** Scientists _____ (permit) to use animals for research.

**7.** The sale of fur products _____ (prohibit).

**8.** Something _____ (do) to stop the pollution of rivers and oceans.

B **GROUP WORK** Compare your statements. Do you agree with one another? If not, why not?

**A:** Young people shouldn't be permitted to vote before age 21. They're not prepared.

**B:** You may have a point, but they could be better informed.

**C:** Maybe, but in my opinion, . . .

# 4 DISCUSSION Controversial topics

A **GROUP WORK** Think of three reasons for, and three reasons against, each idea below. Then discuss your views. As a group, form an opinion about each idea.

requiring employers to offer workers 12 weeks
    of parental leave

paying teachers less when their students fail

banning private cars from the downtown
    areas of big cities

**A:** What do you think about requiring employers to offer workers 12 weeks of parental leave?

**B:** I think it's a good idea. Parents should be allowed to stay with their babies . . .

| offering a different opinion |
| --- |
| That sounds interesting, but I think . . . |
| That's not a bad idea. On the other hand, I feel . . . |
| You may have a point. However, I think . . . |

B **CLASS ACTIVITY** Share your group's opinions and reasons. Who has the most persuasive reasons for and against each position?

## 5 LISTENING Something has got to be done!

▶ **A** Listen to people discuss annoying situations. Number the situations they describe in the correct order from 1 to 3. (There are three extra situations.)

- ☐ using the phone on speaker in public places
- ☐ using a cell phone on a plane
- ☐ posting selfies on social media
- ☐ taking selfies in crowded places
- ☐ not having signs about cell phones in public places
- ☐ texting in a movie theater

▶ **B** Listen again. What solutions do they suggest for each situation?

1. _____
2. _____
3. _____

**C** GROUP WORK Do you agree or disagree with the solutions? What do you think should be done about each problem?

## 6 INTERCHANGE 15 On the wrong side of the law

What if you could make the rules? Go to Interchange 15 on page 130.

## 7 WORD POWER Community issues

**A** PAIR WORK Which of these issues are problems in your community? Check (✓) the appropriate boxes.

- ☐ bullying
- ☐ homelessness
- ☐ inadequate health care
- ☐ irregular trash collection
- ☐ lack of affordable child care
- ☐ noise pollution
- ☐ overcrowded classrooms
- ☐ stray animals
- ☐ street crime
- ☐ vandalism

**B** GROUP WORK Join another pair of students. Which three problems concern your group the most? What should or can be done about them?

vandalism

# 5 LISTENING

Learning Objective: listen for specific information and respond to problems discussed using passive modals

## A [CD 3, Track 30]

- Ask Ss to cover the text and look only at the picture. Ask: "What problems do people have with smartphones? How do you feel about these things?"

### TIP
Use pre-listening activities to prepare Ss for a Listening. Brainstorming or discussing the topic, exploiting the picture and subtitle, and prediction tasks get Ss thinking about what they are going to hear.

- Text uncovered. Explain the task. Ask Ss to read the situations.
- Play the audio program, pausing after each discussion. Ss listen and number the situations. Remind Ss there are three extra situations.

### Audio script
See page T-181.

### Answers
1. texting in a movie theater
2. taking selfies in crowded places
3. using the phone on speaker in public places

## B [CD 3, Track 31]

- Explain the task. Ss listen again to focus on the solutions.
- Pause after each person to give time for the Ss to write.
- Go over the answers with the class.

### Answers
1. People shouldn't be allowed to text at all in movie theaters. Our phones should have a movie mode that people should be required to turn on.
2. Selfies ought to be prohibited at any place with big crowds of people.
3. People should be prohibited from talking on speaker indoors in public places. Offices and public buildings should be required to post signs that prohibit it.

## C Group work

- Explain the task. Ss work in small groups to give their opinions about the situations. Remind them to give a reason and a solution for each situation.

# 6 INTERCHANGE 15

See page T-130 for teaching notes.

## End of Cycle 1

See the Supplementary Resources chart at the beginning of this unit for additional teaching materials and student activities related to this Cycle.

## Cycle 2, Exercises 7–13

# 7 WORD POWER

Learning Objective: discuss social and health issues

## A Pair work

- Explain the task. Ask Ss to read the issues. Point out that these are examples of social issues.
- Use the picture to model the task. Write vandalism on the board. Ask: "Is there too much vandalism in your community?" If so, Ss check (✓) that box.
- Ss work in pairs. Tell Ss that they can respond to issues in their country if they wish.
- Elicit or explain any new vocabulary.

### Vocabulary
**bullying:** intentionally frightening someone who is smaller or weaker (often a problem in schools)
**inadequate:** not acceptable; not up to minimum or basic standards; not able to meet basic needs
**stray animals:** dogs and cats that don't belong to anyone

For more practice with the vocabulary, play **Tic-Tac-Toe** – download it from the website.

## B Group work

- Explain the task. Read the questions.
- Each pair joins another pair. Go around the class and give help as needed.

## 8 CONVERSATION

Learning Objective: use tag questions for opinions in a conversation about social issues

▶ **A** *[CD 3, Track 32]*

- Use the picture to set the scene. Mara is telling Ted about her problems. Ask: "What kinds of problems do you think Mara has?" Ss brainstorm in pairs.

- **Option:** Ask Ss to cover the text and look only at the picture. Ask pairs to tell a story about the people in the picture. Encourage Ss to be creative!

- Tell Ss to listen for what is making life difficult for Mara. Play the audio program several times. Ss listen and take notes.

- Ss open their books and read the conversation. Ss check their notes.

- Elicit or explain any new vocabulary.

- Play the audio program again. Ss listen and read.

- Ss practice the conversation in pairs.

❗ Pairs can practice the conversation using **Say It With Feeling!** – download it from the website.

▶ **B** *[CD 3, Track 33]*

- Explain the task. Read the focus question.

- Play the audio program. Then elicit Ss' answers.

### Audio script

See page T-181.

### Answer

Ted is concerned about what he's going to do after he graduates.

## 9 GRAMMAR FOCUS

Learning Objective: use tag questions to express opinions

▶ *[CD 3, Track 34]*

- Focus Ss' attention on how Ted used tag questions in the previous Conversation. Explain that tag questions are used when we expect someone to agree with us or when we are asking for confirmation.

- Next, focus Ss' attention on the Grammar Focus box. Point out the difference between the two columns. Explain that when a statement is affirmative, the tag question is negative, and vice versa. For example: +/- Health insurance **is** really expensive, **isn't** it?

  -/+Child care **isn't** cheap, **is** it?

- Explain that when *be* is the main verb, *be* is also used in the tag question. Similarly, we use the same modal in the main clause and the tag (e.g., We *should* pay our taxes, *shouldn't* we?).

- However, simple present and past verbs use the auxiliary verb in the tag. Write these examples on the board:

  *Graffiti* <u>makes</u> *everything look ugly,* <u>doesn't</u> *it?*
  *You* <u>found</u> *affordable child care,* <u>didn't</u> *you?*

- Play the audio program. Ss listen and read or repeat.

**A**

- Explain the task.

- Ss complete the task individually. They complete the sentences with tag questions. Go around the class and give help as needed.

- Then Ss compare answers in pairs. Go over answers with the class.

### Answers

1. There aren't enough shelters for the homeless, **are there**?
2. Vandalism makes a neighborhood very unpleasant, **doesn't it**?
3. In overcrowded classrooms, teachers can't give enough attention to students, **can they**?
4. School bullying is a major problem in most schools, **isn't it**?
5. There are more street crimes in big cities than in small towns, **aren't there**?
6. The government should provide adequate health care to everyone, **shouldn't it**?
7. The city doesn't do enough for stray animals, **does it**?
8. It isn't easy to save money these days, **is it**?

**B**

- Explain the task. Read the question.

- Ss work individually. Set a time limit of about ten minutes. Go around the class and give help as needed.

**C** *Group work*

- Explain the task. Ask three Ss to model the conversation.

- Ss work in small groups. Ss take turns reading their statements and giving opinions on others'. Set a time limit of ten minutes.

## 8 CONVERSATION  It's not easy, is it?

**A** Listen and practice.

**Mara:** I need to find a new apartment. I can't stand the noise from all those bars and clubs in my neighborhood anymore.

**Ted:** I can imagine. But it isn't easy to find a nice apartment in a quiet neighborhood, is it?

**Mara:** No, it's not! And my rent is already sky-high. I'm having a hard time making ends meet.

**Ted:** I know. Everything is really expensive nowadays, isn't it?

**Mara:** It sure is. You know, I'm looking for child care for my baby, but I just can't find anything affordable in the area.

**Ted:** The city should provide free child care to working families.

**Mara:** I think so, too. But unfortunately, the mayor doesn't.

**B** Listen to the rest of the conversation. What is Ted concerned about?

## 9 GRAMMAR FOCUS

### Tag questions for opinions

| Affirmative statement + negative tag | Negative statement + affirmative tag |
|---|---|
| Everything is really expensive nowadays, **isn't it**? | It isn't easy to find a nice apartment, **is it**? |
| There are lots of clubs around, **aren't there**? | There aren't any noise pollution laws, **are there**? |
| Mara likes her apartment, **doesn't she**? | Her neighbors don't make much noise, **do they**? |
| The city should provide child care, **shouldn't it**? | You can't sleep because of the noise, **can you**? |

GRAMMAR PLUS see page 146

**A** Add tag questions to these statements. Then compare with a partner.

1. There aren't enough shelters for the homeless, . . . ?
2. Vandalism makes a neighborhood very unpleasant, . . . ?
3. In overcrowded classrooms, teachers can't give enough attention to students, . . . ?
4. School bullying is a major problem in most schools, . . . ?
5. There are more street crimes in big cities than in small towns, . . . ?
6. The government should provide adequate health care to everyone, . . . ?
7. The city doesn't do enough for stray animals, . . . ?
8. It isn't easy to save money these days, . . . ?

**B** What are some things you feel strongly about in your school or city? Write six statements with tag questions.

**C** GROUP WORK  Take turns reading your statements. Other students respond by giving their opinions.

**A:** Public transportation isn't adequate, is it?
**B:** No, it isn't. There should be more bus lines.
**C:** On the other hand, the subway system is very efficient . . .

A law must be passed!  **103**

## 10 PRONUNCIATION Intonation in tag questions

▶ **A** Listen and practice. Use falling intonation in tag questions when you are giving an opinion and expect the other person to agree.

Noise pollution is a serious problem in our city, isn't it?

Governments should offer child care to all working families, shouldn't they?

**B** PAIR WORK Take turns reading the statements with tag questions from Exercise 9, part A. Give your own opinions when responding.

## 11 LISTENING Let's face it.

▶ **A** Listen to people give their opinions about issues in the news. What issues are they talking about?

|   | Issue | Opinions for | Opinions against |
|---|-------|--------------|------------------|
| 1. |       |              |                  |
| 2. |       |              |                  |

▶ **B** Listen again. Write the different opinions that you hear.

**C** GROUP WORK What do you think about the issues in part A? Give your own opinions.

## 12 WRITING There ought to be a law.

**A** Think about a local problem that needs to be solved, and write a persuasive essay suggesting a new law to help solve it. Be creative! Use these questions to help you.

What is the problem, and how does it affect your community?

What can be done to help solve it?

Who might disagree with you, and how will you convince him or her that your law is a good idea?

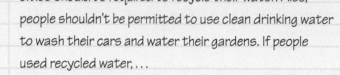

The water crisis affects people all over the world. I think cities should be required to recycle their water. Also, people shouldn't be permitted to use clean drinking water to wash their cars and water their gardens. If people used recycled water, . . .

**B** GROUP WORK Try to convince your classmates to pass your new law. Then vote on it.

# 10 PRONUNCIATION

**Learning Objective:** sound more natural when using tag questions

### ▶ A [CD 3, Track 35]

- Explain that we use falling intonation on tag questions. This shows that we are giving an opinion, not asking a real question. Also, we expect the listener to agree with us.

- Play the audio program. Ss practice. Check Ss' individual pronunciation.

### B *Pair work*

- Ss work in pairs. They take turns reading the tag questions from part A of Exercise 9. Remind Ss to respond with their own opinions.

# 11 LISTENING

**Learning Objective:** listen for main ideas in personal views and opinions about issues in the news, discussed using tag questions

! To set the scene for the Listening, try **Cloud Prediction** – download it from the website. Use these words:

1. entertainment, research, abuse, money, animals
2. supercenter, combined, cheaper, smaller businesses, close

### ▶ A [CD 3, Track 36]

- Explain the task.
- Tell Ss to listen and fill in the issues in the chart. Play the audio program. Pause between issues for Ss to complete the chart.

#### Audio script

See page T-181.

#### Answers

Parts A and B:
1. animals used for entertainment; *for:* they use the profits for research, rescue, and protection of the animals; *against:* animals are punished and abused if they don't do things right; they're kept in horrible conditions; it's not natural for them to be in small spaces

2. supercenters: *for:* the products are cheaper and they provide a lot of jobs for the community; *against:* smaller businesses can't compete with supercenters and they lose a lot of money, either closing down or limiting their products; consumers will have fewer choices when they go shopping

### ▶ B [CD 3, Track 37]

- Explain the task. Remind Ss to listen for key words and take notes.
- Tell Ss to listen and fill in the "for" opinions in the chart first. Play the audio program. Pause between issues for Ss to complete the chart. Ss listen and write.
- Play the audio program again. This time Ss fill in the "against" opinions.
- Ask Ss to write the answers on the board.

### C *Group work*

- Explain the task.
- Ss work in groups. They discuss the issues in part A. Go around the class and listen in. Note errors to go over after the activity.

⚃ For more practice, play **Just One Minute** – download it from the website.

# 12 WRITING

**Learning Objective:** write a persuasive paragraph suggesting a new law to help solve a local problem

### A

- Explain the task. Elicit or explain the meaning of *persuasive essay* (an essay that tries to get people to agree with your opinion or proposal).
- Focus Ss' attention on the picture. Ask Ss to predict what this essay is about. Then read the example essay. Point out the use of opinions and reasons.
- Read the focus questions. Give Ss a few minutes to choose a topic.

- Explain how to organize the essay. The first paragraph should include a brief description of the issue, the writer's opinions, and supporting reasons. The second paragraph should include a proposal for a new law, with recommendations on what needs to be done or reasons for why it will help solve the problem.
- After Ss generate ideas and organize their thoughts, have them write a first draft.

### B *Group work*

- Explain the task. Encourage Ss to ask each other questions about the proposed laws or about their opinions. Have Ss vote by having them write "yes" or "no" on a slip of paper.

**Learning Objectives:** identify main ideas and sequence in an essay; identify arguments for and against plagiarism

## A

- Go over the task.
- Ss read the title of the article and look at the picture. Ask Ss to raise their hands or look up when they are done.
- Elicit answers from the class.
- Ask Ss to look at the title and the picture. Ask them what plagiarism is. (Answer: copying material without giving credit to the source or getting someone else to do your work.)
- Then ask: "What is the first paragraph about?" (Answer: a hypothetical example of plagiarism) Point out that opening with an example to illustrate a broader issue is a common technique in magazine and newspaper articles.

## B

- Ss read the article individually. Encourage Ss to guess the meaning of new words. Remind Ss to circle or underline words they can't guess from context.
- Ss work in pairs or groups to discuss marked words. Ss may look up definitions if needed.
- Elicit or explain any new vocabulary.

### Vocabulary

**plagiarism:** copying someone else's work or ideas
**key:** one of the parts on a keyboard you press with your fingers
**ownership:** the right of owning something
**fairly:** more than average, but less than very
**assume:** think that something is likely to be true
**critique:** to say what is good and bad about something
**masked:** hidden
**spot:** see or notice something or someone
**approach:** a way of doing something
**quote:** repeat what someone has said or written

- Explain the task.
- Ss complete the task individually and answer the questions.
- Go over answers with the class.

- **Option:** Assign the article for homework. Ask Ss to read it once or twice for comprehension. Then they should mark new vocabulary. Tell Ss to list the marked words, use a dictionary to check definitions, and write the definitions on the list. In class, Ss work in groups to discuss and compare their lists.

### Answers

1. to explain what plagiarism is, how it can happen, and how to avoid it
2. because so much material is available and it is not always clear who wrote it
3. Are all of these words my own?

## C

- Explain the task.
- Ss complete the task individually. Ask Ss to read the descriptions and make a decision.
- Go over answers with the class.

### Answers

1. not plagiarism
2. plagiarism – Either he thought it was OK to use the material if he changed it in some ways, or he intended to commit plagiarism.
3. plagiarism – accidental
4. plagiarism – probably intentional

## D *Pair work*

- Explain the task. Read the focus questions.
- Ss discuss the questions in small groups. Tell Ss they can discuss related issues if they wish.
- **Option:** Ss take notes as they talk. Then ask Ss to share ideas with the class.

## End of Cycle 2

See the Supplementary Resources chart at the beginning of this unit for additional teaching materials and student activities related to this Cycle.

**A** Look at the title and the picture. What do you think plagiarism is?

HOME       NEWS       ARTICLES       COMMUNITY

THAT'S PLAGIARISM? _____ POSTED AUGUST 21

If a teacher or your boss called you aside and said that he or she suspected you of plagiarism, how would you react? You'd probably be honestly confused. Nowadays, there are so many sources of information available that you can copy from with a single click. Many people don't even realize that they're committing plagiarism. Whether it's intentional or not, using someone else's information is stealing, and stealing is definitely a big deal.

The confusion about ownership comes from the fact that articles, photos, blogs, and social media posts are so easy to access – and just as easy to copy. When you see the same article on various websites, it's fairly natural to assume that it's public property. If a resource like Wikipedia offers material that can be critiqued and changed by its readers, that must be free for the taking, right? But that simply is not the case. Everything that has been written, drawn, photographed, or recorded, and released to the public, belongs to someone. Even your friends' comments on your social media page belong to them, not to you.

To avoid plagiarism, here are a few basic points to keep in mind. When writing a paper, if you get ideas or wording from someone else's writing, you must include the name of the writer or the source. If you find a few articles that you want to use, and you think taking a few points from each article and combining them makes the content yours, it's just not the case. This kind of "masked" plagiarism is very easy to spot, and it will get you into trouble. But really, just asking yourself a simple question should be enough: "Are all of these words my own?" If the answer is yes, you're in the clear.

In the end, the best approach is to write down the source for any material you quote from directly, and to assume that if it's public, it isn't yours. Plagiarism is a serious problem and can have serious consequences – even if it's totally accidental. Besides, putting ideas into your own words can make you a better writer, and a better thinker as well.

**B** Read the article. Then answer the questions.

**1.** What is the author's main purpose in writing the piece?

**2.** Why might it be easy to commit plagiarism by accident?

**3.** What question should you ask yourself in order to avoid plagiarism?

**C** Look at the following situations. Do you think they are describing plagiarism or not? If they are, do you think it was accidental or intentional?

**1.** Stacy copied a paragraph from a travel website and pasted it into her essay about Aruba. She put it into quotation marks and included the name and link for the website.

**2.** John works for a bank. He copied a paragraph from a website. He changed some words and rearranged some of the sentences. He did not indicate where it came from. He used it in a brochure for the bank.

**3.** Julie read an article online and later wrote her own essay about the same subject. Some of her wording was exactly the same as the online article.

**4.** Mitch borrowed a friend's essay to get some ideas for his own. Their teacher said that their essays were almost identical.

**D** PAIR WORK Sometimes famous musicians get in trouble for putting out songs that sound like someone else's. Do you think this is plagiarism? What, if anything, should be done about it?

# Unit 16 Supplementary Resources Overview

| | After the following SB exercises | You can use these materials in class | Your students can use these materials outside the classroom |
|---|---|---|---|
| **CYCLE 1** | 1 Snapshot | | |
| | 2 Perspectives | | |
| | 3 Grammar Focus | | **SB** Unit 16 Grammar plus, Focus 1<br>**SS** Unit 16 Grammar 1<br>**GAME** Sentence Stacker (Talking about past accomplishments) |
| | 4 Pronunciation | | |
| | 5 Listening | **TSS** Unit 16 Listening | |
| | 6 Word Power | **TSS** Unit 16 Vocabulary Worksheet | **SS** Unit 16 Vocabulary 1–2<br>**GAME** Sentence Runner (Antonyms) |
| | 7 Discussion | **TSS** Unit 16 Writing Worksheet | **WB** Unit 16 exercises 1–5 |
| **CYCLE 2** | 8 Conversation | | **SS** Unit 16 Speaking 1 |
| | 9 Grammar Focus | **TSS** Unit 16 Grammar Worksheet | **SB** Unit 16 Grammar plus, Focus 2<br>**SS** Unit 16 Grammar 2<br>**GAME** Word Keys (Describing goals and possible future accomplishments)<br>**GAME** Say the Word (Past and possible future accomplishments) |
| | 10 Listening | **TSS** Unit 16 Listening | |
| | 11 Interchange 16 | | |
| | 12 Writing | | |
| | 13 Reading | **TSS** Unit 16 Extra Worksheet<br>**TSS** Unit 16 Project Worksheet<br>**VID** Unit 16<br>**VRB** Unit 16 | **SS** Unit 16 Reading 1–2<br>**SS** Unit 16 Listening 1–3<br>**SS** Unit 16 Video 1–3<br>**WB** Unit 16 exercises 6–8 |

| With or instead of the following SB section | You can also use these materials for assessment |
|---|---|
| **Units 15–16 Progress Check** | **ASSESSMENT PROGRAM** Units 15–16 Oral Quiz<br>**ASSESSMENT PROGRAM** Units 15–16 Written Quiz<br>**ASSESSMENT PROGRAM** Units 9–16 Test |

**Key**

| | | | |
|---|---|---|---|
| **GAME:** Online Game | **SB:** Student's Book | **SS:** Online Self-study | **TSS:** Teacher Support Site |
| **VID:** Video DVD | **VRB:** Video Resource Book | **WB:** Online Workbook/Workbook | |

# My Plan for Unit 16

Use the space below to customize a plan that fits your needs.

| With the following SB exercises | I am using these materials in class | My students are using these materials outside the classroom |
|---|---|---|
|  |  |  |
|  |  |  |
|  |  |  |
|  |  |  |
|  |  |  |
|  |  |  |
|  |  |  |
|  |  |  |
|  |  |  |
|  |  |  |
|  |  |  |
|  |  |  |
|  |  |  |

| With or instead of the following SB section | I am using these materials for assessment |
|---|---|
|  |  |
|  |  |
|  |  |

# 16 Reaching your goals

▸ Discuss personal accomplishments
▸ Discuss goals

## 1 SNAPSHOT

### Some Common Goals and Dreams

- [ ] win a competition
- [ ] make a lot of money
- [ ] get a promotion
- [ ] become famous
- [ ] learn to travel light
- [ ] find true love
- [ ] run a marathon
- [ ] learn to live with less
- [ ] be able to help others
- [ ] be respected
- [ ] have a healthy lifestyle
- [ ] plant a tree

*Which of these goals do you think are the most difficult to achieve? Which are the easiest? Why?*
*Do you have the same goals? Check (✓) them.*
*What other goals or wishes do you have?*

## 2 PERSPECTIVES  Personal accomplishments

▶ **A** Listen to people talk about their accomplishments. Match the statements and the people.

1. For me, my greatest accomplishment is the feeling that I've been able to help kids develop their potential and achieve their goals. _____

2. I worked hard in school, but I never managed to get good grades. However, I've just published my first book – and it's a best seller! _____

3. Last year, I ran my first marathon. I didn't win, but I was able to finish it, and I was very proud of myself. _____

4. No one believed in me in the beginning, but I've managed to make a living from my music for the past 5 years. _____

5. I felt I had reached one of my lifetime goals when I managed to quit my nine-to-five job to make a living traveling and sharing my experiences. _____

a. **an amateur athlete**

b. **a teacher**

c. **a writer**

d. **a travel blogger**

e. **a musician**

**B  GROUP WORK** Do you share any similar accomplishments? Which ones?

# 16 Reaching your goals

## Cycle 1, Exercises 1–7

In this unit, Ss discuss personal accomplishments and goals. By the end of Cycle 1, students will be able to discuss personal accomplishments using complex noun phrases with gerunds. By the end of Cycle 2, students will be able to discuss accomplishments and goals using future tenses, including the future perfect.

## 1 SNAPSHOT

**Learning Objective:** discuss personal accomplishments

- Books closed. Elicit examples of common goals and dreams, and write Ss' suggestions on the board. (You can write a few ideas to get them started: *find love, plant a tree, travel.*)

- Books open. Ask Ss to cover up the text and look only at the pictures. Ask which goals and dreams listed on the board they guessed.

- Have Ss uncover the text and read the information.

- Elicit or explain any new vocabulary.

**Vocabulary**
**goal:** something you want to do successfully in the future
**travel light:** make a journey without taking a lot of things with you
**healthy:** good for your health
**lifestyle:** the way that you live
**achieve:** succeed in doing something good, usually by working hard
**wish:** a thing you want to do or that you want to happen

- Read the questions. Ask Ss to think about their answers first.

- Ss work in pairs or small groups. They take turns sharing their responses.

## 2 PERSPECTIVES

**Learning Objectives:** demonstrate understanding of opinions that use complex noun phrases with gerunds in context; discuss the frustrations and rewards of personal accomplishments

### ▶ A [CD 3, Track 38]

- Books closed. Ask: "What do you think a writer wants to accomplish? And a teacher, a musician, an amateur athlete, and a travel blogger?" Write some of the Ss' ideas on the board.

- Books open. Tell Ss to read the statements and try to guess the person that said it.

- Play the audio program, pausing after each speaker.

- Go over answers with the class.

- Elicit or explain any new vocabulary.

**Vocabulary**
**best seller:** a new book or other product that has sold a great number of copies
**marathon:** a race in which people run for about 26 miles/42 km

**proud of one's self:** feeling very pleased about something one has done
**make a living:** earn enough money to buy the things you need
**quit:** leave your job permanently
**nine-to-five job:** a job that begins at nine o'clock in the morning and ends at five o'clock

### Answers

1. b  2. c  3. a  4. e  5. d

- Play the audio program again if needed. Ss listen and read or repeat.

### B Group work

- Explain the task. Read the questions.

- Ss work in pairs or small groups. Ss take turns sharing their responses.

# 3 GRAMMAR FOCUS

**Learning Objective:** use the present perfect and simple past to describe accomplishments

▶ **[CD 3, Track 39]**

- Books closed. Briefly review the differences between simple past and present perfect. Remind Ss of the structure by writing on the board:

  | Simple Past | Present Perfect |
  |---|---|
  | did (negative and question forms) | have/has |
  | was/were | has/have been |

- Remind Ss of these structures by asking for some examples from different Ss.

- Then write the following sentences on the board:

  I **managed** to quit my nine-to-five job two years ago.
  I've **managed** to make a living with my music.

- Elicit the differences between the two sentences (the first one is simple past, it has a defined time in the past; the second is present perfect, it uses *have* and it doesn't have a defined time in the past).

- Books open. Focus Ss' attention on the Grammar Focus box. Read the sentences.

- Play the audio program. Ss listen and read or repeat.

- Explain that *be able to* means "to have the ability to do something" or "the possibility of doing something" and it can be used in both simple past (with *was* and *were*) and in the present perfect (with *have been*).

## A

- Explain the task.
- Ss complete the task individually. Go around the class and give help as needed.

### Possible answers

| | |
|---|---|
| 1. have/haven't | 4. have/haven't |
| 2. have/haven't | 5. was/wasn't |
| 3. have/haven't | 6. have/haven't |

## B *Pair work*

- Explain the task. Ask Ss to compare their answers in part A to check what they have in common.
- Ss work in pairs. They take turns asking and answering the questions.

## C *Group work*

- Explain the task. Ask three Ss to read the example. Then model the task by asking Ss to respond:

  T:  What's something you've been able to do?

  S1: I've been able to travel to interesting places.

- Ss work in small groups. Ss take turns asking questions and giving their own answers. Encourage Ss to ask follow-up questions, and add information.

# 4 PRONUNCIATION

**Learning Objective:** sound more natural by using stress and rhythm in sentences

▶ **A [CD 3, Track 40]**

- Play the audio program. Ss listen and focus on the stressed and unstressed syllables.

- Play the audio program again. Ss listen and repeat. If needed, clap your hands in time to the stress. Ss clap with you.

! For another way to practice stress and unstressed syllables, try **Walking Stress** – download it from the website.

## B *Pair work*

- Ss work in pairs. They take turns reading the sentences in the Grammar Focus Box in Exercise 3. Remind Ss to pay attention to stress and rhythm as they read.

# 3 GRAMMAR FOCUS

GRAMMAR PLUS see page 147

▶ **Talking about past accomplishments**

| With the simple past | With the present perfect |
|---|---|
| I **managed** to quit my nine-to-five job two years ago. | I**'ve managed** to make a living with my music. |
| I **didn't manage** to get good grades in school. | I **haven't managed** to record an album yet. |
| I **was able** to finish the marathon last year. | I**'ve been able** to help kids achieve their goals. |
| I **wasn't able** to travel much on my last job. | I **haven't been able** to achieve many of my goals. |

**A** What are some of your latest accomplishments?
Complete the statements with *have*, *haven't*,
*was*, or *wasn't* to make them true for you.

1. I _____ managed to eat a healthy diet.
2. I _____ been able to help others.
3. I _____ met the person who's right for me.
4. I _____ made an important career move.
5. I _____ able to get a degree.
6. I _____ learned important life skills.

**B** PAIR WORK Compare your sentences in part A.
What accomplishments do you have in common?

**C** GROUP WORK Complete the statements with
your own information. Then share them with
your classmates.

I have been able to _____.   I haven't been able to _____.
I have managed to _____.   I haven't managed to _____.

**A:** I've managed to take a trip abroad.
**B:** What countries did you visit?
**A:** I went to New Zealand three years ago.
**C:** Really? I've always wanted to go to New Zealand. How did you like it?

# 4 PRONUNCIATION Stress and rhythm

▶ **A** Listen and practice. Notice how stressed words and syllables occur
with a regular rhythm.

    ●      ●     ●    ●     ●
I managed to accomplish a lot while I was in college.

   ●    ●      ●     ●     ●
I haven't managed to get a promotion yet.

     ●     ●      ●       ●
I was able to share my experiences with the world.

**B** PAIR WORK Take turns reading the sentences in the grammar box
in Exercise 3. Pay attention to stress and rhythm.

## 5 LISTENING A different perspective

A Listen to two people answer two interview questions. Write the obstacles they faced and what they did about them in the chart.

|  | Mr. Sandberg | Ms. Rowe |
|---|---|---|
| Obstacle |  |  |
| What he or she did |  |  |
| What he or she learned |  |  |

B Listen again. What did each person learn from his or her experience? Complete the chart.

C PAIR WORK Discuss an obstacle that you managed to overcome. What did you learn?

## 6 WORD POWER Antonyms

A Complete the pairs of opposites with the words in the box. Then compare with a partner.

| compassionate | cynical | dependent | rigid | timid | unimaginative |
|---|---|---|---|---|---|

1. adaptable ≠ _____
2. courageous ≠ _____
3. insensitive ≠ _____
4. resourceful ≠ _____
5. self-sufficient ≠ _____
6. upbeat ≠ _____

B GROUP WORK How many words or things can you associate with each word in part A?

A: What words or things do you associate with *resourceful*?
B: Capable.
C: Good at solving problems.

## 7 DISCUSSION Inspirational sayings

A Read the quotes. Which one inspires you the most?

1. The greatest pleasure in life is doing what people say you can't do.
2. Discipline is the bridge between goals and achievements.
3. No matter what you have achieved, somebody helped you.
4. Fall down seven times, stand up eight.
5. Success isn't about how much money you make. It's about the difference you make in people's lives.

B GROUP WORK Discuss and justify your choices.

A: I like the first quote because, even though my friends weren't sure I could do it, I managed to graduate from high school early. That felt great!
B: You must have been resourceful! But someone helped you, too, didn't they?
C: That's why I like the third quote. No one achieves anything all on their own.

## 5 LISTENING

**Learning Objective:** listen for main ideas and take notes on the challenges and rewards of jobs described using the present perfect and simple past

**Audio script**

See page T-182.

▶ **[CD 3, Track 41]**

- Books closed. Ask Ss "What are some challenges you might have if you decided to study abroad, or if you loved a sport but couldn't play it?"
- Ask Ss to predict what they will hear.
- Tell Ss to listen for the answers to the questions. Play the audio program. Ss listen and take notes.

▶ **B [CD 3, Track 42]**

- Play the audio program again, pausing after each speaker so Ss have time to write.
- Give Ss time to fill in the chart.
- Elicit Ss' answers. Ask Ss to give full sentences.

**C Pair work**

- Ss discuss in pairs. Ask one S to take notes and elicit one or two responses from each pair.

### Answers

Parts A and B:

|  | Mr. Sandberg | Ms. Rowe |
|---|---|---|
| Obstacle | He wanted to study abroad in Italy, but his parents wouldn't help him. | She loves soccer, but she's not very good at playing it. |
| What he/she did | He got two jobs and saved money. | She found a job coaching a kids' soccer league. |
| What he/she learned | He could do anything he wanted if he worked hard enough. | You have to be creative dealing with problems. |

## 6 WORD POWER

**Learning Objective:** discuss personalities using synonyms and antonyms

**A**

- Elicit that the word *antonym* means "opposite."
- Ask Ss to read the words in the box. Elicit or explain that they are adjectives that describe people.
- Ss work individually or in pairs to fill in the blanks. Ss compare answers in pairs.

### Answers

1. rigid
2. timid
3. compassionate
4. unimaginative
5. dependent
6. cynical

- **Option:** Ss decide if the adjectives are positive (*P*) or negative (*N*) (e.g., *cynical* = *N*; *upbeat* = *P*).

**B Group work**

- Explain the task. Ask three Ss to model the conversation.
- Ss work in groups. They associate words or ideas with the adjectives in part A. Tell Ss to make whatever associations come to mind.

! For more practice with antonyms, try **Vocabulary Tennis** – download it from the website.

## 7 DISCUSSION

**Learning Objective:** give opinions about inspirational quotes using present perfect and simple past

**A**

- Explain the task. Explain that *inspirational sayings* are bits of advice or positive thoughts that people say to motivate others. Ss choose the quote that inspires them most.

### Vocabulary

**pleasure:** a feeling of happiness or enjoyment
**bridge:** something that connects two things

**B Group work**

- Ask two Ss to model the conversation.
- Ss discuss the quotes in small groups. Encourage Ss to think of at least one reason why they find it inspirational.

### End of Cycle 1

See the Supplementary Resources chart at the beginning of this unit for additional teaching materials and student activities related to this Cycle.

# 8 CONVERSATION

**Learning Objective:** use various verb tenses in a conversation about goals

## ▶ A [CD 3, Track 43]

- Books closed. Elicit or explain that it is common for an interviewer to ask about a job applicant's five-year plan.
- Ask questions to stimulate discussion on goals and accomplishments:

  Where do you see yourself in five years? What do you hope to have accomplished by then?

- Set the scene. Mike is at a job interview. He is talking to an interviewer about what he's achieved and what his plans are.
- Tell Ss to listen to find out how Mike feels about his past, present, and future. Play the audio program. (Note: Ss will have to make inferences.) Elicit ideas.

- Write these questions on the board:

  What has Mike achieved in the last few years? What hasn't he achieved? What two things does he hope he'll have accomplished in five years?

- Play the audio program again. Ss listen and answer the questions. (Answers: He developed a successful app. He hasn't gotten the job, yet. He hopes to have developed many successful apps and to have seen more of the world.)
- Books open. Ss check their answers by reading the conversation.

## B *Class activity*

- Explain the task. Read the focus questions.
- Use the questions for a class discussion.

# 9 GRAMMAR FOCUS

**Learning Objective:** use the future perfect and *would like to have* to describe goals

## ▶ [CD 3, Track 44]

- Play the audio program. Ss listen and read or repeat.
- Review how to form the various structures. Elicit rules and example sentences from Ss.

### *Talking about possible future accomplishments*

**1.** the future perfect (*will have* + past participle)

What do you hope you'<u>ll have learned</u> in the next five years?

I hope (that) I'<u>ll have learned</u> how to cook.

**2.** *would like to have* + past participle

What <u>would you like to have accomplished</u> in the next five years?

I'<u>d like to have bought</u> my own home.

I'<u>d like to have seen/made</u> . . .

### A

- Explain the task.
- Ss complete the sentences individually.
- Ss write four statements about the future. Go around the class and spot-check Ss' answers. Decide if they need more practice with the tenses.

- For more practice with past and future tenses, play **True or False?** – download it from the website. Ss talk about their accomplishments.

## B *Pair work*

- Explain the task. Ask two Ss to read the model conversation.
- Ss discuss their answers in pairs and compare goals. Encourage students to give more information and to ask questions.

- For another way to practice the tenses, try the **Substitution Dialog** – download it from the website. Ss use the Conversation on page 109.

## 8 CONVERSATION  Where do you see yourself?

A  Listen and practice.

**Interviewer:** Tell me a bit more about yourself. What's your greatest accomplishment?

**Mike:** I think my most important accomplishment was the development of a mobile app during my internship last summer.

**Interviewer:** And did you manage to finish the project?

**Mike:** Yes, I was able to deliver the app before the end of my internship, and it has already received lots of positive reviews from customers.

**Interviewer:** That's interesting. And where do you see yourself in five years?

**Mike:** Well, I know your company already hires remote workers, and that's one of my goals for the future. So, five years from now, I hope I'll be working from my laptop in some tropical country . . . a true digital nomad.

**Interviewer:** I see. And what do you hope you'll have achieved by then?

**Mike:** I'd like to have developed many other successful apps. And I hope I'll have seen more of the world.

B  CLASS ACTIVITY  What do you think of Mike's answers? How would you have answered the interviewer's questions?

## 9 GRAMMAR FOCUS

### Describing goals and possible future accomplishments

| With the future perfect | With *would like to have* + past participle |
|---|---|
| What do you hope you**'ll have achieved**? | **What would you like to have** achieved? |
| I hope I**'ll have seen** more of the world. | I**'d like to have developed** many successful apps. |

GRAMMAR PLUS *see page 147*

A  What are some goals you would like to have accomplished in the future? Complete the sentences.

1. By this time next year, I hope I'll have . . .
2. Three years from now, I'd like to have . . .
3. In 10 years, I'd like to have . . .
4. By the time I'm 60, I hope I'll have . . .

Montreal, Canada

B  PAIR WORK  Compare your sentences. What goals do you have in common?

**A:** By this time next year, I hope I'll have finished my English course.

**B:** Me, too. And I'd like to have spent some time in an English-speaking country, like . . .

## 10 LISTENING My dream career

A Listen to three young people describe their plans for the future. What do they hope they will have achieved by the time they're 30?

| | 1. Hugo | 2. Erin | 3. Danny |
|---|---|---|---|
| What they hope they'll have achieved | | | |
| Their reasons | | | |

B Listen again. Why does each person have his or her specific dream? List one reason for each person.

C **PAIR WORK** Who do you think has the most realistic expectations? the least realistic? Why?

## 11 INTERCHANGE 16 A digital nomad

Are you ready to work remotely? Take a quiz and find out.
Go to Interchange 16 on page 131.

## 12 WRITING A personal statement for an application

A Imagine you are applying to a school or for a job that requires a personal statement. Use these questions to organize your ideas. Make notes and then write a draft.

1. What has your greatest accomplishment been? Has it changed you in any way? How?
2. What are some interesting or unusual facts about yourself that make you a good choice for the job or school?
3. What is something you hope to have achieved 10 years from now? When, why, and how will you reach this goal? Will achieving it change you? Why or why not?

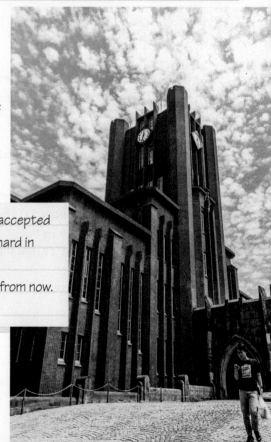

> I think my greatest accomplishment has been getting accepted at a top university in my country. I've always worked very hard in school, and I've had some truly amazing teachers who . . .
>
> There are two things I'd like to have achieved 10 years from now. First, I hope I'll have made a good start on my career . . .

B **GROUP WORK** Share your statements and discuss each person's accomplishments and goals. Who has the most unusual accomplishment or goal? the most realistic? the most ambitious?

# 10 LISTENING

**Learning Objective:** listen for main ideas and take notes about people's future plans and goals

## ▶ A [CD 3, Track 45]

- Read the situation and the question. Present each picture and the person's name in the chart.

- **Option:** Ask Ss to look at the photos and make predictions. Ask: "Which person will probably have a hotel chain? be an architect? be a veterinarian?" Tell Ss to discuss and justify their guesses. Take a poll and write the guesses on the board. Later compare Ss' answers to the chart.

- Tell Ss to listen for what each person hopes to achieve. Play the audio program. Ss listen and take notes.

### Audio script

See page T-182.

---

**TIP**
If Ss have problems understanding the audio program, try to establish where the problem lies. Then replay that segment only.

---

- Elicit Ss' answers around the class. Encourage Ss to give full-sentence answers with the future perfect.

### Answers

Parts A and B:
1. Hugo: he hopes he'll have established his career as a green architect; protecting the environment is important to him, he has lots of ideas for building with recyclable materials, and green building is the architecture of the future
2. Erin: she'll have opened the world's biggest luxury hotel chain; she knows what makes people happy and she knows about luxury
3. Danny: he'll have started working full time as a veterinarian, and by age 35, he'll have his own clinic; he loves animals and they make people happy

## ▶ B [CD 3, Track 46]

- Explain the task. Read the focus question. Play the audio program again and give Ss time to write.

## C *Pair work*

- Ss answer the questions in pairs. Remind them to give reasons for their choices. Ask one S to take notes to share with the class.

- Take a poll and find out who the class thinks have the most and the least realistic expectations.

# 11 INTERCHANGE 16

See page T-131 for teaching notes.

# 12 WRITING

**Learning Objective:** write a personal statement for an application describing accomplishments and goals

## A

- Explain the task. Ss write a personal statement. Ask Ss to read the questions and example.

- Tell Ss to use the questions to guide their writing. Ss first brainstorm accomplishments, then interesting or unusual facts, and finally future goals. Go around the class and give help as needed.

- Ss use their brainstorming notes to compose a first draft.

- **Option:** Assign the task for homework.

## B *Group work*

- Explain the task. Read the focus questions.

- Ss work in small groups. Give Ss the choice of reading the statements silently or of having the writers read their statements to the group. Set a time limit of about ten minutes.

- Ss discuss the questions. Remind Ss to keep the discussion friendly and light-hearted.

- **Option:** Ss role-play an interview for the school or job.

**Learning Objectives:** scan an article about accomplishments and goals and make inferences; identify the meaning of words in context

### A

- Books closed. Ask: "Have you ever known a person that really loves sports?" Elicit Ss' responses around the class.
- Books open. Present the title, picture, and questions. Elicit or remind Ss that *soaring like an eagle* means "to fly high" or "to go after your dreams."
- Ask Ss to scan the article to answer the questions. Tell Ss to raise their hands or look up when they are done. Elicit answers around the class. (Answers: He is from the UK. He participated in ski jumping.)

> **TIP**
> Encourage Ss to use cooperative learning to learn new vocabulary. For example, they can discuss the meaning of the new words in groups.

### B

- Explain the task. Read the questions aloud.
- Ss complete the task individually or in pairs.
- Go over answers with the class.
- Elicit or explain any remaining new vocabulary.

**Vocabulary**
**pretty:** quite, but not extremely
**plenty:** a lot
**make it big:** become very successful or famous
**matter:** be important
**downhill:** towards the bottom of a hill or slope
**elsewhere:** in or to another place
**switch:** change
**hurdle:** a problem or difficulty
**poor eyesight:** unable to see well
**goggles:** special glasses that fit close to your face to protect your eyes
**against all the odds:** in spite of something being very unlikely

**Answers**
1. pretty rarely
2. his weight and his poor eyesight
3. He finished last.

### C

- Explain the task. Ss choose the right answers individually.
- Check the answers with the class.

**Answers**
1. c    2. a    3. c

### D *Pair work*

- Explain the task. Read the focus questions.
- Give Ss time to plan what they want to say.
- Ss discuss the questions with a partner. Remind Ss that they should be able to explain their opinions.
- Ask pairs to share their ideas with the whole class.
- **Option:** Ss role-play. Student A is Michael "Eddie the Eagle" Edwards. Student B is a journalist. Student B interviews Student A about accomplishments and goals. Then Ss change roles and role-play again.

### Hooray! It's the end of the course!

- Take a class vote (through a show of hands or by secret ballot) on whether Ss are interested in doing something special to celebrate the end of the course. If the majority decides they want to, have them make plans:
  1. Brainstorm with the class some ways or ideas on how to celebrate; write them on the board.
  2. Take a class vote on which idea they like the best.
  3. Let a volunteer take over the brainstorming on what kinds of plans the class needs to make and who will be in charge of each part (e.g., choosing the date/place/time; organization of transportation or entertainment; food/drinks; cost per student).
  4. In groups, Ss plan certain parts of the celebration.
  5. Ss celebrate!

## End of Cycle 2

See the Supplementary Resources chart at the beginning of this unit for additional teaching materials and student activities related to this Cycle and for assessment tools.

**A** Scan the article. Where is Michael Edwards from? What sport did he participate in?

# Soaring Like an Eagle

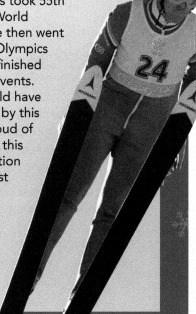

Being highly successful in any field is pretty rare. It takes a combination of natural talent, luck, determination, and plenty of outside support for someone to make it big in sports, entertainment, or business. But what if competing is all that matters to you, whether you are likely to succeed or not? This was the goal of Michael "Eddie the Eagle" Edwards, and that he reached that goal was an amazing achievement.

Born in the U.K. in 1963, Michael was an enthusiastic downhill skier whose dream was to compete for Britain in world-class competitions. He would have liked to represent his country in the 1984 Winter Olympics, but there was a large number of downhill competitors, and Edwards didn't qualify. Seeing his chance elsewhere, he switched to ski jumping. Ski jumping training didn't cost nearly as much, and there was no competition for a place on the British team.

But a number of hurdles could have meant the end of Edwards's dream. He weighed more than most competitors, which put him at a disadvantage. He had no financial support for his training. Poor eyesight meant that he had to wear glasses under his goggles – not a good thing when they steamed up at high altitudes. But he didn't let any of this discourage him. He saw himself as a true lover of the sport who simply wanted the chance to compete. Winning wasn't the point. Having the opportunity to try was all he cared about. And nothing could stop him from trying.

In the end, Edwards took 55th place in the 1987 World Championships. He then went on to the Calgary Olympics in 1988, where he finished last in both of his events. Many athletes would have been embarrassed by this result, but he is proud of his achievement to this day. His determination to persevere against all the odds made him a global hero, and in 2016, the inspiring film *Eddie the Eagle* was made about his life.

**B** Read the article. Answer the questions.

1. According to the writer, how often do people become highly successful?
2. What were two disadvantages that Michael Edwards overcame?
3. How did Edwards do at the Calgary Olympics in 1988?

**C** Choose the correct answers.

1. Michael Edwards chose ski jumping instead of downhill skiing because . . .
   - **a.** it took less skill.
   - **b.** the equipment was cheaper.
   - **c.** there were few British ski jumpers.

2. After the Calgary Olympics, Edwards . . .
   - **a.** felt he had reached his goal.
   - **b.** was embarrassed by his results.
   - **c.** was glad it was over.

3. Michael Edwards is outstanding because of . . .
   - **a.** his determination to win.
   - **b.** his ability to overcome physical disabilities.
   - **c.** his enthusiasm for the sport.

**D** **PAIR WORK** Would you compete in something if you knew you were likely to lose? Why or why not?

## SELF-ASSESSMENT

How well can you do these things? Check (✓) the boxes.

| I can . . . | Very well | OK | A little |
|---|---|---|---|
| Give recommendations and opinions about rules (Ex. 1) | ☐ | ☐ | ☐ |
| Understand and express opinions, and seek agreement (Ex. 2) | ☐ | ☐ | ☐ |
| Describe qualities necessary to achieve particular goals (Ex. 3) | ☐ | ☐ | ☐ |
| Ask about and describe personal achievements and goals (Ex. 4) | ☐ | ☐ | ☐ |

## 1 DISCUSSION It's the rule.

**A PAIR WORK** What kinds of rules do you think should be made for these places? Talk with your partner and make three rules for each. (Have fun! Don't make your rules too serious.)

office            public pool
a health club     an apartment building

**B GROUP WORK** Join another pair. Share your ideas. Do they agree?

**A:** Office workers should all be required to wear the same outfit.

**B:** That sounds interesting. Why?

**A:** Well, for one thing, people wouldn't need to spend so much money on clothes.

## 2 LISTENING My city

**A** Listen to people give opinions about their city. Check (✓) the correct responses to agree with their statements.

1. ☐ Yes, it should.
   ☐ No, it shouldn't.

2. ☐ Yes, it is.
   ☐ No, it isn't.

3. ☐ Yes, they are.
   ☐ No, there aren't.

4. ☐ Yes, it does.
   ☐ Yes, they do.

5. ☐ Yes, we do.
   ☐ No, we don't.

6. ☐ No, there isn't.
   ☐ Yes, it is.

**B PAIR WORK** Come up with three more opinions about your city with a partner. Ask your classmates and see if they agree or disagree.

**A:** There aren't enough nightlife options for teenagers, are there?

**B:** No, there aren't!

# Progress check

## SELF-ASSESSMENT

**Learning Objectives:** reflect on one's learning; identify areas that need improvement

- Ask: "What did you learn in Units 15 and 16?" Elicit Ss' answers.

- Ss complete the Self-assessment. Explain to Ss that this is not a test; it is a way for them to evaluate what they've learned and identify areas where they need additional practice. Encourage them to be honest, and point out they will not get a bad grade if they check (✓) "a little."

- Ss move on to the Progress check exercises. You can have Ss complete them in class or for homework, using one of these techniques:
  1. Ask Ss to complete all the exercises.
  2. Ask Ss: "What do you need to practice?" Then assign exercises based on their answers.
  3. Ask Ss to choose and complete exercises based on their Self-assessment.

## 1 DISCUSSION

**Learning Objective:** demonstrate one's ability to give recommendations and opinions using passive modals

### A *Pair work*

- Explain the task. Ask Ss to read the list of places.

- Elicit one or two examples of fun rules (e.g., *People should be required to use every machine in a health club.*). Write the examples on the board.

- Ss work in pairs. Ss choose a place and talk about possible rules. Remind Ss to use passive modals.

- Ss choose three rules to tell a group. Ss can memorize their rules or write them down.

### B *Group work*

- Explain the task. Ask two Ss to model the conversation.

- Focus Ss' attention on the picture. Ask Ss what would be the *bad* points of the example rule.

- Each pair joins another pair. Pairs take turns telling and discussing their rules.

- Ask each pair to share the most interesting rule the other pair described.

## 2 LISTENING

**Learning Objective:** demonstrate one's ability to listen to, understand, and use tag questions to ask for agreement

### ▶ A *[CD 3, Track 47]*

- Explain the task.

- Ss work in pairs. They decide what tag question matches each person's opinion.

- Play the audio program as many times as needed. Ss listen and check (✓) the correct response.

#### Audio script

See page T-182.

- Go over answers with the class.

#### Answers

| | |
|---|---|
| 1. Yes, it should. | 4. Yes, it does. |
| 2. No, it isn't. | 5. Yes, we do. |
| 3. No, there aren't. | 6. No, there isn't. |

- **Option:** Play the audio program again. Pause after each question. Ask Ss to repeat the question (a paraphrase is OK).

### B *Pair work*

- Explain the task. Ask two Ss to model the conversation.

- Ss work in pairs to write three opinions with tag questions.

- Ask Ss to read their statements aloud. Elicit answers from the rest of the class.

- **Option:** Ss work in pairs to write tag questions to fit any six answers in part A. Then each pair joins another pair. Pairs take turns reading their questions. The other pair answers.

# 3 DISCUSSION

**Learning Objectives:** demonstrate one's ability to identify qualities necessary to achieve certain goals; assess one's ability to describe challenges

## A *Group work*

- Explain the task. Ask Ss to read the goals and qualities. Elicit or explain any new vocabulary.
- Ask two Ss to model the conversation.
- Give Ss time to think of ideas.
- Ss work in small groups and decide on two qualities for each goal.

## B *Pair work*

- Explain the task. Ask two Ss to model the conversation. Point out that B keeps the conversation going by making a comment and then asking a question.
- Ss work in pairs. Ss take turns making statements and asking follow-up questions.
- Go around the class and note use of gerunds, both correct and incorrect.
- Write your notes on the board. Elicit whether the gerunds are used correctly or not. If not, ask the class to correct them.

# 4 ROLE PLAY

**Learning Objective:** demonstrate one's ability to talk about one's own accomplishments and goals using the present perfect and future perfect

- Explain the task.
- Divide the class into pairs, and assign A/B roles. Student As are going to be interviewed. Student Bs are the interviewers.
- Give Ss time to plan what they are going to say. Student As think of their accomplishments and goals. Student Bs read the interview questions and write two more.

- Ss role-play in pairs.
- Ss change roles and repeat the role play.
- **Option:** Ask Ss to write an article about the interview for an imaginary newspaper. The paragraphs can be posted around the room or turned in for you to check.

# WHAT'S NEXT?

**Learning Objective:** become more involved in one's learning

- Focus Ss' attention on the Self-assessment again. Ask: "How well can you do these things now?"
- Ask Ss to underline one thing they need to review. Ask: "What did you underline? How can you review it?"
- If needed, plan additional activities or reviews based on Ss' answers.

## 3 DISCUSSION  Do you have what it takes?

**A  GROUP WORK**  What qualities are needed if you want to accomplish these goals? Decide on two qualities for each goal.

| Goals | Qualities | | |
|---|---|---|---|
| start your own business | adaptable | dependent | self-sufficient |
| live abroad for a year | compassionate | insensitive | timid |
| make a low-budget movie | courageous | resourceful | unimaginative |
| hike across your country | cynical | rigid | upbeat |

**A:** To start your own business, you need to be resourceful.
**B:** Yeah, and you should be courageous too.

**B  PAIR WORK**  Does your partner have what it takes to accomplish the goals in part A? Interview him or her and find out.

**A:** Do you think you're resourceful?
**B:** Yes, I think so. I'm usually good at solving problems.

## 4 ROLE PLAY  Students' profiles

*Student A:*  Student B is going to interview you for the school website.
Think about your accomplishments and goals.
Then answer the questions.

*Student B:*  You are interviewing Student A for the school website.
Add two questions to the notebook paper below.
Then start the interview.

Change roles and try the role play again.

> What have you managed to accomplish in school?
> What would you like to have achieved by the time you graduate?
>
> Are you happy with your home?
> Do you hope you will move someday?
> Where would you like to live?
>
> Have you been able to accomplish a lot in your career?
> Where do you hope you'll be in 5 years?
> _____
> _____

## WHAT'S NEXT?

Look at your Self-assessment again. Do you need to review anything?

# Interchange activities

## INTERCHANGE 1

**Learning Objective:** speak more fluently about one's personality using relative pronouns *who* and *that*, clauses with *it*, and adverbial clauses with *when*

### A *Pair work*

- Ask: "Have you ever taken a personality quiz in a newspaper or magazine?" If so, ask Ss to describe the quiz (e.g., where they took it, what it was about, whether it seemed accurate).

- Give Ss time to read the quiz individually. Tell Ss to circle unfamiliar words.

- Elicit or explain any new vocabulary.

#### Vocabulary
**put (something) off:** wait until later to do something
**face:** do something even though it is difficult
**avoid:** stay away from something
**give up:** stop doing something because you can't do it
**high achiever:** a person who always likes to be best or first
**cool and steady:** calm and not nervous or excited
**carefree:** not worried about anything

- Explain the task.

- Ss work in pairs. They take turns interviewing each other. Encourage Ss to answer quickly, choosing the answer that fits most situations.

- Then Ss add up their partner's "a", "b", and "c" answers. Ss find their partner's personality type and read it aloud to him or her.

### B *Group work*

- Each pair joins another pair to compare scores. Ss also suggest four characteristics for each of the three personality types in part A.

**INTERCHANGE 1** Personality quiz

A **PAIR WORK** What is your personality type? Take turns using the quiz to interview each other. Then tally your answers and find out which category best describes you.

### What's your **personality** type?

1. **When you fail a test, do you:**
   a. get really upset and decide to try much harder next time?
   b. go over your answers and learn from your mistakes?
   c. not care much about it?

2. **When you work on a big project, do you:**
   a. try to finish it as quickly as possible?
   b. work at it over a long period of time?
   c. put it off as long as possible?

3. **When you do an assignment, do you:**
   a. try to do a first-class job so people will notice?
   b. do it as well as you can without worrying too much?
   c. do only what you must to get it done?

4. **When faced with a difficult challenge, do you:**
   a. look forward to facing it?
   b. worry about dealing with it?
   c. try to avoid it?

5. **Do you think the best way to get the most out of a day is to:**
   a. do as many things as possible?
   b. take your time to get things done?
   c. do only those things you really have to?

6. **When something doesn't work out the way you want it to, do you:**
   a. get angry with yourself and others?
   b. think calmly about what to do next?
   c. give up, because it wasn't important anyway?

7. **When people take a long time to finish something, do you:**
   a. get impatient and do it yourself?
   b. gently ask them to do it more quickly?
   c. let them take their time?

8. **When you are learning a new skill, do you:**
   a. work very hard to master it quickly?
   b. do your best and often ask for help?
   c. take your time and enjoy the learning experience?

9. **If you compare your goals with your friends' goals, do you:**
   a. want to accomplish greater things than they do?
   b. hope to achieve similar things in life?
   c. not care if they set higher goals for themselves than you do?

10. **When people are late for appointments, do you:**
    a. get angry and stressed out?
    b. remember that you are sometimes late, too?
    c. not worry, because you are usually late, too?

11. **When people are talking to you, do you:**
    a. not listen and think about other things?
    b. listen and participate in the conversation?
    c. let them talk and agree with everything they say?

**Scoring**
Count how many a, b, and c answers your partner has. If there are . . .

**mostly a answers:** This person is a high achiever but can get very stressed.

**mostly b answers:** This person is the cool and steady type.

**mostly c answers:** This person is the easygoing or carefree type.

B **GROUP WORK** Compare your scores. Then suggest four characteristics of each personality type.

"A high achiever is the kind of person who . . . . He or she can't stand it when . . ."

- Write the example phrases on the board. Ask Ss to complete them. Elicit phrases for the other two personality types. Write them on the board (e.g., *The cool and steady person is someone who . . . . The person who is easygoing doesn't mind it when . . . .*). Remind Ss to use the language from the Grammar Focus boxes on pages 3 and 6.

- Groups discuss their scores and whether they feel the test was accurate.

- Bring the class back together, and help Ss summarize the scores. Ask how many people had more than six "a" answers? more than seven? more than eight? Then ask about "b" and "c" answers.

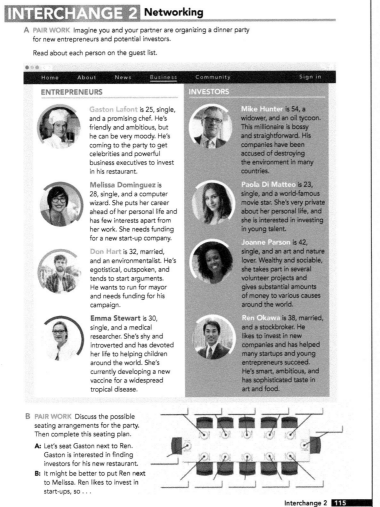

INTERCHANGE 2 Networking

A **PAIR WORK** Imagine you and your partner are organizing a dinner party for new entrepreneurs and potential investors.

Read about each person on the guest list.

**ENTREPRENEURS**

**Gaston Lafont** is 25, single, and a promising chef. He's friendly and ambitious, but he can be very moody. He's coming to the party to get celebrities and powerful business executives to invest in his restaurant.

**Melissa Dominguez** is 28, single, and a computer wizard. She puts her career ahead of her personal life and has few interests apart from her work. She needs funding for a new start-up company.

**Don Hart** is 32, married, and an environmentalist. He's egotistical, outspoken, and tends to start arguments. He wants to run for mayor and needs funding for his campaign.

**Emma Stewart** is 30, single, and a medical researcher. She's shy and introverted and has devoted her life to helping children around the world. She's currently developing a new vaccine for a widespread tropical disease.

**INVESTORS**

**Mike Hunter** is 54, a widower, and an oil tycoon. This millionaire is bossy and straightforward. His companies have been accused of destroying the environment in many countries.

**Paola Di Matteo** is 23, single, and a world-famous movie star. She's very private about her personal life, and she is interested in investing in young talent.

**Joanne Parson** is 42, single, and an art and nature lover. Wealthy and sociable, she takes part in several volunteer projects and gives substantial amounts of money to various causes around the world.

**Ren Okawa** is 38, married, and a stockbroker. He likes to invest in new companies and has helped many startups and young entrepreneurs succeed. He's smart, ambitious, and has sophisticated taste in art and food.

B **PAIR WORK** Discuss the possible seating arrangements for the party. Then complete this seating plan.

**A:** Let's seat Gaston next to Ren. Gaston is interested in finding investors for his new restaurant.

**B:** It might be better to put Ren next to Melissa. Ren likes to invest in start-ups, so . . .

Interchange 2 **115**

# INTERCHANGE 2

**Learning Objective:** speak more fluently about people's personalities using comparisons

## A *Pair work*

- Explain the task. Elicit or explain that professional party planners plan and organize important social events. Ss read about the guests. In part B, Ss will decide where these people should sit at the dinner party.

- Ss can read individually, or pairs can take turns reading paragraphs aloud. Encourage Ss to work together to figure out new vocabulary. If they can't figure out a word, they can check with you, another pair, or a dictionary.

- Elicit or explain any new vocabulary.

## Vocabulary

**guest list:** a list of people that are coming to a party
**ambitious:** having a strong desire for success
**moody:** often unfriendly because of feeling angry or unhappy
**computer wizard:** an expert on computers

**startup:** a small business that has just been started
**environmentalist:** a person who is interested in or studies the environment and who tries to protect it from being damaged by human activities
**egotistical:** considering yourself to be better or more important than other people
**outspoken:** always saying what one thinks
**mayor:** a person who is elected or chosen to lead the group who governs a town or city
**introverted:** quiet and shy
**widower:** a man whose wife has died
**tycoon:** a very powerful, rich business owner
**straightforward:** direct
**entrepreneur:** a business owner

## B *Pair work*

- Ask two Ss to model the conversation.

- Explain the task. Ss will complete a seating plan. They should seat guests next to people they will want to talk to and will not argue with.

- Ss work with the same partner from part A. Tell Ss to make brief notes about their decisions.

- Each pair joins another pair to compare seating plans, or call on a few pairs to present their plans to the class. Ss should give reasons for their choices.

- *Option:* Ss form new pairs and work out seating plans for groups of students in the class or for a group of popular celebrities. Ss share their plans with another pair.

# INTERCHANGE 3

**Learning Objective:** speak more fluently about borrowing and lending using modals, *if* clauses, and gerunds

## A

- Books closed. As a warm-up and review, go around the classroom asking different Ss if you can borrow certain items (e.g., *a pen, watch, comb, dictionary, moped*):

  T: Can I borrow your watch for a minute?

  S1: Well, OK, but please be careful with it.

  T: I will. Thanks. And, uh, Joe, don't you come to school on a moped?

  S2: Yes, I do.

  T: Would you mind lending it to me for about half an hour? I need to take a book back to the library.

  S2: Gee, I'm sorry, but . . .

- Books open. Explain the task. Make sure Ss understand that *be willing* means "would agree to do something."

- Discuss the pictures. Ask different Ss to read the names of the items. Point out the same two choices under each item.

- Give Ss time to decide whether they would be willing to lend each item. Remind Ss to check one of the two boxes. Tell Ss to make sure they have at least three items checked they would rather not lend.

## B *Class activity*

- Ask two Ss to model the conversation. Elicit additional responses to the request about borrowing the tent. Write them on the board.

- Ss go around the class and take turns asking to borrow the items in part A.

- Set a time limit of ten minutes. Tell Ss to make requests of as many classmates as possible. Remind Ss to give the reason they need to borrow each item.

Also remind Ss to give an excuse for not lending something.

- Tell Ss to check off each item that someone agrees to lend them.

- Go around and note problems Ss are having. When time is up, go over the most common problems with the class.

## C *Class activity*

- Find out who was able to borrow every item or the most items on the list.

- *Option:* If time allows, ask Ss to give quick summaries of who was willing to lend them each item and why they needed to borrow it.

## INTERCHANGE 4 Spin a yarn

A **GROUP WORK** Place a pen on the CHARACTER spinner and spin it. Repeat for the other two spinners. Use the elements the pen points at to create a story. If the pen points at YOU DECIDE, you can use any element from that spinner, or you can invent a new one.

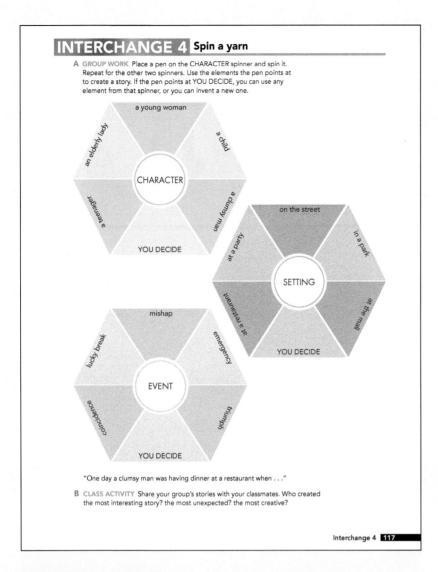

"One day a clumsy man was having dinner at a restaurant when . . ."

B **CLASS ACTIVITY** Share your group's stories with your classmates. Who created the most interesting story? the most unexpected? the most creative?

# INTERCHANGE 4

**Learning Objective:** discuss, take notes on, and complete a story using various past tenses

## A Group work

- Explain the task. Ss will select a character, a setting, and an event from the spinners. Remind Ss that there is no story yet. They will have to create a story with the elements.
- Divide Ss into small groups. Ss come up with a story orally and one S can take notes.
- Elicit or explain any new vocabulary.

- Give groups about five minutes to think of a story. Walk around the class, helping with structure and vocabulary when needed.

### Vocabulary
**clumsy:** awkward in movement or manner

## B Class activity

- Explain the task. Ss share their stories with the class. Ask groups to ask follow-up questions and make comments.
- **Option**: Have each group act out their story for the class.
- After all the stories are told, vote on which was the most creative, interesting, or unexpected.

# INTERCHANGE 5

**Learning Objective:** speak more fluently about customs using *if* and *when* clauses

## A

- Focus Ss' attention on the pictures. Ask: "What do you think is happening in each picture? Do you have similar customs in your country?"

- Model the task by reading the first two or three statements. Ss check those statements that apply to their own culture.

- Ss work individually. Remind Ss to mark any words they are unable to guess from context. They can consult their dictionary after they finish. Go around the class and give help as needed.

- Elicit or explain any new vocabulary.

> **Vocabulary**
> **hug:** put your arms around someone and hold them
> **drop by:** visit someone without calling first
> **split the cost:** share the bill
> **bargain:** ask a store owner to lower the price of something

## B *Pair work*

- Ss compare their answers with a partner. They discuss how many answers are the same and how many are different.

- **Option:** If your background is different from your Ss', go through the chart and explain which statements are true in your own culture.

---

INTERCHANGE 5 **Cultural dos and taboos**

A These statements are generally true about cultural behavior in the United States. Check (✓) those that are true in your country.

### COMPARING CULTURES
*Find out how typical U.S. cultural behavior compares to yours!*

#### SOCIALIZING AND ENTERTAINING

- [ ] **1.** It's OK to start a conversation with a stranger when waiting in line.
- [ ] **2.** People aren't supposed to stand too close to other people when talking.
- [ ] **3.** In general, people wear outdoor shoes inside their homes.
- [ ] **4.** Women often hug their female friends when they meet.
- [ ] **5.** It's not acceptable to ask people how much money they earn or how much they paid for things.
- [ ] **6.** People are expected to call or text before dropping by a friend's house.
- [ ] **7.** When invited to someone's home for dinner, people usually arrive on time.
- [ ] **8.** Gifts are normally opened when received.

#### DINING AND SHOPPING

- [ ] **9.** It's acceptable to eat while walking outside.
- [ ] **10.** Eating is not allowed while shopping in most stores.
- [ ] **11.** When eating in a restaurant, friends either split the cost of the meal or take turns paying.
- [ ] **12.** It's the custom to leave a 15–20% tip for the server at a restaurant.
- [ ] **13.** It's uncommon to bargain when you buy things in stores.

#### AT WORK AND SCHOOL

- [ ] **14.** In an office, people usually prefer to be called by their first names.
- [ ] **15.** Students remain seated when the teacher enters the classroom.

#### DATING AND MARRIAGE

- [ ] **16.** It's acceptable for most teenagers to go out on dates.
- [ ] **17.** People usually decide for themselves who they will marry.

B **PAIR WORK** Compare your answers with a partner. For the statements you didn't check, why do you think these behaviors are different in your country?

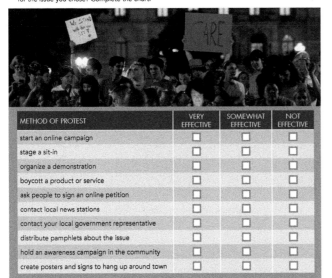
# INTERCHANGE 7

**Learning Objective:** speak more fluently about social, public, and environmental problems using infinitive clauses and phrases

## A

- Explain the task. Give Ss time to read the issues.
- Elicit or explain any new vocabulary.

### Vocabulary

**genetically modified:** Genetically modified plants or animals have had some of their genes (= parts of cells which control particular characteristics) changed.
**shut down:** stop something from operating

- Ask Ss to check (✓) the issue that would upset them the most.
- Books closed. Ask the class to brainstorm methods of protest. You may need to give them one or two examples (use ones from the book) to get them started. Write Ss' ideas on the board.

## B  Group work

- Books open. Ask Ss to go around the class to find other Ss who chose the same issue. Limit group size to five Ss.
- Read the methods of protest in the chart. Note which are the same as the ones the class came up with. Answer any vocabulary questions.

- Groups complete the chart. Encourage Ss to discuss their ideas before checking (✓) any boxes. Explain that it is OK for Ss in the same group to check different columns.
- Ask the groups to plan a strategy for their protest. Tell the groups to choose one S as a secretary to write down the group's ideas.

## C  Class activity

- Group secretaries take turns sharing their group's solutions for each problem. Let other Ss ask questions.
- **Option:** Take a quick class poll (through a show of hands) to find out which solution is the best for each problem.

# INTERCHANGE 6A/B

**Learning Objective:** speak more fluently about problems using *keep* and *need* with gerunds and *need* with passive infinitives

## A

- Books closed. Read the subtitle, "Home makeover." Ask Ss to guess what it means. (It describes the process of suddenly improving the appearance of a home.)

- Divide the class into pairs, and assign A/B roles. Tell Student As to look at Interchange 6A, and Student Bs to look at Interchange 6B.

- Give Ss a few minutes to look at their picture. Tell Ss not to look at their partner's picture.

> **TIP**
> In information gaps, have partners sit across from each other so they can't see their partner's page. Alternatively, have them sit back-to back.

- Explain the task. Say that the instructions and conversations in Interchange 6A and 6B are the same; only the pictures have slight variations.

- Model the task. Write these examples on the board:

  *What's wrong in the living room?*

  *The walls need painting.* OR

  *The walls need to be painted.*

- Then Ss work individually. Set a time limit of about five minutes to list all the problems they see. Ss may use their dictionaries if necessary.

- Go around the class and give help as needed.

---

## INTERCHANGE 6A   Home makeover

### Student A

**A** Look at this apartment. What's wrong with it? First, make a list of as many problems as you can find in each room.

**B** PAIR WORK  Compare your lists. What are the similarities and differences in the problems between your picture and your partner's picture? Ask questions to find the differences.

**A:** What's wrong in the bedroom?
**B:** Well, in my picture, the walls need painting. And the curtains . . .
**A:** Oh, really? In my picture, the walls need to be painted, but the curtains . . . , and the window . . .

Interchange 6a **119**

## INTERCHANGE 6B Home makeover

### Student B

A Look at this apartment. What's wrong with it? First, make a list
of as many problems as you can find in each room.

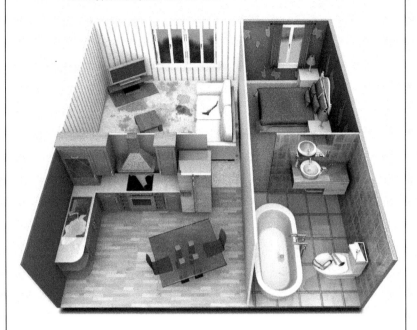

B PAIR WORK Compare your lists. What are the similarities and
differences in the problems between your picture and your
partner's picture? Ask questions to find the differences.

A: What's wrong in the bedroom?
B: Well, in my picture, the walls need painting. And the curtains . . .
A: Oh, really? In my picture, the walls need to be painted, but the
curtains . . . , and the window . . .

## B Pair work

- Explain the task. Ask two Ss
to read the conversation. Ss
find similarities and differences
between the two pictures.

- Ss work in pairs. Set a time limit
of ten minutes. Tell Ss to make
notes on their lists about which
problems are the same (S) and
which are different (D).

### TIP
To check answers at the end of
an information gap activity, it's
helpful to ask Ss to exchange
answers, rather than going
over the answers as a class.

## Possible Answers

Two problems are the same (S)
and nine are different (D):
*What's wrong in the
living room?*
**Student A and Student B:**
The couch has a hole in it./The
couch needs to be fixed./The
couch needs fixing./The couch
needs to be repaired./The
couch needs repairing. (S)
**Student A:** The wallpaper is
peeling./The wallpaper needs
to be replaced./The wallpaper
needs replacing. (D)
**Student B:** The carpet is
dirty./The carpet needs to be
cleaned./The carpet needs
cleaning. (D)

*What's wrong in the kitchen?*
**Student A:** 1. The refrigerator
door is falling off./The
refrigerator needs to be
repaired./The refrigerator
needs repairing. (D) 2. The
stove is damaged./The stove
needs to be repaired./The
stove needs repairing./The
stove doesn't work. (D)
**Student B:** The sink is
leaking./The sink has a leak./
The sink needs to be fixed./
The sink needs fixing. (D)
*What's wrong in the bedroom?*
**Student A and Student B:**
The paint on the wall is
coming off./The walls need
to be painted./The walls
need painting. (S)
**Student A:** 1. The curtains are
torn./The curtains need to be
repaired./The curtains need
repairing. (D) 2. There's a crack
in the window./The window is
broken./The window needs to
be fixed./The window needs
fixing. (D)
*What's wrong in the
bathroom?*
**Student A:** The pipe is
leaking./The pipe needs to be
fixed./The pipe needs fixing. (D)
**Student B:** The toilet is
broken./The toilet needs to
be repaired./The toilet needs
repairing. (D)

# INTERCHANGE 8

## A

- Explain the task. Ask Ss to read the items in the chart. Focus Ss' attention on the first item on the list. Ask: "What are some artistic skills you can think of? Which one would you like to learn? Why?" (e.g., *paint, draw, sing, act, play an instrument*)

- To help Ss get started, model like this:

  T: I'd like to learn how to paint because. . . . Let's see, . . . I've always wanted to learn how to paint. I think it must be nice to be able to capture a moment. And how about you, Cecilia?

  S: Well, some day I'd really like to learn how to draw . . .

- Ss complete the chart individually. Tell Ss to use dictionaries to check spelling and pronunciation of new words they want to use.

- Go around the class and give help as needed.

## B *Class activity*

- Explain the task. Ss ask three classmates for help choosing between things in part A. Ss write classmates' preferences and reasons in the chart. Ask two Ss to model the conversation.

- Write these additional questions on the board:

  *Would you rather . . . ?*

  *Would you prefer to . . . ?*

- Ss go around the class interviewing one another. Remind Ss to include the interviewees' names in the chart. Set a time limit of about ten minutes.

- Go around the class and give help as needed. Make sure Ss are completing their charts.

## C *Group work*

- Give Ss some time to read over their charts and decide who gave the best advice.

- Ask Ss to tell the class about the best advice they received. In a large class, Ss can do this activity in groups.

---

## INTERCHANGE 8 Making choices

**A** Complete this chart with information about yourself. Add one idea of your own.

| | | |
|---|---|---|
| two artistic skills I'd like to develop | | |
| two adventurous activities I'd like to try | | |
| two dances I'd like to learn | | |
| two topics I'd like to learn more about | | |
| two foreign languages I'd like to speak | | |
| two dishes I'd like to learn how to cook | | |
| two volunteer activities I'd like to do | | |
| two courses I'd like to take | | |
| two sports I'd like to play | | |
| two skills I'd like to improve | | |
| two _____ | | |

**B** CLASS ACTIVITY Ask three classmates to help you choose between the things you wrote down in part A. Write their recommendations in the chart.

| Names: | | | |
|---|---|---|---|
| artistic skill | | | |
| adventurous activity | | | |
| dance | | | |
| topic | | | |
| foreign language | | | |
| dish | | | |
| volunteer activity | | | |
| course | | | |
| sport | | | |
| skill | | | |

**A:** I don't know if I'd rather be a graffiti artist or a painter. What do you think?
**B:** Hmm. If I were you, I'd choose graffiti.
**A:** Why graffiti and not painting?
**B:** Well, that kind of street art is very popular nowadays. You could become famous, and . . .

**C** GROUP WORK What are your final choices? Who gave the best advice? Why?

122 Interchange 8

---

## INTERCHANGE 9 Absolutely not!

**A** PAIR WORK Read these comments made by parents. Why do you think they feel this way? Think of two arguments to support each point of view.

Our son wants to go camping with his friends alone. No way!

Our son wants to stay out until midnight. We think that's way too late.

Our son wants to have his hair cut at an expensive salon. What's wrong with a regular barber?

Our son wants a new laptop, but we just bought him one last year. He can have it upgraded instead.

If our daughter insists on having her nails done at a nail salon, she has to pay for it herself.

Our daughter wants to sleep over at friends' houses on weeknights. Absolutely not!

Our daughter wants to have her ears pierced. We're totally against that.

Regardless of the color, we refuse to let our daughter get her hair dyed.

**A:** Why do you think they won't let their son go camping with his friends?
**B:** They probably think he's too young to take care of himself.
**A:** They may also feel that he . . .

**B** PAIR WORK Discuss the parents' decisions. Think of arguments for and against their points of view.

**A:** I think the parents should let their son go camping with his friends.
**B:** Why?
**A:** Because his friends are going, and he needs to learn to take care of himself.
**B:** I don't agree. I think he's too young. Teens shouldn't travel without an adult.

**C** CLASS ACTIVITY Take a vote. Do you agree with the parents? Why?

Interchange 9 **123**

---

# INTERCHANGE 9

**Learning Objective:** speak more fluently about having things done and giving reasons using causatives

## A *Pair work*

- Explain the task. Ss will think of reasons to support the parents' views.
- Give the class some time to read the parents' comments.
- Elicit or explain any new vocabulary.

### Vocabulary

**barber:** a person who cuts men's hair and boys' hair
**have (a computer) upgraded:** get new, up-to-date software or hardware for a computer
**have (a person's) nails done:** get one's fingernails painted at a salon
**have (a person's) ears pierced:** have holes made in one's ears for earrings
**get (a person's) hair dyed:** have one's hair colored

- Model the conversation with a S. Complete the conversation with an idea of your own. Then elicit other ideas from the class.

- Ss work in pairs. Remind Ss to think of two arguments to support each point of view. Ss can take notes of their arguments.
- Each pair joins another pair to compare arguments.
- **Option:** Ask Ss to share their arguments with the whole class or write them on the board.

## B *Pair work*

- Ss think of arguments for and against the decisions. Elicit some examples from the first situation.
- Ss work with the same partner from part A. Ss can take notes of their arguments.
- Each pair joins another pair to compare arguments.
- **Option:** Ask Ss to share their arguments with the whole class or write them on the board.
- **Option:** Ss suggest additional parent-child conflicts for the class to discuss and vote on.

## C *Class activity*

- For each issue, have a class vote on whether Ss agree with the parents. Tally the results on the board for each issue.
- Ask Ss to share their reasons with the class.

# INTERCHANGE 10A/B

**Learning Objective:** speak more fluently about world events using time references

## A *Pair work*

- Find out if any Ss know what *history buff* means. (Answer: A history buff is someone who is interested in and knows a lot about history.)

- Explain the task.

- Divide the class into pairs, and assign A/B roles. Ask the Student As to look at Interchange 10A and the Student Bs to look at Interchange 10B. Tell Ss not to look at their partner's page.

- Tell Ss to read their ten quiz questions. Ask Ss to mark any words they don't understand or know how to pronounce. Point out that the quiz answers are in boldface.

- Now gather all the Student As and quietly explain any words they ask about. Ss may also use their dictionary.

- Elicit or explain any new vocabulary.

> ### Vocabulary
> *Student A's quiz (Interchange 10A)*
> **play:** perform as a character in a play or movie
> **activist:** a person who believes strongly in political or social change and takes part in activities such as public protests
> **penicillin:** a type of antibiotic (= a medicine that kills bacteria)
> **thermometer:** a device used for measuring temperature, especially of the air or in a person's body

- Model rising and falling intonation patterns in these questions of choice. If needed, ask the Student As to repeat quietly in unison. Remind Ss not to give away the correct answer by reading it differently from the other choices.

---

### Student A

**A** PAIR WORK Ask your partner these questions. Put a check (✓) if your partner gives the correct answer. (The correct answers are in **bold**.)

Frida Kahlo

Volkswagen Beetle

Alexander Fleming

## TEST YOUR KNOWLEDGE

1. What nationality was the painter Frida Kahlo? Was she Spanish, **Mexican**, or Argentinian?

2. What was the first capital of the United States? Was it **Philadelphia**, New York, or Boston?

3. Who played 007 in the first James Bond movie? Was it Roger Moore, **Sean Connery**, or Pierce Brosnan?

4. When was the first Volkswagen Beetle car built? Was it during the 1920s, **1930s**, or 1940s?

5. Was Nelson Mandela a political activist from India, Angola, or **South Africa**?

6. When did the British return Hong Kong to China? Was it in 1987, **1997**, or 2007?

7. Who discovered penicillin? Was it **Alexander Fleming**, Charles Darwin, or Albert Einstein?

8. Which planet is closest to the sun? Is it Mars, **Mercury**, or Venus?

9. What Italian astronomer invented the thermometer in 1593? Was it Copernicus, Isaac Newton, or **Galileo**?

10. When did the first MP3 player hit the market in the US? Was it in 1978, 1988, or **1998**?

**B** PAIR WORK Answer the questions your partner asks you. Then compare quizzes. Who has the most correct answers?

**C** CLASS ACTIVITY Think of three more questions of your own. Can the rest of the class answer them?

---

- Now work with the Student Bs in the same way.

- Elicit or explain any new vocabulary.

> ### Vocabulary
> *Student B's quiz (Interchange 10B)*
> **former:** of an earlier time, but not now
> **magnetic compass:** an instrument used for finding direction as it always points to magnetic north
> **lightbulb:** a rounded glass container with a thin thread of metal inside that produces light when an electric current goes through it

- Set a time limit of about five minutes. Ask the Student As to start. Tell Ss to read each question on their quiz to their partner. Remind Ss to write a check (✓) when their partner gives the correct answer.

---

## B *Pair work*

- Now tell the Student Bs to ask their quiz questions. Again, set a time limit of about five minutes.

- When time is up, tell pairs to total their quiz scores to find out who had more correct answers.

- Designate these winners as the class "history buffs."

- Remind Ss to tell their partners the correct answers to items they missed.

## C *Class activity*

- Explain the task. Ss write three more questions of choice like those in the quiz.

- Ss work individually or in pairs to write the questions.

- Ss take turns standing up and asking their questions. Tell Ss to call on others who have raised their hands to answer the questions.

# INTERCHANGE 11

**Learning Objective:** speak more fluently about regrets and hypothetical situations using *would have* + past participle and *if* clauses in the past

## A *Pair work*

- Explain the task. Read the example sentences as a model. Then show Ss how to toss a coin and advance on the game board.
- Ss play the board game in pairs.
- Go around the class and give help as needed.

## B *Class activity*

- Read the questions. Elicit or explain the meaning of *responsible* (showing good judgment, making good choices) and *rebellious* (refusing to follow rules).
- Give Ss time to plan what they will say.
- Ask different Ss if they were responsible or rebellious when they were younger. Encourage Ss to give examples to explain why, and encourage other Ss to ask follow-up questions.
- **Option:** Ss write a paragraph about things people have done that they wish they could change. Ss hand it in to you to check, or ask Ss to share their paragraphs in pairs or small groups.

---

## INTERCHANGE 11   Good choices, bad choices

**A PAIR WORK** Play the board game. Follow these instructions.

1. Use small pieces of paper with your initials on them as markers.
2. Take turns tossing a coin:

 Move one space.

**Heads**

 Move two spaces.

**Tails**

3. When you land on a space, tell your partner what is true. Then say how things would have been different. For example:
"When I was younger, I didn't pay attention in class. If I had paid attention in class, I would have gotten better grades."
OR
"When I was younger, I paid attention in class. If I hadn't paid attention in class, I wouldn't have won a scholarship."

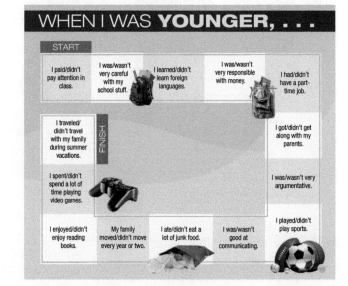

**WHEN I WAS YOUNGER, . . .**

| | |
|---|---|
| START | |

- I paid/didn't pay attention in class.
- I was/wasn't very careful with my school stuff.
- I learned/didn't learn foreign languages.
- I was/wasn't very responsible with money.
- I had/didn't have a part-time job.
- I got/didn't get along with my parents.
- I traveled/didn't travel with my family during summer vacations.
- FINISH
- I spent/didn't spend a lot of time playing video games.
- I was/wasn't very argumentative.
- I enjoyed/didn't enjoy reading books.
- My family moved/didn't move every year or two.
- I ate/didn't eat a lot of junk food.
- I was/wasn't good at communicating.
- I played/didn't play sports.

**B CLASS ACTIVITY** Who was responsible when they were younger? Who was rebellious? Tell the class.

## INTERCHANGE 12 Advertising taglines

**A** PAIR WORK Read these popular slogans for products.
Match the slogans with the product types.

| | | |
|---|---|---|
| 1. Think different. _____ | | **a.** a soft drink |
| 2. Unforgettable happens here. _____ | | **b.** a technology company |
| 3. Taste the feeling. _____ | | **c.** an amusement park |
| 4. All the news that's fit to print. _____ | | **d.** sports clothing |
| 5. Impossible is nothing. _____ | | **e.** potato chips |
| 6. Bet you can't eat just one. _____ | | **f.** a daily newspaper |
| 7. Stay with us, and feel like home. _____ | | **g.** fast food |
| 8. Reach out and touch someone. _____ | | **h.** automobiles |
| 9. I'm loving it. _____ | | **i.** a game console |
| 10. Live in your world. Play in ours. _____ | | **j.** a hotel |
| 11. Melts in your mouth, not in your hands. _____ | | **k.** a telephone service |
| 12. Built for the road ahead. _____ | | **l.** chocolate candy |

**B** PAIR WORK Join another pair and compare your answers.
Then check your answers at the bottom of the page.

**C** GROUP WORK Think of a product. Then create your own slogan for it and
add a logo. Consider a design and colors that are suitable for the product.

**A:** Any ideas for a product?
**B:** What about an online store for used toys?
**C:** Sounds interesting. Let's try to think of some catchy slogans.
**D:** How about, "Play again!"? Or maybe . . .

**D** CLASS ACTIVITY Present your slogans to the class.
Who has the catchiest ones?

1. b; 2. c; 3. a; 4. f; 5. d; 6. e; 7. j; 8. k; 9. g; 10. i; 11. l; 12. h

# INTERCHANGE 12

**Learning Objective:** speak more
fluently about advertising products
using various ways of giving reasons

- Note: Bring some magazine ads
  to class, or ask Ss to bring some.

## A Pair work

- Focus Ss' attention on the
  title. Elicit or explain that
  *tagline* means "a short,
  easily remembered phrase
  that a company uses in its
  advertisements."

- Explain the task. Ss try to identify
  what product each slogan is
  advertising.

- Ask Ss to read the slogans. Point
  out that these slogans are real.
  All have been used to advertise
  well-known companies or
  products.

- Ss work in pairs to match the
  slogans to the products. Set
  a time limit of about seven
  minutes. Go around the class and
  give help as needed.

## B Pair work

- Ss join another pair and compare
  their answers. Then they check
  their answers at the bottom of
  the page.

## C Group work

- Explain the task. Elicit or explain
  that a logo is a picture, design, or
  symbol that represents a business
  or helps to advertise a product.

- Have four Ss read the example
  conversation.

- Tell Ss they can imagine the
  slogan, logo, and any other
  design elements as part of a print
  ad, an online ad, or some other
  type of ad.

- **Option:** To further prepare Ss
  for the task, show examples of
  advertisements with slogans
  and logos. Have Ss discuss
  what they like and dislike about
  them, including the design and
  colors, or have Ss find their own
  examples outside of class and
  bring them in for discussion.

- Ss work in groups to think of a
  product, slogan, and logo. One
  S records the group's ideas. Go
  around the room and offer help
  as needed.

## D Class activity

- Groups present their ideas to the
  class. Give Ss time to practice
  their presentations. Encourage Ss
  to draw a mock-up or draft of the
  advertisement.

- Each S presents a different aspect
  of their advertising campaign (the
  slogan, the logo, and the design
  and color of the ad). Encourage
  Ss to ask for more information.

- **Option:** The class votes on
  the business that is (1) most
  interesting and (2) most likely to
  succeed.

# INTERCHANGE 13

**Learning Objective:** speak more fluently when speculating about what might have happened using past modals

## A Pair work

- Explain the task. Focus Ss' attention on the pictures. Ask two Ss to model the conversation.
- Write questions on the board to help guide Ss:

  Describe the situation or event
  What's the situation in the first picture?
  What is the man doing?
  Guess what happened
  What do you think happened?
  Why did it happen?
- Read the useful expressions.
- Ss work in pairs. Ss take turns talking about what might have happened.
- **Option:** After pairs discuss the pictures, they choose one of the pictures and write a paragraph about what might have happened.
- Set a time limit of about ten minutes. Go around the class and give help as needed.
- **Option:** If pairs have trouble coming up with vocabulary, brainstorm with the whole class on each picture. Write Ss' suggestions on the board.
- **Option:** Ss can do part A for homework. In the next class, pairs compare their interpretations and stories. Then they choose the four most interesting ones for part B.

## B Group work

- Explain the task.
- Each pair joins another pair. Ss take turns telling their stories for each picture.

- Groups choose their favorite story about each situation. Groups practice telling their stories.
- Groups then take turns sharing their best stories around the class.
- **Option:** Take a quick class poll to find out which group's story was the best or most creative for each picture.

---

A PAIR WORK What do you think might have happened in each situation? Talk about possibilities for each situation.

Pete made a fortune in the stock market. He's now working at a burger joint.

Lisa went grocery shopping yesterday afternoon. She hasn't come back home yet.

Jim was the best salesperson in the company for the past 10 years. He just got fired.

Clara had everything ready for her dream vacation in Tahiti. She's on the bus heading to her parents' home.

**A:** Maybe Pete made some bad investments.
**B:** Or he might have spent all his money on . . .

**useful expressions**

Maybe he/she was . . . when . . .      He/She may have . . . when . . .
Or perhaps he/she was . . .            He/She might have . . .

B GROUP WORK Agree on one explanation for each situation and share it with the class. Be ready to answer any questions.

## INTERCHANGE 14 Celebrities

**A** Prepare to play a guessing game.

- Write the names of five celebrities on slips of paper. Names can include people in history, movie stars, singers, politicians, writers, etc.
- Mix all the slips in a bag.

Adele

**B** GROUP WORK Each player takes turns picking a slip for his or her group to guess.

**A:** She's a celebrity who was born in London.
**B:** Is she a movie star?
**A:** No, she's a singer and songwriter who has a beautiful voice.
**C:** I think I know the answer. It's . . .

**C** CLASS ACTIVITY Which celebrities were easier to guess? Which were the most difficult? Who gave the best clues?

Nico Rosberg

Sofia Vergara

Albert Einstein

Sally Ride

# INTERCHANGE 14

**Learning Objective:** speak more fluently about the entertainment industry using defining and non-defining relative clauses

## A

- Explain the task.
- Give Ss time to think of famous people and write five names on individual slips of paper.
- Go around the class and give help as needed.

## B Group work

- Explain the task. Ask three Ss to model the conversation.
- Ss work in groups and try to guess the celebrity.

- Set a time limit of about seven minutes. Go around the class and listen in. Note any problems, especially with relative clauses.
- When time is up, write some of the problems on the board. Elicit Ss' help in correcting them.

## C Class activity

- Explain the task. Give groups time to plan what to say.
- Ask the groups to present their ideas to the class. Ask Ss to share the speaking.
- **Option:** Each group writes up a description of celebrities to hand to you.

# INTERCHANGE 15

**Learning Objective:** speak more fluently about and give different opinions on offenses and punishments using passive modals

## A *Pair work*

- Explain the task. Ask Ss to read the offenses and possible punishments. Ask two Ss to model the conversation.

- Elicit or explain any new vocabulary.

> ### Vocabulary
> **disabled:** having an illness, injury, or condition that makes it difficult to do the things that other people do
> **permit:** an official document that allows you to do something
> **fare:** the price that you pay to travel on an aircraft, train, bus, etc.
> **pickpocketing:** stealing things from people's pockets
> **seat belt:** a strap that you fasten across your body when traveling in a vehicle

- *Option:* Ask Ss to identify as many offenses as they can in the pictures.

- Ss work in pairs to discuss ideas and complete the chart. Tell Ss they can write more than one punishment if they wish.

## B *Group work*

- Explain the task. With the class, brainstorm useful phrases for agreeing, disagreeing, and convincing others.

- Each pair joins another pair. Remind Ss to use a variety of expressions. Go around the class and give help as needed.

- *Option:* Ask groups to come to an agreement on one punishment for each offense. Then ask groups to share a few punishments they agreed on. Ask Ss to explain their choices. This can be done as a written assignment and turned in.

---

## INTERCHANGE 15 On the wrong side of the law

**A** PAIR WORK What punishment (if any) is appropriate for each possible offense? Why? Complete the chart.

| OFFENSE | PUNISHMENT |
|---|---|
| 1 parking in a disabled parking space without a permit | _____ |
| 2 posting offensive comments online | _____ |
| 3 leaving trash on public streets | _____ |
| 4 riding the subway without paying the fare | _____ |
| 5 failing to clean up after a dog | _____ |
| 6 pickpocketing | _____ |
| 7 scratching paint off another person's car | _____ |
| 8 crossing the street in dangerous places | _____ |
| 9 driving without a seat belt | _____ |
| 10 riding a motorcycle without a helmet | _____ |
| 11 hacking into a government computer | _____ |
| 12 _____ (your own idea) | _____ |

**A:** What do you think should be done about people who park in a disabled parking space without a permit?
**B:** They should be required to pay a heavy fine because it may cause problems for people with disabilities.
**A:** I don't agree. I think . . .

**B** GROUP WORK Join another pair of students. Then compare and discuss your lists. Do you agree or disagree? Try to convince each other that you are right!

> **possible punishments**
> receive a warning
> spend some time in jail
> pay a fine
> lose a driver's license
> get suspended
> do community service
> be banned from using the Internet

## INTERCHANGE 16 A digital nomad

**A** PAIR WORK Interview your partner. Would he or she be a happy digital nomad?

### Is the digital nomad lifestyle **right for you?**

Do you dream of working from a beach paradise? Are you ready to hit the road and make a living while traveling the world? Take our quiz and find out.

1. Have you traveled much before?
   - ☐ **a.** I've traveled with my family in our country.
   - ☐ **b.** Not yet, but I hope to have seen more of the world by the time I retire.
   - ☐ **c.** I've been to a couple of continents and seen some amazing things!

2. Are you resourceful?
   - ☐ **a.** Well, I can always count on my friends to help me when I need it.
   - ☐ **b.** Yes, and I can always find the answers I need on the Internet.
   - ☐ **c.** Yes, I'm good at finding opportunities everywhere.

3. When you pack for a long weekend, what do you take with you?
   - ☐ **a.** A big suitcase with everything I might need – you never know what might happen.
   - ☐ **b.** A small bag with the essentials.
   - ☐ **c.** A toothbrush and a change of clothes. I like to travel light.

4. Are you flexible and adaptable?
   - ☐ **a.** I try to be, but I don't always succeed.
   - ☐ **b.** Yes, if you give me some time to adjust.
   - ☐ **c.** Definitely. I've managed to survive under the most challenging circumstances.

5. Have you ever traveled all by yourself?
   - ☐ **a.** Of course not. I need family and friends around at all times.
   - ☐ **b.** No, but I think I'd enjoy it.
   - ☐ **c.** Sure. I often take vacations alone. It's a great opportunity to meet new people.

6. Are you ready to give up a fixed salary?
   - ☐ **a.** No. I need to have a steady income. It's important for me to know how much money I'll be making for the next 12 months.
   - ☐ **b.** Well, I can live on very little money – I've done it before.
   - ☐ **c.** I'm good at managing my money, and I always have some savings, so that wouldn't be a problem.

7. Are you self-motivated, or do you depend on others to get you going?
   - ☐ **a.** I need to know that my boss or my teachers are around and that I can count on them.
   - ☐ **b.** It depends. If I'm really involved with a project, I'm more independent; if not . . .
   - ☐ **c.** Definitely. I know what I have to do, and I always finish the work on time.

8. How do you feel about changes?
   - ☐ **a.** I like to have a set routine. Changes make me feel uncomfortable.
   - ☐ **b.** They can be a challenge, but they also help me grow.
   - ☐ **c.** Changes are always welcome. New things inspire and motivate me.

**Score the quiz by counting the number of a's, b's, and c's.**
**Mostly a's:** The digital nomad lifestyle is not for you.
**Mostly b's:** You'd probably be happy being a digital nomad, but you might miss your current life.
**Mostly c's:** What are you doing here? Go grab your things and hit the road!

**B** CLASS ACTIVITY Compare your findings. Who is ready to become a digital nomad?

- Tell pairs to take turns interviewing each other and check (✓) one of the three choices for each question.
- Go around the class and give help as needed.

**B** *Class activity*

- Explain the task.
- Conduct a class poll. Ask Ss to read each question and the three choices while you count how many Ss (through a show of hands) checked each one.

# INTERCHANGE 16

**Learning Objective:** speak more fluently about the challenges, frustrations, and rewards of accomplishments using the present perfect and simple past

## A *Pair work*

- Explain the task. Read the title. Elicit or explain that a "digital nomad" is a person that earns money off the Internet, so they can work from anywhere in the world. Ask Ss to read the survey questions.
- Elicit or explain any new vocabulary.

### Vocabulary

**retire:** leave your job and stop working, usually because you are old
**resourceful:** good at finding ways to solve problems
**count on my friends:** be confident that you can depend on someone
**pack:** put your things into bags
**succeed:** achieve a goal
**steady:** at a regular or constant rate
**savings:** money that you have saved, usually in a bank
**self-motivated:** able and willing to work without being told what to do

# Grammar plus

### 1 Relative pronouns  /page 3/

> ■ A relative pronoun – *who* or *that* – is necessary when the pronoun is the subject of the clause: I'd love to meet someone **who/that** is considerate. (NOT: I'd love to meet ~~someone is considerate.~~)
>
> ■ When the pronoun is the object of the clause, *who* and *that* can be left out: I'd like a roommate **who/that** I have a lot in common with. OR I'd like a roommate I have a lot in common with.

Complete the conversation with *who* or *that*. Put an ✗ when a relative pronoun isn't necessary.

**A:** Ana, have you met Clint – the guy __✗__ Laurie is going to marry?

**B:** Oh, Clint and I have been friends for years. In fact, I'm the one _____ introduced Laurie and Clint.

**A:** Do you think they're right for each other?

**B:** Definitely. They're two people _____ have a lot in common – but not *too* much.

**A:** What does that mean?

**B:** Well, you don't want a partner _____ doesn't have his or her own interests. Couples _____ do everything together usually don't last very long.

**A:** I guess you're right, but the opposite isn't good, either. My last girlfriend was someone _____ I had nothing in common with. She wasn't the kind of girl _____ I could talk to easily.

**B:** Well, you can talk to *me* easily. . . .

### 2 *It* clauses + adverbial clauses with *when*  /page 6/

> ■ In sentences with an *it* clause + an adverbial clause with *when*, the word *it* refers to and means the same as the adverbial clause with *when*. The *it* in these sentences is necessary and cannot be left out: I hate **it when** people talk on a cell phone in an elevator. (NOT: ~~I hate when~~ people . . .) **It** bothers me **when** people talk on a cell phone in an elevator. (NOT: ~~Bothers~~ me when people . . .)

Rewrite the sentences using the words in parentheses.

1. I can't stand it when people call me before 8:00 A.M. (it really bothers me)
   *It really bothers me when people call me before 8:00 a.m.*

2. It upsets me when I don't have enough time to study for an exam. (I hate it)
   _____

3. I don't mind it when friends talk to me about their problems. (it doesn't bother me)
   _____

4. I don't like it when I forget a co-worker's name. (it embarrasses me)
   _____

5. It makes me happy when my friends send me videos. (I love it)
   _____

6. I hate it when I have to wait for someone. (it upsets me)
   _____

## 1 Gerund phrases  page 9

> ■ A gerund phrase as a subject takes a singular verb: Taking care of children **is** a rewarding job. (NOT: Taking care of children ~~are~~ a rewarding job.)
>
> ■ There are some common verb + preposition expressions (for example, *dream about, feel like, talk about, think about*) and adjective + preposition phrases (for example, *good/bad at, excited by/about, interested in, tired of, used to*) that are followed by a gerund: I'm **thinking about looking for** a new job. I'm **tired of working** long hours.

Complete the sentences with the correct gerund forms of the verbs in the box.

| ✓ become | have | make | stand | travel |
|----------|------|------|-------|--------|
| change | learn | solve | take | work |

1. My brother's very interested in _____*becoming*_____ a flight attendant. He dreams about _____ to new places.
2. I'm excited about _____ a Japanese class next semester. I enjoy _____ languages.
3. You wouldn't like _____ in a restaurant. You'd get tired of _____ on your feet throughout the long shifts!
4. Our teacher is very good at _____ problems. Maybe she should think about _____ careers to become a guidance counselor.
5. _____ a living as a photographer could be challenging. _____ an impressive portfolio is really important to attract new clients and employers.

## 2 Comparisons  page 11

> ■ When making general comparisons with count nouns, use *a/an* + singular noun or no article + plural noun: **A pilot** earns more than **a flight attendant**. **Pilots** earn more than **flight attendants**. (NOT: ~~The~~ pilots earn more than ~~the~~ flight attendants.)

Make comparisons with the information below. Add articles and other words when necessary.

1. architect / more education / hairstylist
   An architect needs more education than a hairstylist.
2. college professor / earn more / elementary school teacher

   _____
3. nurses / worse hours / psychiatrists

   _____
4. working as a police officer / as dangerous / being a firefighter

   _____
5. taxi driver / not as well paid / electrician

   _____
6. being a tour guide / less interesting / being an actor

   _____

# UNIT 3

## 1 Requests with modals, *if* clauses, and gerunds  page 17

> ■ Use the simple past form – not the gerund or simple present form – after *if* with *Would you mind . . . ?* and *Would it be all right . . . ?*: **Would you mind if I used** your car? **Would it be all right if I used** your car? (NOT: Would you mind if I ~~using~~ your car? OR Would it be all right if I ~~use~~ your car?)

Read the situations. Then complete the requests.

1. You want to borrow a friend's underwater camera for a diving trip.
   **A:** I was wondering if <u>I could borrow your underwater camera.</u>
   **B:** Sure. That's fine. Just please be careful with it.

2. You want to use your roommate's computer.
   **A:** Is it OK _____
   **B:** You can use it, but please don't drink near it.

3. Your neighbor has a car. You need a ride to class.
   **A:** Would you mind _____
   **B:** I'd be glad to. What time should I pick you up?

4. You want your brother to help you move on Saturday.
   **A:** Can you _____
   **B:** I'm sorry. I'm busy all weekend.

5. You would like a second piece of your aunt's cherry pie.
   **A:** Would it be all right _____
   **B:** Yes, of course! Just pass me your plate.

6. You want to borrow your cousin's red sweater.
   **A:** Could you _____
   **B:** Sorry. I don't like it when other people wear my clothes.

## 2 Indirect requests  page 20

> ■ In indirect requests with negative infinitives, *not* comes before – not between – the infinitive: Could you tell Allie **not to be** late? (NOT: Could you tell Allie ~~to not be~~ late?)

Complete the indirect requests. Ask someone to deliver the messages to Susie.

1. Are you busy this weekend?          →  Could <u>you ask Susie if she's busy this weekend?</u>
2. Do you want to hang out with me?     →  Can _____
3. Text me.                            →  Can _____
4. Do you know my address?             →  Can _____
5. Don't forget to write.              →  Could _____
6. What are you doing Saturday?        →  Can _____
7. Do you have plans on Sunday?        →  Could _____

# UNIT 4

## 1 Past continuous vs. simple past  *page 23*

> ■ Verbs for non-actions or states are rarely used in the past continuous: I **wanted** to stop, but I couldn't. (NOT: I ~~was wanting~~ to stop . . . )

Circle the best forms to complete the conversations.

**1. A:** How **did you break** / **were you breaking** your arm?
   **B:** It's a crazy story! Ramon and I **rode** / **were riding** our bikes in the park when a cat **ran** / **was running** out in front of me. I **went** / **was going** pretty fast, so when I **tried** / **was trying** to stop, I **went** / **was going** off the road and **fell** / **was falling**.
   **A:** That's terrible! **Did you go** / **Were you going to** the hospital after it **happened** / **was happening**?
   **B:** Yes. Luckily, we **weren't** / **weren't being** too far from City Hospital, so we **went** / **were going** there.

**2. A:** You'll never guess what **happened** / **was happening** to me this morning!
   **B:** What?
   **A:** Well, I **brushed** / **was brushing** my teeth when suddenly the water **went** / **was going** off. I **had** / **was having** toothpaste all over my mouth, and I couldn't wash it off.
   **B:** So what **did you do** / **were you doing**?
   **A:** Fortunately, I **had** / **was having** a big bottle of water in the refrigerator, so I **used** / **was using** that water to rinse my mouth.

## 2 Past perfect  *page 25*

> ■ Use the past perfect to show that one past action happened before another past action:
> I **wasn't able to** pay for lunch because I **had left** my wallet at work.
> PAST ——————X————————————X———— NOW
>      had left my wallet      wasn't able to pay

Combine the two ideas into one with a past event and a past perfect event. Use *when* or *because*.

**1.** The museum closed. A thief stole a famous painting earlier.
   *The museum closed because a thief had stolen a famous painting earlier.*

**2.** We finished cleaning the house. Then our guests arrived.

_____

**3.** Someone robbed my house yesterday. I left the window open.

_____

**4.** There was no food in the house. We forgot to stop at the supermarket.

_____

**5.** I called her three times. She finally answered.

_____

**6.** I knew about the problem. Your brother told me about it.

_____

## 1 Noun phrases containing relative clauses   page 31

■ The relative pronoun *who* or *that* can be left out in noun phrases as subjects and as objects. These four sentences have exactly the same meaning: One thing I'd be nervous about is getting lost. One thing that I'd be nervous about is getting lost. Getting lost is one thing I'd be nervous about. Getting lost is one thing that I'd be nervous about.

Answer the questions using the words in parentheses. Write each sentence two ways. Leave out the relative pronouns.

*If you went to live in a foreign country, . . .*

**1.** Who would you miss a lot? (person: my best friend)

**a.** One person I'd miss a lot is my best friend.

**b.** My best friend is one person I'd miss a lot.

**2.** What would you be very interested in? (things: the food and the music)

**a.** _____

**b.** _____

**3.** What would you be worried about? (something: not understanding the customs)

**a.** _____

**b.** _____

**4.** Who would you stay in touch with? (people: my brother and sister)

**a.** _____

**b.** _____

**5.** What would you feel insecure about? (thing: speaking a new language)

**a.** _____

**b.** _____

## 2 Expectations   page 33

■ Use the base form of a verb – not the gerund – after these expressions for expectations: *be the custom to, be supposed to, be expected to, be acceptable to*: It's the custom to **arrive** a little late. (NOT: It's the custom to ~~arriving~~ a little late.)

Complete the sentences with the clauses in the box.

it's not acceptable to show up without calling first.
it's the custom for them to sit across from each other.
you're expected to reply within a few days.
you're supposed to bring a gift.
✓ you're supposed to shake his or her hand.

**1.** When you meet someone for the first time, _you're supposed to shake his or her hand._

**2.** When a friend sends you an email, _____

**3.** If you want to visit someone, _____

**4.** If you invite a married couple to dinner, _____

**5.** When you go to a birthday party, _____

## 1 Describing problems 1 　page 37

> ■ The simple past and the past participle of regular verbs are the same: I **chipped** the vase. The vase is **chipped**. BUT Many irregular verbs have different simple past and past participle forms: I **tore** my jacket. My jacket is **torn**.

Complete the conversations with the correct words from the box.

| are stained | has a dent | ✓ have a tear | is broken | is scratched |
|---|---|---|---|---|
| has a chip | has a stain | is a hole | is leaking | some damage |

1. **A:** Oh, no! These jeans _____*have a tear*_____ in them.
   **B:** And they _____, too.
2. **A:** This table has _____ on top.
   **B:** I know. The wood _____ because my son drags his toy cars on it.
3. **A:** Why are you drinking out of that glass? It _____ in it.
   **B:** Oh, I didn't see it. That's why it _____.
4. **A:** Someone hit my car today. Look! The door _____ in it.
   **B:** I see that. Your back light _____, too.
5. **A:** I bought this blouse yesterday, but I have to take it back. There _____ in it.
   **B:** It's really cute, but that's not the only problem. It _____ on it, too.

## 2 Describing problems 2 　page 39

> ■ Use the past participle – not the present participle or gerund – with passive forms: The oven needs to be **fixed**. (NOT: The oven needs to be ~~fixing~~.)

**A** Complete the conversation with the verbs in parentheses.
Use *need* + passive infinitive in A's lines and *need* + gerund in B's lines.

**A:** Look at this place! A lot of work _____*needs to be done*_____ (do) before we move in.
**B:** You're not kidding. Let's make a list. First, the walls _____*need painting*_____ (paint).
**A:** Right. And the windows _____ (wash). Add the rug to your list:
　　 It really _____ (clean). Do you think it _____ (dry-clean)?
**B:** No, I think we can do it ourselves. It _____ (shampoo).
　　 We can rent a machine for that.
**A:** And what about the ceiling fan? I think it _____ (replace).
　　 Fans aren't too expensive.
**B:** OK. I've added it to the list. And what should we do with all this old furniture?
**A:** It _____ (throw out)! I think the landlord should take care of that, though.

**B** Complete the blog with the correct form of *keep* and the verb in parentheses.

I _____*keep having*_____ (have) technical problems. My computer _____ (crash), and my printer _____ (jam). I have to _____ (put) a new battery into my mouse because it _____ (die). The letters on my keyboard _____ (stick), too. I _____ (think) things will get better, but they just _____ (get) worse. Time for some new electronics!

# UNIT 7

### 1 Passive with prepositions  page 45

■ The prepositions *by, as a result of, because of, though,* and *due to* have similar meanings. They are used in sentences that describe cause and effect; they introduce the cause.

Match phrases from each column to make sentences. (More than one answer may be possible.)

| Subject | Effect | Cause |
|---|---|---|
| **1.** The environment | is being contaminated due to | improper disposal of medical waste. |
| **2.** Our soil | is being harmed by | deforestation to make paper products. |
| **3.** Infectious diseases | are being endangered due to | hybrid cars. |
| **4.** Many different species | has been affected because of | the use of pesticides on fruits and vegetables. |
| **5.** Our air quality | has been reduced as a result of | the destruction of their habitats. |
| **6.** Smog pollution | have been spread through | climate changes like global warming. |

### 2 Infinitive clauses and phrases  page 47

■ The form of *be* that follows the first infinitive must agree with the subject:
The best way to reduce pollution **is** to improve public transportation.
BUT The best ways to reduce homelessness **are** to build more public housing and provide free health care.

**A** Match the phrases.

**1.** What are the best ways to make __*e*__
**2.** And the best way to do that is _____
**3.** The best ways to reduce _____
**4.** One way to improve _____
**5.** Another way to make _____

a. people safer is to make the air healthier.
b. to create a larger police force.
c. people's quality of life is to help them feel safe.
d. air pollution are to ban cars and control industry.
e. this city a better place to live?

**B** Complete the conversation with the sentences above.

**A:** _What are the best ways to make this city a better place to live?_
**B:** Well, _____
**A:** That's right. _____
**B:** I agree. _____
**A:** Yes. Good air quality is key. _____
**B:** Maybe it's time to share our ideas with the mayor. Get out your phone.

# UNIT 8

## 1 *Would rather* and *would prefer* page 51

> ■ In negative statements with *would rather* and *would prefer*, the word *not* comes after the verbs: I**'d rather not**/I**'d prefer not** to take any courses this semester. (NOT: I ~~wouldn't rather~~/I ~~wouldn't prefer~~ to . . .)

Write questions and responses using the words in parentheses.

**1. A:** _Would you prefer to take classes during the day or at night?_
   (prefer / take classes / during the day / at night)
**B:** _____
   (rather / take classes / at night)

**2. A:** _____
   (rather / study / business / education)
**B:** _____
   (prefer / become / a teacher)

**3. A:** _____
   (prefer / sign up for / an art course / a computer course)
**B:** _____
   (prefer / not / take / any classes this semester)

**4. A:** _____
   (rather / take up / an individual sport / a team sport)
**B:** _____
   (rather / not / take up / either)

## 2 *By* + gerund to describe how to do things page 53

> ■ In negative sentences that express comparison with *by* + gerund and *but*, *not* comes before *by*: A good way to improve your accent is **not by watching** TV **but by talking** to native speakers. In negative sentences with *by* that give advice without a comparison, *not* comes after *by*: A good way to improve your accent is **by not imitating** non-native speakers.

Combine the two ideas into one sentence using *by* + gerund.

**1.** You can build your vocabulary. Write down new words and expressions.
   _One way to build your vocabulary is by writing down new words and expressions._
**2.** There is a good way to improve your accent. You can mimic native speakers.
   _____
**3.** Students can improve their listening skills. They can listen to English-language podcasts.
   _____
**4.** Hardworking students improve their grammar. They don't repeat common mistakes.
   _____
**5.** You can become fluent. Don't translate everything. Try to think in English.
   _____
**6.** You can become a good conversationalist. Don't just talk with others.
   Talk to yourself when you're alone, too.
   _____

**1 Get or have something done** page 59

> ■ Sentences with *get/have* + object + past participle are passive. BUT Don't use any form of *be* before the past participle: Where can I **have** my watch **fixed**? (NOT: Where can I have my watch ~~be~~ fixed?)

Rewrite the statements as questions with *Where can I get/have . . . ?*
Then complete B's answers with the information in parentheses.

**1.** I want to have someone shorten these pants.
   **A:** _Where can I have these pants shortened?_
   **B:** _You can have them shortened at Tim's Tailoring._ (at Tim's Tailoring)

**2.** I need to get someone to repair my computer.
   **A:** _____
   **B:** _____ (at Hackers Inc.)

**3.** I need to have someone prepare my taxes.
   **A:** _____
   **B:** _____ (by my accountant)

**4.** I'd like to get someone to cut my hair.
   **A:** _____
   **B:** _____ (at Beauty Barn)

**5.** I need to have someone paint my apartment.
   **A:** _____
   **B:** _____ (by Peter the Painter)

**2 Making suggestions** page 61

> ■ Use the base form of a verb – without *to* – after *Maybe you could . . .* and *Why don't you . . . ?*: Maybe you could **join** a book club. (NOT: Maybe you could ~~to~~ join a book club.) Why don't you **join** a book club? (NOT: Why don't you ~~to~~ join a book club?)

Complete the conversations with the correct form of the verbs in parentheses.

**A:** I'm having trouble meeting people here in the city. Any ideas?

**B:** I know it's hard. Why don't you _____ (join) a gym? That's usually a good place to meet people. Or maybe you could _____ (take) a class at the community college.

**A:** What about _____ (check out) the personal ads? Do you think that's a good way to meet people?

**B:** I wouldn't recommend doing that. People never tell the truth in those ads. But it might be a good idea _____ (find) a sports team. Have you thought about _____ (play) a team sport – maybe baseball or volleyball?

**A:** I'm not very good at most sports, but I used to play tennis.

**B:** There you go! One option is _____ (look up) tennis clubs in the city and see which clubs have teams people can join.

**A:** Now, that's a great idea. And I could always use the exercise!

## 1 Referring to time in the past  page 65

> - Use *since* with a particular time: The UN has been in existence **since** 1945.
>   Use *for* with a duration of time: The UN has been in existence **for** about the last 70 years.
> - Use *in* and *during* with a specific period of time: Rock 'n' roll became popular **in/during** the 1950s.
> - Use *from* and *to* to describe when something began and ended: World War II lasted **from** 1939 **to** 1945.

Complete the conversation with the words in the box. (Use some of the words more than once.)

| ago | during | for | from | in | since | to |
|-----|--------|-----|------|-----|-------|-----|

**A:** Hey, Dad. Did you use to listen to the Beatles?

**B:** Of course. In fact, I just listened to one of their records a few days _____*ago*_____.
Do you realize that the Beatles's music has influenced other musicians _____ over 50 years? They were the greatest!

**A:** Well, I just found some interesting information about them. I'll read it to you: "The Beatles were a well-known British band _____ the 1960s. They performed together _____ 10 years – _____ 1960 _____ 1970. _____ 2003, the Beatles released *Let it Be*, even though one of the original members had been dead _____ 1980 and another had died _____ 2001. The original album had been recorded _____ 1969 and was in the studio safe _____ 34 years before the new, remixed album was released."

**B:** That *is* interesting. It's pretty amazing that people have listened to the Beatles _____ both the twentieth and the twenty-first centuries, isn't it?

## 2 Predicting the future with *will*  page 67

> - In sentences referring to time, the preposition *by* means "not later than." Don't confuse *by* with *within*, which means "some time during." Use *by* with points in time; use *within* with periods of time: **By** 2050, we will have eliminated starvation around the world. (NOT: ~~Within~~ 2050, . . .) **Within** the next five years, people will have invented mobile phone apps for nearly everything! (NOT: ~~By~~ the next five years, . . .)

Circle the correct verb forms to complete the conversation.

**A:** What do you think you **will do / will be doing** five years from now?

**B:** I'm not sure. Maybe I **will get / will have gotten** married by then. How about you?

**A:** I **will be finishing / will have finished** medical school, so I **will be doing / will have done** my internship five years from now.

**B:** So you **won't be living / won't have lived** around here in five years, I guess. Where do you think you **will live / will have lived**?

**A:** Wherever I get my internship.

## 1 Time clauses  page 73

> ■ Use the past perfect in the main clause with *until* and *by the time*. This shows that one of the past events happened before the other: Until I got my driver's license, I **had** always **taken** public transportation. By the time I got my driver's license, all of my friends **had** already **gotten** theirs.

Circle the correct time expression to complete each sentence.

1. After / (Until) I traveled overseas, I hadn't known much about different cultures.
2. After / **Before** I got a full-time job, I had to live on a very limited budget.
3. **By the time** / **Once** I finished high school, I had already taken three college courses.
4. **As soon as** / **Before** I left for college, my mother turned my room into her office.
5. **Once** / **Until** I left home, I realized how much my family meant to me.
6. **By the time** / **The moment** you have a child, you feel totally responsible for him or her.

## 2 Expressing regret and describing hypothetical situations  page 75

> ■ Conditional sentences describing hypothetical situations often refer to both the present and the past:
> If I**'d finished** college, I**'d have** a better job now.
>   past              present
> (NOT: If I'd finished college, I'd ~~have had~~ a better job now.)

A Write sentences with *should (not) have* to express regret about each person's situation.

1. Sarah was very argumentative with her teacher, so she had to stay after school.
   *Sarah shouldn't have been argumentative with her teacher.*
2. Ivan didn't save up for a car, so he still has to take public transportation.

3. Jon was very inactive when he was in college, so he gained a lot of weight.

4. Lisa didn't stay in touch with her high school classmates, so now she has very few friends.

5. Tony didn't study Spanish in school, so he's not bilingual now.

B Rewrite your sentences in part A, changing them to hypothetical situations.

1. *If Sarah hadn't been argumentative with her teacher, she wouldn't have had to stay after school.*
2. 

3. 

4. 

5.

## 1 Describing purpose  page 79

> ■ Don't use *for* immediately before an infinitive: **To have** a successful business, you need a lot of luck. (NOT: ~~For~~ to have a successful business, you need a lot of luck.)

**A** Complete the sentences with *in order to* or *in order for*.

1. ____In order for____ a supermarket to succeed, it has to be clean and well organized.
2. _____ stay popular, a website needs to be accurate and visually attractive.
3. _____ run a profitable furniture store, it's important to advertise on TV.
4. _____ a restaurant to stay in business, it needs to have "regulars" – customers that come often.
5. _____ establish a successful nail salon, it has to have a convenient location.
6. _____ an online business to survive, it needs to have excellent pictures of the merchandise it's selling.

**B** Rewrite the sentences in part A without *In order*.

1. ___For a supermarket to succeed, it has to be clean and well organized.___
2. _____
3. _____
4. _____
5. _____
6. _____

## 2 Giving reasons  page 81

> ■ *Because* and *since* have the same meaning, and they can begin or end a sentence: **Because/Since** the food is always fantastic, Giorgio's is my favorite restaurant. = Giorgio's is my favorite restaurant **because/since** the food is always fantastic.
>
> ■ Don't confuse *because* and *because of*. *Because* introduces an adverb clause and is followed by a subject and verb, while *because of* is a preposition and is followed by a noun object: **Because** Giorgio's is so popular, we should get there early. Giorgio's is popular **because of** its food and service.

Circle the correct words to complete the conversation.

**A:** I had to go downtown today **because / because of / due to** I needed to mail a package at the post office. **Due to / For / Since** I was only a few blocks from Main Street, I went over to Martin's. Did you know that Martin's has gone out of business? I'm so upset!

**B:** That's too bad, but I'm not surprised. A lot of family-owned shops are closing **because / because of / since** the construction of shopping malls.

**A:** Yeah, and don't forget about all the megastores that are popping up everywhere. **Because / For / The reason why** people prefer to shop there is to save money. Everyone loves a megastore **because / due to / since** the low prices and the huge selection.

**B:** Not me! I loved Martin's **for / since / the reason that** their beautiful clothes and friendly salespeople. When you were there, you almost felt like family. You'll never get that at a megastore!

### 1 Past modals for degrees of certainty `page 87`

■ Use the past modal *could have* to express possibility. BUT Use *couldn't have* when you are almost 100% sure something is impossible: I suppose he **could have gotten** stuck in traffic, but he **couldn't have forgotten** his own birthday party.

Complete the conversations with past modals *must (not) have, could (not) have,* or *may/might (not) have*. Use the degrees of certainty and the verbs in parentheses. (More than one answer may be possible.)

1. **A:** Yoko still hasn't called me back.
   **B:** She _might not have gotten_ your message. (it's possible – not get)

2. **A:** What's wrong with Steven?
   **B:** Oh, you _____ the news. His dog ran away. (it's almost certain – not hear)

3. **A:** I went to see the Larsens today, but they didn't answer the door.
   **B:** Was their car there? If so, they _____ in the backyard. (it's possible – be)

4. **A:** Fabio said he was going to the party last night, but I didn't see him.
   **B:** Neither did I. He _____ there then. (it's not possible – not be)

5. **A:** I can't find my glasses, but I know I had them at work today.
   **B:** You _____ them at the office. (it's possible – leave)

6. **A:** Marc's new car looks really expensive.
   **B:** Yes, it does. It _____ a fortune! (it's almost certain – cost)

### 2 Past modals for judgments and suggestions `page 89`

■ In advice with *would have*, the speaker means, "If I were you, . . ."

Read each situation and choose the corresponding judgment or suggestion for an alternative past action.

**Situation**

1. Sue forgot her boyfriend's birthday. _b_
2. Tim got a speeding ticket. _____
3. Ruth still hasn't paid me back. _____
4. Bill lied to us. _____
5. I spent an hour making Joe dinner, and he didn't even thank me. _____
6. Carol came over for dinner empty-handed. _____

**Judgment/Suggestion**

a. I wouldn't have lent her money.
b. She should have put it on her calendar.
c. He should have told the truth.
d. He shouldn't have gone over the limit.
e. She should have brought something.
f. I wouldn't have cooked for him.

# UNIT 14

## 1 The passive to describe process _page 93_

■ The modals *have to* and *need to* must agree with the subject; other modals, like *may be*, have only one form: Each character **has to/needs to** be drawn by the animators.

Put the words in the correct order to make sentences.

**1.** overnight / business / A / started / small / isn't / .
  A small business isn't started overnight.

**2.** to / plan / business / a / written / First, / be / has / .
  _____

**3.** research / Next, / done / be / market / should / .
  _____

**4.** needs / competition / to / the / Then / identified / be / .
  _____

**5.** online / ads / posted / be / Classified / may / .
  _____

**6.** work / are / employees / hired / can / start / the / so / Finally, / .
  _____

## 2 Defining and non-defining relative clauses _page 96_

■ Use either *who* or *that* in defining relative clauses about people: A set designer is an artist **who/that** makes important contributions to a theater production. BUT Use only *who* in non-defining relative clauses about people: A set designer, **who** makes important contributions to a theater production, has to be very creative. (NOT: A set designer, ~~that~~ makes . . .)

■ Use commas before and after a non-defining clause: A gossip columnist**,** who writes about celebrities and scandals**,** often gets to go to fabulous parties.

Combine these sentences with *who* or *that*. Add a comma wherever one is necessary.

**1.** A cartoon animator creates animated scenes for movies and games. He or she needs to have a high level of technical know-how.
  A cartoon animator, who needs to have a high level of technical know-how, creates animated scenes for movies and games.

**2.** A screenwriter is a talented person. He or she develops a story idea into a movie script.
  A screenwriter is a talented person that develops a story idea into a movie script.

**3.** Voice-over actors are usually freelancers. They give voice to characters in animated movies and video games.
  _____

**4.** Casting directors choose an actor for each part in a movie. They have usually been in the movie business for a long time.
  _____

**5.** High-budget movies always use big stars. The stars are known around the world.
  _____

**6.** Movie directors are greatly respected. They "make or break" a film.
  _____

## 1 Giving recommendations and opinions  page 101

> ■ *Ought to* has the same meaning as *should*, but it's more formal:
> Traffic signs **ought to** be obeyed. = Traffic signs **should** be obeyed.

A student committee is discussing rules for their school. Complete speaker B's sentences with appropriate passive modals. (More than one answer is possible.)

**1. A:** Students must be required to clean off the cafeteria tables after lunch.

    **B:** I disagree. Students <u>shouldn't be required</u> to do that. That's what the cafeteria workers are paid to do.

**2. A:** Teachers shouldn't be allowed to park in the student parking lot.

    **B:** Why not? Teachers _____ to park wherever a space is available. After all, they're here for us.

**3. A:** A rule has to be made to ban the use of cell phones in school.

    **B:** I don't think a rule _____. Students may need their phones for emergency purposes.

**4. A:** Students mustn't be permitted to use calculators during math exams.

    **B:** Sometimes we _____ to use them, especially when we're being tested on more complicated concepts than simple arithmetic.

**5. A:** Something has got to be done to control the noise in the hallways.

    **B:** Students _____ to talk to each other between classes, though. They aren't disturbing anyone when classes aren't in session.

**6. A:** Teachers must be required to remind students about important exams.

    **B:** That's unnecessary. On the contrary, students _____ to follow the syllabus and check important dates on the course websites.

## 2 Tag questions for opinions  page 103

> ■ Tag questions added to statements in the simple present and simple past use the corresponding auxiliary verb in the tag: You **agree** with me, **don't** you? You **don't agree** with me, **do** you? You **paid** the rent, **didn't** you? You **didn't pay** the electric bill, **did** you?

Check (✓) the sentences if the tag questions are correct. If they're incorrect, write the correct tag questions.

**1.** Food is getting more and more expensive, ~~is it~~? _____<u>isn't it</u>_____

**2.** Supermarkets should try to keep their prices down, shouldn't they? _____✓_____

**3.** People don't buy as many fresh fruits and vegetables as they used to, don't they? _____

**4.** We have to buy healthy food for our children, don't we? _____

**5.** Many children go to school hungry, won't they? _____

**6.** Some people can't afford to eat meat every day, don't they? _____

**7.** We can easily live without eating meat every day, can we? _____

**8.** A lot of people are having a hard time making ends meet these days, haven't they? _____

## 1 Talking about past accomplishments  page 107

> ■ When talking about past accomplishments and including a specific time, use the simple past – not the present perfect: I **was** able to complete my degree last year. (NOT: I've been able to complete my degree last year.)

Complete the sentences about people's accomplishments. Use the verbs in parentheses. (More than one answer is possible.)

**In the last 5 years, Ana . . .**

1. _____managed to finish_____ (finish) college.
2. _____ (pay) all her college loans.
3. _____ (start) her own company.
4. _____ (move) to the city.
5. _____ (make) some new friends.

**In the past year, Bill . . .**

6. _____ (buy) a new car.
7. _____ (take) a vacation.
8. _____ (get) a promotion at work.
9. _____ (learn) to cook.
10. _____ (visit) his grandparents in the south.

## 2 Describing goals and possible future accomplishments  page 109

> ■ When talking about future accomplishments and goals, use *in* to refer to a period of time: I hope I'll find a new job **in** the next two months. Use *by* to talk about a time limit in the future: I hope I'll find a new job **by** the end of September. = I hope I'll find a new job not later than the end of September.

Complete the conversation. Use the verbs in parentheses. (Sometimes more than one answer is possible.)

**Louise:** So, Mike, what do you hope you _will have accomplished_ (accomplish) five years from now?

**Mike:** I hope I _____ (complete) medical school, and I _____ (start) my residence in a good hospital.

**Louise:** What about your personal goals? What _____ (achieve) by then?

**Mike:** Well, I _____ (meet) that special someone, and, maybe, I _____ (get) married by then. What about you? What are your goals?

**Louise:** Well, I hope I _____ (finish) culinary school in the next five years, and I _____ (manage) to work with some famous chef.

**Mike:** Good plan! What about opening your own restaurant?

**Louise:** That will take some more time, but by the time I'm 35, I hope I _____ (open) my own bistro – Chez Louise.

**Mike:** I can hardly wait. I just love your food.

# Grammar plus answer key

## Unit 1

### 1 Relative pronouns
- A: Ana, have you met Clint – the guy **X** Laurie is going to marry?
- B: Oh, Clint and I have been friends for years. In fact, I'm the one **who/that** introduced Laurie and Clint.
- A: Do you think they're right for each other?
- B: Definitely. They're two people **who/that** have a lot in common – but not *too* much.
- A: What does that mean?
- B: Well, you don't want a partner **who/that** doesn't have his or her own interests. Couples **who/that** do everything together usually don't last very long.
- A: I guess you're right, but the opposite isn't good, either. My last girlfriend was someone **X** I had nothing in common with. She wasn't the kind of girl **X** I could talk to easily.
- B: Well, you can talk to *me* easily. . . .

### 2 It clauses + adverbial clauses with *when*
2. I hate it when I don't have enough time to study for an exam.
3. It doesn't bother me when friends talk to me about their problems.
4. It embarrasses me when I forget a co-worker's name.
5. I love it when my friends send me videos.
6. It upsets me when I have to wait for someone.

## Unit 2

### 1 Gerund phrases
1. My brother's very interested in **becoming** a flight attendant. He dreams about **traveling** to new places.
2. I'm excited about **taking** a Japanese class next semester. I enjoy **learning** languages.
3. You wouldn't like **working** in a restaurant. You'd get tired of **standing** on your feet throughout the long shifts!
4. Our teacher is very good at **solving** problems. Maybe she should think about **changing** careers to become a guidance counselor.
5. **Making** a living as a photographer could be challenging. **Having** an impressive portfolio is really important to attract new clients and employers.

### 2 Comparisons
*Answers may vary. Some possible answers:*
2. A college professor earns more than an elementary school teacher.
3. Nurses have worse hours than psychiatrists.
4. Working as a police officer is as dangerous as being a firefighter.
5. A taxi driver isn't as well paid as an electrician.
6. Being a tour guide is less interesting than being an actor.

## Unit 3

### 1 Requests with modals, *if* clauses, and gerunds
*Answers may vary. Some possible answers:*
2. A: Is it OK **if I use your computer?**
   B: You can use it, but please don't drink near it.
3. A: Would you mind **giving me a ride to class?**
   B: I'd be glad to. What time should I pick you up?
4. A: Can you **help me move on Saturday?**
   B: I'm sorry. I'm busy all weekend.
5. A: Would it be all right **if I had another piece of pie?**
   B: Yes, of course! Just pass me your plate.
6. A: Could you **lend me your red sweater?**
   B: Sorry. I don't like it when other people wear my clothes.

### 2 Indirect requests
2. Can you ask Susie if she wants to hang out with me?
3. Can you ask/tell Susie to text me?
4. Can you ask Susie if she knows my address?
5. Could you tell Susie not to forget to write?
6. Can you ask Susie what she's doing on Saturday?
7. Could you ask Susie if she has plans on Sunday?

## Unit 4

### 1 Past continuous vs. simple past
1. A: How **did you break** your arm?
   B: It's a crazy story! Ramon and I **were riding** our bikes in the park when a cat **ran** out in front of me. I **was going** pretty fast, so when I **tried** to stop, I **went** off the road and **fell**.
   A: That's terrible! **Did you go** to the hospital after it **happened**?
   B: Yes. Luckily, we **weren't** too far from City Hospital, so we **went** there.
2. A: You'll never guess what **happened** to me this morning!
   B: What?
   A: Well, I **was brushing** my teeth when suddenly the water **went** off. I **had** toothpaste all over my mouth, and I couldn't wash it off.
   B: So what **did you do**?
   A: Fortunately, I **had** a big bottle of water in the refrigerator, so I **used** that water to rinse my mouth.

### 2 Past perfect
2. We had finished cleaning the house when our guests arrived.
3. Someone robbed my house yesterday because I had left the window open.
4. There was no food in the house because we had forgotten to stop at the supermarket.
5. I had called her three times when she finally answered.
6. I knew about the problem because your brother had told me about it.

## Unit 5

### 1 Noun phrases containing relative clauses
2. a. Two things (that) I'd be very interested in are the food and the music.
   b. The food and the music are two things (that) I'd be very interested in.
3. a Something (that) I'd be worried about is not understanding the customs.
   b. Not understanding the customs is something (that) I'd be worried about.
4. a. Two people (who/that) I'd stay in touch with are my brother and sister.
   b. My brother and sister are two people (who/that) I'd stay in touch with.
5. a. One thing (that) I'd feel insecure about is speaking a new language.
   b. Speaking a new language is one thing (that) I'd feel insecure about.

### 2 Expectations
2. When a friend sends you an email, **you're expected to reply within a few days.**
3. If you want to visit someone, **it's not acceptable to show up without calling first.**
4. If you invite a married couple to dinner, **it's the custom for them to sit across from each other.**
5. When you go to a birthday party, **you're supposed to bring a gift.**

## Unit 6

### 1 Describing problems 1
1. A: Oh, no! These jeans **have a tear** in them.
   B: And they **are stained**, too.
2. A: This table has **some damage** on top.
   B: I know. The wood **is scratched** because my son drags his toy cars on it.
3. A: Why are you drinking out of that glass? It **has a chip** in it.
   B: Oh, I didn't see it. That's why it **is leaking**.
4. A: Someone hit my car today. Look! The door **has a dent** in it.
   B: I see that. Your back light **is broken**, too.

5.  A:  I bought this blouse yesterday, but I have to take it back. There **is a hole** in it.
    B:  It's really cute, but that's not the only problem. It **has a stain** on it, too.

## 2 Describing problems 2

**A**

A:  Look at this place! A lot of work **needs to be done** before we move in.

B:  You're not kidding. Let's make a list. First, the walls **need painting**.

A:  Right. And the windows **need to be washed**. Add the rug to your list: It really **needs to be cleaned**. Do you think it **needs to be dry-cleaned**?

B:  No, I think we can do it ourselves. It **needs shampooing**. We can rent a machine for that.

A:  And what about the ceiling fan? I think it **needs to be replaced**. Fans aren't too expensive.

B:  OK. I've added it to the list. And what should we do with all this old furniture?

A:  It **needs to be thrown out**! I think the landlord should take care of that, though.

**B**

I **keep having** technical problems. My computer **keeps crashing**, and my printer **keeps jamming**. I have to **keep putting** a new battery into my mouse because it **keeps dying**. The letters on my keyboard **keep sticking**, too. I **keep thinking** things will get better, but they just **keep getting** worse. Time for some new electronics!

# Unit 7

## 1 Passive with prepositions

*Answers may vary. Some possible answers:*

2.  Our soil is being contaminated due to the use of pesticides on fruits and vegetables.
3.  Infectious diseases have been spread through improper disposal of medical waste.
4.  Many different species are being endangered due to the destruction of their habitats.
5.  Our air quality has been affected because of deforestation to make paper products.
6.  Smog pollution has been reduced as a result of hybrid cars.

## 2 Infinitive clauses and phrases

**A**

2. b    3. d    4. c    5. a

**B**

B:  Well, **one way to improve people's quality of life is to help them feel safe.**

A:  That's right. **And the best way to do that is to create a larger police force.**

B:  I agree. **Another way to make people safer is to make the air healthier.**

A:  Yes. Good air quality is key. **The best ways to reduce air pollution are to ban cars and control industry.**

B:  Maybe it's time to share our ideas with the mayor. Get out your phone.

# Unit 8

## 1 *Would rather* and *would prefer*

1.  A:  Would you prefer to take classes during the day or at night?
    B:  I'd rather take classes at night.
2.  A:  Would you rather study business or education?
    B:  I'd prefer to become a teacher.
3.  A:  Would you prefer to sign up for an art course or a computer course?
    B:  I'd prefer not take any classes this semester.
4.  A:  Would you rather take up an individual sport or a team sport?
    B:  I'd rather not take up either.

## 2 *By* + gerund to describe how to do things

2.  A good way to improve your accent is by mimicking native speakers.
3.  Students can improve their listening skills by listening to English-language podcasts.
4.  Hardworking students improve their grammar by not repeating common mistakes.
5.  You can become fluent not by translating everything but by trying to think in English.
6.  You can become a good conversationalist not just by talking with others but by talking to yourself when you're alone, too.

# Unit 9

## 1 Get or have something done

2.  A:  Where can I get/have my computer repaired?
    B:  You can get/have it repaired at Hackers Inc.
3.  A:  Where can I get/have my taxes prepared?
    B:  You can get/have them prepared by my accountant.
4.  A:  Where can I get/have my hair cut?
    B:  You can get/have it cut at Beauty Barn.
5.  A:  Where can I get/have my apartment painted?
    B:  You can get/have it painted by Peter the Painter.

## 2 Making suggestions

A:  I'm having trouble meeting people here in the city. Any ideas?

B:  I know it's hard. Why don't you **join** a gym? That's usually a good place to meet people. Or maybe you could **take** a class at the community college.

A:  What about **checking out** the personal ads? Do you think that's a good way to meet people?

B:  I wouldn't recommend doing that. People never tell the truth in those ads. But it might be a good idea **to find** a sports team. Have you thought about **playing** a team sport – maybe baseball or volleyball?

A:  I'm not very good at most sports, but I used to play tennis.

B:  There you go! One option is **to look up** tennis clubs in the city and see which clubs have teams people can join.

A:  Now, that's a great idea. And I could always use the exercise!

# Unit 10

## 1 Referring to time in the past

A:  Hey, Dad. Did you use to listen to the Beatles?

B:  Of course. In fact, I just listened to one of their records a few days **ago**. Do you realize that the Beatles's music has influenced other musicians **for** over 50 years? They were the greatest!

A:  Well, I just found some interesting information about them. I'll read it to you: "The Beatles were a well-known British band **during/in** the 1960s. They performed together **for** 10 years – **from** 1960 **to** 1970. **In** 2003, the Beatles released a new version of their classic album *Let it Be*, even though one of the original members had been dead **since** 1980 and another had died **in** 2001. The original album had been recorded **in** 1969 and was in the studio safe **for** 34 years before the new, remixed album was released."

B:  That *is* interesting. It's pretty amazing that people have listened to the Beatles **in** both the twentieth and the twenty-first centuries, isn't it?

## 2 Predicting the future with *will*

A:  What do you think you **will be doing** five years from now?

B:  I'm not sure. Maybe I **will have gotten** married by then. How about you?

A:  I **will have finished** medical school, so I **will be doing** my internship five years from now.

B:  So you **won't be living** around here in five years, I guess. Where do you think you **will live**?

A:  Wherever I get my internship.

# Unit 11

## 1 Time clauses

2.  **Before** I got a full-time job, I had to live on a very limited budget.
3.  **By the time** I finished high school, I had already taken three college courses.
4.  **As soon as** I left for college, my mother turned my room into her office.
5.  **Once** I left home, I realized how much my family meant to me.
6.  **The moment** you have a child, you feel totally responsible for him or her.

## 2 Expressing regret and describing hypothetical situations

**A**

2.  Ivan should have saved up for a car.
3.  Jon shouldn't have been inactive when he was in college.
4.  Lisa should have stayed in touch with her high school classmates.
5.  Tony should have studied Spanish in school.

**B**

*Answers may vary. Some possible answers:*

2. If Ivan had saved up for a car, he wouldn't have to take public transportation.
3. If Jon hadn't been inactive when he was in college, he wouldn't have gained a lot of weight.
4. If Lisa had stayed in touch with her high school classmates, she wouldn't have very few friends.
5. If Tony had studied Spanish in school, he would be bilingual now.

# Unit 12

## 1 Describing purpose
**A**
2. **In order to** stay popular, a website needs to be accurate and visually attractive.
3. **In order to** run a profitable furniture store, it's important to advertise on TV.
4. **In order for** a restaurant to stay in business, it needs to have "regulars" – customers that come often.
5. **In order to** establish a successful nail salon, it has to have a convenient location.
6. **In order for** an online business to survive, it needs to have excellent pictures of the merchandise it's selling.

**B**
2. To stay popular, a website needs to be accurate and visually attractive.
3. To run a profitable furniture store, it's important to advertise on TV.
4. For a restaurant to stay in business, it needs to have "regulars" – customers that come often.
5. To establish a successful nail salon, it has to have a convenient location.
6. For an online business to survive, it needs to have excellent pictures of the merchandise it's selling.

## 2 Giving reasons
A: I had to go downtown today **because** I needed to mail a package at the post office. **Since** I was only a few blocks from Main Street, I went over to Martin's. Did you know that Martin's has gone out of business? I'm so upset!
B: That's too bad, but I'm not surprised. A lot of family-owned shops are closing **because of** the construction of shopping malls.
A: Yeah, and don't forget about all the megastores that are popping up everywhere. **The reason why** people prefer to shop there is to save money. Everyone loves a megastore **due to** the low prices and the huge selection.
B: Not me! I loved Martin's **for** their beautiful clothes and friendly salespeople. When you were there, you almost felt like family. You'll never get that at a megastore!

# Unit 13

## 1 Past modals for degrees of certainty
*Answers may vary. Some possible answers:*
2. A: What's wrong with Steven?
   B: Oh, you **must not have heard** the news. His dog ran away.
3. A: I went to see the Larsens today, but they didn't answer the door.
   B: Was their car there? If so, they **could have been** in the backyard.
4. A: Fabio said he was going to the party last night, but I didn't see him.
   B: Neither did I. He **couldn't have been** there then.
5. A: I can't find my glasses, but I know I had them at work today.
   B: You **might have left** them at the office.
6. A: Marc's new car looks really expensive.
   B: Yes, it does. It **must have cost** a fortune!

## 2 Past modals for judgments and suggestions
2. d   3. a   4. c   5. f   6. e

# Unit 14

## 1 The passive to describe process
2. First, a business plan has to be written.
3. Next, market research should be done.
4. Then the competition needs to be identified.
5. Classified ads may be posted online.
6. Finally, employees are hired so the work can start.

## 2 Defining and non-defining relative clauses
3. Voice-over actors, who give voice to characters in animated movies and video games, are usually freelancers.
4. Casting directors, who have usually been in the movie business for a long time, choose an actor for each part in a movie.
5. High-budget movies always use big stars that are known around the world.
6. Movie directors, who "make or break" a film, are greatly respected.

# Unit 15

## 1 Giving recommendations and opinions
*Answers may vary. Some possible answers:*
2. A: Teachers shouldn't be allowed to park in the student parking lot.
   B: Why not? Teachers **should be allowed** to park wherever a space is available. After all, they're here for us.
3. A: A rule has to be made to ban the use of cell phones in school.
   B: I don't think a rule **has to be made**. Students may need their phones for emergency purposes.
4. A: Students mustn't be permitted to use calculators during math exams.
   B: Sometimes we **should be permitted** to use them, especially when we're being tested on more complicated concepts than simple arithmetic.
5. A: Something has got to be done to control the noise in the hallways.
   B: Students **should be allowed** to talk to each other between classes, though. They aren't disturbing anyone when classes aren't in session.
6. A: Teachers must be required to remind students about important exams.
   B: That's unnecessary. On the contrary, students **should be required** to follow the syllabus and check important dates on the course websites.

## 2 Tag questions for opinions
3. do they
4. ✓
5. don't they
6. can they
7. can't we
8. aren't they

# Unit 16

## 1 Talking about past accomplishments
*Answers may vary. Some possible answers:*
2. has managed to pay
3. has been able to start
4. was able to move
5. managed to make
6. was able to buy
7. has managed to take
8. has managed to get
9. has been able to learn
10. has managed to visit

## 2 Describing goals and possible future accomplishments
Louise: So, Mike, what do you hope you will have accomplished five years from now?
Mike: I hope I'**ll have completed** medical school and I'**ll have started / 'd like to have started** my residence in a good hospital.
Louise: What about your personal goals? What **would you like to have achieved** by then?
Mike: Well, I'**d like to have met** that special someone, and, maybe I'**ll have gotten** married by then. What about you? What are your goals?
Louise: Well, I hope I'**ll have finished** culinary school in five years, and I'**ll have managed / 'd like to have managed** to work with some famous chef.
Mike: Good plan! What about opening your own restaurant?
Louise: That will take some more time, but by the time I'm 35, I hope I'**ll have opened** my own bistro – Chez Louise.
Mike: I can hardly wait. I just love your food.

# Appendix

## IRREGULAR VERBS

| Present | Past | Past Participle | Present | Past | Past Participle |
|---------|------|-----------------|---------|------|-----------------|
| (be) am/is, are | was, were | been | leave | left | left |
| become | became | become | lend | lent | lent |
| begin | began | begun | let | let | let |
| bite | bit | bitten | light | lit | lit |
| blow | blew | blown | lose | lost | lost |
| break | broke | broken | make | made | made |
| bring | brought | brought | meet | met | met |
| build | built | built | pay | paid | paid |
| burn | burned | burned | put | put | put |
| buy | bought | bought | quit | quit | quit |
| catch | caught | caught | read | read | read |
| choose | chose | chosen | run | ran | run |
| come | came | come | say | said | said |
| cost | cost | cost | see | saw | seen |
| cut | cut | cut | sell | sold | sold |
| do | did | done | send | sent | sent |
| dream | dreamed/dreamt | dreamed/dreamt | shine | shined/shone | shined/shone |
| drink | drank | drunk | shoot | shot | shot |
| drive | drove | driven | show | showed | shown |
| eat | ate | eaten | sink | sank | sunk |
| fall | fell | fallen | sit | sat | sat |
| feel | felt | felt | speak | spoke | spoken |
| fight | fought | fought | spend | spent | spent |
| find | found | found | stand | stood | stood |
| fly | flew | flown | steal | stole | stolen |
| forget | forgot | forgotten | stick | stuck | stuck |
| forgive | forgave | forgiven | sweep | swept | swept |
| get | got | gotten | swim | swam | swum |
| give | gave | given | take | took | taken |
| go | went | gone | teach | taught | taught |
| grow | grew | grown | tear | tore | torn |
| have | had | had | tell | told | told |
| hear | heard | heard | think | thought | thought |
| hold | held | held | throw | threw | thrown |
| hurt | hurt | hurt | upset | upset | upset |
| keep | kept | kept | wake | woke | woken |
| know | knew | known | wear | wore | worn |
| lay | laid | laid | write | wrote | written |

# 1 Language summary

## VOCABULARY

**Nouns**
accomplishment
advice
background
belief
entrepreneur
marriage
play-date
respect
roommate
sense of humor

**Pronouns**
herself
himself
someone
something

**Adjectives**
*Personalities*
direct
easygoing
egotistical
encouraging

friendly
helpful
inflexible
modest
outgoing
(un)predictable
(un)reliable
sensitive
serious
steady
stingy
stubborn
supportive
temperamental

**Other**
close (friend)
endless
ideal

**Verbs**
*Modals*
can
should
would

**Other**
accomplish
bother
brag
can't stand
find
get (angry/annoyed)
go out (with)
have (a sense of humor/in common/
fun [with])
hope
improve
keep (up with)
make (friends)
pursue
remove
suit
treat (someone to dinner)

**Adverb**
anytime

**Preposition**
during (a movie)

## EXPRESSIONS

**Expressing likes and dislikes**
What kind of . . . do you like?
   I like people who/that . . .
   I'd like someone who/that . . .
   I like/love (it when) . . .
   I don't mind it when . . .
   It makes me happy when . . .

**Asking for more information**
What else?

**Complaining**
I can't stand it when . . .
It annoys/bothers/upsets me when
. . .
I hate it when . . .

**Expressing agreement and disagreement**
For me, . . .
I think . . .
I agree.
I'm not sure I agree.
I feel the same way.

    *Interchange* Teacher's Edition 3 © Cambridge University Press 2017    Photocopiable

## VOCABULARY

### Nouns
**Jobs/Occupations/Careers**
(guidance) counselor
(software) developer
(marketing) director
doctor
entrepreneur
environmentalist
fashion designer
firefighter
flight attendant
game tester
hairstylist
intern
(freelance) journalist
(project) manager
mayor
politician
psychiatrist
(news) reporter
researcher
stockbroker
(kindergarten) teacher
(computer) technician
tour guide

tycoon
veterinarian

**Other**
(dis)advantage
computer wizard
field (of research)
greenhouse
guest list
(job) lead
membership
perk
stability
startup
volunteer work
widower

### Adjectives
ambitious
awful
challenging
demanding
fantastic
frustrating
luxurious
moody

outspoken
rewarding
social
stimulating
straightforward
stressful
tedious
tiny

### Verbs
be worth
earn
make up for
picture
seem
sound
train

### Adverbs
furthermore
perhaps
probably

### Conjunctions
as
but

## EXPRESSIONS

**Giving an opinion**
In my opinion, . . .

**Interpreting information**
It sounds like . . .

**Expressing personal preferences**
I'd be interested in . . .
I'd get tired of . . .
I'm very excited by . . .
I'd enjoy . . .
I think I'd be good at . . .
I wouldn't be very good at . . .

**Disagreeing**
I'm not so sure.

That's not true.
I disagree!

**Beginning a series**
First of all, . . .

**Adding information**
In addition, . . .
For example, . . .
Furthermore, . . .
However, . . .
On the other hand, . . .
In conclusion, . . .

**Expressing surprise**
Really?

**Expressing enthusiasm**
Guess what . . . .
That's great!

## VOCABULARY

**Nouns**
apology
favor
matter
sleeping bag

**Adjectives**
bored
cool
important

**Verbs**
accept (an apology/an invitation/a request)
act (out)
decline (a request)
do (a favor)
find (out)
finish
get along
give (a gift)
give up

handle
have (a party)
help (out)
ignore
keep (quiet)
look at
lose (interest)
make (a phone call/a request/noise)
move (away)
offer (an apology)
owe (an apology)
pick up
receive (a compliment/a gift/an invitation/a phone call)
return (a favor/a phone call/a compliment)
spend
take care (of)
turn down (an invitation)
worry

**Adverb**
almost

## EXPRESSIONS

***Talking on the telephone***
Hi, . . . . This is . . .
    Oh, hi, . . . . What's up?

***Making, accepting, and declining requests***
Can I . . . ?/Could you. . . , please?
    Yes./Sorry, but . . .
Is it OK if I . . . ?
    Of course.
Would it be all right/OK if I . . . ?
    No problem.
Do you mind if I . . . ?/Would you mind if I . . . ?
    No, I don't mind.
I was wondering if I could . . .
    Sure, that's fine.

***Thanking someone***
Thanks a million./Thanks. I really appreciate it.
Sure.

***Making indirect requests***
Could you tell . . . (that) . . . ?
Please tell . . . (that) . . .
Would you ask . . . if/whether/to . . . ?
Can you tell . . . (not) to . . . ?
Can/Could you ask . . . if/whether . . . ?
Please ask . . . if/whether . . .
Can/Could you ask . . . what/when . . . ?

***Apologizing***
I'm sorry.
I'm really sorry.
Sorry.

# 4 Language summary

## VOCABULARY

### Nouns

**Events**
coincidence
dilemma
disaster
emergency
lucky break
mishap
mistake
mystery
triumph

**Other**
achievement
brain
desire
destruction
driver
Earth
elevator
(good) fortune
"ick" factor
lice
outbreak
package

podcast
police
runner
selfies
sidewalk
sleep deprivation
suffering
thrift shop
trashcan
trip
weight loss

### Adjectives
believable
complex
connected
dangerous
healthy
inaccurate
incredible
puzzling
quick
satirical
several
sudden
suspicious

trustworthy
understandable
unexpected

### Verbs
**Modals**
be (un)able to
might

**Other**
burn off (calories)
gain
interrupt
involve
lock up
look for
run into
run out (of)
work out

### Adverbs
as
unfortunately
while

### Preposition
off

## EXPRESSIONS

**Reacting to a story**
What happened?
That's terrible!

# 5 Language summary

## VOCABULARY

**Nouns**
behavior
challenge
cheek
chopsticks
cooking
concern
culture
culture shock
custom
elbow
expectation
eye-opener
handshake
host
language
meal
outsider
pamphlet
taboo

**Adjectives**
*Feelings*
anxious
(un)comfortable
confident
curious
embarrassed
enthusiastic
excited
fascinated
homesick
insecure
nervous
uncertain
worried

**Other**
lively
passionate
picky

**Verbs**
drop by
feel

get used to
get sick
go out (on a date)
greet (someone)
hang out with
have (a baby)
hug
miss
plan
point out
split (= divide evenly)
take (photographs)
take off
tip
turn down

**Adverbs**
abroad
along
appropriately
especially
(the) most

**Preposition**
in (public)

## EXPRESSIONS

**Expressing emotions**
One thing/Something (that) I'd be (anxious/excited/ . . . ) about is . . .

**Asking for permission**
Is it all right to . . . ?

**Describing expectations**
You're supposed to . . .
You aren't supposed to . . .
You're expected to . . .
It's the custom to . . .
It's not acceptable to . . .

**Expressing an opinion/ a feeling**
Oh, how (nice/awful/ . . . )!

*Interchange* Teacher's Edition 3 © Cambridge University Press 2017   Photocopiable

## VOCABULARY

### Nouns
#### Electronics
battery
computer (screen)
oven
printer
refrigerator
remote/temperature control
TV (screen)
washing machine

#### Other
charge
complaint
crack
damage
lens(es)
(suitcase) lining
mug
pick-up
pitcher
receipt
refund
scratch
seller
shirt
stain
store credit
tablecloth

tear
temperature
tenant
vase
warranty

### Pronoun
everything

### Adjectives
#### Past participles
chipped
cracked
damaged
dented
made
scratched
stained
torn

#### Other
dirty
reliable
throwaway

### Verbs
bill
book
break
crash
deliver
die
drop
flicker
freeze
have (an eye for)
highlight
jam
leak
pick up
pretend
purchase
repair
replace
rip
rush
skip
spot
state
work (= function)

### Adverbs
hardly ever
right away/now

## EXPRESSIONS

### Offering help
Can I help you?
What can I do for you?

### Describing problems
What's wrong with it?
    It's torn/stained/damaged/scratched/cracked/chipped/worn.
What exactly is the problem?
    It has a tear/a hole/a stain/some damage.
    There are a few scratches.
    There's a crack.
    It's leaking./It has a leak.

# 7 Language summary

## VOCABULARY

### Nouns

**World problems**
e-waste
extinction
famine
global warming
government corruption
(the) homeless
infectious diseases
overbuilding
political unrest
pollution
poverty
unemployment
violence

**The Earth**
air
birds
coral reef
ecosystem
fish
marine life
oil
plant
rain forest
river
soil
wildlife

**Other**
chemical
demonstration
destruction
executive

factory
farm(land)
health
industry
lack
landfill
law
livestock
management
petition
politician
(training) programs
publicity
recession
recycling
reduction
shelter
sit-in
(news) station
(heavy) traffic

### Adjectives
accountable
affordable
clear
destructive
hungry
innovative
invasive
low-income
poisonous
underground
unemployed
unforgettable
urban

vocational

### Verbs
boycott
contaminate
create
decompose
deplete
displace
dive
educate
fight
harm
hunt
ignore
improve
make (a living)
provide
pump
reduce
run (a story)
threaten
trash
voice (= share/talk about)

### Adverbs
outside
too

### Prepositions
against (the law)
as a result of
because of
due to
on (the street)

## EXPRESSIONS

**Describing problems**
The . . . are being . . . by . . .
(The) . . . is being . . . because of/due to . . .
The . . . have been . . . through . . .
(The) . . . has been . . . as a result of . . .

**Offering solutions**
One thing to change things is to . . .
Another way to stop them is to . . .
The best way to help is to . . .

**Talking about what will happen**
What if . . . ?
Well, then . . .

**Identifying something**
What's the name of . . . ?
   It's called . . .

   Interchange Teacher's Edition 3 © Cambridge University Press 2017   Photocopiable

# 8 Language summary

## VOCABULARY

### Nouns

**Language learning**
accent
idiom
pronunciation
vocabulary

**Learning paths and study methods**
conference
internship
job shadowing
language course
lecture
online course
professional course
study group
traditional course
(private) tutor

**Personal qualities and skills**
artistic skills
communication skills
competitiveness
concern for others
cooperation
creativity
money management

perseverance
problem solving
self-confidence
self-discipline
time management
tolerance

**Other**
application (of skills)
approach
attorney
budget
clutter
curriculum
daily planner
dish
finance
foreign language
martial arts
outdoors
play
public defender
public speaking
sitcom
surrounding
volunteer activities

### Adjectives
identical
native
practical
private
right (= correct)
shy
useful

### Verbs
attend
claim
concentrate
expect
get (a degree/a raise/license)
improve
join
learn (about)
manage
prefer
set up
sing along
study (on your own)
take (a class/a course [on/in])
volunteer

### Adverbs
correctly
totally

## EXPRESSIONS

### Asking about preferences
Would you rather . . . or . . . ?
   I'd rather (not) . . .
Would you prefer to . . . or . . . ?
   (I think) I'd prefer . . . to . . .
   I'd prefer (to) . . .
   Let's . . .
   I'd rather not./I'd prefer not to.

### Asking for personal information
How's (your French class/ . . . ) going?
   Not bad.

### Talking about learning methods
You could . . . by . . .
   That's a good idea.
I . . . by . . .
Maybe I should try that!
A good way to . . . is by . . .

### Admitting something
To tell you the truth, . . .

## VOCABULARY

### Nouns

**Services**

car wash
(carpet/house) cleaning
dry cleaning
language tutoring
laundry
(home) repairs

**Other**

(home) appliance
assignment
belongings
budget
disease
fiancée
groceries
jogging

perseverance
portrait
self-confidence
stage
weeknight

### Adjectives

affordable
annual
capable
ground-breaking
lethal
optimistic
overweight

### Verbs

**Phrasal verbs**

break up with
come up with

cut down on
get along with
keep up with
look forward to
put up with
take care of

**Other**

argue
post
spend (time)
upgrade

### Adverbs

absolutely
constantly
deeply
easily
endlessly

## EXPRESSIONS

**Talking about things you need to have done**

Where can I have/get . . . ?
    You can have/get . . .

**Asking for and giving advice**

What can I do?
What about . . . ?
Have you thought about . . . ?
Why don't you . . . ?
Maybe you could . . .
One option is (to) . . .
It might be a good idea to . . .

**Replying to advice**

Um, I don't think so.

**Expressing frustration**

This is so depressing!

## VOCABULARY

### Nouns
**Historic events**
achievement
assassination
catastrophe
discovery
election
epidemic
invention
natural disaster
terrorism/terrorist act

**Other**
billion
century
compass
debut
existence
fad

human
humankind
impact
penicillin
roof garden
sensation
space
speculation
trend

### Adjectives
biodegradable
major
overnight

### Verbs
alter
appreciate
become
come on

cure
hit
hold
release
retain
rip
set up
spread
steal
take place

### Adverb
quickly

### Prepositions
during
for (50 years)
in (existence/1989)
since
within (the next 5 years)

## EXPRESSIONS

**Talking about historical events**
When did . . . begin?
   During/In the (1910s/ . . .).
   About . . . years ago.
How long was the . . . ?
   From . . . to . . . ./For . . . years.
How long has the . . . been in existence?
   Since . . ./For about the last . . . years.
   For over . . . years.

**Making a prediction**
I guess . . .

# 11 Language summary

## VOCABULARY

### Nouns
apology
bank account
blackmail
crush
driver's license
essay
financial advisor
grade
high school
importance
internship
(student) loan
milestone
paycheck
promotion
regret
relationship
sabotage
sense
sleepover
teamwork
turning point

### Pronouns
myself
yourself

### Adjectives
*Behavior and personality*
ambitious
argumentative
carefree
(im)mature
naive
pragmatic
rebellious
(ir)responsible
selfish
short-fused
sophisticated
wise

*Other*
heartfelt
tough

### Verbs
blame
borrow
become (a parent)
feel
get (a credit card/a paycheck/married)
hurt
look something up
lose
move away
reject
retire
save (money)
spend (time)
stay (in touch)
take care of (yourself)
take out (a loan)
yell

### Adverbs
not . . . anymore
seriously
somehow

## EXPRESSIONS

**Describing yourself in the past**
By the time I, . . .
The moment I . . .
Before I got my first job, . . .
Once I left home, . . .
After I traveled overseas, . . .
As soon as I left home, . . .
Until I moved to (Alaska), . . .

**Describing regrets about the past**
I should have . . ./I shouldn't have . . .

**Describing hypothetical situations**
If I had . . . , I would have . . .
If I had . . . , I wouldn't be . . .

**Asking for clarification**
How do you mean?

# 12 Language summary

## VOCABULARY

### Nouns

**Businesses**
(clothing) boutique
coffee shop
health club
megastore
supermarket

**Other**
advertising
barrage
concept
goddess
package
puzzle
reason
self-discipline
slogan
tagline
time-span
(personal) trainer
upset stomach
wait

### Adjectives

**Qualities for success**
affordable
athletic
attractive
charming
clever
convenient
dependable
effective
entertaining
industrious
informative
knowledgeable
muscular
persuasive
tough
unforgettable
well written

### Other
brand new
catchy
crowded
ever-changing
everlasting
flexible
funny
inexpensive
packed
profitable
shocking
trendy

### Verbs
attract
be seen
dive
grab
succeed

### Adverbs
directly
importantly
worldwide

## EXPRESSIONS

**Describing the purpose of something**
In order to . . . , you need to . . .
(In order) for a/an . . . to . . . , it has to . . .
To . . . , it's a good idea to . . .

**Giving reasons**
I like . . . because . . .
It's so popular because of the . . .
The reason people . . . is to . . .
Due to . . .

**Hypothesizing**
I think another reason why . . . is . . .
It could be . . .

**Accepting an invitation**
I thought you'd never ask!

## VOCABULARY

### Nouns

**Reactions**
assumption
criticism
demand
excuse
prediction
suggestion
suspicion
warning

**Other**
announcement
cafeteria
check
doorbell
explanation
fear
fight
flare
haircut
hint
in-laws
mess
nephew
pet peeve

pipe
sci-fi
sewer
sister-in-law
spaceship
trumpet

### Pronoun
one

### Adjectives
complicated
dated
giant
high-pitched
inconsiderate
overnight
tricky
understanding

### Verbs
argue
baffle
blame
borrow
chew
clean up

cut
fall (asleep)
fire
flee
hear
interrupt
lend
make up (an excuse)
pack
pretend
ring
slip (one's mind)
squeal
take place
turn
wash (the dishes)
withdraw
yawn

### Adverbs
besides
constantly
previously

### Conjunction
however

## EXPRESSIONS

**Judging past actions**
You should/shouldn't have . . .
I wouldn't have . . .

**Suggesting alternative past actions**
You could have . . .
I would have . . .

**Expressing approval of someone's action**
. . . did the right thing.

*Interchange* Teacher's Edition 3 © Cambridge University Press 2017 Photocopiable

## VOCABULARY

**Nouns**

*Movies*

character
detail
film
location
role
scene
script
set
shot
special effects
storyboard
studio
(movie) theater

*Media professions*

actor
band manager
club DJ
(game) designer
(production/technical/editorial)
director

editor
game animator
gameplay programmer
(art/photo) editor
news photographer
quality assurance analyst
songwriter
storyboard artist
stunt person
talk show host
(lighting/sound-effects) technician
web content manager

*Other*

clerk
computer graphics
crowd
jury
stage
thousands (of)

**Adjectives**

amazing
challenging

computer-animated
entirely
final
full-length
in-demand
nonexistent
rude
standard

**Verbs**

beat
complete
deal (with)
depend
pack
rehearse
run
shoot (the movie)

**Adverb**

simultaneously

**Preposition**

on (stage)

## EXPRESSIONS

**Explaining or identifying someone**
. . . is the person who/that . . .

**Asking for an explanation**
Can I ask why that is?

**Saying you haven't decided yet**
I'm considering . . .

**Talking about an opportunity**
You get to . . .

## VOCABULARY

### Nouns
**Social issues**
bullying
child care
health care
homelessness
noise pollution
parental leave
stray animal
street crime
trash collection
vandalism

**Other**
big deal
citizen
fare
fur
helmet
(health) insurance
key
leash
mayor

ownership
permit
plagiarism
rail
research
royalties
seat belt
shelter
sidewalk
source

### Adjectives
affordable
(un)attended
disabled
inadequate
irregular
offensive
organic
overcrowded
soundproof
unmarried

### Verbs
assume
ban
belong
critique
deserve
face
fail
feed
litter
make ends meet
pass
permit
pickpocket
pretend
require
ride (a bike)
spot

### Adverbs
fairly
nowadays
unfortunately

## EXPRESSIONS

**Making a recommendation**
People ought to/should be required to . . .
People shouldn't be allowed to . . .
Something has (got) to be done to . . .
A rule has to be made to . . .
Laws must be passed to . . .
People mustn't be permitted to . . .

**Acknowledging an opinion and offering a different one**
That sounds interesting, but . . .
I think . . .
That's not a bad idea. On the other hand, I feel that . . .
You may have a point. However, I think . . .

**Asking for and giving reasons**
Why?/Why not?
    Well, I don't think . . .
    Well, for one thing, . . .

## VOCABULARY

**Nouns**
accomplishment
best seller
competition
degree
discipline
eagle
goal
goggles
grade
hurdle
internship
lifetime
marathon
nomad
pleasure
promotion
savings
skill
personal statement
wish

**Adjectives**
adaptable
compassionate
courageous
cynical
dependent
downhill
healthy
(un)imaginative
insensitive
resourceful
rigid
self-motivated
self-sufficient
steady
timid
upbeat

**Verbs**
achieve
count (on someone)

deliver
develop
manage (to)
pack
proud
quit
retire
share
soar
succeed
switch

**Adverbs**
ahead
elsewhere
plenty
pretty

**Pronouns**
myself
yourself

## EXPRESSIONS

**Describing challenges, frustrations, and rewards**
The most unusual/realistic/ambitious/rewarding thing about . . . is . . .

**Describing past accomplishments**
I've managed to . . .
I managed to . . .
I've been able to . . .
I was able to . . .

**Talking about future accomplishments**
What do you hope you'll have achieved?
    I hope I'll have . . .
    I'd like to have . . .

# Audio scripts

## 1 That's my kind of friend!
### ② Conversation (p. 2)

**B** Listen to Joe and Roy discuss Lisa after they had dinner together. What did Roy think of her?

*Joe:* So, what did you think of Lisa?

*Roy:* Well, I was worried at first – especially when I saw that she rode a motorcycle. I thought she might be one of those girls who is into heavy metal music and stuff like that. You know what I mean?

*Joe:* But she's pretty normal, right?

*Roy:* Yeah, and she's smart and funny . . . and very pretty, too.

*Joe:* I knew you'd like her.

*Roy:* Yeah, I do. She's my kind of girl.

*Joe:* So are you two going to get together again?

*Roy:* I hope so. I got her number, and I'll text her tomorrow. Do you think she liked me?

*Joe:* I think so. She seemed to be having a good time, too. But I guess you're going to have to get in touch with her and find out.

### ⑤ Listening (p. 4)

**A** Listen to conversations that describe three people. Are the descriptions positive or negative? Check the box.

#### 1. Emma

*Rob:* So Courtney, how are things with your new roommate? Emma, right?

*Courtney:* Yeah, Emma. Things are OK.

*Rob:* That doesn't sound good.

*Courtney:* Well, I'm a little annoyed.

*Rob:* What happened?

*Courtney:* So we take turns cleaning the apartment. It was her turn this week, and she still hasn't done anything. Then today she left for her parents' house for the entire weekend.

*Rob:* Do you think she forgot?

*Courtney:* Well, I asked her about it before she left, and she wasn't very nice. She said she didn't need another mom and that she'd do things when she had time. She's not easy to talk to.

*Rob:* Well, she might do it Sunday night when she gets back. If she doesn't, then talk to her.

*Courtney:* Yeah, I'll wait and see. Thanks, Rob.

#### 2. Mrs. Leblanc

*Natalie:* Hey Jen. What's new with that internship in Paris? Did your French teacher help you with the application?

*Jen:* Mrs. Leblanc? Yeah, she was a huge help. She reviewed my French and even gave me some good ideas.

*Natalie:* That's great! She sounds so helpful.

*Jen:* She really is. I often tell her that, and she just laughs. She won't take credit for anything.

*Natalie:* You know, my sister says she's the best teacher she's ever had. She's taking a French class now with another teacher, but she still writes Mrs. Leblanc with questions.

*Jen:* And Mrs. Leblanc doesn't mind?

*Natalie:* Nope. She says she's happy to help.

*Jen:* She's so sweet. It's people like her that make me want to be a teacher.

*Natalie:* Oh, yeah? Would you teach French?

*Jen:* French? Hmm. I'm not so sure. Let's see if I get this internship in Paris first.

#### 3. Pablo

*Man 1:* Hey, remember that it's Pablo's birthday next Friday.

*Man 2:* Oh, that's right! What's the plan?

*Man 1:* I haven't heard of anything. He's always organizing parties for other people. Let's plan something for him this time.

*Man 2:* Great idea! Would he get mad if we invited all his friends?

*Man 1:* No, he'd love it! And Pablo never gets mad, anyway. Let's do dinner at his favorite Indian restaurant. You know how he loves curry.

*Man 2:* Perfect. I'll invite his friends, and you can take care of the dinner reservation.

*Man 1:* OK, but for how many people?

*Man 2:* He has a lot of friends. Let's say fifteen for now, and I'll let you know if it changes.

*Man 1:* He's going to love this!

**B** Listen again. Write two adjectives that describe each person in the chart.

## 2 Working 9 to 5
### ⑦ Conversation (p. 11)

**B** Listen to the rest of the conversation. What is Tyler going to do at the resort?

*Emma:* So, what will you be doing at the beach resort?

*Tyler:* Nothing that great, actually. I'll be working with the entertainment staff, you know, making sure the guests are having a good time.

*Emma:* That sounds interesting to me. What exactly will you have to do?

*Tyler:* Well, during the day, I'll have to organize activities and games for adults and children. And then we have to take part in evening activities, you know, shows, parties . . .

*Emma:* I see. It sounds like your days will be pretty long.

*Tyler:* For sure. And the job is six days a week.

*Emma:* Wow! You mean you only have one day off?

*Tyler:* Yeah. But the resort is in such a beautiful place that I think it's worth it. Besides, the pay is really good.

*Emma:* You know what? I'm beginning to think that the job at the website isn't so bad after all.

## 10 Listening (p. 12)

**A** Listen to Caden talk to Janelle about his job as a video game tester. Which parts of the job does he like and dislike? Check *Like* or *Dislike*.

*Janelle:* Hey, Caden!

*Caden:* Janelle! Hey!

*Janelle:* I haven't seen you in awhile. How have you been?

*Caden:* Oh, all right. I'm so happy it's Friday.

*Janelle:* Oh, yeah? Hard week?

*Caden:* Every week is a hard week. I feel like time goes by so slowly at work.

*Janelle:* Do you still have that job testing video games?

*Caden:* Yeah. I think the last time I saw you, I was just starting and I was really excited about it. But honestly, Janelle, it's just not as fun as I thought it would be.

*Janelle:* Why is that?

*Caden:* I mean, I don't want to sound ungrateful. I know it's better paid than a lot of jobs, and my hours are more flexible than most, but it's making me hate video games. I thought I was going to play the games and suggest ways to improve them, but I have to play the same parts over and over again and make mistakes to see what happens. I basically run hundreds of tests on every detail of the game.

*Janelle:* Oh, I guess that wouldn't be very fun.

*Caden:* And when I play video games on the weekends, I keep noticing little things that I would report for work. I can't play games like I used to and just enjoy them.

*Janelle:* So, do you think you want to change fields?

*Caden:* Well, that's the thing. Because I am always playing them, I'm constantly thinking of new ideas for games. I have lists at home. So, I'm still passionate about video games, but I'm just tired of testing other people's ideas.

*Janelle:* Why don't you go back to school so you can become a software developer? You know, you could develop your own games. I think with the experience you have now, you'd be really good at that.

*Caden:* Yeah, I've thought of that. If I keep working at this job for a while, I could afford to go back to school. Do you think that's a good idea?

*Janelle:* Definitely. Then when you finish school, you can look for a job designing games. Who knows? Maybe this company where you're working now would hire you.

*Caden:* Hey, anything's possible! Thanks for the talk, Janelle. I'm going to look at universities this weekend.

**B** Listen again. What does Caden decide to do?

## Units 1–2 Progress check
## 2 Listening (p. 14)

**A** Listen to Suki and Andy discuss these topics. Complete the chart.

**1. Websites**

*Andy:* I can't stand it when you want to read an article on a website and they make you sign up. What if I don't like it? Why don't they let you read a few articles before making you subscribe?

*Suki:* Yeah, that's annoying. Then you sign up, and they send you emails every day. I don't need more emails!

**2. Children**

*Suki:* I love children, but I hate it when people let kids cry in a restaurant. I know children cry, but parents should try to calm them down in a restaurant.

*Andy:* Yeah, or when you're on a bus or plane and the kid behind you keeps kicking your seat.

**3. Taxi drivers**

*Andy:* Doesn't it bother you when taxi drivers are dishonest? They'll take longer routes to charge you more money. I always feel like I have to pay attention.

*Suki:* I know what you mean! Or sometimes they say they don't know the area, and you don't know if they're lying. Every taxi should have a GPS!

**4. Restaurant servers**

*Suki:* It upsets me when restaurant servers get annoyed if you order something cheap off the menu. I understand they want a bigger tip, but they shouldn't be impolite.

*Andy:* I hate it when they don't write down your order. They think they can memorize it, and then they get it wrong. And I never complain because I think they might do something to my food.

## 3  Lend a hand.
## 2 Conversation (p. 16)

**B** Listen to two more calls Keiko makes. What else does she need help with? Do her friends agree to help?

**1.**

*Hunter:* Hi, Keiko.

*Keiko:* Hi, Hunter. I was wondering if you could do me a favor.

*Hunter:* That depends.

*Keiko:* Well, I'm moving this weekend, so I'll be really busy taking everything over to my new apartment. Would it be OK if I left my goldfish at your place for the weekend?

*Hunter:* Your fish? Sure. I'll be around all weekend, and I love watching those little guys swim around in the tank.

*Keiko:* Thanks a lot. Is it OK if I come by with them on Friday?

*Hunter:* That's fine.

**2.**

*Claire:* Claire Dawson.
*Keiko:* Hi, Claire. It's Keiko.
*Claire:* Oh, hello. How are you?
*Keiko:* Pretty good, thanks. Listen, the reason I'm calling is I have a really big favor to ask you.
*Claire:* OK. What is it?
*Keiko:* Remember I told you that I'm moving this weekend?
*Claire:* Yeah, I remember.
*Keiko:* Well, I was wondering if you could help me pack my stuff.
*Claire:* Gee, Keiko, I'd really love to help you out, but I'm going away this weekend. It's my mother's birthday, and I promised to go visit her.
*Keiko:* Oh, OK. I understand. Anyway, how are things? I haven't seen you for ages.
*Claire:* Oh, you know, work, work, work!

## 5 Listening (p. 18)

**A** Listen to three telephone conversations. Write down what each caller requests. Does the other person agree to the request? Check *Yes* or *No*.

**1. Jesse**

*Maria:* Hello?
*Jesse:* Hi, Maria. This is Jesse.
*Maria:* Oh, hi. How's it going?
*Jesse:* It's going well! Listen, I was wondering if I could borrow your electric mixer.
*Maria:* My mixer? Don't tell me *you* are going to bake!
*Jesse:* I know. I'm having my friends from my study group over this weekend, and I want to make dessert. And I want it to be perfect! I love that chocolate cake recipe you have. So, what do you say?
*Maria:* Well, I have bad news. It's broken. I've been meaning to get it fixed, but I haven't gotten around to it yet. But you know, you can buy a cheap mixer at the store.
*Jesse:* Hmm. I don't know. Maybe I'll just go to a bakery.

**2. Liz**

*Samuel:* Hello?
*Liz:* Hi, Samuel. It's Liz.
*Samuel:* Hi, Liz. What's up?
*Liz:* Do you remember talking about that book yesterday? The one about that man's trip through Asia?
*Samuel:* Yeah, of course.
*Liz:* Would it be all right if I borrowed it? I need a good book for my vacation next week.
*Samuel:* No problem. But you'll have to tell me what you think!
*Liz:* Definitely! Thanks, Samuel.

**3. Min-jun**

*Silvia:* Hello?
*Min-jun:* Hi, Silvia. It's Min-jun.
*Silvia:* Hey! What's up?
*Min-jun:* Not much. I was wondering if I could ask you for a favor.

*Silvia:* Sure.
*Min-jun:* Well, I have to go out of town next week. Could you watch Daisy while I'm gone?
*Silvia:* Who's Daisy?
*Min-jun:* You know – Daisy, my cat.
*Silvia:* Oh. Your cat. I don't know, Min-jun. I'm not crazy about cats. Their hair gets everywhere, and . . .
*Min-jun:* Not Daisy. She's really clean . . . and loving. I bet you'll love cats after watching her.
*Silvia:* Yeah, maybe, but I'm not sure about my roommate.
*Min-jun:* Oh, that's right. I forgot you live with someone now. Well, what if I gave you the keys to my place and you stayed here?
*Silvia:* Well, I guess that would work. You do live close by.
*Min-jun:* Great! I really appreciate it. Why don't you come over tonight so I can show you where everything is?
*Silvia:* OK, but you owe me one!

## 4 What happened?
## 5 Listening (p. 24)

**A** Listen to three news stories. Number the pictures from 1 to 3. There is one extra picture.

**1.**

*Man:* A teenagers' soccer game in Australia took an unexpected turn on Saturday when an escaped bull decided to join the game. The players were running toward the goal when the bull charged the field. It began chasing the 14-year-old boy who had the ball. Luckily, the boy was fast, and managed to get out of the way. Apparently bored with the soccer game, the bull left the field as suddenly as it had entered it, leaving players and viewers shocked at what they had just witnessed.

**2.**

*Woman:* A 19-year-old by the name of Matt is lucky to be alive and well. Matt was watching TV at his grandmother's home in Missouri last Thursday when a terrible storm started. While he was talking to his grandmother, the storm intensified into a tornado, ripping the walls off the house and sucking him in. The tornado took Matt over 1,300 feet before dropping him in an abandoned field. After flying through the air at 150 miles per hour, it's safe to say that Matt had the ride of his life!

**3.**

*Man:* Early Tuesday morning in Ontario, two police officers were chasing a car thief when they suddenly lost control of their vehicle and drove into a river. Surprisingly, the thief went back to the scene of the accident and helped rescue the officers from the river. The local police department dropped all charges against the thief for saving the officers' lives.

**B** Listen again. Take notes on each story.

## 7 Conversation (p. 25)

**B** Listen to the rest of the conversation. What did Milo have stolen once? Where was he?

*Milo:* I had something similar happen last year.
*Carol:* Really?
*Mio:* Yeah. It was when I was overseas. I was on my way to the airport, so I was standing on the side of the road with my bags, trying to figure out the bus schedule. Anyway, this group of guys came by and asked if they could help me. Their English wasn't very clear, and I couldn't really understand what they were saying. Finally, they left, and when I looked down, I realized my carry-on bag had disappeared. It had my wallet in it with all my money, my credit card, and my phone. Luckily, I had put my airline ticket and my passport in my backpack.
*Carol:* How awful! So what did you do?
*Milo:* I went inside a restaurant and asked to use their phone. First, I called the police and reported the theft. Then I called my credit card company. I was able to get some cash, and by the time I got home, I had a new credit card waiting for me.

# Units 3–4 Progress check
## 4 Listening (p. 29)

Listen to each situation. Number the events from 1 to 3.

**1.**

*Man 1:* Even though she had gotten sick while she was on vacation, she went back to work on Monday.

**2.**

*Woman 1:* John called me last week, but I never got the message. I'd changed phone numbers.

**3.**

*Woman 2:* I'd been really nervous about the job interview, so when I left the office, I felt relieved.

**4.**

*Man 2:* When my cousin stopped by, I was watching a movie. We went out for coffee to catch up when the movie was over.

# 5 Expanding your horizons
## 7 Conversation (p. 33)

**B** Listen to the rest of the conversation. If you are invited to someone's house in Germany, when are you expected to arrive? What can you bring as a gift?

*Olivia:* What are some of the customs in Germany?
*Klaus:* Well, when you're invited to someone's house, you can also take flowers. Not red roses, chrysanthemums, carnations, or lilies, but most other flowers are fine.
*Olivia:* When should you arrive? Should you arrive a little early?

*Klaus:* No, never. You're expected to arrive on time. Punctuality is very important in Germany. If you're going to be more than 15 minutes late, it's important to call the host. It's also the custom to write a short thank-you note the following day.
*Olivia:* I like that. I wish we did that here more often. To me, it shows good manners.

## 9 Listening (p. 34)

**A** Listen to people describe customs they observed abroad. Complete the chart.

**1. Carla**

*Carla:* I lived in Saudi Arabia for a while. Women put something over their head and wear clothing that covers the whole body. At first, I felt uncomfortable and found it a real nuisance, but after a while, I got used to it and even started to like it. You feel really secure, and you also don't have to worry about what to wear all the time.

**2. Nate**

*Nate:* When I lived in Spain, I was surprised at how late in the evening people eat. When you're invited to dinner, you're expected to come around nine o'clock, and you usually don't start dinner until ten. And people stay really late – sometimes until two in the morning or even later. I found that difficult. How do you get up and go to work the next day after eating and talking until three in the morning?

**3. Shauna**

*Shauna:* One thing that I had to get used to when I was traveling in South Korea was the way people make noise when they drink soup. I think it's because they want to show that they're really enjoying their food so they make a slurping noise. It bothered me at first, but then I got used to it. I guess it's because when I was growing up, it wasn't acceptable to make noise at the dinner table.

# 6 That needs fixing.
## 4 Listening (p. 38)

**A** Listen to three customers return items they purchased. Complete the chart.

**1. Evie**

*Store clerk:* Hello. How can I help you?
*Evie:* Yes, I bought this dress yesterday. Here's the receipt. I was at an important business dinner, bent over to pick something up, and the zipper in the back ripped! See?
*Store clerk:* Oh, my. Yes, I see.
*Evie:* Luckily, I was sitting down, but I had to pretend I was cold and wear my husband's jacket all night. Then the server turned up the heat because he thought I was cold! I was sweating all night!
*Store clerk:* I'm so sorry, ma'am. Let me take care of this and give you your money back.

### 2. Darren

*Manager:* Welcome to Electronics City!

*Darren:* I'd like a refund for this broken coffeemaker.

*Manager:* Hmm. It's pretty stained and damaged. Do you have the receipt?

*Darren:* How can I have a receipt for something I bought four years ago?

*Manager:* Sir, without a receipt, we can't give you a refund. And the warranty on these is two years, so if it's been four, we can't help you.

*Darren:* Just give me a new one then. I need my coffee!

*Manager:* Unfortunately, we can't give away coffeemakers, but I can show you some on sale. Just follow me.

### 3. Gisela

*Gisela:* Excuse me. I bought this laptop two days ago, opened it, and found this scratch on the screen!

*Employee:* Oh, that is a bad scratch! But we don't sell this brand.

*Gisela:* That's impossible. I was here last week. Look at this receipt.

*Employee:* Ma'am, this is from Electronics City, our competitor. We're Electronics World.

*Gisela:* Oh, that's right! I bought my tablet here and my laptop there! How embarrassing!

*Employee:* Don't worry! I'm sure Electronics City will take care of it. And let us know if you need any help with your tablet.

*Gisela:* Will do! Thank you!

## 6 Conversation (p. 38)

**B** Listen to another tenant's call with Mr. Leroy. What's the tenant's problem?

*Mr. Leroy:* Hello?

*Mr. Harris:* Hello. Is this the manager?

*Mr. Leroy:* Yes, this is Mr. Leroy.

*Mr. Harris:* This is Carl Harris in Apartment 10C.

*Mr. Leroy:* Yes. How can I help you, Mr. Harris?

*Mr. Harris:* I'm having a problem with the electricity.

*Mr. Leroy:* What sort of problem with the electricity?

*Mr. Harris:* Well, it keeps going off and coming back on again.

*Mr. Leroy:* I see. Is it just the lights, or is it the appliances, too?

*Mr. Harris:* Let me check. . . . No, the refrigerator is OK, so it must be just the lights.

*Mr. Leroy:* I guess the fuse box needs to be checked. I'll come up and take a look at it right away.

*Mr. Harris:* Thanks so much.

## 10 Listening (p. 40)

**A** Listen to a conversation between two friends. Answer the questions.

*Aaron:* Hayley! Where have you been? I've been texting you all morning.

*Hayley:* Sorry, Aaron. My phone keeps freezing. And the camera isn't working! I'm going to go buy a new phone after class.

*Aaron:* You'll spend a ton of money on a new phone. Why don't you just fix it?

*Hayley:* I don't trust repair technicians. They charge you for parts you don't need, or they supposedly fix it, but a few days later, the same problem comes back! I don't have time for that.

*Aaron:* I agree there are a lot of dishonest ones, but I know someone. My phone kept shutting off, and this guy only charged me $50 to fix it! And my phone has worked perfectly ever since.

*Hayley:* Yeah, Aaron, but we have different phones. Everyone says mine is more complicated.

*Aaron:* This guy is a genius. He won't charge you if he can't fix it. Plus, Hayley, you shouldn't throw electronics away if you can fix them. It's terrible for the environment. I read this article about how we're becoming a throwaway culture.

*Hayley:* A throwaway culture?

*Aaron:* Yeah, we throw things away instead of trying to fix them.

*Hayley:* Well, I think companies don't make things, especially electronics, as well as they used to. The quality of everything just isn't as good as before.

*Aaron:* Oh, I agree. The article mentioned that, too, but it made a good point. If the companies are making things worse than before, why should we buy more? That's what the companies want. It's better to give a local repair technician some money and help small businesses. And you'll spend less, too.

*Hayley:* I guess I see your point. So this guy guarantees his work?

*Aaron:* Yep! Why don't we stop by his shop after class?

*Hayley:* All right, you convinced me, Aaron.

**B** Listen again. What is a "throwaway culture"?

## Units 5–6 Progress check
### 3 Listening (p. 43)

**A** Listen to three tenants complain to their building manager. Complete the chart.

**1.**

*Tenant 1:* Hello, Mr. Frost. I was wondering if you could change the lightbulb out front. It keeps flickering, and it's going to go out.

*Mr. Frost:* I'll take care of it later. I'm really busy right now, and besides, it's still light outside.

*Tenant 1:* But it'll be dark when I get home tonight.

*Mr. Frost:* I'd love to help, but somebody borrowed my ladder.

*Tenant 1:* Well, you know, I have a chair! And if you give me a lightbulb, I can ask my son to change it. OK?

*Mr. Frost:* Oh! OK. Here . . . take a lightbulb from one of my lamps so you know it works.

*Tenant 1:* Thank you!

**2.**

*Tenant 2:* Uh, excuse me, Mr. Frost.

*Mr. Frost:* Yeah?

*Tenant 2:* Uh, I was wondering if you could do something about my next-door neighbor's dog? It's been barking and keeping me up all night.

*Mr. Frost:* Dogs bark. That's what they do.

*Tenant 2:* Yes, but they don't have to bark all night. This is three nights in a row.

*Mr. Frost:* Have you seen the size of that dog? You want me to go up there? That dog could hurt me!

*Tenant 2:* Well, I need my sleep!

*Mr. Frost:* Look, look. I tell you what. I'll call your neighbor and ask if he can keep his dog quiet.

*Tenant 2:* OK. Thank you!

**3.**

*Tenant 3:* Mr. Frost.

*Mr. Frost:* Mrs. Albano.

*Tenant 3:* I have a problem.

*Mr. Frost:* What is it now?

*Tenant 3:* It's my kitchen window. It's jammed shut. I can't open it anymore.

*Mr. Frost:* Mrs. Albano, I'm not sure how I can help you.

*Tenant 3:* Well, it needs to be opened. Can you try?

*Mr. Frost:* That's not really part of my job. Maybe you could try putting some vegetable oil on it.

*Tenant 3:* I don't think so. I'll call my cousin George to come over to take a look at it. He's a weightlifter.

# 7 What can we do?
## 5 Listening (p. 46)

**A** Listen to three people describe some serious environmental problems. Check the problem each person talks about.

**1. Morgan**

*Morgan:* Wait, don't throw that out!

*Man:* Why not?

*Morgan:* Recycle it. I've been reading a lot about how much trash we produce and what happens to all of it – and it really has me worried.

*Man:* Why?

*Morgan:* Well, it seems that the easiest way to dispose of trash is by burying it in landfills – land that could be used by farmers to grow food and other things. The problem is that in many countries the dumping areas have already been filled up, and it's hard to find places to start new ones. Of course, no one wants trash buried in their neighborhood, but it has to go somewhere!

*Man:* So what's the solution?

*Morgan:* Well, there is no easy solution; however, many cities are trying to do more recycling so that they can reduce the amount of stuff that goes into the landfills.

**2. Dalton**

*Woman:* I love my new computer, but I don't know what to do with my old one. It's so outdated. I know I shouldn't just throw it away.

*Dalton:* Well, you're right about that. Not disposing of electronic devices and other appliances properly is a huge problem these days, not just here but all over the world. Many people don't know what to do with their old phones, computers, video game systems, TV sets, refrigerators. . . . There are dangerous chemicals in these products, and they have to be handled in the right way.

*Woman:* So what are we supposed to do?

*Dalton:* Well, e-waste is not going away. With all the new technology these days, there's more e-waste than ever before. The solution is to dispose of it responsibly.

The good news is that there are more and more e-waste processing centers where professionals take these products and separate them into their various parts. Many of the parts can be reused, of course.

**3. Kendall**

*Kendall:* You know, you always hear about air pollution, but not many people are aware of the problem of water pollution.

*Man:* You mean in the oceans?

*Kendall:* No. I mean polluted drinking water. It's a problem in almost every major city in the world. Almost all our rivers and lakes – where we get our drinking water – are being polluted in some way by businesses, farms, homes, industries, and other sources. And even though the water most of us drink is treated, it's still not a hundred percent pure.

*Man:* So what's the solution?

*Kendall:* Well, it's a complicated problem to solve, but basically what's involved is treating all waste products more carefully so that dangerous chemicals and bacteria don't get into our water supply.

**B** Listen again. What can be done to solve each problem? Complete the chart.

## 7 Conversation (p. 47)

**C** Listen to the rest of the conversation. What do Cindy and Otis decide to do?

*Otis:* Wait a minute. Before we do anything, shouldn't we make sure that we've got our facts straight?

*Cindy:* Absolutely. The best thing to do is to monitor the situation over the next couple of weeks to see what exactly is happening.

*Otis:* How do we do that?

*Cindy:* Well, we can take pictures of the river and even take water samples to see how bad the situation is. We can get some friends to help.

*Otis:* OK. And then maybe I should talk to my uncle about it.

*Cindy:* That would be fantastic.

# 8 Never stop learning.
## 2 Perspectives (p. 50)

**A** Listen to a survey that a school is conducting about student preferences. Check the student's answers.

*Interviewer:* OK. Let's start. 1. Would you rather study on your own or join a study group?

a. I'd rather study on my own.

b. I'd rather join a study group.

c. I'd rather do both.

*Man:* I guess I'd rather join a group.

*Interviewer:* 2. Would you rather take an art course or a professional course?

a. I'd rather take an art course.

b. I'd rather take a professional course.

c. I'd rather not take either.

*Man:* Hmm. I'd rather not take either. . . . I think I'd rather take a language course.

*Interviewer:* 3. Would you prefer to take an online course or a traditional course?

a. I'd prefer to take an online course.

b. I'd prefer to take a traditional course.

c. I'd prefer not to take either. I'd prefer to hire a private tutor.

*Man:* Let's see. . . . I'd prefer to take an online course.

## 5 Listening (p. 52)

**A** Listen to a conversation between a student and his guidance counselor. Check the suggestions the guidance counselor gives.

*Ms. Mooney:* Hello, Ivan! How great to see you. How are your classes going?

*Ivan:* Well, OK, Ms. Mooney, but I think I'd rather be studying psychology. I chose civil engineering as my major, but this psychology class that I took was amazing. I'd even stay after class to talk to the professor about the material. I never do that in my other classes.

*Ms. Mooney:* That's great! But psychology is a big change from civil engineering.

*Ivan:* Exactly! What if I change majors and regret it later? I'm getting good grades in my engineering classes, but I'm bored. Psychology was really interesting, but it wasn't as easy. Maybe I should just do what's easy.

*Ms. Mooney:* Don't do what's easy. Do what you love. But you only took one psychology class, right? Perhaps you need to learn more about the field.

*Ivan:* So you think I should take more classes?

*Ms. Mooney:* Yes, you could. Have you ever heard of informational interviews? That's an option, too.

*Ivan:* What are they?

*Ms. Mooney:* You find people with jobs in the fields you're interested in and sit down with them and ask them about their work. You know, the day-to-day stuff, what they like, what they don't like, how many years they had to study. It's like an interview, but just to learn about the job.

*Ivan:* That sounds great! So I could talk with a civil engineer *and* a psychologist?

*Ms. Mooney:* Sure. And you could even shadow some of these professionals.

*Ivan:* Shadow them?

*Ms. Mooney:* Job shadowing is when you follow someone around at their job and experience it from their perspective. Think of it like an internship, but you're only watching. You can shadow someone for a few hours or several times if you'd prefer. You

know, before I became a guidance counselor, I was a banker.

*Ivan:* You were a banker, Ms. Mooney?

*Ms. Mooney:* Yes, for 10 years. But after doing some volunteer work with finance students, I realized I'd rather help people than crunch numbers. So I did informational interviews and job shadowing, and here I am! And I love being a guidance counselor! So, what do you say? Shall we find some professionals you can talk to?

*Ivan:* Yes, please! I need all the information I can get.

## 8 Conversation (p. 52)

**B** Listen to two other students, Rick and Nia, explain how they learn new words. Who uses technology to study? Who organizes words by category?

**Rick**

I keep a record of new words I come across. Then I make up study cards. I write the word on one side of the card and the meaning on the other side. Oh, and I always include at least one sentence with the word in it. Then I go through the cards whenever I have some spare time – like when I'm waiting for my laundry to dry or on the bus – and study the words until I know them by heart. Every week or so, I organize the cards into categories: You know, I put all the words together that have to do with food . . . or work . . . or home . . . or school . . . whatever I can find that my new words have in common.

**Nia**

I keep a vocabulary list on my phone. It's organized alphabetically. Whenever I hear or read a new word, I add it to the list. I also try to put down some key information about the word – you know, whether it's a noun or a verb, and some examples of how it's used. I go through the list and study the words as often as I can. I really believe that the only way to learn new words – even in your own language – is by memorizing them.

## 10 Discussion (p. 53)

**A** Listen to James and Sophia describe how they developed two skills. How did they learn? Complete the chart.

**1. James**

*James:* I have a huge fear of speaking in front of people. Seriously, I'd rather do anything else. And I'm a lawyer, so it's all about *how* you speak and present your case. I decided to take a public speaking course, and the teacher taught me some great tips. By memorizing the first line of my speech, by looking out in the audience and focusing on just one person at a time, and, of course, by practicing a ton in that class, I was finally able to improve. Oh, and I always exercise before a presentation to calm my nerves!

**1. Sophia**

*Sophia:* I love to speak in public. People think if you love public speaking, then it's easy – but that's not true. I work for a non-profit organization, so I give lots of speeches to convince people to donate money. I would tell stories and jokes, ask the audience questions, but they wouldn't donate money. I was too spontaneous, and I wasn't reaching them. So I started to organize my ideas. By putting my stories at the beginning of my speech and ending with numbers and facts, I had a bigger impact. I'm still spontaneous, but hard facts and data are hard to forget, so I always end with those.

### 2. James

*James:* I remember I was so excited to learn how to drive. I was 15 when my dad gave me my first lesson in a parking lot. He taught me the basics and then wanted me to drive home on a busy street that first day! He said that by learning on the road with other drivers, I would never forget the basics. That was my dad. My mom was another story. She was so nervous that we never left the parking lot! I never practiced with her again. And it took her six months to get in the car with me, even after I got my license!

### 2. Sophia

*Sophia:* I'm from New York City, where most people don't even learn to drive until they're older. But not me. I first tried when I was 16 with my mom. I wanted to visit a friend, so we went in my mom's car. I thought by going slowly, I'd be fine. But I hadn't thought about parking, and in the city, parking is impossible! After 30 minutes of trying to park and almost hitting two cars, I just wanted to go home. But my mom insisted we keep practicing, so we drove outside the city, where I finally could relax and get comfortable driving!

## Units 7–8 Progress check
### 3 Listening (p. 57)

**A** Listen to people talk about recent events and activities in their lives. What events and activities are they talking about? What two qualities does each person's behavior demonstrate? Complete the chart.

### 1. Kate

*Kate:* I did it! I did it!
*Man:* Did what, Kate? What happened?
*Kate:* I can't believe it!
*Man:* Kate! Calm down! What happened?
*Kate:* I got it! I got into the company I auditioned for!
*Man:* Really? That's fantastic! But I thought you auditioned and didn't make it.
*Kate:* That's right. And I felt really sad about it for a while because I know I have potential. I started thinking maybe I just needed to work harder, so I started dancing again on my own. And by practicing every day, I got better and better. Then I saw in the newspaper that auditions were being held again. I knew I could do it, so I went in, auditioned, and made it!
*Man:* That's great. Congratulations!

### 2. Mark

*Mark:* I could just kick myself.
*Woman:* Come on, Mark, it could happen to anyone.
*Mark:* I lost the game for us. All I had to do was kick it past the goalie.
*Woman:* Yeah, but that goalie is tough to get by.
*Mark:* No way. There was no one in the way. Everyone else was at the other end of the field.
*Woman:* Yeah, but we all miss one sometimes.
*Mark:* Well, my teammates aren't going to lose another game because of me.

### 3. Iris

*Man:* Iris, when did you start doing this?
*Iris:* Oh, a few months ago.
*Man:* What made you start?
*Iris:* Well, it was my brother who inspired me. I've always wanted to paint or draw, but he was the artistic one. His paintings have been sold for big money at galleries, and, well, I had never even picked up a brush. But I started saving money every month until I had enough for this painting class. I'm so glad I did.
*Man:* You're not bad, you know. I love the colors in this portrait.
*Iris:* Thanks.
*Man:* Who is it?
*Iris:* It's you.

## 9 Getting things done
### 10 Listening (p. 62)

**A** Listen to a conversation between three friends on New Year's Eve. Check the resolution each person has and write their friends' suggestions.

*Edward:* That food was delicious, you guys. How many years have we all spent New Year's Eve together, Hannah?
*Hannah:* Five years! I just posted our annual picture. Your mom already liked it, Selena.
*Selena:* Of course she did! And now my favorite part: New Year's resolutions! Edward?
*Edward:* I need to stop procrastinating on my big project for grad school. I still haven't started it because I get so easily distracted.
*Hannah:* I've said this before, Edward, but you need to cut down on those distractions. How can you work with the TV on? And your roommate's music! I could never put up with that.
*Edward:* I know. It's hard because I get along with him so well. But he is a big distraction. And well, you know how I love TV.
*Selena:* Yeah, but you'd finish your project a lot faster without them. Have you thought about going to the library? Work hard for a few hours, then go home and watch all the TV you want!
*Edward:* Hmm, that's not a bad idea. I've never tried working at the library. What about you, Selena?
*Selena:* I want the energy I used to have at school! Now I'm just always tired at work.

*Hannah:* I think you need to exercise, Selena. You sit down all day at a desk and then go home and sit more. Of course you're tired! I found this great app that has quick and effective exercises you can do in your living room!

*Edward:* Yeah, but she needs to leave the living room. Selena, maybe you could start some outdoor exercise, like hiking, swimming, or jogging. You need to take better care of yourself.

*Selena:* I hate jogging, but I've always liked swimming. You swim, don't you, Edward?

*Edward:* Yes, and I love it. Why don't you come with me to the pool this week? Push yourself to start exercising three times a week, and I'll push myself to go to the library.

*Selena:* Perfect. That leaves us with Hannah, our social media queen.

*Hannah:* Ugh, I need to come up with an idea to save my relationship. I think my boyfriend might break up with me.

*Selena:* What happened?

*Hannah:* He says I'm addicted to my phone and social media, but it's my job! I'm a social media analyst! I *have* to constantly be online.

*Edward:* Yeah, but you shouldn't be working online ALL the time, Hannah. Everyone needs a break.

*Selena:* What about taking a couple hours off from your phone every night?

*Hannah:* Every night?

*Edward:* Hannah, work is important, but it isn't everything.

*Hannah:* I just don't want my work to suffer and lose my job.

*Selena:* You'll be better at your job if you're not always working. Try it for a few nights.

*Hannah:* Yeah, maybe you're right. Guys, why can't life be easy like it used to be?

*Edward:* Like when we were 12?

*Selena:* Welcome to being an adult! Happy New Year!

# 10   A matter of time

## 🔟 Listening (p. 68)

**A** Listen to people discuss changes that will affect these topics in the future. Write down two changes for each topic.

### 1. Crime

*Woman:* Well, I think crime will completely change in the future.

*Man:* How so?

*Woman:* Nowadays people use their debit and credit cards more than they use cash. How we spend money is changing. I think there will be less street crime in the future. Crime will become more intelligent and digital. There will be more computer hacker criminals.

*Man:* That sounds more serious.

*Woman:* I know! Crimes will definitely become more severe. Instead of stealing some cash from my purse, a criminal could go online to my bank account and steal a lot more. It's scary to think about.

### 2. Space travel

*Woman:* Do you really think people will live in space in the future? I don't know if I believe that.

*Man:* Oh definitely. I think within 100 years, people will be living on other planets.

*Woman:* Really? Like you and I could be living on another planet?

*Man:* Well, not in our lifetime. But I think within the next 50 years, humans will have traveled to other galaxies.

*Woman:* Yes, I agree with that. And what about extraterrestrial life? Will we have made contact with aliens from other galaxies?

*Man:* I don't know, but if we do, I sure hope they're friendly!

### 3. Environment

*Man:* Every time I read the newspaper, there's another environmental disaster. Do you think environmental problems will eventually become a thing of the past?

*Woman:* Definitely. There are some amazing ideas to clean up our oceans. I think in the next 20 years, we will have cleaned up all the trash in the oceans.

*Man:* I sure hope so. Some of those garbage patches in the ocean are larger than some countries!

*Woman:* I know. I read that nonbiodegradable trash is the biggest problem in the oceans and on land.

*Man:* Nonbiodegradable trash, like plastic?

*Woman:* Exactly. I think in the next 30 years, we will have eliminated plastic and found materials to use that are better for the environment.

### 4. Energy

*Man:* You know, I was reading this article about energy of the future. Fossil fuels like oil and coal have become our main energy sources.

*Woman:* Yeah, but we need safer energy.

*Man:* This article says we're making progress with other kinds of energy. It predicts that in 50 years, we will be using only green energy sources, like wind and solar energy.

*Woman:* Wouldn't that be wonderful?

*Man:* And it said that with electronic devices, we won't have to wait for them to charge. We'll be able to charge our phones or computers in just a few minutes.

### 5. Money

*Man:* With all the technology we use every day, sometimes it feels strange that we're still using paper money that can rip or get damaged.

*Woman:* Yeah, it seems old-fashioned next to credit cards with chips and sensors, doesn't it? It's just a matter of time before paper money isn't made at all anymore.

*Man:* You think so?

*Woman:* Definitely. No one will use cash and everyone will have cards.

*Man:* If that happens, then I think everyone in the world will eventually use the same currency.

*Woman:* So only one currency and no more cash? It sounds a lot easier, but I'm sure there will be new problems, too.

*Man:* Oh, there always are!

# Units 9–10 Progress check

## 3 Listening (p. 71)

**A** Listen to people discuss the questions. Write the correct answers.

**1.**

*Man:* Did I ever tell you that when I was little, I wanted to be an astronaut?

*Woman:* No, you didn't.

*Man:* I remember watching Neil Armstrong land on the moon. Do you remember the date?

*Woman:* July 20, 1969, right?

*Man:* That's right!

**2.**

*Man:* Hey, we should start planning a trip for the next World Cup.

*Woman:* Yeah! That would be exciting.

*Man:* I was watching this documentary. Did you know that in the first World Cup in Uruguay, only 13 countries participated?

*Woman:* Wow, what a difference! I think there were 32 countries in the last tournament.

*Man:* Yeah, a lot has changed since 1930!

**3.**

*Man:* What are you reading?

*Woman:* It's an article about the Chernobyl nuclear disaster. They're talking about what the contaminated area is like now. Did you know that a few hundred elderly people never left Chernobyl? They didn't want to leave their homes.

*Man:* I can't believe that. It seems so dangerous.

*Woman:* Do you remember the year?

*Man:* It was in 1986, right?

*Woman:* Yep! Good memory.

**4.**

*Boy:* Mom, can you help me with this project?

*Woman:* Sure, what is it about?

*Boy:* I'm talking about the *Titanic*, but I need one more fact.

*Woman:* Let me see. Ah, I know that they took from 1909 to 1911 to build it. More than 3,000 people helped build it.

*Boy:* Really? That's perfect! Thanks, Mom!

**5.**

*Man:* It's almost the anniversary of the Indian Ocean tsunami. Do you remember that?

*Woman:* Oh, yeah! How could I forget?

*Man:* Did you know it took only 15 minutes after the quake for the waves to reach the coast of Sumatra?

*Woman:* Wow, that's fast! Let me see if I remember the date. It was in 2004, right?

*Man:* Yep, December 26, 2004.

*Woman:* I read the waves were 100 feet high in some places. Can you imagine?

# 11 Rites of passage

## 2 Conversation (p. 72)

**B** Listen to the rest of the conversation. What was an important turning point for Jim? for Luke?

*Luke:* So that was a turning point in your life.

*Jim:* One of them. But the most important was becoming a parent. When your cousin Bella was born, my life changed completely, and I changed, too. Before that, I never used to worry about the future. But then I realized I was responsible for another person and that made me take life more seriously. What about you? Have you had any life-changing experiences yet?

*Luke:* Well . . . I guess making the basketball team really changed my life. For the first time, other people really depended on me to do my best. Since I'm an only child, I hadn't had much experience working with others before I joined the team.

*Jim:* That's great.

*Luke:* Yeah, I learned how to be a team player and not be so selfish. And our team, we really grew up together over the past four years. It was so rewarding when our hard work paid off, and we won the championship last year!

## 4 Listening (p. 74)

**A** Listen to three people describe important events in their lives. Complete the chart.

*Mark:* Good morning, listeners! I'm Mark Markinson and we're back talking about turning points – those moments when something happens in our lives and afterward we're never quite the same. Let's go to our first caller, Nari.

*Nari:* Hi, Mark! I'm South Korean and came to Boston by myself when I was 17. Transitioning was hard. I had studied English, but had never practiced with anyone. I was so nervous at first, and the second week I had to buy a cell phone. I was terrified, but the salesperson understood my first question and I understood his answer! The moment that happened, I knew I was going to be OK with my English and get my dream job in Boston. So I guess buying a cell phone was my turning point with my English.

*Mark:* Thank you, Nari! And your English sounds great! Let's go to Anthony.

*Anthony:* Hi, Mark! Well, I started working for myself one year ago.

*Mark:* What made you decide to do it, Anthony?

*Anthony:* I was doing graphic design for this company, and I was bored. I didn't like the company or town I lived in. I wanted to work for myself. I'd say my turning point was the day I started looking for my own clients online. As soon as I did that, I knew I was serious. I started doing freelance work, saving money, and one year later I quit my job and moved to Chicago.

*Mark:* Love those entrepreneur stories! We have time for one more call.

*Karina:* Hi, I'm Karina. I'm a doctor, but I didn't always know that was my calling. My aunt had cancer and I took care of her during the hardest part of her treatment. After she finished treatment, she told me I had taken better care of her than any doctor. That's when I knew I wanted to help people like her. So my aunt's sickness was my turning point to decide my career.

*Mark:* And I'm sure your aunt is very proud. Thank you for sharing, Karina. And listeners, that's all the time we have for today. I'm Mark Markinson; Have a great day!

**B** Listen again. What do these three people have in common?

## 🔟 Listening (p. 76)

**A** Listen to a conversation between three friends about regrets. Write two regrets that each person has.

*Ray:* Hey, Ariana! You should come to the movies with Kira and me on Saturday.

*Kira:* Yeah, come with us, Ariana! It'll be fun!

*Ariana:* I wish I could, but I have to write a paper for that writing course I'm taking.

*Kira:* What's it about?

*Ariana:* My biggest regret in life. I mean, that's a big question! I have regrets, but just one?

*Ray:* Well, what are they?

*Ariana:* I've always said I should have spent more time with my grandma while she was alive. And I shouldn't have waited so long to start learning Arabic. If I'd talked more with my extended family, I could have learned it ages ago. I guess I have lots of regrets. What about you guys?

*Ray:* Hmm. I think my biggest regret is from when I was a kid. There was this really mean bully at school. I mean, every day he would tease me because of my glasses, or my grades, or something I was wearing. There was always a reason. And I never defended myself. I just let him say what he wanted and make me feel terrible. And I regret that. I should've talked to him. I should've been more confident.

*Kira:* Don't be so hard on yourself, Ray. You were a kid. And what's important is that you learned from that situation, and you won't let people bully you again.

*Ray:* True. So, do you have regrets, Kira?

*Kira:* Well, I didn't take many difficult classes in high school. I should have been more ambitious. And I didn't do any activities after school. I could've done more volunteer work and helped people more in my spare time. But honestly, I don't believe in regrets. I've learned lessons from my mistakes and have become a better person. No regrets, just lessons learned.

*Ariana:* You know what, Kira? I like that idea for my paper. "No regrets, just lessons learned."

*Ray:* Perfect! Now go work on your paper so you can go to the movies with us!

**B** Listen again. Which friend feels differently about regrets? How does he or she feel?

## 12 Keys to success
## 9 Listening (p. 82)

**A** Listen to radio commercials for three different businesses. What are two special features of each place?

**Fitness For Life**

*Announcer:* You said you'd start working out next month, right? Or after you finish that big project at work? Did you know that you can make something a habit in 21 days? Take our bet at Fitness For Life. Sign up for one month and we'll throw in a personal trainer for your first 21 days. That's right, your own personal trainer free for 21 days! People love Fitness For Life because of our qualified trainers, state-of-the-art fitness equipment, dynamic group classes, and nutritional guidance to start eating and feeling better as soon as possible. Fitness For Life, where you come first.

**Beauty To Go**

*Woman 1:* So what time are we meeting for dinner tomorrow?

*Woman 2:* I don't know if I'll have time! I have to go to the hair salon after work. And I have no idea when I'll get home because traffic has been horrible lately. I wish I had a good beauty salon closer to home.

*Woman 1:* What about Beauty To Go? They go to your house!

*Woman 2:* My house? But I don't have all the equipment and products.

*Woman 1:* No, they bring everything with them. Just go online to their site, select what you want, where you live, and the time you want them there, and that's it! The professionals are amazing!

*Woman 2:* What a great idea! But isn't it expensive? I mean, since they come to me with all the supplies, they must charge a lot.

*Woman 1:* Not at all. Since they don't pay for a fancy hair salon, they're actually cheaper! And you can't beat the convenience! They even brought magazines for me to look at while they did my nails.

*Announcer 2:* Beauty To Go. When and where you want, beauty has never been this easy.

**Like-New Repair Services**

*Announcer:* Cracked screen? Slow camera? Short battery life? You depend on your smartphone every day to live your life. So why should you let it slow you down? But don't go buy a new smartphone! Let trusted repair technicians at Like-New Repair Services fix your phone for a fraction of the cost. We'll diagnose the problem for free. And if we can't fix it, you don't pay for it. So what have you got to lose? Like-New Repair Services. Don't let your phone slow you down.

**B** Listen again. Complete the slogan for each business.

# Units 11–12 Progress check
## 3 Listening (p. 85)

**A** Listen to a career coach discuss some factors necessary to work for yourself. Write down the three factors that you hear.

*Woman:* Many of us dream about working for ourselves. No boss, working at home . . . sounds great, right? It is, but it's also difficult. You'll work harder than you ever have and not only that, a lot of it will be for free. What do I mean? The first factor in your success is knowing your field. I'm talking about becoming an expert in your type of work. Know your competition. Be ready to explain why you are better than them. Learn how potential clients can find you. Be on every site for freelancers in your field. Remember: Research is knowledge and knowledge is power. If your clients trust that you know what you're talking about, they will come back to you.

Have you ever heard the saying, "It's not *what* you know, but *who* you know"? Networking is everything! Sure, it's important to have a strong online presence, but never underestimate the people you already know. I'm talking about old colleagues and bosses, family, friends, acquaintances, neighbors. These are people who know you and often know your work. You never know who may be a potential client.

Feeling overwhelmed yet? That's OK! And that's why it's so important to establish small goals every week. You have a lot of work to do. The third factor in your success is organizing all of your work into small goals, or realistic tasks. Don't write down a goal to "learn about competition." Find out the names of three competitors and find out all you can about those three. Goals should be realistic. Only then can you accomplish them, make progress, and be a successful freelancer!

**B** Listen again. In your own words, write why each factor is important.

# 13 What might have been
## 2 Conversation (p. 86)

**B** Listen to the rest of the conversation. What happened?

*Ava:* Look! There's Tyler coming down the street.

*Chris:* Hey, Tyler, what happened?

*Tyler:* You won't believe how stupid I was. I came outside to take the trash to the garbage can, and I locked myself out. And worst of all, my cell phone was locked inside.

*Chris:* So that's why you didn't answer my call.

*Tyler:* Yeah, and I couldn't call you because I didn't remember your number.

*Chris:* That's the trouble with smartphones! Nobody remembers anyone's number anymore. So, what did you do?

*Tyler:* I walked to the gas station and called a locksmith. He said he would arrive in about half an hour. He

must be on his way. I'm sorry for all this. You guys must be starved.

*Ava:* Well, I brought some dessert. . . . Would anyone care for a piece of pie?

## 5 Listening (p. 87)

**B** Listen to the explanations for the two events in part A and take notes. What *did* happen? How similar were your explanations?

**1.**

*Woman:* Last Saturday was a long day! We were going to my grandparents' 50th anniversary party, and we had to catch a plane at 7 a.m. We planned to get there early to spend time with my family. But during the night we lost power, so our alarm clock never woke us up. We got up two hours late, missed our flight, and had to catch the next plane. We even changed into our clothes for the party at the airport to save time! It was a close call, but we arrived just when everyone was sitting down to dinner. I'm so glad we made it, but what a stressful trip!

**2.**

*Man:* You wouldn't guess it from her size, but our little dog Sheba is really adventurous. She loves to play in our backyard and chase birds, but when we come home, she is always waiting for us by the door. But yesterday when my daughter and I got home, we couldn't find Sheba anywhere. My poor daughter was so upset she couldn't stop crying! Someone must've left the back gate open, and she must've escaped. Luckily, my neighbor saw her running down the street and was able to pick her up. Ten minutes after we got home, she knocked on the door with Sheba in her arms. What a relief!

## 11 Listening (p. 90)

**A** Listen to descriptions of three situations. What would have been the best thing to do in each situation? Check the best suggestion.

**1.**

*Simon:* Hey, what's this? Wow! A gold ring!

*Woman:* Simon found a gold ring on a busy sidewalk. It looked like an expensive ring. He wanted to give it back to the owner, but he thought the person who lost it might return to look for it. So he left the ring on the sidewalk.

**2.**

*Jana:* No one is ever going to want to hire me.

*Man:* Jana got fired from her last job because she was rude to a customer. She just applied for a new job, but she lied and said she had quit her last job. The manager called her old boss and found out what really happened.

**3.**

*Martin:* I trusted my boss.

*Woman:* Martin discovered that $1,000 was missing from the company account, so he asked his boss about it. His boss admitted he borrowed the money without permission, but he promised to return it next week. Three days later, Martin's boss disappeared, and now more money is missing from the company account.

# 14 Creative careers

## 2 Conversation (p. 92)

**B** Listen to the rest of the conversation. Who helps Clara choose the voice actors?

*Clara:* I see there's another question. You, in the red shirt, please.

*Jill:* Yes. I'm curious: Do you, as the director, get to choose the actors for the voices?

*Clara:* I do. But for big-budget animated movies, I often get help from a casting director.

*Jill:* Can I ask why that is?

*Clara:* A casting director can help you get big names. And when popular stars are used, it can bring a wider audience to an animated film, which, of course, means more money can be made.

*Jill:* Is it pretty hard to get movie stars? Wouldn't they rather be working on live action movies?

*Clara:* Actually, no! You'd be surprised. Some big names in Hollywood want to work on animated films because they want to do a movie their kids will love. And I love that!

## 4 Listening (p. 93)

**A** Listen to Casey and Grant talk about things that often happen in movies. Number the parts of a movie in the order they are mentioned.

*Grant:* So, what did you think of the movie?

*Casey:* Well, the acting was good, but I thought it was too predictable.

*Grant:* What do you mean, predictable?

*Casey:* I could tell what was going to happen, even before it happened on screen! All of these action movies have the same basic story.

*Grant:* I don't think so! What about *Star Wars*? That movie is totally different from this one.

*Casey:* Well, OK, this movie is set in Washington, D.C., not in space – but the basic formula is the same. First, the main character is introduced – the good guy.

*Grant:* Right. We had Luke Skywalker in *Star Wars*, and in this one, we have the president of the United States.

*Casey:* Exactly. Then a problem is presented. Right? Usually, the problem is bad guys who do something wrong, and the good guys have to stop them. That's when the action really starts.

*Grant:* Of course – because it's an action movie!

*Casey:* Right. So, like Luke has to save Princess Leia and fight Darth Vader. Or, like in this movie, the president has to fight enemy soldiers trying to take over the White House.

*Grant:* And then . . . something bad happens, and it seems like all hope is lost.

*Casey:* Exactly! In this movie, it seemed like the president was winning, but then the bad guys kidnapped his family.

*Grant:* And in *Star Wars*, Princess Leia's planet was destroyed.

*Casey:* But it's all really just a test of our heroes' strength and determination!

*Grant:* Wow! OK, it really does seem like there are some similarities. So then, finally, we get to some good stuff. Like the president setting a trap for the enemy soldiers!

*Casey:* Yes! A new plan is put into action. Remember how the Death Star spaceship had one weakness? Luke and the rebels planned to destroy the ship.

*Grant:* And in the end, the bad guy is defeated. Luke destroys the Death Star, Princess Leia is safe, and Darth Vader is spun off into space!

*Grant:* Thank goodness, right? And in this movie, the president's family is saved and the soldiers are sent to jail. It's a feel-good ending.

*Casey:* And that's the most important part!

**B** Listen again. For each movie part above, write an example from the movies the friends discuss.

# Units 13–14 Progress check

## 1 Listening (p. 98)

**A** Listen to three conversations. Where do you think each conversation takes place? What do you think might have happened? Take notes.

**1.**

*Man:* Help! Help! Can anyone hear me? Help! Please call the manager!

*Woman:* Hello? Is someone in there?

*Man:* Yes! I'm stuck between the second and third floors! Please help me get out!

*Woman:* Won't it open?

*Man:* No! Get the manager, please!

*Woman:* OK! I'll get some help! Stay right there!

**2.**

*Man:* Oh, no! Not again! I thought you got it fixed.

*Woman:* Yeah, I did! And they said that it shouldn't freeze anymore.

*Man:* Well, something's not right. And it's too late to call anyone. Maybe there's something we can do.

*Woman:* Let's just wait until morning and see how it is then.

**3.**

*Man:* Well. I'll certainly never eat here again! And I'll tell all my friends not to come here either!

*Man:* I do apologize. I . . . I'm afraid he's just started working here, but I don't think he's going to last long . . . not after this!

# 15 A law must be passed!

## 5 Listening (p. 102)

**A** Listen to people discuss annoying situations. Number the situations they describe in the correct order from 1 to 3. (There are three extra situations.)

**1.**

*Woman:* Well, that was a great movie, but that guy in front of us texting the whole time was really annoying!

*Man:* I agree! The light from his cell phone really distracted me.

*Woman:* I think people shouldn't be allowed to text at all in the movie theater. Our phones should have a movie mode that people should be required to turn on. You know – like airplane mode when you're on a plane, but for movies!

*Man:* Hey, movie mode! The screen wouldn't light up and distract other people. I love that idea!

**2.**

*Man:* Ouch! That woman just stepped on my foot trying to take a selfie. I can't believe we're at this historic monument, and I'm being bothered with other people's selfies!

*Woman:* Something has really got to be done about this whole selfie phenomenon.

*Man:* You know, I read that selfies have been banned at many tourist destinations, like at museums and monuments.

*Woman:* Really? I think that's great! Selfies ought to be prohibited at any place with big crowds of people. Whatever happened to just asking people to take a picture of you?

**3.**

*Woman:* I thought I was going to go crazy in that waiting room!

*Man:* Why? Was it crowded?

*Woman:* No, there was only one other man in there, but he was talking with his phone on speaker the whole time! I could hear his entire conversation with his co-worker. A rule has to be made that prohibits people from talking on speaker indoors in public places. It's so unnecessary!

*Man:* I agree. Offices and public buildings should be required to post signs that prohibit that. It's very disrespectful.

**B** Listen again. What solutions do they suggest for each situation?

## 8 Conversation (p. 103)

**B** Listen to the rest of the conversation. What is Ted concerned about?

*Mara:* Oh, listen to me. I'm always complaining, aren't I? Anyway, how are things with you?

*Ted:* Oh, not bad, but I'm still not sure what I'm going to do after I graduate.

*Mara:* Yeah, it's hard to find a job these days, isn't it?

*Ted:* It's not that. I'm just not sure if going to engineering school was the right thing to do.

*Mara:* What do you mean?

*Ted:* I only have a few more months before I graduate, and now I'm wondering why I did this. I don't want to be an engineer. It all seems like a waste of time now.

*Mara:* So what are you going to do?

*Ted:* Well, I'd like to move to Hawaii and set up a surfing school, but I think my parents would flip.

## 11 Listening (p. 104)

**A** Listen to people give their opinions about issues in the news. What issues are they talking about?

**1.**

*Woman:* Wow, that documentary about animals in entertainment was a little hard to watch. I mean, I love watching animals do tricks at amusement parks and circuses, but I had no idea how much they can suffer.

*Man:* Yeah, some of those animals are kept in horrible conditions. That's just not right! Then they're punished and abused if they don't do what they're supposed to. And the only benefit is that the owners are making money. In most cases, they're not trying to improve the animals' living conditions. If it weren't for those animals, they wouldn't make any of that money!

*Woman:* I know. It's awful, isn't it? But I feel like some places have the right idea, too. They use the animals for entertainment, but they make sure the animals are taken care of, and they use part of the profits to rescue other animals and do research. Research, rescue, and protection of the animals. That seems more acceptable, doesn't it?

*Man:* I guess, but how do we make sure that all places are acting responsibly and doing those things? I still think that animals should be in their natural habitats, not in some small space so they can help humans make money. It's just not natural.

**2.**

*Man:* I just read in the paper that a supercenter is going to open just five minutes outside of town.

*Woman:* A supercenter? Like a drugstore, supermarket, and discount store all combined into one?

*Man:* Exactly. I think it's great. The products are cheaper, and it will provide a lot of jobs for the community.

*Woman:* I agree that the products are cheaper and it does create jobs, but what about the smaller family-owned stores in town? All those small markets and clothing stores and pharmacies will now have to compete with this supercenter. And a lot of those smaller businesses will lose a lot of money because, let's face it, they can't compete.

*Man:* I guess I hadn't thought about the impact on the small businesses in town.

*Woman:* And not only that, but I think we'll lose a lot of variety. If these smaller businesses start losing money, they will either close down or start limiting their products. Then we'll have fewer choices when we go shopping.

*Man:* Yeah, I guess big companies aren't always good for small businesses, are they?

**B** Listen again. Write the different opinions that you hear.

# 16  Reaching your goals
## ⑤ Listening (p. 108)

**A** Listen to two people answer two interview questions. Write the obstacles they faced and what they did about them in the chart.

*Interviewer:* Thank you, Mr. Sandberg. Can you tell me about an accomplishment that you are proud of?

*Mr. Sandberg:* I was lucky to have my parents' help paying for my education. But when I decided I wanted to study abroad in Italy, both my parents thought it was a complete waste of my time. I tried to convince them, but in the end they told me that if I went, they wouldn't help me financially. So I decided I would pay for it myself. I was able to get two jobs and for one year before my trip, all I did was work and study. But I did it! I managed to save enough money and study in Italy like I wanted. That experience taught me that I could do anything I wanted if I worked hard enough.

*Interviewer:* Ms. Rowe, please tell me about an obstacle you managed to overcome.

*Ms. Rowe:* Well, one thing you must know about me is that I love soccer. Unfortunately, I'm not very good at playing it, and it took me years to finally accept that. But I didn't want to give up on soccer. I just needed a new approach. I started investigating and managed to find a job coaching a kids' soccer league. I discovered I was really good at it. I understood their frustration and energy. That experience taught me that we have to be creative dealing with problems. We shouldn't give up on what we love, but sometimes we have to think about what we love with a different perspective to find a solution.

**B** Listen again. What did each person learn from his or her experience? Complete the chart.

## ⑩ Listening (p. 110)

**A** Listen to three young people describe their plans for the future. What do they hope they will have achieved by the time they're 30?

### 1. Hugo

*Hugo:* Protecting the environment is something that is really important to me. We only have one chance with our planet, so we need to keep finding new ways to live that don't destroy it. By the time I'm 30, I'd like to have established my career as a green architect. I have lots of ideas for building with recycled materials, and there are so many environmentally friendly ways to create energy. I think green building is the

architecture of the future, and I want to be a huge part of that!

### 2. Erin

*Erin:* I know what makes people happy and I know about luxury. That's why by the time I turn 30, I'll have opened the world's biggest luxury hotel chain, and it'll be a huge success! I don't have any money right now, but I know I can convince rich people to invest in my hotel. I'll start with one hotel in every major European city. And then, by the time I'm 40, I'd like to have retired so I can travel all over the world and stay in my hotels.

### 3. Danny

*Danny:* Ever since I was little, I've loved animals. We always had pets in my family – cats, birds, even snakes – and they always made me so happy. That's why I'm going to veterinary school. I want to take care of animals so they can make other people happy. I hope that by the time I'm 30, I'll have started working full time as a veterinarian. My dream is to have my own clinic five years after that.

**B** Listen again. Why does each person have his or her specific dream? List one reason for each person.

# Units 15–16 Progress check
## ② Listening (p. 112)

**A** Listen to people give opinions about their city. Check the correct responses to agree with their statements.

**1.**

*Woman:* The city should have more nighttime buses, shouldn't it?

**2.**

*Man:* It isn't easy to find good housing, is it?

**3.**

*Woman:* There aren't enough taxis in the city, are there?

**4.**

*Man:* The community center has great exercise classes, doesn't it?

**5.**

*Woman:* We need to raise money for the new soccer field, don't we?

**6.**

*Man:* There isn't much crime in this neighborhood, is there?

# Workbook answer key

## 1 That's my kind of friend!

### Exercise 1

2. The Wongs like meeting new people and having friends over for dinner. They're one of the most <u>outgoing</u> couples I know.
3. You can't trust Alice. She always promises to do something, but then she never does it. She's pretty <u>unreliable</u>.
4. James wants to be an actor. It's hard to break into the business, but his family is very <u>supportive</u> of his dream.
5. I never know how to act around Lisa! One minute she's in a good mood, and the next minute she's in a bad mood. She's so <u>temperamental</u>.

### Exercise 2

**A**

*Opposites with –in*
incompetent, independent, inexperienced, inflexible, informal, insensitive
*Opposites with un-*
unattractive, uncooperative, unhelpful, unpopular, unreasonable, unreliable

**B**

Answers will vary.

### Exercise 3

A: I'm looking for someone <u>x</u> I can go on vacation with.
B: Hmm. So what kind of person are you looking for?
A: I want to travel with someone <u>who / that</u> is easygoing and independent.
B: Right. And you'd probably also like a person <u>who / that</u> is reliable.
A: Yeah, and I want someone <u>x</u> I know well.
B: So why don't you ask me?
A: You? I know you too well!
B: Ha! Does that mean you think I'm someone <u>who / that</u> is high-strung, dependent, and unreliable?
A: No! I'm just kidding. You're definitely someone <u>x</u> I could go on vacation with. So, . . . what are you doing in June?

### Exercise 4

Answers will vary.

### Exercise 5

**A**

introvert, extrovert, thinker, feeler, sensor, and intuitive

**B**

Answers will vary.

**C**

Answers will vary.

### Exercise 6

1. b   I like it when people are easygoing and friendly.
2. d   I don't mind it when people are a few minutes late for an appointment.
3. c   It upsets me when rich people are stingy.
4. a   It embarrasses me when someone criticizes me in front of other people.

### Exercise 7

Answers will vary. Possible answers:

2. I love it when someone gives me a gift.
3. It bothers me when someone listens to loud music on the bus.
4. It makes me happy when I finish work for the day.
5. I can't stand it when I'm stuck in traffic.
6. It upsets me when people talk on their phones at the movies.

### Exercise 8

Answers will vary. Possible answers:

2. It bothers me when someone wants to argue with me.
   I can't stand it when someone gets angry about something unimportant.
3. I don't mind it when someone looks at their phone during mealtime.
   It doesn't bother me when someone does work while they eat.
4. It upsets me when my kids leave their toys all over the apartment.
   It makes me angry when people don't clean up their mess.

### Exercise 9

Answers will vary.

### Exercise 10

1. I can tell Simon anything, and I know he won't tell anyone else. I can really <u>trust</u> him.
2. Kay has a very high opinion of herself. I don't like people who are so <u>egotistical</u>.
3. It bothers me when people are too serious. I prefer people who are <u>easygoing</u> and have a good sense of humor.
4. I like it when someone expresses strong <u>opinions</u>. Hearing other people's views can really make you think.
5. Lisa is very rich, but she only spends her money on herself. She's very <u>stingy</u>.

# 2 Working 9 to 5

## Exercise 1

### A

2. green researcher <u>a</u>
3. guidance counselor <u>b</u>
4. organic food farmer <u>e</u>
5. social media manager <u>c</u>
6. software developer <u>d</u>

### B

Answers will vary. Possible answers:
1. An accountant is someone who manages people's finances and money.
2. A fashion designer is someone who creates clothes.
3. A flight attendant is someone who takes care of passengers on a plane.

## Exercise 2

### A

awful <u>N</u>          fantastic <u>P</u>
boring <u>N</u>         fascinating <u>P</u>
challenging <u>P</u>   frightening <u>N</u>
dangerous <u>N</u>     interesting <u>P</u>
difficult <u>N</u>     rewarding <u>P</u>

### B

Answers will vary.

## Exercise 3

### A

work   with computers – learn new software programs
       as a high school coach – teach discipline and fitness
be     a university professor – do research
       a writer – work independently

### B

*Teri:* So, what kind of career would you like, Jack?
*Jack:* Well, I'm not exactly sure. *Being a writer* could be interesting. Maybe blogging about something I'm interested in.
*Teri:* Hmm. I don't know if I'd like that because I'd have to write every day.
*Jack:* What do you want to do, then?
*Teri:* Well, I'm not sure either! I'd love <u>working as a high school coach</u>. I'd really enjoy being with teenagers all day and <u>teaching discipline and fitness</u>. On the other hand, I'd be interested in <u>working for an airline</u>.
*Jack:* Really? What would you like about that?
*Teri:* Well, I'd love <u>traveling to different countries</u> all over the world.
*Jack:* Oh, I could never do that! I think it would be very tiring work.

### C

Answers will vary. Possible answers:
A: So, what kind of career would you like?
B: Well, I'm not exactly sure. <u>Working with computers might be fun.</u>
A: That sounds interesting. But I wouldn't like it because <u>learning new software programs seems complicated.</u>
B: What do you want to do then?
A: Well, I'd love <u>being a university professor.</u>
B: <u>Really? Why do you think you would like that?</u>
A: <u>I really like doing research.</u>

## Exercise 4

### A

1. architect
2. freelance artist
3. house painter
4. website designer
5. bus driver
6. preschool teacher

### B

1. making things, building, space needs to be constructed, at the office
2. working for yourself, paint pictures
3. rooms, colors that customers choose
4. show on the Internet, good eye for art, knowledge of the latest technology
5. attention on the road
6. take care of children, I teach, I play games, I read books

## Exercise 5

2. A chef's <u>assistant</u> has <u>worse hours than</u> a waiter.
3. A dog <u>walker</u> is <u>better paid than</u> a student intern.
4. A house <u>painter</u> earns <u>more than</u> a camp counselor.
5. A park <u>ranger</u> is <u>not as well paid as</u> a landscaper.
6. Being a yoga <u>instructor</u> is <u>not as difficult as</u> being a professor.
7. Being an interior <u>decorator</u> is <u>more interesting than</u> being a sales assistant.
8. A guidance <u>counselor</u> has <u>more responsibility than</u> a gardener.

## Exercise 6

1. Chonglin works <u>at / in</u> the best Chinese restaurant in Los Angeles.
2. I think working <u>with</u> other people is more fun than working alone.
3. I would hate working <u>in / with</u> the media. It would be nerve-racking!
4. Working <u>with / as</u> a dance instructor sounds great.
5. Working <u>in / at</u> an office is less interesting than working <u>on</u> a cruise ship.

## Exercise 7

Answers will vary. Possible answers:
2. A: Working in a travel agency provides better benefits than working as a tutor.
   B: Yes, but working as a tutor is more challenging than working in a travel agency.
3. A: A tour guide doesn't make as much money as a tennis instructor.
   B: That's true. And a tour guide has to work longer hours than a tennis instructor.
4. A: Taxi drivers have a shorter workweek than office assistants.
   B: Yes, and being an office assistant sounds less boring than being a taxi driver.

## Exercise 8

Answers will vary.

# 3 Lend a hand.

## Exercise 1

### A

2. Would you mind giving me a ride home after class?
3. Is it OK if I turn down your TV?
4. Do you mind if I use your cell phone?
5. I was wondering if I could borrow your car for the weekend.
6. Could you tell me how to get to the subway?

### B

Answers will vary. Possible answers:
2. Would you mind feeding my cat?
3. I was wondering if you could collect my mail.
4. Do you mind checking on my house a few times?
5. Could you water my plants?

## Exercise 2

Answers will vary.

## Exercise 3

Answers will vary. Possible answers:
2. A: Would you mind washing the dishes? I'm late for class.
   B: Sorry, but they're your dirty dishes.
3. A: I was wondering if you could do these chores over the weekend. I have to prepare for my meeting on Monday.
   B: I'd like to, but I have a lot of work to do this weekend.

## Exercise 4

### A

Less formal: make a statement with *need*; use an imperative.
More formal: ask about ability; be polite – use *may*; ask for permission, express curiosity; state the request negatively; apologize; give a hint.

### B

|  | Less formal | More formal | Type |
|---|:---:|:---:|:---:|
| **1.** Close the door. | ✓ |  | 2 |
| **2.** It's really cold in here. |  | ✓ | 9 |
| **3.** Could you possibly move your car? |  | ✓ | 3 |
| **4.** May I borrow your dictionary? |  | ✓ | 4 |
| **5.** I was wondering if you could help me with this assignment. |  | ✓ | 6 |
| **6.** I need some help moving to my new apartment. | ✓ |  | 1 |
| **7.** I'm sorry, but I can't stand loud music. |  | ✓ | 8 |
| **8.** I don't suppose I could borrow your camera. |  | ✓ | 7 |

## Exercise 5

### A

| Noun | Verb | Noun | Verb |
|---|---|---|---|
| apology | _apologize_ | invitation | _invite_ |
| compliment | _compliment_ | permission | _permit_ |
| explanation | _explain_ | request | _request_ |

### B

1. accepting an apology
2. giving a compliment
3. asking for a favor
4. declining a request
5. making a request

## Exercise 6

1. My phone didn't work for a week. The phone company <u>offered</u> an apology and took $20 off my bill.
2. A friend of mine really loves to <u>receive</u> compliments, but he never gives anyone else one. I don't understand why he's like that.
3. Diane is always talking on the phone. She makes a lot of calls, but she rarely <u>returns</u> mine. Maybe she never listens to her voice mail!
4. I need to <u>ask for</u> a favor. Could you please give me a ride to school tomorrow? My bike has a flat tire!

## Exercise 7

1. A: Is Silvia Vega there, please?
   B: No, she isn't. Would you like to leave a message?
   A: Yes, please. This is Karen Landers calling from Toronto. Could you tell her _that my flight arrives at 7:00 P.M. on Tuesday_? Would <u>she mind meeting me in the International Arrivals area</u>?
   B: OK, I'll give her the message.
2. A: Can I speak to Mark, please?
   B: I'm afraid he's not here. Do you want to leave a message?
   A: Yes, please. This is Ed. Please <u>ask him if I can borrow his scanner</u>. And if it's OK, could you <u>ask him when I can pick it up</u>?
   B: Sure, I'll leave him the message.
3. A: Could I speak to Mike, please?
   B: I'm sorry, but he's not here right now.
   A: Oh, OK. This is Mr. Maxwell. I'd like to leave a message. Could <u>you tell him that the meeting is on Thursday at 10:30 A.M.</u>? Could <u>you also tell him not to forget to bring his report</u>?
4. A: I'd like to speak to Katy, please.
   B: She's not here right now. Can I take a message?
   A: Yeah. This is Andy Chow. Can <u>you ask her if she's going to the conference tomorrow</u>? And would <u>you ask her what time it starts</u>?
   B: OK, I'll give Katy your message.

## Exercise 8

*Dan:* So, is there anything I can do to help for the party?
*Mark:* Yeah. I have a list here. Would it be all right _if I borrowed your wireless speaker_? Mine isn't working very well.
*Dan:* Sure. And I'll bring two extra speakers. We'll have amazing sound.
*Mark:* Thanks.
*Dan:* No problem. Now, what about food?
*Mark:* Well, I thought maybe a salad. Would you mind <u>bringing a big salad</u>, too?
*Dan:* Well, OK. And how about drinks?
*Mark:* Well, could you <u>ask Kelly to get some soda</u>? And please tell her <u>not to be late</u>. Last time we had a party, she didn't arrive till eleven o'clock, and everyone got really thirsty!
*Dan:* I remember.
*Mark:* One more thing – I was wondering if you could <u>buy dessert</u>.
*Dan:* Um, sure. All right. But, uh, would you mind if I <u>borrow some money</u> to pay for it?

## Exercise 9

Answers will vary. Possible answers:
2. Would you ask Annie to stop by and talk to me?
3. I was wondering if I could borrow your guitar.
4. Could you ask Mitch when he's coming over?
5. Would you mind lending me your hairbrush?

# 4 What happened?

## Exercise 1

**1.** A 69-year-old grandmother in Paris <u>went</u> to the bathroom – and <u>stayed</u> there for twenty days. What happened? As she was <u>locking</u> the door, the lock <u>broke</u>. She could not open the door. She <u>shouted</u> for help, but no one <u>heard</u> her because her bathroom had no windows. After nearly three weeks, the woman's neighbors <u>wondered</u> where she was. Firefighters broke into her apartment and <u>found</u> her in a "very weakened" state. While she was <u>waiting</u> to be rescued, she <u>drank</u> warm water.

**2.** A woman was <u>behaving</u> strangely when she <u>entered</u> the Bangkok airport. While she was <u>checking in</u> for an overseas flight, she <u>had</u> difficulty with a very large bag. The check-in clerk <u>became</u> suspicious and <u>decided</u> to X-ray the bag. The X-ray <u>showed</u> an image that looked like an animal. When airport staff <u>opened</u> the bag, they saw that a baby tiger was <u>sleeping</u> under lots of toy tigers. The tiger was taken to a rescue center for wildlife, and the woman was arrested.

## Exercise 2

Answers will vary. Possible answers:

**2.** I was using my computer when it suddenly stopped working.
**3.** While we were playing tennis, my racket broke.
**4.** As I was taking a shower, the water got cold.
**5.** I was cooking dinner when I burned my finger.

## Exercise 3

**1.** A: Guess what happened to me last night! As I <u>*was getting*</u> (get) into bed, I <u>heard</u> (hear) a loud noise like a gunshot in the street. Then the phone <u>rang</u> (ring).
   B: Who was it?
   A: It was Luisa. She always calls me late at night, but this time she had a reason. She <u>was driving</u> (drive) right past my apartment when she <u>got</u> (get) a flat tire. It was very late, so while we <u>were changing</u> (change) the tire, I <u>invited</u> (invite) her to spend the night.

**2.** A: I'm sorry I'm so late, Erin. I was at the dentist.
   B: Don't tell me! While you <u>were sitting</u> (sit) in the waiting room, you <u>met</u> (meet) someone interesting. I know how you are, Matt!
   A: Well, you're wrong this time. The dentist <u>was cleaning</u> (clean) my teeth when she suddenly <u>got</u> (get) called away for an emergency. So I just sat there waiting for two hours with my mouth hanging open!

## Exercise 4

### A

The story is about Andre Botha and Evan Geiselman. It took place at the Pipeline in Oahu, Hawaii.

### B

**1.** Andre Botha is a two-time champion in bodyboarding.
**2.** Evan Geiselman excels at surfing.
**3.** The Pipeline is located in Oahu, Hawaii.
**4.** You can help an unconscious person start breathing by breathing into their mouth / by hitting their chest.
**5.** Two lifeguards brought Evan Geiselman to the hospital.
**6.** Respect and care for people help make bodyboarding and surfing such wonderful sports.

## Exercise 5

Answers will vary.

## Exercise 6

Andy and I <u>*had just gotten*</u> engaged, so we went to a jewelry store to buy a wedding ring. We <u>had just chosen</u> a ring when a masked man <u>came in</u>. After the robber <u>took</u> Andy's wallet, he <u>demanded</u> the ring. I <u>had just handed</u> it to him when the alarm <u>started</u> to go off, and the robber <u>ran off</u>. We were so relieved! But then the sales assistant <u>told</u> us we had to pay for the ring because I <u>gave</u> it to the robber. We <u>had just told</u> her that we wouldn't pay for it when the police arrived and <u>arrested</u> us! What a terrible experience!

## Exercise 7

### A

**1.** What an emergency!
**2.** What a triumph!
**3.** What a dilemma!

### B

Answers will vary. Possible answers:
remote: <u>far away</u>
mainland: <u>larger land close to an island</u>
skip: <u>miss</u>
remarkably: <u>amazingly</u>
promotion: <u>a higher position</u>
resign: <u>quit</u>

## Exercise 8

**1.** In 2011, two divers <u>*discovered*</u> the remains of a 200-year-old shipwreck while they <u>were diving</u> off the coast of Rhode Island, in the eastern United States.
**2.** After an art show <u>opened</u> in New York, it was discovered that someone <u>had hung</u> a famous painting by Henri Matisse upside down.
**3.** In 2015, workers <u>found</u> a chemistry lab from the 1840s while they <u>were repairing</u> a building at the University of Virginia in the United States. The lab was behind a wall of the current building.
**4.** Chile's Calbuco volcano <u>surprised</u> residents of Santiago when it erupted in 2015. Before that, an eruption of Calbuco <u>had not happened</u> for over 40 years.

## Exercise 9

| Day | Name | Country | Name | Country |
|---|---|---|---|---|
| Sunday | Mr. Simpson | Singapore | ____ | ____ |
| Monday | Ms. Johnson | United States | Mr. Grant | Mexico |
| Tuesday | Mr. James | Australia | Ms. Marshall | Brazil |

# 5 Expanding your horizons

## Exercise 1

**2.** The first time I traveled abroad, I felt really <u>depressed</u>. I was alone, I didn't speak the language, and I didn't make any friends.

**3.** I just spent a year in France learning to speak French. It was a satisfying experience, and I was <u>fascinated</u> by the culture.

**4.** At first I really didn't like shopping in the open-air markets. I felt <u>uncomfortable</u> because so many people were trying to sell me something at the same time.

**5.** When I arrived in Lisbon, I was nervous because I couldn't speak any Portuguese. As I began to learn the language, though, I became more <u>confident</u> about living there.

**6.** Before I went to Alaska last winter, I was very <u>worried</u> about the cold. But it wasn't a problem because most buildings there are well heated.

**7.** When I was traveling in Southeast Asia, I couldn't believe how many different kinds of fruit there were. I was <u>curious</u> to try all of them, so I ate a lot of fruit!

**8.** It was our first trip to Latin America, so we were <u>uncertain</u> about what to expect. We loved it and hope to return again soon.

## Exercise 2

Answers will vary.

## Exercise 3

### A

Answers will vary. Possible answers:
Try new things.; Talk to locals.; Read about the country's history and current events.; Go to museums, concerts, and other cultural events.

### B

Answers will vary. Possible answers:
You can find articles like this in travel magazines, travel blogs, brochures for study abroad programs, training materials for international workers, etc.
It was written for people who are traveling to a foreign country.

### C

Answers will vary. Possible answers:
**1.** culture: the way of life of a particular people that reflects their attitudes and beliefs
**2.** culture shock: a feeling of confusion that results from suddenly experiencing a culture with customs that are not familiar to you
**3.** appreciate: to be aware of something, or to understand that something is valuable
**4.** stereotypes: ideas that are used to describe a particular type of person or thing

### D

Answers will vary.

## Exercise 4

Answers will vary. Possible answers:
**2.** it's the custom to send a card.
**3.** it's the custom to return it as soon as possible.
**4.** it's the custom to bring dessert or a beverage.

## Exercise 5

### A

**2.** Denmark and Spain
**3.** Egypt and New Zealand
**4.** France and the United States

### B

**1.** In Spain, you're expected to arrive to dinner a few minutes late.
**2.** In France, it's not the custom to tip at a restaurant.
**3.** In Egypt, when you're invited to dinner, you're not supposed to offer to pay for your dinner.
**4.** In Japan, you're not supposed to kiss your friends.
**5.** In Bali, Indonesia, it's not acceptable to wear shorts and a T-shirt in a temple.

## Exercise 6

Answers will vary.

## Exercise 7

Answers will vary.

# 6 That needs fixing.

## Exercise 1

### A

Answers may vary.

| chipped | cracked | dented | leaking |
|---------|---------|--------|---------|
| glasses | chair | bike | car |
| plate | glasses | car | sink |
| sink | plate | chair | |
| | sink | | |

| scratched | stained | torn |
|-----------|---------|------|
| bike | blouse | blouse |
| car | carpet | carpet |
| chair | chair | tablecloth |
| glasses | tablecloth | |
| plate | | |

### B

2. The blouse is torn. *or* There's a tear in the blouse.
3. The carpet is stained. *or* There's a stain on the carpet.
4. The bicycle is dented. *or* There's a dent in the bicycle.
5. The sink is leaking. *or* There's a leak in the sink.
6. The chair is cracked. *or* There's a crack in the chair.
7. The plate is chipped. *or* The plate has a chip in it.
8. The tablecloth is torn. *or* There's a tear in the tablecloth.
9. The glasses are cracked. *or* There's a crack in the glasses.

## Exercise 2

### A

Answers will vary. Possible answer:
Average people who have problems with products or conflicts with companies / organizations would read articles like these. The magazine can give them tips on how to deal with the problems and solve the conflicts.

### B

| | Problems | What *Consumer* magazine did | Received money? | |
|---|----------|------------------------------|---------|---|
| | | | Yes | No |
| 1 George's trip | *delay in Madrid* / missed connections in NY | contacted airline in Madrid and discovered European airlines pay for delays | ✓ | |
| 2 Diane's vacation | stolen car / responsible for paying for car | contacted rental car agency and discovered that credit card company will pay for stolen car | | ✓ |

## Exercise 3

2. The screws on these glasses are too loose. They need to be tightened. *or* They need tightening.
3. The blades on these scissors are too dull. They need to be sharpened. *or* They need sharpening.
4. This faucet is too tight. It needs to be loosened. *or* It needs loosening.
5. These pants are too long. They need to be shortened. *or* They need shortening.
6. This street is too narrow. It needs to be widened. *or* It needs widening.

## Exercise 4

*Jack:* Guess what? Someone broke into my car last night!
*Mia:* Oh, no. What did they take?
*Jack:* Nothing! But they did a lot of damage. The lock needs to be repaired. And the window needs to be replaced / needs replacing.
*Mia:* It was probably some young kids having "fun."
*Jack:* Yeah, some fun. I think they had a party in my car! The seats need to be cleaned / need cleaning.
*Mia:* How annoying. Does the car drive OK?
*Jack:* No, it feels strange. The gears keep sticking, so they need to be fixed / need fixing. And the brakes need to be checked / need checking right away.
*Mia:* Well, I guess you're lucky they didn't steal it!
*Jack:* Yeah, lucky me.

## Exercise 5

Answers will vary.

## Exercise 6

### A

2. c
3. b
4. e
5. d
6. a

### B

2. A DVD is stuck in the DVD player. The DVD needs to be removed. (*or* The DVD needs removing.)
3. The speaker wire is damaged. It needs to be repaired (*or* It needs repairing.)
4. The dresser mirror is cracked. It needs to be replaced (*or* It needs replacing.)
5. The stove door is scratched. It needs to be repainted (*or* It needs repainting.)
6. The table legs are loose. They need to be tightened and glued (*or* They need tightening and gluing.)

### C

Answers will vary.

## Exercise 7

2. Your computer screen is so dirty. It needs to be cleaned.
3. Something is wrong with your TV screen. It keeps flickering. It's time to get a new one.
4. I hate this printer. It keeps jamming. The copies won't come out.
5. Be careful – your cup is chipped. I don't want you to cut yourself.
6. The buttons on this remote control keep sticking. Do you have something to clean it with?
7. Do you realize your jeans are torn in the back?
8. Your bathroom faucet keeps leaking. Do you want me to try to fix it?
9. My new glasses already have a scratch on one of the lenses. How did that happen?
10. Did your laptop freeze again? I find that so annoying.
11. This old scanner doesn't work at all anymore. It needs to be fixed.
12. The battery in my cell phone keeps dying. I should buy a new one.

# 7 What can we do?

## Exercise 1

2. The taste of drinking water has been ruined by chlorine and other additives.
3. New illnesses have been caused by certain agricultural pesticides.
4. Our crops are being destroyed because of pollution from cars and trucks.
5. Dangerous chemicals are being released by factories.
6. Many people's health has been damaged as a result of breathing smog every day.
7. More severe droughts have been created through the lack of rainfall.
8. Our forests and wildlife are being threatened by global warming.

## Exercise 2

### A

| Verb | Noun | Verb | Noun |
|------|------|------|------|
| *contaminate* | contamination | educate | education |
| contribute | contribution | pollute | pollution |
| create | creation | populate | population |
| deplete | depletion | protect | protection |
| destruct | destruction | reduce | reduction |

### B

Answers will vary.

## Exercise 3

2. One way to inform the public about factories that pollute the environment is through educational programs on TV.
3. In many countries around the world, threatened animal and plant species are being protected by strict laws.
4. Agricultural pesticides are damaging the soil in many countries.
5. Poverty is an enormous problem in many large cities where whole families can only afford to live in one room.

## Exercise 4

### A

Answers will vary. Possible answer:
Fleece is an inexpensive, lightweight synthetic fiber used to make clothing. Common fleece items are shirts, jackets, pants, and blankets.

### B

1. False. In the developing world, 70% of people buy fleece.
2. True.
3. True.
4. False. More than 1,500 particles of fleece may separate during washing.
5. False. Fish do consume particles of fleece.
6. False. We still do not know what people are going to do about this problem.

## Exercise 5

### A

2. i  3. g  4. e  5. f  6. c  7. b  8. a  9. h

### B

1. During the recent recession, 30 percent of the businesses in my town closed, and a large part of the population didn't have jobs.
2. It seems like there are more dangerous infectious diseases these days, like swine flu and the Zika virus.
3. There's so much violence in this city. I'm afraid to walk on the streets alone at night because I don't feel safe.
4. Before you travel to a foreign country, make sure there are no dangerous political situations going on there. It can be unsafe to visit countries that are experiencing political unrest.
5. In the 1800s, a large portion of Irish potato crops were destroyed by disease. Because potatoes were a major part of the Irish diet, there was a major famine and over 1.5 million people died.
6. People in this country don't trust the police or city officials because there is a lot of government corruption.

## Exercise 6

1. A: A big housing developer wants to build an apartment complex in Forest Hill Park. I think that's terrible, but what can we do?
   B: *One thing to do is to complain to the Parks Department about it.*
   A: That's a good idea.
   B: Another thing to do is to organize a public meeting to protest the threat to public property.
2. A: Personally, I'm worried about violence in the city. The streets are not safe at night.
   B: One thing to do is to educate young people about its dangers.
3. A: You know, there's a lot of corruption in our city government.
   B: The best way to fight government corruption is to report it to the local newspaper.
   A: Yeah, the bad publicity might help to clean things up a bit.
4. A: There are so many unemployed people in this city. I just don't know what can be done about it.
   B: One thing to do is to create more government-funded jobs.
5. A: What worries me most is the number of homeless people on the streets.
   B: One way to help is to create more public housing projects.
   A: I agree.
   B: Another thing to do is to donate money to charities that provide shelters and food.

## Exercise 7

Answers will vary. Possible answers:

2. These days, a lot of endangered animals are being killed by hunters and poachers.
   The best way to stop this practice is to strengthen hunting and poaching laws.
3. During the past few years, lots of trees have been destroyed by acid rain. One thing to do about it is to minimize industrial pollution.
4. Underground water is being contaminated by agricultural pesticides.
   The best way to deal with the problem is to make sure factories are not polluting the groundwater.
5. Too many people have been affected by infectious diseases in the past few years.
   The best way to stop this is to educate people about diseases and vaccinations.

## Exercise 8

Answers will vary.

# 8 Never stop learning.

## Exercise 1

1. I'm interested in human behavior, so I'm planning to take a class in <u>psychology</u>.
2. I want to take a course in <u>business</u>, such as commerce or accounting.
3. I'd prefer not to study <u>nursing</u> because I'm not very comfortable in hospitals.
4. I'd really like to work in Information Technology, so I'm thinking of taking courses in <u>computer science</u>.

## Exercise 2

### A

2. Would you rather/Would you prefer to study part time or full time?
3. Would you rather/Would you prefer to have a boring job that pays well or an exciting job that pays less?
4. Would you rather/Would you prefer to take a long vacation once a year or several short vacations each year?

### B

Answers will vary.

## Exercise 3

### A

Answers will vary.

### B

Answers will vary.

## Exercise 4

Answers will vary.

## Exercise 5

### A

Answers will vary.

### B

1. (par. 1) Massive Online Open Courses (MOOCs for short) are designed for students who cannot afford, cannot get to, or simply don't want to attend classes in a university classroom.
2. (par. 3) Because a MOOC doesn't cost anything, students don't have to worry about losing money if they decide to drop the class. And many of them ultimately do.
3. (par. 2) However, almost half of the professors who have taught a MOOC believe that the coursework is as demanding as the work done in a traditional university class.
4. (par. 4) Some professors fear that in the future there may be two kinds of university courses: expensive and superior courses at a traditional university where small groups of students meet in classes with their professors, and inexpensive and inferior massive online courses where students will never meet their professors nor even their fellow students.

### C

Answers will vary.

### D

Answers will vary.

## Exercise 6

2. A good way to keep in touch with old friends is <u>by using social media</u>.
3. You can make new friends <u>by going out more often</u>.
4. The best way to save money is <u>by cooking at home</u>.
5. You could stay in shape <u>by exercising regularly</u>.
6. I stay healthy <u>by eating good food</u>.
7. One way to learn self-confidence is <u>by studying dance</u>.

## Exercise 7

1. Robin shows her <u>concern for others</u> by volunteering to help people with cancer.
2. When I was young, I didn't understand the importance of <u>money management</u>. But when I started paying my own bills, I realized it's an important skill.
3. I learned <u>creativity</u> from my parents. They taught me the importance of using my imagination and making art.
4. Gina always gets upset with people who disagree with her. I wish she would show more <u>tolerance</u>.
5. I recently joined a choir, and I love it. But you need a lot of <u>perseverance</u>, because you have to practice the same piece of music for weeks before you're ready to perform it!

## Exercise 8

### A

1. Alex is always on time for everything. He's never even five minutes late. He keeps track of everything on his calendar. I wish I were as good at <u>time management</u> as Alex is.
2. Frank finds school very hard, but no one tries harder than he does. He always spends the whole weekend at the library trying to keep up with his studies. He shows great <u>perseverance</u>.
3. Melissa always wants to do better than everyone else. In school, she always tries to get the best grades. Her favorite sport is field hockey because she's the best player in the school. No one needs to teach Melissa <u>competitiveness</u>.
4. Jennifer has more <u>creativity</u> than any of her classmates. She writes fascinating stories that show she has a wonderful imagination. She's also very artistic and does very interesting paintings.

### B

Answers will vary.

## Exercise 9

### A

Answers will vary.

### B

Answers will vary.

# 9 Getting things done

## Exercise 1

**2.** house painting
**3.** dry cleaning
**4.** computer repair
**5.** language tutoring
**6.** home repairs

## Exercise 2

### A

**2.** check my blood pressure
**3.** do my nails
**4.** fix my computer
**5.** print my photos
**6.** remove a stain
**7.** shorten my pants

### B

Answers will vary. Possible answers:
**2.** A: Where can I get my blood pressure checked?
    B: You can get it checked at Dr. Fieldstone's office.
**3.** A: Where can I get my nails done?
    B: You can get them done at Super Nails.
**4.** A: Where can I have my computer fixed?
    B: You can have it fixed at Seabreeze Computer Repair.
**5.** A: Where can I get my photos printed?
    B: You can get them printed at Main Street Photo.
**6.** A: Where can I have a stain removed?
    B: You can get it removed at Mike's Cleaners.
**7.** A: Where can I get my pants shortened?
    B: You can have them shortened at the tailor shop on Lily Street.

## Exercise 3

**2.** You can have your shoes repaired at Kwik Fix.
**3.** You can have your clothes dry-cleaned at Dream Clean.
**4.** You can have your carpets cleaned by Carpet World.
**5.** You can have your nails done at Nail File.
**6.** You can have your car washed at Jimmy's.
**7.** You can have your washing machine fixed by Hal's Repairs.
**8.** You can have your eyes examined at Eye to Eye.

## Exercise 4

### A

Answers will vary.

### B

**1.** False. Adult children no longer enjoy receiving furniture from their parents.
**2.** False. Boomers are Americans born after World War II.
**3.** True.
**4.** True.
**5.** False. The next step in downsizing could be for millennials to share houses and large apartments.

## Exercise 5

Answers will vary.

## Exercise 6

**1.** I don't know how my grandmother <u>keeps up with</u> all the new technology. She's better at understanding new gadgets than I am!
**2.** My cousin didn't know what to do for her mother's 60th birthday, but she finally <u>came up with</u> the idea of a surprise picnic with the whole family.
**3.** Ilene has done it again! She only met Chris two months ago, and already she has <u>broken up with</u> him. Why doesn't she try to work out any problems?
**4.** After Michelle saw her doctor, she decided to <u>cut down on</u> eating fast food. She wants to lose some weight and start exercising again in order to keep fit.
**5.** We're really lucky in my family because we all <u>get along with</u> each other very well.
**6.** I've done pretty badly in my classes this semester, so I'm not really <u>looking forward to </u>receiving my grades.
**7.** I can't <u>put up with </u>that loud music anymore! I can't stand hip-hop, and I'm going to tell my neighbor right now.
**8.** I've been getting sick a lot lately, and I often feel tired. I really need to start <u>taking care of</u> my health.

# 10 A matter of time

## Exercise 1
**2.** discovery
**3.** terrorist act
**4.** achievement
**5.** assassination
**6.** natural disaster

## Exercise 2
**2.** The cell phone was invented about 45 years <u>ago</u>.
**3.** Brasília has been the capital city of Brazil <u>since</u> 1960.
**4.** The first laptop was produced <u>in</u> 1981.
**5.** Mexico has been independent <u>for</u> more than 200 years.
**6.** World War II lasted <u>from</u> 1939 <u>to</u> 1945.
**7.** Vietnam was separated into two parts <u>for</u> about 20 years.
**8.** East and West Germany have been united <u>since</u> 1990.

## Exercise 3

### A

| Noun | Verb | Noun | Verb |
|---|---|---|---|
| achievement | <u>*achieve*</u> | existence | <u>exist</u> |
| assassination | <u>assassinate</u> | exploration | <u>explore</u> |
| demonstration | <u>demonstrate</u> | explosion | <u>explode</u> |
| discovery | <u>discover</u> | invention | <u>invent</u> |
| discrimination | <u>discriminate</u> | transformation | <u>transform</u> |
| election | <u>elect</u> | vaccination | <u>vaccinate</u> |

### B
**2.** In World War I, many soldiers were <u>vaccinated</u> against typhoid, a deadly bacterial disease.
**3.** Aung San, the man who led Myanmar to independence, was <u>assassinated</u> in 1947. No one is certain who killed him.
**4.** The European Union has <u>existed</u> since 1957.
**5.** Until the 1960s, there were many laws that <u>discriminated</u> against African Americans in certain regions of the United States.
**6.** In 1885, Louis Pasteur <u>discovered</u> a cure for rabies when he treated a young boy who was bitten by a dog.
**7.** In recent years, teams of experts in countries such as Cambodia and Angola have been safely <u>exploding</u> land mines in order to rid those countries of these dangerous weapons.
**8.** One of the few parts of the world that has not been <u>explored</u> much is Antarctica. The extreme climate makes it dangerous to travel far from research centers.

## Exercise 4

### A

Vaccinations are injections given to people to prevent a disease. They usually contain a weakened or dead form of the disease.

### B

| Date | Event |
|---|---|
| **1.** Early 16th century | *Smallpox killed much of the native population in South America.* |
| **2.** End of the 18th century | Smallpox was responsible for the death of about one in ten people around the world. |
| **3.** 1796 | Dr. Edward Jenner vaccinated a boy with cowpox and, two months later, with smallpox. The boy did not get smallpox. |
| **4.** 1800 | The Royal Vaccine Institution was founded in Berlin, Germany. |
| **5.** 1801 | Napoleon opened a vaccine institute in Paris, France. |
| **6.** 1967 | The World Health Organization started a vaccination program. |
| **7.** 1977 | The last known case of smallpox was recorded in Somalia. |
| **8.** Future challenge | The future of vaccinations aims at eradicating malaria, Zika virus, and dengue. |

## Exercise 5

### A
**2.** many people <u>will be wearing</u> temperature-controlled body suits.
**3.** most people <u>will be driving</u> cars that run on fuel from garbage.
**4.** people <u>will be competing</u> in a new Olympic event – mind reading.
**5.** Answers will vary.
**6.** Answers will vary.

### B
**2.** ties for men <u>will have gone</u> out of fashion.
**3.** scientists <u>will have discovered</u> a cheap way of getting drinking water from seawater.
**4.** medical researchers will have found a cure for cancer.
**5.** Answers will vary.
**6.** Answers will vary.

## Exercise 6
Answers will vary.

## Exercise 7
Answers will vary.

## Exercise 8
Answers will vary.

# 11 Rites of passage

## Exercise 1

### A

Answers will vary.

### B

Answers will vary.

## Exercise 2

**2.** I just spent a horrible evening with Patricia. She questioned and criticized everything I said. I wish she weren't so <u>argumentative</u>.

**3.** My sister is very <u>naive</u>. She trusts everyone and thinks everyone is good.

**4.** Once I turned 16, I became less <u>rebellious</u>, and my parents started to let me do what I wanted.

**5.** Eric is really <u>ambitious</u>. He wants to own his own business by the time he's 25.

**6.** I wish I could be like Susie. She's so <u>carefree</u> and never seems to worry about anything.

## Exercise 3

Answers will vary.

## Exercise 4

### A

He learned that he is ambitious because he loves to compete and to win. He doesn't want to be a runner-up.

### B

Answers will vary. Possible answers:

**1.** sprint: <u>a short, very fast foot-race</u>

**2.** runners-up: <u>those who didn't win first place / those who won second, third, or fourth place</u>

**3.** launched himself into: <u>began for first time</u>

**4.** prestigious: <u>very important</u>

**5.** ecstatic: <u>very happy</u>

**6.** record time: <u>fast enough to break a record</u>

### C

Answers will vary.

## Exercise 5

Answers will vary. Possible answers:

**2.** I shouldn't have been so argumentative.

**3.** I should have gotten a different job.

**4.** I shouldn't have bought the TV.

**5.** I should have studied computer science.

**6.** I shouldn't have been so rebellious.

**7.** I should have refused to let my friend copy my homework.

**8.** I should have put the date in my calendar.

**9.** I shouldn't have been so naive.

**10.** I should have told my friend that I liked her hair.

## Exercise 6

### A

**2.** If we'd made a reservation, we would have eaten already.

**3.** If I'd put on sunscreen, I wouldn't have gotten a sunburn.

**4.** If you had let me drive, we would have arrived by now.

**5.** If I'd ignored your text in class, I wouldn't have gotten in trouble.

### B

Answers will vary.

## Exercise 7

*Hector:* I've made such a mess of my life!

*Scott:* What do you mean?

*Hector:* If I *hadn't accepted* a job *as soon as* I graduated, I <u>would have traveled</u> around South America all summer – just like you did. You were so carefree.

*Scott:* You know, I shoul<u>dn't have gone</u> to South America. I should <u>have taken</u> the great job I was offered. <u>After</u> I returned from South America, it was too late.

*Hector:* But my job is so depressing! <u>The moment</u> I started it, I hated it – on the very first day! That was five years ago, and nothing's changed. I should <u>have looked</u> for another job right away.

*Scott:* Well, start looking now. I posted my résumé online last month, and five companies contacted me right away. If I <u>hadn't posted</u> my résumé, no one <u>would have contacted</u> me. I accepted one of the job offers.

*Hector:* Really? What's the job?

*Scott:* It's working as a landscape gardener. <u>The moment</u> I saw it, I knew it was right for me.

Hector: But for me right now, the problem is that I get a very good salary and I just bought a house. If I <u>hadn't bought</u> the house, I <u>would be able to</u> take a lower paying job.

*Scott:* Well, I guess you can't have everything. If I <u>had</u> a better salary, I <u>would buy</u> a house, too.

# 12 Keys to success

## Exercise 1

2. <u>In order for</u> a movie to be entertaining, it has to have good actors and an interesting story.
3. <u>In order to</u> succeed in business, you often have to work long hours.
4. <u>In order to</u> attract new members, a sports club needs to offer inexpensive memberships.
5. <u>In order to</u> speak a foreign language well, it's a good idea to use the language as often as possible.
6. <u>In order for</u> a clothing store to succeed, it has to be able to find the latest fashions.

## Exercise 2

2. For a clothes store to be profitable, it has to have talented salespeople.
3. In order to manage your own business, you have to work extremely long hours.
4. In order for an advertisement to be persuasive, it has to be clever and entertaining.
5. In order to run a successful automobile company, you have to provide excellent customer service.
6. In order for a reality TV show to be successful, it has to have drama and interesting characters.

## Exercise 3

2. I learned a lot about how to run a successful bookstore from taking that class. I found it very <u>informative</u>.
3. Annie has so many interesting ideas, and she's always thinking of new projects. She's very <u>clever</u>.
4. Debra is a salesperson, and she's good at her job. She's so <u>persuasive</u> that she sells three times as much as her co-workers.
5. Matthew is one of the top models in Milan. He goes to the gym every day, so he looks really <u>muscular</u>.
6. Before opening a new store, it's important to think through all of your ideas and have a <u>clear business plan</u>.
7. My new job has great benefits. We have unlimited time off, excellent health insurance, and <u>flexible working hours</u>.

## Exercise 4

Answers will vary.

## Exercise 5

### A

Answers will vary.

### B

Answers will vary.

## Exercise 6

### A

The secret that the company sells is the three indigenous Latin-American plants that were replaced by wheat: chia seeds, amaranth, and quinoa.

### B

Answers will vary. Possible answers:
1. comeback: something that returns to favor
2. indigenous: native, original of a place
3. to prominence: become popular or well-known
4. superfood: a very healthy food
5. went out of favor: no longer popular
6. rumor has it: people are saying

## Exercise 7

Answers will vary.

## Exercise 8

### A

1. I'm not <u>knowledgeable</u> enough about tools to be a successful salesperson in a hardware store. I'm familiar with some common tools, but I don't know how to use most tools.
2. To be successful, personal trainers need to be fit and <u>muscular</u>.
3. *Weekend Talk* ran for only three months because it was so boring. For a TV show to be successful on Saturday evenings, it really has to be <u>entertaining</u>.
4. I wouldn't be a good <u>salesperson</u> because I'm not very persuasive.
5. I found a fantastic news website this morning. It's really <u>informative</u>. It has very detailed stories about local and international news.
6. For a salesperson to be persuasive, he or she has to be <u>clever</u> with words.
7. Kate is so <u>athletic</u>. She plays soccer, tennis, and basketball, and she's excellent at all three sports.
8. I like this store, but it's not very <u>affordable</u>. Even the small items are expensive.

### B

Answers will vary. Possible answers:
1. To apply for a job, you should write a good résumé.
2. To be an effective personal trainer, you have to listen to your clients' needs.
3. For a restaurant to be successful, it has to have delicious food at good prices.
4. For students to get good grades, they should study hard and do their best.
5. To learn a new language, it's a good idea to practice every day.

# 13 What might have been

## Exercise 1

Answers will vary. Possible answers:
2. They might have gone to get a cup of coffee.
3. A friend might not have come to his birthday party.
4. Someone must have hit her car.
5. They must have won the game.
6. It must have been in the oven too long.

## Exercise 2

Answers will vary.

## Exercise 3

Answers will vary. Possible answers:
2. They could have built it for ceremonies and celebrations.
3. They could have drawn pictures.
4. They may have learned the languages.
5. They may have built rowboats.
6. They might have used sailboats.

## Exercise 4

### A

Answers will vary.

### B

Answers will vary. Possible answers:
1. Bigfoot is a gigantic, hairy, mysterious man-like creature that lives in the forests of the Pacific Northwest and avoids people.
2. Answers will vary.
3. The most popular possibility is Gigantopithecus.
4. Most scientists believe that Gigantopithecus walked on its hands and legs because its weight would have been too much for the legs and ankles to carry. *or* The bones of this ape have only been found in Asia.
5. Answers will vary.

## Exercise 5

### A

Answers will vary.

### B

Answers will vary. Possible answers:
2. I would have slept in my car until the morning.
3. I would have asked them to throw away their trash.
4. I would have asked them not to make any noise in the evenings.
5. I wouldn't have loaned it to him.

## Exercise 6

### A

| Noun | Verb | Noun | Verb |
|---|---|---|---|
| assumption | *assume* | prediction | predict |
| criticism | criticize | suggestion | suggest |
| demand | demand | suspect | suspect |
| excuse | excuse | warning | warn |

### B

2. Christopher shouldn't have suggested having a beach party. It was so dark, I stepped in a hole and hurt my ankle.
3. Andy bought an expensive ring and gave it to Millie for her birthday. A year later, he asked her to marry him. When she said no, he made an outrageous demand. He said he wanted his ring back!
4. I shouldn't have warned my co-worker not to be late for work so often. It was really none of my business.
5. Lori said she was late because she got caught in traffic. Hmm. I've heard that excuse before.
6. Kevin shouldn't have assumed I would still be awake at midnight. I was asleep when he called.
7. I thought that my roommate had taken my wallet, but I found it at the bottom of my bag. I shouldn't have suspected that my roommate took it. He would never do something like that.
8. James shouldn't have criticized me for wearing jeans and a T-shirt to a friend's party. He always has negative things to say.

## Exercise 7

Answers will vary. Possible answers:
2. A: Judy never responded to my invitation.
   B: She must not have received it. You should have called her.
3. A: Matt hasn't answered his phone for a week.
   B: He could have gone on vacation. He might not have told you, though – sometimes he's very inconsiderate.
4. A: I can never get in touch with Kathy. She never returns phone calls or answers texts!
   B: Yeah, I have the same problem with her. Her voice mail may have run out of space. She should have gotten a new phone service by now.
5. A: Thomas is strange. Sometimes he works really hard, but sometimes he seems pretty lazy. Last week, he hardly did any work.
   B: Well, you know, he might not have felt well. Still, he should have told you that he was sick.
6. A: I ordered a book online a month ago, but it still hasn't arrived.
   B: They could have had a problem with the warehouse, but they should have let you know.

# 14 Creative careers

## Exercise 1

*Anna:* Putting on a fashion show must be really fun!

*Marcus:* Yeah, but it's also challenging. All the clothes have to *be numbered* so that the models wear them in the right sequence. And they also have to <u>be marked</u> with the name of the right model.

*Anna:* What happens if something <u>is worn</u> by the wrong model?

*Marcus:* Well, if it doesn't fit, it looks terrible! First impressions are very important. A lot of clothes <u>are sold</u> because they look good at the show.

*Anna:* Do you have to rehearse for a fashion show?

*Marcus:* Of course! There's more involved than just models and clothes. Special lighting <u>is used</u>, and music <u>is played</u> during the show.

*Anna:* It sounds complicated.

*Marcus:* Oh, it is. And at some fashion shows, a commentary may <u>be given</u>.

*Anna:* A commentary? What do you mean?

*Marcus:* Well, someone talks about the clothes as they <u>are shown</u> on the runway by the models.

*Anna:* It sounds like timing is really important.

*Marcus:* Exactly. Everything has to <u>be timed</u> perfectly! Otherwise, the show may <u>be ruined</u>.

## Exercise 2

1. Often, special music has to be <u>written</u> for a film.
2. A play may be <u>rehearsed</u> for several weeks before it is shown to the public.
3. Designing <u>clothes</u> for actors to wear requires a lot of creativity.
4. Newspapers are <u>delivered</u> to stores after they are printed.
5. <u>Sound effects</u> are added after the film has been put together.

## Exercise 3

1. Nowadays, all sorts of things *are produced* in factories, including lettuce! At one food factory, fresh green lettuce <u>is grown</u> without sunlight or soil. Here is how it <u>is done</u>.
2. Lettuce seedlings <u>are placed</u> at one end of a long production line. Conveyor belts <u>are used</u> to move the seedlings slowly along. The tiny plants <u>are exposed</u> to light from fluorescent lamps.
3. They have to <u>be fed</u> through the roots with plant food and water that <u>is controlled</u> by a computer.
4. Thirty days later, the plants <u>are collected</u> at the other end of the conveyor belts.
5. They may <u>be delivered</u> to the vegetable market the same day.

## Exercise 4

### A

1. has been <u>created</u>
2. are <u>concerned</u>
3. was passionately <u>interested</u> in
4. was soon <u>noticed</u>
5. be <u>interviewed</u>
6. were relevant, intelligent, and <u>inspired</u>

### B

1. False. He moved to London around 2007.
2. False. His family and friends read his blog.
3. True
4. True
5. False. They started after *The Business of Fashion*.
6. False. Passionate interest is fundamental to success in blogging.

## Exercise 5

Answers will vary. Possible answers:

1. An editorial director, who tells the reporters what news stories to cover, chooses only the most interesting stories.
2. A game animator, who creates detailed graphics for computer games, is a skilled artist.
3. A storyboard artist, who illustrates plans for individual scenes for a movie, is a creative person.
4. Stunt people perform dangerous moves in films and TV shows that have a lot of action scenes.
5. TV sitcoms include actors and actresses that are recognized by television viewers around the world.

## Exercise 6

2. c
3. a
4. h
5. b
6. f
7. d
8. e

## Exercise 7

Answers will vary.

## Exercise 8

2. Next, <u>new walls are built</u>.
3. Then <u>the walls are painted</u>.
4. After that, <u>new lighting is installed</u>.
5. Then <u>new furniture is delivered</u>.
6. Finally, <u>the restaurant is reopened</u>.

# 15 A law must be passed!

## Exercise 1

Answers will vary. Possible answers:
2. People shouldn't be allowed to eat on the subway.
3. People shouldn't be permitted to play loud music in their apartments.
4. Dogs should be required to wear leashes.

## Exercise 2

Answers will vary. Possible answers:
2. Something must be done to reduce traffic on the freeways.
3. Bicyclists must have their own bike lanes.
4. A law has got to be passed to stop people from looking at their phones when they're crossing the street.

## Exercise 3

Answers will vary.

## Exercise 4

Answers will vary. Possible answers:
2. A: People mustn't be allowed to write unkind things about others on social networking sites.
   B: That's not a bad idea. On the other hand, I feel that people should be allowed to express their opinions about anything.
3. A: Public transportation should be provided free of charge.
   B: That's interesting, but I think that free public transportation would result in increased taxes for everyone.
4. A: I think people ought to be required to buy hybrid cars.
   B: Do you? I'm not sure everyone can afford a hybrid car.
5. A: In my opinion, all plastic containers should be banned.
   B: You may have a point. However, I think that some plastic containers, such as food storage containers, are necessary.

## Exercise 5

### A

Possible answer:
A revenge story describes an action someone took to get back at someone who was hurting or taking advantage of him or her in some way. It's usually a mean or controversial action. Marcy's friend was taking advantage of Marcy's kindness and generosity and forcing her to pay for meals when they ate out together, so Marcy did the same thing to her. Jonathan's neighbors were neglecting the rabbits, so he stole them to protect and save them. Chad's neighbor didn't care that the leaky air conditioner was making it difficult for Chad to sleep, so Chad turned the air conditioner off without telling the neighbor.

### B

Answers will vary.

### C

Answers will vary.

## Exercise 6

3. You can easily spend all your money on food and rent, can't you?
4. Some unemployed people don't really want to work, do they?
5. Health care is getting more and more expensive, isn't it?
6. There are a lot of homeless people downtown, aren't there?
7. Some schools have overcrowded classrooms, don't they?
8. Laws should be passed to reduce street crime, shouldn't they?

## Exercise 7

### A

| Noun | Verb | Noun | Verb |
|---|---|---|---|
| advertisement | advertise | pollution | pollute |
| bully | bully | prohibition | prohibit |
| improvement | improve | provision | provide |
| offense | offend | requirement | require |
| permission | permit | vandalism | vandalize |

### B

Answers will vary.

## Exercise 8

Answers will vary. Possible answers:
2. For: It might stop children from being bullies.
   Against: Parents, not schools, should be responsible for their children's behavior.
3. For: It's important to keep the city clean.
   Against: There are other more important things to spend tax money on.
4. For: Every animal's life is important.
   Against: There aren't enough animal shelters to care for every stray animal.

## Exercise 9

*Gina:* You know, I just moved into this new apartment building, and I thought everything would be really great now.
*Alec:* What's the problem?
*Gina:* Well, yesterday, the manager gave me a copy of the house rules. I found out that I can't park my moped on the sidewalk in front of the building anymore.
*Alec:* But people shouldn't be permitted to park their bikes or mopeds there.
*Gina:* Why not? There isn't any other place to park, is there? I guess I'll have to park on the street now.
*Alec:* I'm sorry that parking somewhere else will be inconvenient, but don't you agree that people shouldn't be allowed to block the sidewalk or the entrance to the building?
*Gina:* Well, you may have a point, but parking spaces for all types of cycles need to be provided for renters here. All renters with a car have a parking space, don't they?
*Alec:* Well, yes, you're right. You should go to the next renters' meeting and discuss the issue with everyone else.
*Gina:* That's not a bad idea. My voice ought to be heard as much as anyone else's – I think I will!

# 16 Reaching your goals

## Exercise 1
2. volunteer
3. student
4. actor
5. parent
6. nurse

## Exercise 2

### A
Answers will vary. Possible answers:
1. social worker: *help people, get to know the community*
2. university professor: *educate people, write books*
3. small-business owner: *be your own boss, help the community*
4. emergency-room nurse: *help people, have an exciting job*

### B
Answers will vary. Possible answers:
1. As a social worker, Jane hopes she'll *have helped poor and elderly people in her community*. She'd also like to have *made a lot of good friends*.
2. As a university professor three years from now, Paul hopes he'll have *effectively educated people about world history*. He'd also like to have *written a book within five years*.
3. By this time next year, Jake, a small business owner, would like to have *hired three new employees*. In addition, he hopes he'll have *opened two additional stores in the next three years*.
4. In the next five years, Amy, an emergency-room nurse, hopes she'll have *helped save a lot of lives*. In addition, she'd like to have *gotten promoted to head nurse*.

## Exercise 3
Answers will vary.

## Exercise 4

### A
Rupert Isaacson is from London. His parents are from Africa. He went to visit the Bushmen of the Kalahari Desert.

### B
Challenge: *Rupert faced the challenge of his son's autism.*
Solution: *One of the solutions was to use horses to help his son.*

### C
1. Autism affects people's ability to communicate and interact socially.
2. They went to Mongolia to help with Rowan's autism.
3. The Horse Boy Foundation is a school that teaches people how to use horses for healing.
4. Rowan is the host of *Endangerous*.
5. Answers will vary. Possible answers: He wrote the books *The Healing Land* and *The Long Ride Home*. He produced the documentaries *Horse Boy* and *Endangerous*. He started The Horse Boy Foundation to help people with autism.

## Exercise 5
1. It's not good to be timid if you're an emergency-room nurse.
2. If teachers are going to be successful, they have to be resourceful.
3. You have to be adaptable if you work as a volunteer.
4. If you take a job far from your family and friends, you have to be self-sufficient.
5. One of the most important things about working with children is being positive and not cynical.
6. Being a role model for troubled youths requires someone who is strong and compassionate.

## Exercise 6
1. A
2. G
3. A
4. G
5. G
6. G

## Exercise 7

### A
2. get a promotion / a house
3. learn new skills
4. make a change
5. meet someone special
6. pay off debts / a house

### B
Answers will vary.

## Exercise 8

### A
Answers will vary.

### B
Answers will vary.

# CREDITS

**The authors and publishers acknowledge the following sources of copyright material and are grateful for the permissions granted. While every effort has been made, it has not always been possible to identify the sources of all the material used, or to trace all copyright holders. If any omissions are brought to our notice, we will be happy to include the appropriate acknowledgements on reprinting and in the next update to the digital edition, as applicable.**

Key: Ex = Exercise, T = Top, B = Below, C = Center, CL = Center Right, TR = Top Right, BR = Below Right, TL = Top Left, TC = Top Center, BL = Below Left, BC = Below Center, L = Left, R = Right, CL = Center Left, B/G = Background.

## Illustrations

**Mark Duffin:** 39, 115, 119, 120; **Thomas Girard** (Good Illustration): 86; **Dusan Lakicevic** (Beehive Illustration): 18, 24; **Gavin Reece** (New Division): 43.

## Photos

Back cover (woman with whiteboard): Jenny Acheson/Stockbyte/GettyImages; Back cover (whiteboard): Nemida/GettyImages; Back cover (man using phone): Betsie Van Der Meer/Taxi/GettyImages; Back cover (woman smiling): PeopleImages.com/DigitalVision/GettyImages; Back cover (name tag): Tetra Images/GettyImages; Back cover (handshake): David Lees/Taxi/GettyImages; screenshots on p. x from Interchange 5e Self-study, Jack C. Richards with Jonathan Hull and Susan Proctor; screenshots on pp. xi–xiv from Interchange 5e Student's Book 3, Jack C. Richards with Jonathan Hull and Susan Proctor; screenshots on p. xv (T) & p. xvi (T) from Interchange 5e Self-study, Jack C. Richards with Jonathan Hull and Susan Proctor; screenshot on p. xvi (B) from Interchange 5e Games, Jack C. Richards with Jonathan Hull and Susan Proctor; screenshot on p. xvii from Interchange 5e Student's Book 3, Jack C. Richards with Jonathan Hull and Susan Proctor; screenshot on p. xviii (T) from Interchange 5e Teacher's Edition 3, Jack C. Richards with Jonathan Hull and Susan Proctor; screenshot on p. xviii (B) from Interchange 5e Complete Assessment Program, Jack C. Richards with Jonathan Hull and Susan Proctor; p. xix (woman with whiteboard): Jenny Acheson/Stockbyte/GettyImages; p. xix (whiteboard): Nemida/GettyImages; screenshots on p. xix from Interchange 5e Student's Book 3, Jack C. Richards with Jonathan Hull and Susan Proctor; screenshot on p. xx (L) from Interchange 5e Supplementary Resources Overviews, Jack C. Richards with Jonathan Hull and Susan Proctor; screenshot on p. xx (R) from Interchange 5e Teacher's Resource Worksheets, Jack C. Richards with Jonathan Hull and Susan Proctor; p. xxiii (TL): Hill Street Studios/Blend Images/GettyImages; p. xxiii (BR): Hill Street Studios/Blend Images/GettyImages; p. xxiii (BL): track5/E+/GettyImages; p. xxiii (TR): fstop123/E+/GettyImages; p. 2 (header), p. iv (Unit 1): Tony Anderson/Taxi/GettyImages; p. 2 (T): Steve West/Taxi Japan/GettyImages; p. 2 (B): PhotoInc/E+/GettyImages; p. 4 (CR): Thomas Barwick/Iconica/GettyImages; p. 4 (BR): Gary Burchell/GettyImages; p. 5 (T): Shawna Hansen/Moment Open/GettyImages; p. 5 (B): Andersen Ross/Stockbyte/GettyImages; p. 6: Mel Yates/Cultura/GettyImages; p. 7: Heath Korvola/Stone/GettyImages; p. 8 (header), p. iv (Unit 2): Kelvin Murray/Taxi/GettyImages; p. 8 (TR): Paul Bradbury/Caiaimage/GettyImages; p. 8 (Lia): Tetra Images/Brand X Pictures/GettyImages; p. 8 (Josh): NicolasMcComber/E+/GettyImages; p. 8 (Ed): XiXinXing/GettyImages; p. 8 (Rose): Tim Robberts/The Image Bank/GettyImages; p. 8 (Jeff): T2 Images/Cultura/GettyImages; p. 8 (Mei): Yagi Studio/DigitalVision/GettyImages; p. 8 (Anna): Ron Levine/DigitalVision/GettyImages; p. 8 (Mike): Jon Feingersh/Blend Images/GettyImages; p. 9 (student): Nycretoucher/Stone/GettyImages; p. 9 (volunteer): asiseeit/E+/GettyImages; p. 9 (business): Thomas Barwick/Stone/GettyImages; p. 9 (movie set): bjones27/E+/GettyImages; p. 10: Sue Barr/Image Source/GettyImages; p. 11: JAG IMAGES/Cultura/GettyImages; p. 12: Edge Magazine/Future/Future Publishing/GettyImages; p. 13 (T): Gary Burchell/Taxi/GettyImages; p. 13 (C): Hero Images/GettyImages; p. 13 (B): asiseeit/E+/GettyImages; p. 14: Juanmonino/E+/GettyImages; p. 15 (CR): Hero Images/GettyImages; p. 15 (BR): kali9/E+/GettyImages; p. 16 (header), p. iv (Unit 3): Hero Images/GettyImages; p. 16 (T): CREATISTA/iStock/Getty Images Plus/GettyImages; p. 16 (B): Tetra Images/GettyImages; p. 17: Maskot/GettyImages; p. 18 (Sara): Tim Robberts/Taxi/GettyImages; p. 18 (Kim): monkeybusinessimages/iStock/Getty Images Plus/GettyImages; p. 19 (T): Kirsty Lee/EyeEm/GettyImages; p. 19 (Ex 9a): Sam Edwards/Caiaimage/OJO+/GettyImages; p. 19 (Ex 9b): Tetra Images-Rob Lewine/Brand X Pictures/Getty Images; p. 20: Roy Mehta/Iconica/GettyImages; p. 21: Tetra Images/GettyImages; p. 22 (header), p. iv (Unit 4): Tom Merton/Caiaimage/GettyImages; p. 22 (news): Rune Johansen/Photolibrary/GettyImages; p. 22 (health): Peter Dazeley/Photographer's Choice/GettyImages; p. 22 (trending topics): Jess Nichols/EyeEm/GettyImages; p. 22 (arts): Daniel Allan/Cultura/GettyImages; p. 22 (science): Don Klumpp/The Image Bank/GettyImages; p. 22 (tech): Georgijevic/E+/GettyImages; p. 23: Highwaystarz-Photography/iStock/Getty Images Plus/GettyImages; p. 25: Rachel Lewis/Lonely Planet Images/GettyImages; p. 25 (Carol): Jetta Productions/Blend Images/GettyImages; p. 25 (Milo): JohnnyGreig/E+/GettyImages; p. 26: elvira_gumirova/GettyImages; p. 26 (B/G): Anna Bryukhanova/GettyImages; p. 27: artpipi/E+/GettyImages; p. 28: JGI/Jamie Grill/Blend Images/GettyImages; p. 29: Matt Dutile/Image Source/GettyImages; p. 30 (header), p. iv (Unit 5): Image Source/DigitalVision/GettyImages; p. 30 (T): William King/Taxi/GettyImages; p. 30 (B): PBNJ Productions/Blend Images/GettyImages; p. 31: Felix Hug/Lonely Planet Images/GettyImages; p. 32: Nachosuch/iStock/Getty Images Plus/GettyImages; p. 33: John Fedele/Blend Images/GettyImages; p. 34 (T): Dave & Les Jacobs/Blend Images/GettyImages; p. 34 (B): Kay Chernush/Stockbyte/GettyImages; p. 35 (B): Westend61/GettyImages; p. 35 (TR): Rafael Elias/Moment/GettyImages; p. 36 (header), p. iv (Unit 6): Thomas Barwick/Iconica/GettyImages; p. 36 (CR): Peter Cade/The Image Bank/GettyImages; p. 37 (photo 1): p6opov/iStock/Getty Images Plus/GettyImages; p. 37 (photo 2): Michael Blann/DigitalVision/GettyImages; p. 37 (photo 3): Shannon Miller/Moment/GettyImages; p. 37 (photo 4): xril/iStock/Getty Images Plus/GettyImages; p. 38 (TR): Creatas/Creatas/Getty Images Plus/GettyImages; p. 38 (BR): caviarliu/iStock/Getty Images Plus/GettyImages; p. 38 (Leory): Monty Rakusen/Cultura/GettyImages; p. 38 (Heather): Hero Images/GettyImages; p. 40: Jupiterimages/PHOTOS.com/Getty Images Plus/GettyImages; p. 41: Image Source/GettyImages; p. 42: Jamie Grill/GettyImages; p. 43: Klaus Vedfelt/DigitalVision/GettyImages; p. 44 (header), p. iv (Unit 7): Hero Images/GettyImages; p. 44 (B): Todd Wright/Blend Images/GettyImages; p. 45 (TL): Anne Rippy/Photographer's Choice/GettyImages; p. 45 (TC): TongRo Images Inc/TongRo Images/GettyImages; p. 45 (TR): Visuals Unlimited, Inc./Thomas Marent/Visuals Unlimited/GettyImages; p. 45 (BL): mshch/iStock/Getty Images Plus/GettyImages; p. 45 (BC): Marcos Alves/Moment/GettyImages; p. 45 (BR): Ailime/iStock/Getty Images Plus/GettyImages; p. 46: Michael Krasowitz/Photographer's Choice/GettyImages; p. 47: Photofusion/Universal Images Group/GettyImages; p. 48 (TL): jinga80/iStock/Getty Images Plus/GettyImages; p. 48 (TR): Biris Paul Silviu/Moment Mobile ED/GettyImages; p. 48 (BL): 101cats/iStock/Getty Images Plus/GettyImages; p. 48 (BR): inFocusDC/iStock/Getty Images Plus/GettyImages; p. 49 (TR): Cigdem Sean Cooper/Moment Open/GettyImages; p. 49 (BL): Antonio Busiello/robertharding/GettyImages; p. 50 (header), p. iv (Unit 8): akindo/DigitalVision Vectors/GettyImages; p. 51: Hill Street Studios/Blend Images/GettyImages; p. 52: Wavebreakmedia Ltd/Wavebreak Media/Getty Images Plus/GettyImages; p. 53: MarioGuti/iStock/Getty Images Plus/GettyImages; p. 54 (T): Dave & Les Jacobs/Blend Images/Getty Images Plus/GettyImages; p. 54 (B): JGI/Jamie Grill/Blend Images/GettyImages; p. 55: Apeloga AB/Cultura/GettyImages; p. 56: John Lund/DigitalVision/GettyImages; p. 57: mediaphotos/iStock/Getty Images Plus/GettyImages; p. 58 (header), p. vi (Unit 9): Robert D. Barnes/Moment/GettyImages; p. 58 (automotive): Reza Estakhrian/Iconica/GettyImages; p. 58 (car wash): energyy/iStock/Getty Images Plus/GettyImages; p. 58 (computer repair): Tetra Images/GettyImages; p. 58 (security repair): fatihhoca/iStock/Getty Images Plus/GettyImages; p. 58 (carpet cleaning): leezsnow/E+/GettyImages; p. 58 (home repair): sturti/E+/GettyImages; p. 58 (laundry cleaning): kali9/E+/GettyImages; p. 58 (tutoring): Hill Street Studios/Blend Images/GettyImages; p. 59 (Jessica): imagenavi/GettyImages; p. 59 (Peter): g-stockstudio/iStock/Getty Images Plus/GettyImages; p. 59 (Barry): Maskot/GettyImages; p. 59 (Tricia): Andersen Ross/GettyImages; p. 60: MachineHeadz/iStock/Getty Images Plus/GettyImages; p. 61: Morsa Images/DigitalVision/GettyImages; p. 62 (L): James And James/Photolibrary/GettyImages; p. 62 (C): Jose Luis Pelaez Inc/Blend Images/GettyImages; p. 62 (R): Dan Dalton/Caiaimage/GettyImages; p. 63: Paul Morigi/Getty Images Entertainment/Getty Images North America/GettyImages; p. 64 (header), p. vi (Unit 10): Kypros/Hulton Archive/GettyImages; p. 64 (1975): Jason Todd/DigitalVision/GettyImages; p. 64 (1982): Photofusion/Universal Images Group Editorial/GettyImages; p. 64 (1996): Kimberly Butler/The LIFE Images Collection/GettyImages; p. 64 (2004): Graffizone/E+/GettyImages; p. 64 (2006): Future Publishing/Future/GettyImages; p. 64 (2013): Jacob Ammentorp Lund/iStock/Getty Images Plus/GettyImages; p. 65 (T): Mark Dadswell/Getty Images Sport/Getty Images AsiaPac/GettyImages; p. 65 (B): Leanna Rathkelly/Photographer's Choice/GettyImages; p. 66: Steve Sands/FilmMagic/GettyImages; p. 67 (T): Walter Bibikow/AWL Images/GettyImages; p. 67 (B): ferrantraite/Vetta/GettyImages; p. 68 (BR): JGI/Jamie Grill/Blend Images/GettyImages; p. 68 (crossing slackline): Ascent Xmedia/The Image Bank/GettyImages; p. 69 (B/G): vladimir zakharov/Moment/GettyImages; p. 69: Willie Maldonado/The Image Bank/GettyImages; p. 70: Jonas Gratzer/LightRocket/GettyImages; p. 71 (T): NASA/The LIFE Picture Collection/GettyImages; p. 71 (B): Hero Images/GettyImages; p. 72 (header), p. vi (Unit 11): Hero Images/GettyImages; p. 72 (T): SW Productions/Photodisc/GettyImages; p. 72 (B): Hero Images/GettyImages; p. 73: martinedoucet/E+/GettyImages; p. 74: Jamie Kingham/Image Source/GettyImages; p. 75 (L): Rick Gomez/Blend Images/GettyImages; p. 75 (R): Simon Winnall/Taxi/GettyImages; p. 76: Elenathewise/iStock/Getty Images Plus/GettyImages; p. 77 (R): FilippoBacci/E+/GettyImages; p. 77 (L): Comstock Images/Stockbyte/GettyImages; p. 78 (header), p. vi (Unit 12): Jose Luis Pelaez Inc/Blend Images/GettyImages; p. 78: Martin Barraud/Caiaimage/GettyImages; p. 79: Martin Poole/The Image Bank/GettyImages; p. 80 (T): Tim Robberts/GettyImages; p. 80 (B): Chris Ryan/Caiaimage/GettyImages; p. 81: Anadolu Agency/Anadolu/GettyImages; p. 82: Car Culture/Car Culture®Collection/GettyImages; p. 83 (B): Gary Burke/Moment/GettyImages; p. 83 (T): UpperCut Images/GettyImages; p. 84: Tetra Images/GettyImages; p. 85: ullstein bild/GettyImages; p. 86 (header), p. vi (Unit 13): Manfred Gottschalk/Lonely Planet Images/GettyImages; p. 86: Image Source/GettyImages; p. 87 (L): James Lauritz/Photodisc/GettyImages; p. 87 (R): RichLegg/E+/GettyImages; p. 88 (T): Sweet Wedding/GettyImages; p. 88 (B): Gogosvm/iStock/Getty Images Plus/GettyImages; p. 89: LisaValder/E+/GettyImages; p. 91 (T): serdjophoto/iStock/Getty Images Plus/GettyImages; p. 91 (B): Ian Cuming/Ikon Images/GettyImages; p. 92 (header), p. vi (Unit 14): bjones27/E+/GettyImages; p. 92 (BR): GUILLAUME SOUVANT/AFP/GettyImages; p. 93 (T): GUILLAUME SOUVANT/AFP/GettyImages; p. 93 (B): Highwaystarz-Photography/iStock/Getty Images Plus/GettyImages; p. 94 (TL): B. O'Kane/Alamy; p. 94 (TC): Hill Street Studios/Blend Images/GettyImages; p. 94 (TR): Tom and Steve/Moment/GettyImages; p. 94 (CL): Daniela White Images/Moment/GettyImages; p. 94 (C): Lucia Lambriex/Taxi/GettyImages; p. 94 (BR): Caiaimage/Sam Edwards/OJO+/GettyImages; p. 94 (B): Hero Images/GettyImages; p. 95 (TL): Mads Perch/Iconica/GettyImages; p. 95 (TR): Plume Creative/DigitalVision/GettyImages; p. 95 (BL): Sam Edwards/Caiaimage/GettyImages; p. 95 (BR): asiseeit/E+/GettyImages; p. 96: Gary Houlder/Taxi/GettyImages; p. 97 (R): FREDERICK FLORIN/AFP/GettyImages; p. 97 (L): Tim Robberts/The Image Bank/GettyImages; p. 98: Image Source/GettyImages; p. 99 (TL): Vico Collective/Michael Shay/Blend Images/GettyImages; p. 99 (TR): Eric Audras/ONOKY/GettyImages; p. 99 (BR): Morsa Images/DigitalVision/GettyImages; p. 100 (header), p. vi (Unit 15): Dominic Burke/Photographer's Choice/GettyImages;